...nan and ... the
... ... of which are studies of
criminology and sexuality past and present. The best known of
these are the *Outsider Cycle*, *Origins of the Sexual Impulse* and
A Casebook of Murder.

Donald Seaman was on the staff of the *Daily Express* for
twenty-five years, working variously as a crime reporter, fea-
ture-writer and foreign correspondent, before moving to
Cornwall, where he is a near neighbour of Colin Wilson. He
has written eight thrillers and one exposé of the intelligence
network, *The Great Spy Scandal*.

COLIN WILSON AND
DONALD SEAMAN

An Encyclopedia of
Scandal

GRAFTON BOOKS

A Division of the Collins Publishing Group

LONDON GLASGOW
TORONTO SYDNEY AUCKLAND

Grafton Books
A Division of the Collins Publishing Group
8 Grafton Street, London W1X 3LA

Published by Grafton Books 1987

First published in Great Britain by
George Weidenfeld and Nicholson Ltd 1986

ISBN 0-586-07177-6

Printed and bound in Great Britain by
Collins, Glasgow

Set in Times

The photographs in this book are reproduced by permission of the
following:
Associated Press 3 (*bottom*), 8 (*bottom*), 16 (*top*); *BBC Hulton Picture
Library* 1 (*top*), 16 (*bottom*); *Mansell Collection* 4; *National Film
Archive* 6; *National Portrait Gallery* 3; *Popperfoto* 1 (*middle*), 7
(*bottom*), 9 (*bottom*), 12 (*bottom*), 14 (*top* and *middle*), 15 (*bottom*);
Syndication International 5, 7 (*top*), 8 (*top*), 9 (*top*), 10 (*top left* and
bottom), 11, 12 (*top* and *middle*), 13, 14 (*bottom*), 15 (*top* and
middle), 16 (*middle*); *Topham Picture Library* 1 (*bottom*), 2, 10 (*top
right*).

Contents

6 *Contents*

Contents   7

Introduction

by Colin Wilson

When Donald Seaman, my co-author on *An Encyclopedia of Modern Murder*, suggested following it up with an Encyclopedia of Scandal, I must admit that my first reaction was unenthusiastic. Murder has always interested me because it is one of the extremes of human nature; by comparison, an interest in scandal seems a rather discreditable form of self-indulgence, like a passion for chocolate éclairs. Then I began to think about some of the classic scandals – the South Sea Bubble, the Mayerling affair, the Dreyfus case, the rector of Stiffkey, the Fatty Arbuckle 'rape', the Profumo scandal – and I saw that I was being narrow minded. The great scandals afford the same opportunity to study the curious complexities of human nature as the famous criminal cases.

The next problem was to decide precisely what constitutes a scandal. A good starting point seemed to be Henry Fielding's remark: 'Love and scandal are the best sweeteners of tea.' That is to say, a scandal is any event that 'lets the cat out of the bag' and provides material for interesting gossip. That is why the best scandals seem to involve the downfall of some respectable person as a result of sexual misdemeanours. The case of the rector of Stiffkey is probably the archetypal sexual scandal. But then, anyone who reads the case of the Reverend Harold Davidson will agree that this gentle and rather silly little man did not really deserve to be defrocked and – quite literally – thrown to the lions. On the other hand, the Reverend Henry Ward Beecher, that deafening foghorn of virtue, was undoubtedly a less-deserving case – at least it is known that he seduced the wives of two of his friends – and he succeeded in convincing his flock that he was a persecuted saint and remaining in his pulpit to the end of his days. If Harold Davidson deserved to be included, then Ward Beecher certainly did. So the element of 'downfall' had to be removed from our definition of scandal.

As I began to work on the book, I began to see an altogether more interesting common factor. When Professor Joad decided to save a few shillings by lying to a ticket collector about where he had boarded the train, he must have known that his career would be destroyed if he was caught. When Colonel Valentine Baker cast his eyes on Miss Rebecca Dickinson on the Portsmouth train and decided he wanted to possess her, he must have known that it could mean total ruin if she screamed. When Sir Gordon Cumming decided to cheat at cards when sitting at the same table as the Prince of Wales, he must have realized that detection would mean the end of his career as an 'officer and gentleman'. So why did they do it? Because they were dual personalities. Joad was a highly respected philosopher who wrote books about morals; another part of him was a greedy and dishonest adolescent who had a streak of meanness. Baker was a brave man and an honest soldier; but there was a part of him that regarded every girl as his legitimate prey (a feeling shared by his self-indulgent friend the Prince of Wales). As to Sir Gordon Cumming, it will never be known why a wealthy landowner decided to add a few chips to his pile and so gain a small sum of which he had no need; there was obviously some fundamental split between the lieutenant-colonel of the Scots Guards and the gambler who felt a compulsion to cheat.

There is an ultimate stupidity about most criminals, even when they happen to be highly intelligent; they are a disturbing example of what William James calls 'a certain blindness in human beings'. With people involved in scandal, it is not so much blindness as a kind of astigmatism. They want the world to see them as respectable, but there is an element of childish egoism that they somehow feel they 'deserve' to indulge. A successful psychiatrist told me that as soon as she found herself alone in someone else's house, she experienced an immediate compulsion to go and look in the drawers. She admitted that this dated back to childhood, when her parents went out and she was free to explore the 'forbidden' places of their bedroom.

In *The Idiot*, there is a scene at a party where all the characters decide to tell one another the most shameful thing they have ever done – proof that Dostoevsky recognized this same 'split' as a fundamental part of human nature.

It is here that we can begin to grasp the deeper reasons for the fascination of scandal. Simone de Beauvoir remarked about Albert Camus that he often talked to her of an idea that obsessed him: that one day it had to be possible to write the Truth. 'The truth, as she saw it, was that in Camus the gap between his life and his writing was wider than in many others', says Herbert Lottman, Camus's biographer. Camus was an incorrigible seducer who found girls irresistible; his marriage dissolved because of this problem and he spent much of his time living in hotels where he could entertain his mistresses more freely. It must have seemed ironic to this man, who knew he was regarded as one of the major intellectual figures of his time, to have to go through the usual trivial patter necessary to get a girl into bed. He knew he was not interested in her personally, that all he wanted was to get her to remove her clothes. Yet he was supposed to be a humanist who taught the importance of personal relationships. In a deeper sense, he undoubtedly believed in compassion and personal relationships. So how could it be possible to tell the exact truth about oneself? The same point emerges in a story Lottman tells about Sartre and Camus getting drunk and staggering back home in the early hours of the morning. 'To think', said Sartre, 'that in a few hours I'll be lecturing in the Sorbonne about the writer's responsibility.' He was not suggesting that there was something hypocritical about a 'serious' writer being drunk; only noting that the Sartre who stood up to speak to the students and the Sartre who was now weaving his way homeward were not quite the same person.

Now obviously, the simplest and crudest way of 'not being the same person' is to be a hypocrite, like Tartuffe. And that is why scandal intrigues us: because it suggests that truth has finally triumphed and the hypocrite stands exposed. But it is never quite as simple as that. The Reverend Harold Davidson did not believe for a moment that he was a hypocrite which is why he fought so bitterly to reinstate himself in the church.

Lord Byron and Oscar Wilde were certainly not hypocrites; in fact, they did their best to drop very broad hints about their 'secret sins' in their writings. (In the case of Wilde, I have always suspected some masochistic element that unconsciously connived at his own discovery and downfall.) H. G. Wells was not in the least hypocritical about his love life – and indeed, he went out of his way to drop broad hints about it in many of his novels. Yet when confronted with a scandal – in the case of the young lady who tried to commit suicide on his carpet – he hastily contacted his friends on the newspapers and made sure nothing appeared in print. He had recognized – what becomes very clear in this book – that scandal is a kind of distorting mirror that obscures the truth just as much as it reveals it. This is because scandal is based on wishful thinking. The public wants to be shocked in order to confirm its own sense of virtue.

This is why scandal can be so stupid and dangerous. Fatty Arbuckle caused the accidental death of a young girl by landing on her with his full weight when she had a distended bladder. The simple explanation was not enough for the American public, and rumours began to circulate that he had raped her with a bottle, that his member was abnormally large, and so on. Arbuckle, being a naïve and good-natured soul, totally failed to grasp what was happening, and was convinced that the public would once again take him to its heart if he was allowed the opportunity to make more films. What he failed to understand was that as a film star, he was already a kind of myth. He was the archetypal clown, like Buttons in the pantomime. After the death of Virginia Rappe, he became a different type of myth – the ravening monster. (All fairy tales of monsters have sexual overtones – think of Dracula bending over a sleeping girl . . .) He had become a victim of the psychological distortion mechanism.

Hollywood is, of course, one enormous distorting mirror – which is why the section on Hollywood scandal is the longest in this book. Robert Harrison, the publisher of Hollywood's most successful scandal magazine, explained its success by saying, 'Americans like to read about things which they are afraid to do themselves.' But I am inclined to see this as an oversimplification. Would most people really have liked to launch the South Sea Bubble, or sodomize telegraph boys in cheap hotel rooms, or be involved in the bribery of politicians? Obviously not. What interests us is the contrast between myth and reality that becomes apparent when a scandal explodes. Writers are particularly obsessed by this contrast because every writer sees it as his task to tell his own particular kind of truth. This occupation has its own dangers, as Graham Greene discovered when he reviewed a Shirley Temple film for *The Spectator* in the 1930s and found himself in court on a libel charge. Evidentaly irritated by the sugary sweetness of the Shirley Temple image, Greene attempted to administer his own corrective by suggesting that her main appeal was to dirty old paedophiles; her studio was so enraged that they sued Greene on the grounds that he had accused them of procuring Miss Temple for immoral purposes. But why did the studio bother to sue the film critic of a small-circulation magazine? The answer must be that they felt Greene was trying to prick the balloon, destroy the illusion, and their living depended on maintaining illusions.

This, then, is why we all enjoy reading about scandal: because we all enjoy seeing over-inflated balloons explode. Yet this, as I have pointed out, is also a kind of illusion. Arbuckle was not really an over-inflated balloon, even if he looked like one. Oscar Wilde was not really a monster of perversity. Harold Davidson was not really a satyr. President Nixon was certainly not half as corrupt as his Democratic opponents made him out to be. Scandal specializes in half-truths.

This is why the range of this book is so wide and why some of its 'cases' – for example H. G. Wells and Bertrand Russell – do not, strictly speaking, qualify as scandals. Scandal lies in the nature of a human being rather than in the chain of events that caused a public commotion. Some scandals, when examined objectively, dwindle to microscopic proportions, and we realize that this is because they were never really scandals in the first place. This applies especially to political scandals, which are usually inflated out of all proportion by journalists and opposition politicians. When I was in Washington in 1966, I had dinner at the house of a Georgetown hostess who had been a close friend of President Kennedy. When I asked whether it was true that Kennedy had been a notorious womanizer, everyone looked shocked and reproachful and I was assured that there was absolutely no truth in the story. By the time the revelations of Judith Exner – and other of the president's ex-mistresses – began to appear, no one really cared any more. A recent paperback on Kennedy prints on its cover the story that when Jackie Kennedy came back from a journey, she found a pair of panties under the president's pillow; she tossed them at Kennedy with the comment, 'You'd better return these – they're not my size.' If Kennedy's opponents had got hold of that story in the early 1960s, it would have been blown up into a major scandal; Kennedy would have been branded a lecherous beast, a faithless husband, a danger to national security. Twenty years or so later, the same story provokes admiring chuckles; it proves that Kennedy was masculine and virile and willing to take risks – in fact, precisely the kind of man who ought to be president . . .

It was on that same trip to America that, in a university in the Mid-West, I met the wife of a professor who had written a book about Somerset Maugham. We discussed Maugham's rather negative attitude towards women and I suggested that it might be a consequence of his homosexuality. She was horrified and asked me where I had heard such vicious gossip. She and her husband had known Maugham intimately, she assured me, and there was not the slightest truth in the story. Fifteen years after Maugham's death, Ted Morgan's biography appeared and made it clear why the professor and his wife had never even suspected Maugham's homosexuality. He was frantically obsessed with a desire to preserve his secret. And Morgan's book also makes it clear that this obsession turned him into one of the most unpleasant characters ever to achieve literary celebrity.

Maugham is, in fact, the perfect example of the observation that scandal lies in the nature of a human being rather than in the chain of events that causes the public commotion. He belongs to a type that could be called the 'scandal-personality'. These are men for whom there is a wide gap between the private life and the public *persona*. Morgan's book is full of examples. In 1928 Maugham wrote a novel called *Cakes and Ale* into which he put a vicious portrait of his friend Hugh Walpole. Walpole was deeply hurt and wrote to ask Maugham why he had done it. Maugham assured him solemnly that he was mistaken; nothing had been further from his thoughts than to portray his old friend. Maugham even asked J. B. Priestley to assure Walpole that he was not the original of the character in the novel.

Three years later, a novelist named Elinor Mordaunt decided to give Maugham a taste of his own medicine in a novel called *Gin and Bitters*. It is about a novelist who spends much of his time travelling in the Far East, staying as a guest in the homes of English residents, then putting spiteful portraits of them into his novels. Maugham was in the habit of doing precisely this. Elinor Mordaunt's sketch of his personality has a deadly precision: 'He secretes bile as snakes secrete poison in their fangs: the bite of sheer venom.' This was true; Morgan gives many examples of Maugham's tendency to nurse grudges. Even the physical portrait of him is unmistakable: '. . . a small, dark man, proud of his smallness, rather sallow, showing even then yellow pouches under his dark eyes: eyes as sad and disillusioned as those of a sick monkey.'

Walpole instead of rejoicing in the attack, advised Maugham to prevent its publication in England. Maugham replied blandly, 'I do not mind very much what anyone says about me.' But it was a lie; when the novel appeared in England, Maugham sued the publisher and forced him to withdraw it.

Every reader of Morgan's biography must end by feeling that if ever a man deserved to have his come-uppance, it was Maugham. He was a walking time bomb of scandal. Regrettably, it never happened. So Maugham does not figure in the present book. But in the course of compiling my half, it became increasingly clear to me that most of the people involved in scandals have the same basic flaws as Maugham and that they were simply less lucky. Most of us have to learn to accept that it is impossible to tell – or to live – the whole truth. But the 'scandal personality' seems to derive a certain pleasure from double standards. He likes to tell himself that 'everybody does it', and that the trick is simply not to get found out.

What it really amounts to is that the 'scandal personality' is determined to protect and justify the spoilt child inside himself, usually at the expense of other people. He does this by refusing to recognize it as such. So Joad pandered to his own meanness, Maugham to his spite, MacPherson to his untruthfulness, Wells to his libertinism, Novello to his weakness and conceit, Davidson to his capacity for self-deceit. In fact, the capacity for self-deceit seems to be a lowest common multiple among the people in this book. The 'scandal personality' is basically a confidence trickster who also tricks himself.

ARBUCKLE, Fatty
A Star's Disgrace

The scandal that wrecked the career of film comic 'Fatty' Roscoe Arbuckle – and tarnished the image of Hollywood – occurred after a three-day drinking party in 1921.

Arbuckle was born on 24 March 1887 in Smith Center, Kansas, USA and named Roscoe Conklin Arbuckle. He worked as a plumber's assistant, then became a performer in carnivals and vaudeville – for all his enormous weight (330 lb or 21 stone) he was incredibly agile. At the age of twenty-one he was hired as an extra by the Selig Polyscope Company and he made his first one-reel comedy – *The Sanitarium* – in 1910. He was hired by Mack Sennett and made a dozen films in 1913 including *Fatty's Day Off* and *Fatty's Flirtation*. His attraction lay in his cherubic innocence – the good nature that he radiated was obviously genuine. Neither, for a Hollywood star, was he unusually sex-orientated; the girls he worked with found him protective and 'big brotherly'. His reputation was a great deal better, for example, than that of his co-star Charlie Chaplin. In 1917, he moved with Sennett to Jesse Lasky's Artcraft, and wrote and directed most of his own films. He gave Buster Keaton a start in life. When he made a film for Paramount, a banner over the gate read: Welcome To The Prince Of Whales. But an all-night party laid on in his honour by Jesse Lasky in Boston on 6 March 1917, almost led to scandal. Twelve party girls were paid over $1,000 for their night's work. But some Boston resident who peered through the transom and saw Fatty stripping on a table with several girls called the police. It is alleged that Lasky, Adolph Zukor and Joseph Schenck ended by paying the district attorney and mayor $10,000 to overlook the incident.

In 1921, Arbuckle signed a contract worth $3 million and he

decided to celebrate with a party in the St Francis Hotel in San Francisco. He arrived from Bay City on the evening of Saturday 3 September 1921, and took a suite, as well as three rooms on the twelfth floor, in the unlikely event that anyone should want to sleep. By the following afternoon, the party was in full swing, with about fifty guests, including such Hollywood cronies as Lowell Sherman and Freddy Fishback, and a number of pretty actresses. Arbuckle, separated from his wife, had asked his friend Bambina Maude Delmont to invite a girl he particularly admired – the starlet Virginia Rappe. The two women were staying at the nearby Palace Hotel, together with Virginia's agent.

Twenty-five-year-old Virginia Rappe was a model from Chicago, who had achieved public notice when her face appeared on the sheet music of 'Let Me Call You Sweetheart'. She was a pretty, fresh-faced girl, the type Hollywood liked to cast as a milkmaid – dressed in a check frock and sunbonnet she looked the essence of female innocence. According to film-maker Kenneth Anger (in *Hollywood Babylon*) this appearance was misleading. 'An offer came from Sennett, and she went to work on his lot, taking minor parts. She also did her share of sleeping around, and gave half the company crabs. This epidemic so shocked Sennett that he closed down his studio and had it fumigated.' Arbuckle had been pursuing Virginia – without success – for five years. She found him unattractive and was later quoted as having said: 'I'd sooner go to bed with a jungle ape than have that fat octopus groping at me.' But since Arbuckle was now an influential figure in the film world and Virginia was still an unknown starlet, she was willing to make certain compromises to advance her career.

On Labour Day, Monday, 5 September 1921, the party was still going, and Virginia had come from the Palace Hotel, accompanied by a 'bodyguard'. Arbuckle was still dressed in pyjamas, carpet slippers and a bathrobe. Most of the other guests were in a similar state of *déshabillé*. Virginia refused champagne and accepted a gin and orange. She was drinking her third – and was anxious to get to the bathroom, which seemed to be constantly occupied – when Arbuckle grabbed her and steered her into a bedroom, winking at his friends and commenting: 'This is what I've been waiting for.'

A few minutes later, there were screams from the bedroom. Suddenly, the party noises died away. Maude Delmont went and tried the bedroom handle, calling, 'Virginia, what's happening?' There were more screams. Maude Delmont picked up the telephone and called down for the manager. The assistant manager, H. J. Boyle, rushed into the suite just as the door of bedroom 1219 burst open and Arbuckle appeared with Virginia's hat perched on his head at an absurd angle. He gave an innocent smile and did a little dance on the carpet. Back in the room, Virginia was making groaning sounds. Fatty's good temper seemed to slip and he said to Maude Delmont, 'Get her dressed and take her back to the Palace.' And when Virginia started to scream again he yelled, 'Shut up, or I'll throw you out of the window.'

Virginia was lying on the bed, almost nude, with her clothes scattered around her. She was moaning, 'I'm dying, I'm dying. He hurt me.' They tried to dress her, but her blouse was badly torn – it had obviously been ripped from her by force.

The house doctor was sent for and Virginia was moved to another room, still moaning. Arbuckle seemed to feel she was 'putting it on', perhaps to blackmail him into offering her a part, and snapped, 'Shut up. You were always a lousy actress.'

She was in pain for the next three days, often becoming unconscious. She was transferred to a nursing home, where she died. The doctor who performed the autopsy discovered that her bladder was ruptured. The result was death from peritonitis. What had happened seemed clear. Arbuckle had flung himself on her with his full weight when she had a full bladder and it had ruptured like a balloon. When it was reported to the coroner, police interviewed hospital staff to find out who was behind the accident. The next morning newspaper headlines all over the country talked about the orgy that had ended in rape and death.

An inquest found that Arbuckle was 'criminally responsible' for Virginia's death and recommended that he should be charged with manslaughter. Even before he went on trial in November, his career was in ruins. The fat, innocent man who made everybody laugh was really a 'sex fiend'. Rumour had it that his penis was so enormous that it had ruptured her bladder. But Arbuckle's friend Al Seminacher introduced a note of horror when he told people that Arbuckle had used a large piece of ice from the ice bucket to penetrate Virginia. Rumour added that he had first assaulted her by introducing a champagne bottle.

Church groups and women's clubs demanded that his films should be withdrawn from circulation, and that unreleased films should never be shown. It was hardly necessary. No one could laugh at Arbuckle when they remembered that this innocent, babylike character had torn off a girl's clothes and raped her. A 'Fatty lynching' mood swept the country: in Wyoming, cowboys shot up the screen of a cinema showing an Arbuckle short; in Hartford, Connecticut, women tore down the screen.

Arbuckle was released on bail. His trial began in November; he denied doing any harm to Virginia and his lawyers did their best to suggest that she was little better than a prostitute. After forty-three hours deliberation, a jury was in favour of acquitting Arbuckle by ten to two but a majority verdict was not good enough and a mis-trial was declared. At his second trial, the jury found him guilty by ten to two and again they were dismissed. On 12 April 1922, a third jury found him innocent, and the foreman added: 'Acquittal is not enough. We feel a grave injustice has been done him and there is not the slightest proof to connect him in any way with the commission of a crime.' Outside the court, Arbuckle told newsmen, 'My innocence of the hideous charge preferred against me has been proved.' But it made no difference. Comedy depends upon a make-believe world in which no one does any real harm and everything is a joke. Fatty's 'rape' had introduced a brutal element of reality. This was the real reason why he remained unforgiven.

The $3 million contract was cancelled and his unreleased films were suppressed. It cost the studio $1 million. His friend Buster Keaton suggested he should change his name to Will B. Good. In fact, he directed a few comedy shorts under the name of William Goodrich. He toured America's backwoods in second-rate farces, but some of them were booed off the stage. In 1931 he pleaded in *Photoplay*: 'Just let me work . . . I think I can entertain and gladden the people that see me.' He seemed incapable of grasping that the case had somehow undermined the public's willingness to laugh at him.

He began to drink heavily: in 1931 he was arrested in Hollywood for drunken driving. Yet in 1933, his luck seemed to be turning. Warner Brothers took the risk of hiring him to make several short comedies. But after a celebration party in a New York hotel on 28 June 1933, he returned to his room and died of a heart attack. He was forty-six years old.

THE BACCARAT SCANDAL
The Tranby Croft Case

His Highness Edward Albert, Prince of Wales – the son of Queen Victoria – seems to have been in many ways a rather unsavoury character. He was an incorrigible seducer of women, who spent most of his time drinking, playing cards, and indulging in slightly sadistic forms of horseplay. At least one of his friends – Christopher Sykes – ruined himself trying to keep up with the Prince's extravagant way of life. Another, Sir William Gordon Gordon Cumming, Bart, a Scottish land-owner, also owed his ruin – although in a slightly less direct manner – to his spoiled and unreliable friend.

Gordon Cumming seems to have been rather a disagreeable character, noted for his rudeness and boorishness; the *Sporting Times* described him as 'possibly the handsomest man in London, and certainly the rudest'. On meeting a medical acquaintance in the courtyard of Buckingham Palace he is said to have enquired: 'Hello, is one of the servants sick?'

On 8 September 1880, the Prince of Wales was a guest at Tranby Croft, the house of Arthur Wilson, a rich Hull ship-owner. By his special request, Gordon Cumming had also been invited to Tranby Croft. Cumming was at the time a lieutenant-colonel in the Scots Guards.

After a late dinner, the guests listened to some music, then settled down to play baccarat – a card game which has something in common with both roulette and bingo. A dealer hands out a card, face downwards, to two sets of players who sit on either side of him. The aim is to get eight or nine. The dealer looks at his own two cards, and he may 'declare'. Or he may offer another card to the two lots of players. When either a player or the dealer has eight or nine, he has won. It is a game of chance. The players may stake what they like on the game, and the dealer, like the croupier in roulette, either wins or loses.

The players must sit with their money – or counters representing money – in front of them. The cheating of which Gordon Cumming was accused consisted in quietly adding a few counters to his stake after the cards had been declared in his favour. It was the son of the house, Arthur Stanley Wilson, who thought he saw Gordon Cumming doing this. He quietly drew the attention of another guest, Berkeley Levett, to this. Levett watched carefully and was soon convinced that he had also seen Gordon Cumming add to his stake after he had won, so increasing his winnings. Later that evening, when the game was finished, he told his mother, and his brother-in-law, Lycett Green, what he had seen. It was decided that the best thing to do was to watch Gordon Cumming carefully the next evening to see if he cheated again.

They did this on the evening of 9 September and five of them – Lycett Green and his wife, and the two Wilson parents and their son – were all convinced they saw Gordon Cumming cheating.

Now this was a serious business – not because of the money involved – for Gordon Cumming had only won £228 in two nights' play but because he was there at the invitation of the Prince of Wales. Edward Albert – later Edward VII – already had a bad reputation as a gambler and ladies' man, and was often pilloried in the Press. The first thought of his hosts – and they seem to have been social climbers – was to save the Prince from scandal.

Other guests were let into the secret, including Lord Coventry and his assistant General Owen Williams, a close friend of Gordon Cumming. The Prince was told by Coventry that Gordon Cumming had been seen cheating at baccarat, then Coventry and General Williams went to Gordon Cumming, who was in the smoking room, and told him that he had been accused by Lycett Green and young Wilson of cheating at baccarat. Gordon Cumming was indignant and said, 'Do you believe the statements of a parcel of inexperienced boys?' After dinner, Coventry, Williams and the Prince of Wales all confronted Gordon Cumming, who continued to insist on his innocence. And later, a document was presented to Gordon Cumming, which he was asked to sign. It declared that, in exchange for the silence of the witnesses against him, Gordon Cumming would solemnly undertake never again to play cards. If he did not sign it, he was told, he would have to leave the house immediately and be proclaimed a cheat on every racecourse in England. Gordon Cumming decided to sign.

Far from 'hushing up' the scandal, all this secrecy only made it a better subject for gossip. By the next day it was being openly discussed on Doncaster Racecourse. And three months later, on 27 December 1890, Gordon Cumming received an anonymous letter from Paris saying that the scandal was being discussed in Paris and Monte Carlo. Belatedly, he decided to sue. He was demanding an apology from the Wilsons, the Lycett Greens, and Berkeley Levett. Understandably, they refused. Gordon Cumming's solicitors issued a writ for slander.

Sir Edward Clarke was briefed for the prosecution and Sir Charles Russell for the defence – Russell had a reputation of being quite as rude and arrogant as Gordon Cumming. The judge was the Lord Chief Justice himself, the Right Honourable John Duke Bevan Coleridge, a close friend of Russell.

The case opened on 1 June 1891. The defence was one of justification – that Gordon Cumming had not been slandered because he really had cheated. There were no spectacular revelations and no dramatic surprises. The Prince of Wales appeared in the witness box but his evidence was neither for nor against Gordon Cumming. The prosecution failed to shake the witnesses who thought they had seen Gordon Cumming cheat, although he scored a few good points. Gordon Cumming explained that he signed the paper 'because it was the only way to avoid a terrible scandal'. Clarke's final speech was so brilliant that it looked for a while as if Gordon Cumming had won after all. But the judge's summing up was against Gordon Cumming, his central point being that surely an innocent man would not have signed a paper virtually admitting his guilt. One writer on the case had described the summing up as 'polished, skilful and fiendishly unfair'. The jury took only thirteen minutes to find the defendants not guilty. They were awarded their costs. Gordon Cumming – now a socially ruined man – slipped out of court immediately after the verdict. The crowd hissed the jurors, and even tried to attack the defendants as they left the court; this was probably due less to a conviction that Gordon Cumming was innocent than to an intense dislike of the Prince of Wales.

The following day, Gordon Cumming married his 21-year-old fiancée, an American heiress named Florence Garner, who had stuck to him throughout his ordeal. She remained convinced to the end of her life that her husband had been deliberately 'framed' by the Prince of Wales because of a disagreement about a lady. It is true that 'Bertie' (as the Prince was known) was a petty and vindictive man – but there seems to be no evidence for Lady Gordon Cumming's assertion. The Gordon Cummings spent most of their lives on their Scottish estate and seem to have been reasonably happy together.

BAKER, Colonel Valentine
Attempted Rape on a Train

The attempt of Colonel Valentine Baker to rape a young lady on a train was one of the most widely publicized scandals of the 1870s.

On the afternoon of 17 June 1875, a 21-year-old girl named Rebecca Kate Dickinson boarded the Portsmouth to London train at Midhurst, in Sussex. She was alone in the compartment when 49-year-old Colonel Valentine Baker, until recently commanding officer of the 10th Hussars, entered the train at Liphook. Miss Dickinson was a pretty, self-possessed young lady who was on her way to Switzerland for a holiday. Colonel Baker was Assistant Quartermaster-General at Aldershot, a highly distinguished soldier who was an intimate friend of the Prince of Wales. He was also a married man, with two young daughters.

Baker made polite conversation for the first fifty minutes of the journey, apparently the ultra-respectable English gentleman exchanging commonplaces with a girl young enough to be his daughter or even granddaughter. But when the train pulled out of Woking, and London was half an hour away, he suddenly asked her if she often travelled alone. When she said she didn't, he asked her if they could meet on the train at some future time. She said no. He asked her name and she declined to tell him. He asked if he could write to her and she said no. He then closed the window and sat down next to her. When she asked him to sit further away he said, 'Don't be cross', and put his arm round her waist. 'You must kiss me, darling.' She struggled to her feet but he forced her down again and held her down with his weight while he kissed her again and again on the lips. 'If I give you my name will you get off?' she asked.

Instead of replying he sank in front of her, thrust one hand up her dress and began to fumble with his flies with the other.

She struggled to her feet and tried to smash the window with her elbow; then she lowered it and screamed. Baker pulled her back so violently that she was half suffocated. She twisted the door handle and began to climb out backwards. 'Get in, dear!' said the colonel in great alarm. And he offered to get out of the other door in an effort to calm her. But she knew the other door was locked.

She could see two men looking out of the window of the next compartment as she balanced on the running board and she shouted, 'How long before the train stops?' But their answer was carried away by the roar of the engine and the wind.

At 4.45 the train passed through Walton station and a bricklayer called William Burrowes saw a young lady standing on the running board, clinging to the handle of the door; someone inside the compartment seemed to be preventing her from falling by holding on to her other arm. The stationmaster signalled to Esher and there the train stopped. As it began to slow down, Baker said urgently, 'Don't say anything – you don't know what trouble you'll get me into. Say you were frightened.'

Railway officials at Esher wanted to know what had happened but she was too upset and exhausted to say much. Baker was told to go into another compartment. A clergyman named Baldwin Brown got in with Miss Dickinson and travelled with her to London.

At Waterloo, Miss Dickinson, Colonel Baker and the Reverend Brown were taken to the Inspector's office. Baker must have been relieved when she declined to go into details about her complaint. She gave her name and address; so did Baker. And then the Reverend Brown escorted her to her brother's house – he was a doctor living in Chesterfield Street. At this point, Rebecca Dickinson apparently wanted to forget the whole thing but her brother pointed out that Baker might do the same thing to other girls. So, reluctantly, she agreed to report the matter to the police.

The news items about the case caused widespread interest

and astonishment. Valentine Baker was the kind of soldier who had created the British Empire; he was also the author of a number of books on cavalry tactics. He was the younger brother of the explorer Sir Samuel Baker, who had journeyed to the source of the Nile. It was true that he was the son of a merchant, not a 'gentleman', but the Victoria era was the age of opportunity, and no one held this against him, least of all the future King Edward VII, his close friend. Surely there must be some mistake? Why should such a man risk his career and reputation to assault a girl on a train?

Three days after the assault, Baker was arrested at Guildford. His trial took place at Croydon Assizes on 2 August 1875, a Bank Holiday Monday. Huge crowds gathered outside the courtroom long before the trial was due to start at 10.30 A.M. Two well-dressed ladies even tried to get in through a window. Many peers were in court, including Lord Lucan and the Marquess of Tavistock. A rumour was going about that those in 'high places' had arranged for the whole thing to be dropped, so there was some relief when the Grand Jury found a True Bill and Mr Justice Brett refused to postpone the trial. There was so much noise coming from the crowds outside – disappointed at being unable to get in – that the case had to be adjourned for ten minutes while the police tried to restore order. Then Mr Sergeant Parry, QC, for the prosecution, called Miss Dickinson into the witness box. But he declined to increase her distress by asking her a single question. So the defence lawyer, Henry Hawkins, cross-examined her. He elicited the interesting fact that part of the conversation between Liphook and Woking had been about hypnotism and that Colonel Baker had told Miss Dickinson that he thought she could be mesmerized. She also detailed other topics they had discussed, including the murder of a certain Mr Walker. The defence was obviously trying to establish that Miss Dickinson's openness, her willingness to engage in animated conversation, had probably convinced the Colonel that a kiss might not be rejected.

But the evidence against the colonel was serious. He had fairly certainly intended rape – otherwise, why had he unbuttoned his flies? The guard had noticed that they were undone at Esher. And so had the two gentlemen in the carriage that Baker transferred into. He had also put his hand up her skirt, although it had apparently gone no further than above the top of her boot.

The judge's summing up emphasized that Baker's chief concern had apparently been to save Miss Dickinson from falling from the running board and he indicated that he could see no evidence that there was 'intent to ravish'. This was on the grounds that Baker had hoped to win the girl's consent to intercourse by 'exciting her passions'. The jury took the hint. Baker was found not guilty of intent to ravish but guilty of indecent assault and common assault. The judge then told Baker sternly that, 'Of all the people who travelled in the train that day, you were the most bound to stand by and defend a defenceless woman. Your crime is as bad as it could be.' And he sentenced Baker to a year in jail – without hard labour – and a fine of £500.

The Press, on the whole, felt it was a just verdict – most people had believed that this friend of royalty would be acquitted. But the general public seemed to feel that Baker had got off too easily – a mere year in 'honourable detention', then back to the old life.

But Baker was disgraced. He tried to resign his commission and was told that he was to be cashiered. It was widely believed that this was due to Queen Victoria's intervention. (The Queen was not fond of her rakish son – or his friends.) It is true that, in Horsemonger Lane jail, Baker was treated with due consideration, allowed to wear his own clothes, to send out for his food and to receive his friends more or less as he wished. But the knowledge that he had involved his family in the most degrading kind of public scandal was enough to turn him into a psychological wreck. Three months after his imprisonment, it was reported that he was critically ill. *The Times* published a letter from his wife assuring his 'many friends' that he was no longer in danger of his life but admitting that his condition caused her much distress.

He served his full term; then, with his wife and two young daughters he left England. He became a lieutenant-general in the Ottoman army and fought bravely during the Russo-Turkish war. Then he went to Egypt and accepted an appointment as a commander of police. He attempted unsuccessfully to relieve Tokar during the Sudan war but his poorly trained force was destroyed. He himself was seriously wounded in a later action. When he came back to London to recuperate, a cheering crowd greeted him at Victoria Station. His friends tried hard to get him reinstated in the British army. But their efforts were a failure – almost certainly due to Queen Victoria's determination that the would-be rapist would never again become a soldier of the Queen. Baker died of heart failure, after an attack of typhoid, on 12 November 1887, twelve years after the Dickinson case. The Queen finally relented and cabled that Baker was to be buried in Cairo with full military honours.

The mystery remains: why did Baker do it? In court he swore solemnly that the facts were not as Miss Dickinson represented them. His supporters took this to mean that she had given him some encouragement. He also spoke of her 'exaggerated fear'. Did he mean that he believed she had been willing to be kissed but had become alarmed when he had shown signs of being carried away?

But the theory that Baker gave way to an 'irresistible impulse' will not hold water. He was a highly disciplined soldier and discipline means the ability to resist 'impulses'. Yet this in itself suggests another explanation. Baker was a close friend of the Prince of Wales who spent much of his time bedding attractive women. So it is easy to understand that Baker may have regarded Rebecca Dickinson as a challenge, the natural prey of a dashing cavalry officer. But when he asked her if he might see her again, he was promptly rebuffed. For a man who is accustomed to giving orders and having them obeyed – and probably dominating his own wife and daughters with the natural authority of a sultan – this must have seemed an intolerable humiliation. He might have withdrawn stiffly into his shell and passed the rest of the journey to London in sulky silence. But he was not that kind of man; he was used to pressing on in the face of odds. He asked her name and again was rebuffed. The distinguished soldier, the friend of royalty, was being snubbed by a mere 'chit of a girl'. By this time he was probably burning with humiliation – and with the feeling that perhaps, after all, he was making a fool of himself. The author of a book on cavalry tactics had mistimed his charge. If he drew back now, he would remember this for the rest of his life with a shock of outraged vanity. The soldier had to act. He stood up and closed the window . . .

BEECHER, Henry Ward

The Preacher and the Adoring Disciples

Beecher was one of the most celebrated preachers of the nineteenth century. He was almost ruined by a scandal in which he was accused of adultery with one of his flock.

Henry Ward was born in Litchfield, Connecticut, USA, in June 1813, the eighth of thirteen children of the Reverend Lyman Beecher. He had been a shy child with a stammer and his scholastic performance had been abysmal until he went to Amherst College at the age of seventeen. At twenty-four he became minister to a small congregation at Lawrenceburg, Indiana, and began to develop his preaching talent. He was fundamentally an actor: he preferred to stand or sit on a platform rather than in a pulpit and told anecdotes with a wealth of gesture and facial expression that made his audience feel they were in a theatre. On one occasion, he mimed catching a fish so perfectly that a man in the front row jumped up crying, 'By God, he's got him!' Physically speaking, Beecher was not unusually attractive, with a round face, thick lips, a fleshy nose and shoulder-length hair. But his congregation found him magnetic and women adored him. A book of his called *Seven Lectures to Young Men* appeared in 1844 and became something of a bestseller. Yet for many years he was regarded simply as one of the preacher-sons of the far more famous Lyman Beecher. In 1847, he was persuaded to move east by Henry C. Bowen, a Brooklyn businessman, whose young wife was an admirer of Beecher. Within three years, his sermons were attracting audiences of more than 2,000, and he had the largest congregation in America.

As he grew older, Beecher gradually changed his stance from that of a narrow, hell-fire revivalist preacher to a liberal who advocated women's rights and Darwinian evolutionism, and opposed slavery. In 1861, Bowen made Beecher the editor of his newspaper *The Independent*. A young man named Theodore Tilton, who passionately admired Beecher, had been given the job of managing editor, largely due to Beecher's insistence. In 1855, Beecher had married Theodore Tilton to a pretty, dark-eyed young woman named Elizabeth Richards who like her husband regarded Beecher with adoration. *The Independent* became one of America's most widely read newspapers, largely due to Beecher's regular contribution, 'The Star Papers'. It was partly through the influence of Theodore Tilton that Beecher preached liberal doctrines.

In 1862, the attractive and popular Lucy Bowen died at the age of thirty-eight; she had borne ten children. On her death bed she beckoned her husband to move closer and whispered into his ear a confession that stunned him. She had been committing adultery with Henry Ward Beecher. Henry Bowen was in a difficult position. He was convulsed by jealousy and resentment: the man he had brought from Indiana and made editor of his newspaper had been his wife's lover. Beecher's column ceased to appear in *The Independent* and, not long after, Beecher himself left for England to preach the doctrines of anti-slavery. It was many years before he and Bowen renewed their friendship. When Beecher returned from England, Tilton insisted that he should become a regular visitor at his house; he wanted to share his friend with his wife. If anyone had told him that this would one day involve sharing his wife with his friend, he would have been furiously indignant; no one believed more deeply than Tilton in Beecher's total honesty and integrity.

Theodore Tilton, like Henry Ward Beecher, had started life as a highly orthodox young man who would 'rather have had my right hand cut off than have written a letter on the Sabbath.' Yet when he had met the seventeen-year-old Elizabeth Richards – known to all as Libby – their passion had been so intense that they consummated their love before Beecher joined them in wedlock. Ten years after their marriage, Tilton began to experience 'doubts' – about Christ's divinity, the absolute authority of the Bible, and other such weighty matters. Libby was horrified and Beecher had to comfort and soothe her. While her husband was away lecturing, Libby wrote him long letters in which she spoke freely of her love for Beecher. Neither she nor her husband experienced any misgivings; both believed implicitly that the highest form of love is wholly spiritual, and that such love casts out carnal desire. So Libby went on playing with fire, assuring herself that she was part of a 'blessed trinity' rather than an eternal triangle. In 1867, Beecher signed a contract to write a novel for which he was to receive the record sum of $24,000. (His sister was Harriet Beecher Stowe, author of *Uncle Tom's Cabin*.) He would bring the novel – *Norwood* – to Libby's house to ask her advice.

In August 1868, the Tiltons' baby son, Paul, died of cholera. Soon afterwards, Theodore Tilton set out on another of his lecture trips. On 9 October Libby went to hear Beecher deliver a speech at the Brooklyn Academy of Music and was overwhelmed with admiration. On the following day, Libby called on him at his home. That afternoon the inevitable happened: Libby became his mistress. It seems to have been Beecher who took the lead, since she later explained that she had 'yielded to him' in gratitude for the sympathy he gave her on the death of her child. Beecher had apparently assured her that their love was divine and that having sexual intercourse was its proper and valid expression, like a handshake or a kiss. He insisted that she should guard their secret – he called it 'nest hiding', borrowing the terminology from bird-watching. Not long after this, Beecher called on Libby at her home at 174 Livingston Street in Brooklyn, and once again they made love. After that, they made love on a number of occasions, at their respective homes, and in 'various other places'.

But the delicate, romantic Libby was not made for adultery. It began to prey on her mind. Beecher enjoyed sex much more than she did and wanted to make love every time they were alone. He obviously enjoyed it so much that Libby began to wonder whether it could be true that their relationship was blessed by God. In the summer of 1870, Libby went to pass the hot months – as was her custom – at Schoharie, New York. But on 3 July tormented by conscience, she returned to Brooklyn and confessed everything to her husband.

Tilton was deeply shaken. His initial reaction, understandably, was to denounce the 'white sepulchre', but his wife had preceded her confession with the demand that he would not harm the person implicated. His mind was still in confusion the next day when he went to his office. He admitted later that his chief desire was to find some excuse for his wife. He decided that '. . . she sinned as one in a trance. I don't think she was a free agent. I think she would have done his bidding if, like the heathen-priest in the Hindoo-land, he had bade her fling her child into the Ganges . . .' In this he showed a great deal of insight – there can be no doubt that Lib Tilton regarded herself as Beecher's slave, to do with as he would. Tilton then decided that he would not denounce Beecher, but that his punishment would be that Lib herself would go and tell him that she had confessed to her husband. Having decided 'in my secret self to be a conqueror', Tilton experienced a kind of ecstasy; for the next two weeks, 'I walked the streets as if I scarcely touched the ground.' Then human nature asserted itself. He had to tell somebody. One evening three prominent figures in the feminist movement came to the house and Tilton unburdened himself about the 'lecherous scoundrel who has defiled my bed'. When he came back from seeing two of the ladies home, the third – a woman named Sue Anthony – had to interpose herself between Tilton and his wife as he railed at her. She was later to allege that Libby Tilton then confessed in detail to her adultery with Beecher.

Libby then made the immense mistake of telling her mother – a psychotic and an impossible lady named Mrs Nathan B. Morse – about her affair. Mrs Morse had separated from her second husband after trying to strangle him to death. She hated Tilton and adored Beecher. Now she glimpsed the marvellous possibility that Libby might divorce Tilton and marry Beecher; she set about promoting this end by gossiping all over Brooklyn about the scandal, writing abusive letters to her son-in-law, and insinuating letters to Beecher that began 'My dear son . . .'

On Christmas Eve that year, Lib Tilton suffered a miscarriage; she later referred to it as 'a love babe' and there seems no doubt that she believed the child to be Beecher's. She was in a state of agonized misery. Her husband hardly ever spoke to her – he spent much of his time at the house of a friend called Frank Moulton, who became his confidant – and on one occasion, she went to the graveyard and lay down on the grave of her two dead children until a keeper made her move on.

Mrs Morse's gossip finally reached the ears of Henry Bowen, the other man Beecher had cuckolded. He immediately saw it as a marvellous opportunity to get his own back on Beecher without compromising the reputation of his dead wife (he had now remarried). Bowen asked Tilton to go and see him and then proceeded to accuse Beecher of being an inveterate seducer. According to Bowen, Beecher was even a rapist – he had thrown down a well-known authoress on the sofa and taken her by force. The story of Beecher's seduction of the former Mrs Bowen was repeated. Finally, Tilton was persuaded to write a letter to Beecher, ordering him to renounce his ministry and quit Brooklyn 'for reasons he well understood'. Bowen promised to deliver this. But Bowen was playing a double game. He was too much of a coward to want to confront Beecher openly. What he wanted to do was to pretend he was the friend of both parties, while setting them at one another's throats. He went to Beecher, gave him the letter, then assured him that he was on his side and that Tilton was himself a seducer of many women. (This seems to be true – Tilton apparently admitted to one of Bowen's employees, Oliver Johnson, that he had even slept with one of his mistresses in his own home.) Meanwhile, Tilton decided to use Frank Moulton as a go-between; he made his wife write a confession of her adultery, then sent Moulton to tell Beecher about it. This was the first Beecher knew about Libby's confession of adultery.

Beecher now went to see Libby, who was still in bed after her miscarriage. And he succeeded in persuading her to write a letter in which she declared that her confession had been untrue, wrung out of her by her husband's jealousy. There followed more to-ing and fro-ing between the various parties which ended finally in an uneasy truce between Beecher and the wronged husband. Beecher heaved a sigh of relief; it looked as if his sins would not find him out after all.

But he had reckoned without an extraordinary lady named Victoria Woodhull, an ardent 'women's libber' of the period, who became known as 'Mrs Satan' because she preached the doctrine of 'free love'. Victoria Woodhull was, in her way, as remarkable a character as Beecher himself. She was the daughter of a riverboat gambler and maidservant, and as a child she discovered she was psychic. She became a clairvoyant and spirit medium. At fifteen she married an alcoholic doctor named Woodhull, to whom she bore a child. She divorced him when she met a spiritualist named Colonel Blood but allowed Woodhull to continue living in the household. Then she made her greatest conquest: she and her equally remarkable sister Tennessee Claflin persuaded one of America's richest men, old Commodore Vanderbilt, that they could heal his various ailments with 'magnetism'. Vanderbilt fell in love with Tennessee (or Tennie C, as Victoria's younger sister preferred to spell it). He set them up in a brokerage business and financed a magazine called *Woodhull and Claflin's Weekly*, in which Victoria preached her doctrines of free love, attacked the rich (though not, of course, Vanderbilt) and espoused Marxism.

On 22 May 1871, Victoria published in the *World* a letter in which she praised free love 'in its highest, purest sense as the only cure for immorality', and stated that people who attacked her were hypocrites. 'I know of one man, a public teacher of eminence, who lives in concubinage with the wife of another public teacher.' And she sent Theodore Tilton a message asking him to come and see her. Tilton had by now been sacked by Bowen, but with the help of Beecher, had started another magazine called *The Golden Age*. He was curious to see the notorious 'free lover' and hurried round to her office. He found her to be a highly attractive woman in her early thirties who seemed far less formidable than he expected – even when she showed him her letter in the newspaper. Soon he and Victoria became good friends – in fact, Victoria was later to declare that they became lovers. Tilton no doubt told himself that he was only trying to prevent a scandal by keeping Victoria friendly. Victoria Woodhull also met Beecher and admitted that she found him a magnetic and attractive personality. But when Beecher declined to introduce Victoria at a suffragette meeting (where he knew she was going to preach free love), Tilton stepped into the gap. It did his reputation no good at all to be publicly associated with 'Mrs Satan' and her scandalous doctrines. Unfortunately, Victoria was so carried away by her new popularity with the women's movement (which had formerly regarded her as a crank) that she allowed herself to denounce her former protector Commodore Vanderbilt as a capitalist; he promptly dropped her. In May 1872, Victoria announced that she was standing as the first woman president of the United States, with a Negro reform leader as her running mate. She was infuriated when Tilton declined to support her cause and instead declared his support for Horace Greeley. (Because of the bad reputation he was acquiring, Tilton's support did Greeley no good at all.) Victoria Woodhull became increasingly angry and embittered. And finally she did what Beecher had always feared she would do: she told the whole story of his affair with Libby Tilton and the subsequent 'cover up', in her magazine. The result was as sensational as she had hoped. The magazine sold 100,000 copies and could have sold many times that number – copies began to change hands for as much as $40. A young man named Anthony Comstock, the vice-warden for the Young Men's Christian Association, saw the story, was outraged at this smear on the saintly Henry Ward Beecher, and was responsible for the arrest of the Claflin sisters for sending indecent material through the United States mails. Victoria and Tennessee went to jail. But the damage was done. The whole country was now gossiping about the Beecher-Tilton scandal. Six months later, when Victoria and her sister were acquitted (on the grounds that their accusations did not constitute pornography), everyone in the country wanted to know whether Tilton was a cuckold and Beecher was a seducer.

Beecher's own congregation increased his problems by insisting on expelling Tilton from the church. If, as Beecher insisted, he was innocent of adultery, then Tilton was a wicked traducer. Tilton, who had so far been more or less on Beecher's side (at least in wanting to suppress the scandal), now began to smoulder with resentment. This was not assuaged when Beecher decided to air the scandal by holding a 'trial' in his own church and Libby was persuaded to leave her husband and take Beecher's side. The church committee, predictably, decided that Beecher was not guilty. Tilton was branded as a liar. On 24 August 1874, Tilton swore out a complaint against Beecher, charging him with having wilfully alienated his wife's affections.

The Beecher-Tilton trial began on 11 January 1875, and lasted until 2 July. The whole nation was agog. Beecher spent much of his time in court; so did his sour-faced wife Eunice (known locally as 'the Griffin'). Beecher took the line that he had never, at any time, sinned with Libby Tilton, but that he fully acknowledged his guilt in having allowed her to idolize him to the exclusion of her husband – this, he claimed, was the meaning of some of the letters he had written admitting his guilt.

During those six months, the American public had more than its fill of scandal. It learned that Beecher was accused of seducing Lucy Bowen as well as Lib Tilton. One newspaper cartoon showed a Brooklyn businessman locking his wife in a huge safe with a notice on the door Proof Against Fire And Clergymen, while another showed a hatter who sold the 'new style of Brooklyn hat' – with horns on it. The public also learned that the wronged husband was not entirely innocent. He was alleged to have seduced the seventeen-year-old daughter of a congressman named Lovejoy in Winsted, Connecticut, and to have made an unsuccessful attempt to seduce a young girl who formed part of his household; this girl, Elizabeth Turner, told how Tilton had laid on her bed, kissed her, and put his hand 'down her neck' (i.e. on her breast). On another occasion he had come into her bedroom when she was fast asleep and carried her out; if he had failed to seduce her, it was plainly not for want of trying. The story of Tilton's 'affair' with Victoria Woodhull was also raked up. On the other hand, various servants testified to having seen Beecher in situations of intimacy with Libby Tilton; even her own brother reluctantly admitted that he had walked into the room and seen Beecher and Libby separating with obvious embarrassment. Libby herself, like Beecher, denied any misconduct.

The jury was out for eight days; it was unable to reach a unanimous verdict but voted nine to three against Tilton. Beecher's supporters regarded this as a triumph and he left the court like a conquering hero. His trials were not quite over, however. Frank Moulton sued Beecher for malicious prosecution but the suit was dismissed. Then Henry Bowen demanded that the Plymouth church committee should try Beecher for adultery with Lucy Bowen. The committee disbelieved him and Bowen, like the Moultons, was expelled from the church. Beecher made a lecture tour of the country and although he was booed in many places, he never failed to draw enormous crowds. When he died, thirteen years later (in 1887) his popularity with his own congregation was as great as ever.

Theodore Tilton also continued to lecture but his fortunes declined. He left the country in 1883, to settle finally in Paris, where he wrote novels and romantic poetry, and spent his days in a café playing chess. Libby, deserted by her husband and her lover, became a schoolteacher; she remains the most pathetic figure in the case. The Woodhull sisters both married rich men, and Victoria died in 1927, at the age of eighty-nine.

In retrospect, it is difficult not to agree with the reporter who wrote: 'Mankind fell in Adam and has been falling ever since, but never touched bottom until it got to Henry Ward Beecher.'

BELCHER, John and STANLEY, Sydney
The Board of Trade Bribery Scandal

Britain's first post-World War II political scandal erupted in the autumn of 1948, after rumours swept the country that huge bribes were being paid to certain Ministers and public servants in return for official favours. The central figures in the investigation which followed were: John Belcher, MP, Parliamentary Secretary at the Board of Trade, George Gibson, a former director of the Bank of England, football-pools promoters, brothers Abe and Harry Sherman, and a Polish 'Mister Fixit' named Sydney Stanley. It was a scandal which ended John Belcher's career both as a Minister and an MP, even though no reliable evidence was found to support any major allegation of improbity against him. By its negative findings, however, the Tribunal of Inquiry – known as the Lynskey Tribunal, after the judge who presided – effectively dispelled the wider rumours of corruption which threatened the Socialist government of the day, since most had originated from Sydney Stanley's own lies and greed. Even those ministerial offences which were uncovered seem, in retrospect, less of an exposé of graft than a mirror of the times we lived in; times of such austerity that something as trivial as the gift of a suit, or an expenses-paid night out at the dogs, was held to be enough of a bribe to 'improperly influence' a member of His Majesty's government.

In the late 1940s, food, clothing and petrol were still rationed in Britain. Alcoholic drink was in short supply, cigarettes were sold under the counter and most household utensils were unobtainable. Ministers and civil servants assumed an almost divine importance, since import licences were required for every commodity. Weary of waiting for the good times to return, ordinary men and women who would never normally dream of breaking the law, bought scotch, nylons, perfume and anything else said to have 'fallen off the back of a lorry', from the booming, coupon-free Black Market.

It was against this backcloth of nationwide 'fiddling' that rumours started to circulate of vast bribes being paid to certain Ministers and key public servants. So insistent were they that Prime Minister Clement Attlee set up a Tribunal under Mr Justice Lynskey to inquire into them. Its principal task was to investigate the relation between junior Minister John Belcher and contact man Sydney Stanley, the Pole with fingers in many a financial pie. The Bank of England's Mr Gibson, newly appointed chairman of the North Western Electricity Board, was likewise called to give evidence. So, too, was Mr Glenvil Hall, Financial Secretary to the Treasury, while Mr Hugh Dalton, Chancellor of the Exchequer, also appeared at his own request, although he knew Sydney Stanley only slightly. (Both Hugh Dalton and Glenvil Hall were completely exonerated of any complicity in the scandal.) As well as the various companies in which Stanley was interested, the Tribunal also inquired into the business transactions and relations between Shermans Pools and the Board of Trade.

Compared, say, with contemporary corruption scandals (like that involving former Japanese Premier Tanaka, who took a £1 million pound bribe, *see* page 390) the findings of the Lynskey Tribunal seem very small beer indeed. Mr Belcher accepted from his friend Sydney Stanley gifts of a gold cigarette case, a week's stay for his wife and himself at a hotel in Margate, free drinks, hospitality including the odd night out at a dog-track or boxing match, and a new suit. (The Minister told the Tribunal how he arrived one day at Sydney Stanley's flat wearing trousers which had a patch sewn over a cigarette burn. Stanley, who appeared genuinely shocked, took him to a tailor where he was measured for the new suit – although, said Belcher piously, before accepting it he handed over the twenty-six clothing coupons required under the existing regulations.)

In return for these 'benefactions', the Minister gave Stanley free access to his private office and in the House of Commons, or went himself to Stanley's flat to meet various people. The Tribunal concluded that because of the obligation he felt he owed Stanley, Belcher used his ministerial powers to help some of them, including one Margate businessman and another from Bognor Regis. In a separate case, he accepted gifts of wine and spirits from Glasgow businessman Sir Maurice Bloch; in return, he used his influence to obtain for Sir Maurice the licence he sought to import sherry casks from Spain. When he was asked by the Attorney-General why he had not told the Lord Chancellor of his gold cigarette case, or the visits to the dog-track, Mr Belcher said his mind was occupied 'with the specific allegations'. The Tribunal concluded, however, that, 'There is no reliable evidence to show that Mr Belcher received any sums of money in respect of any of the transactions which we have investigated, or indeed in respect of any transactions.'

The Tribunal also heard how football-pools promoters Abe and Harry Sherman handed over £10,000 in two equal amounts to Sydney Stanley. He told them the money was needed to bribe Solicitor-General Sir Frank Soskice ('very expensive') and Minister John Belcher ('a very big spender') to drop a Board of Trade prosecution against them. Stanley further asked for money over and above the £10,000, as there were other people 'who had to be looked after' – including, he said, payments to Mrs Belcher 'at her request'. Belcher said that when the Shermans told him this, he found the story so 'preposterous' that he was unable to take it seriously. And although he did take the political decision not to proceed with the case, the Tribunal found, 'We are not satisfied that Mr Belcher received the sum of £5,000 or any other sum in respect of his decision to withdraw the Sherman Pools prosecution, or that he received the sums of £50 or any other sum a week from Mr Stanley, or that Mrs Belcher ever received any money from Mr Stanley.' Similarly, it found that 'Sir Frank Soskice had never met Mr Stanley or any of the Shermans, and was in no way concerned with any of the proceedings against Shermans Pools', while the allegation that he shared in any of the cash paid to withdraw the prosecution 'had no foundation in fact'.

Although John Belcher denied that he had been influenced in any way by Stanley's gifts, his acceptance of them spelled the end of his political career. Like many before him, he discovered too late that 'in scandal as in robbery, the receiver is always thought as bad as the thief . . .' On 13 December 1948, as soon as he completed his evidence and without waiting for the Tribunal to announce its findings, he resigned his office as Minister. His letter to Attlee was long and contrite; the response was curt and cool. 'My dear Belcher', wrote the Prime Minister, 'I have received your letter of December 13. I am certain you have taken the right step in offering to resign your office. I greatly regret the circumstances which have made it necessary for you to do this and for me to accept your resignation, but you will not, I am sure, expect me at the present time to comment on the contents of your letter.' Although Belcher said at the time he had every intention to continue as an MP, the pressures on him continued to mount, and on 3 February 1949 he also resigned his seat as the member for Sowerby, in the West Riding of Yorkshire.

In a personal statement to the House he apologized for his part in making the Lynskey Tribunal necessary, but added, 'My regret is tempered by the knowledge that – in the result – most of the wilder rumours affecting Ministers, officials and others have been dispelled.' Of the Sherman prosecution, he commented, 'It has been suggested that I exceeded my authority in the action which I took. I wish merely to point out that I took the action as a result of an instruction from my senior Minister . . . had I yielded to human emotion . . . it is altogether probable I would have ordered the prosecution to continue, because I was irritated by the activities of the individual concerned.' The Tribunal, however, ruled that his written statement to the Lord Chancellor 'contained a misstatement about the withdrawal of the prosecution, and that it showed a marked lack of candour.'

The Lynskey Tribunal strongly attacked Sydney Stanley for his role in the affair. 'The allegations which led to the appointment of this Tribunal were that large sums of money were being, or had been paid, to some Ministers and some public servants. These allegations in our view were largely the result of the statements and activities of Mr Sydney Stanley . . . We are satisfied that for his own purposes he represented to various persons that upon payment by them to him of substantial sums he could secure licences for various purposes and also assistance from different ministries, and in particular the Board of Trade, and that he was able to do this by paying part of the money received by him to the Minister and officials who would have to deal with these matters. Mr Stanley is a man who will make any statement, whether true or untrue, if he thinks it is to his own advantage to do so. He was able, however, to give colour to his statements because Mr Belcher, Mr Gibson and Mr Key [Charles William Key, MP, cleared by the Tribunal of improperly receiving gifts] received him on apparently friendly terms, and it is not therefore surprising that rumours arose and that these baseless allegations of payments of large sums of money were made.'

It was also sharply critical of George Gibson, who turned down an offer of a £10,000-a-year company chairmanship from Sydney Stanley. '[His] reputation and high standing, not only in the Labour Party but in the public life of the country, gave him great influence. His advice and his word would carry great weight with any of his colleagues, whether inside or outside the Government.' Stanley offered him the £10,000-a-year job in an attempt '. . . to induce Mr Gibson as a public servant to assist in obtaining from the Treasury, upon the recommendation of the Capital Issues Committee, permission for a public issue of the shares of the new company' – and, said the Tribunal, 'Mr Gibson realized the reason for the offer.' Although he refused it, preferring instead the security of his Electricity Board appointment, he '. . . continued to assist Mr Stanley in his efforts to secure this permission for a public issue, and to assist in any other enterprise in which Mr Stanley sought his help. We are satisfied that Mr Gibson did this in the hope of material advantage to himself, although in fact all that he received apart from some trivial gifts was the present of a suit of clothes.' The Tribunal also referred to a 'misleading statement' in a letter Gibson wrote, which led to a meeting between Sydney Stanley and Glenvil Hall, the Financial Secretary to the Treasury.

Mr Gibson issued a brief statement from his home at Chorlton-cum-Hardy, in Manchester, when the findings were published. 'I have only had an opportunity of seeing a brief synopsis of the tribunal report, but I am deeply shocked and grieved at the findings, with which I cannot agree. I must reserve further comment until I have carefully studied the full report.'

Following John Belcher's resignation as an MP, Mr Attlee told the House that a committee was to be set up to look into the activities of contact men, and said it had been decided 'conducive to the public good' that Sydney Stanley should be deported. Stanley eventually went to live in Israel.

BRITISH SPY SCANDAL
Russian Agents in MI5 and MI6

The cloak-and-dagger flight to Moscow by British diplomats Burgess and Maclean in the summer of 1951 – following a tip-off from another highly placed traitor that Maclean was about to be interrogated on suspicion of treason – quickly erupted into the greatest spy scandal in the nation's history. Today it holds the dubious distinction of also being the longest-running: still the echoes rumble on, with a number of vital questions left unanswered by the authorities after more than thirty-four years – a situation which some might consider a scandal in itself, in any self-professed democratic society.

That there was a long-term Soviet conspiracy to infiltrate the British Establishment over the past half-century, with the security/intelligence network as its principal target, is no longer in doubt. With many of the original conspirators now either dead or beyond the reach of the law, the marathon spy scandal turns on a single issue: the extent to which that network was penetrated from the 1930s onward and its present state of efficiency. It was brought to a head in July 1984 when a retired senior MI5 officer, who had himself chaired an internal inquiry into KGB penetration of the service dating back to Burgess-Maclean days – and who insists that it has since failed to protect itself adequately against further treachery – risked prosecution under the Official Secrets Act to call publicly for a full official inquiry into the matter.

The extent of the Soviet conspiracy was underlined by the long list of spy trials between 1946, when Allan Nunn May – a friend of Burgess and first of the atom spies – was jailed for ten years, and 1984, when MI5 officer Michael Bettaney was sentenced to twenty-three years' imprisonment, also for spying for Russia. No single spy case, however, evoked as great a storm as the joint defection of Burgess and Maclean; while the sense of public outrage and frustration was similarly reflected in each of the subsequent scandals which arose directly from it.

These included the clandestine flight of Mrs Maclean with her three young children from Geneva in 1953 to rejoin her husband – with Soviet connivance – behind the Iron Curtain, while the British Secret Service, which apparently considered it unethical to shadow her, searched in vain for the two missing traitors. Next came the scandal of H. A. R. ('Kim') Philby, the 'Third Man' in the Burgess-Maclean defection, who was officially cleared of any involvement by the Foreign Secretary of the day, Harold Macmillan – only to defect himself eight years later, after first being restored to the payroll of the Secret Service he had successfully betrayed for so long. Then there was the scandal of traitor Anthony Blunt, the so-called 'Fourth Man' in the Burgess-Maclean saga. Art historian Blunt, a wartime MI5 officer and Surveyor of the Queen's Pictures, was awarded a knighthood while under interrogation on suspicion of spying for Russia – the classic case of the right hand of the Establishment not knowing what the left was doing. Blunt finally confessed to being a Soviet agent in 1964, in return for a promise of immunity against prosecution, but was not unmasked until 1979 following the publication of Andrew Boyle's book on spies within the Establishment *The Climate of Treason*. Blunt's guilt was then officially confirmed by Mrs Thatcher in the House of Commons, whereupon he was stripped of his knighthood by the Palace.

No sooner had the storm over Blunt's treachery, made all the more heinous because of his royal appointment, died down than a new and even bigger spy scandal emerged. In 1981, author and journalist Chapman Pincher revealed in his book *Their Trade is Treachery* that the man suspected of being the most damaging Soviet penetration agent of all inside MI5 was none other than its former Director General, Sir Roger Hollis. Hollis, who joined MI5 before World War II, served as head of 'Section F' – the department responsible for keeping watch on all Soviet operations in Britain – before his promotion, first to deputy Director General and finally head of the service from 1956 until his retirement in 1965.

Pincher told how, '. . . early in 1980 the Prime Minister, Margaret Thatcher, was warned about a hushed-up security scandal affecting MI5 which was infinitely more explosive than the exposure of the Russian spy, Anthony Blunt. The Home Secretary, William Whitelaw, and the Attorney-General, Sir Michael Havers, were also told that in 1974 Lord Trend, formerly Sir Burke Trend and Secretary of the Cabinet for a decade, was secretly called from retirement to conduct an unprecedented inquiry. He was asked to give an independent judgment on the appalling probability that Sir Roger Hollis, a long-serving Director General of MI5, had been a Russian spy for almost thirty years.'

Not unnaturally, Chapman Pincher's disclosures caused a sensation. Hollis, however, was not charged with any offence, far less found guilty in a court of law for on 26 March 1981 Mrs Thatcher told the Commons the inquiry had concluded that Sir Roger was not a spy. Pincher stuck to his guns and in July 1984, the Prime Minister's statement was challenged in turn by retired MI5 officer (and 'mole-catcher') Peter Wright, who had earlier chaired a secret internal committee of inquiry into Soviet penetration of the security service. He insisted in both Press and television interviews that, 'Those of us intimately concerned with the investigation believed that Hollis . . . had been a long-term Soviet penetration agent in MI5.' Although he agreed there was no legal proof of treason, he maintained that 'intelligence-wise, it is 99 per cent certain he was a spy.' He also alleged that Mrs Thatcher had been given 'a lot of facts which are not correct. She was advised by the security service, who were anxious that there should not be a high-level independent inquiry into the service that might . . . drag skeletons out of the cupboard they would not want revealed.'

Mr Wright further claimed that MI5 had since failed to protect itself adequately against further penetration and cited the case of Michael Bettaney, a serving MI5 officer who was sentenced to twenty-three years' imprisonment only four months earlier, as the most recent example. He said it was a situation which had been allowed to develop because there had been a cover-up of the truth both by politicians and members of the service. 'I want to go before the Security Commission, or any other suitable form of inquiry, to argue my case,' he said. 'And I am not going to give up until they have listened to me.' The spy scandal which so many British governments had hoped was dead and buried was very much alive again.

From the outset, the hurried and even amateurish joint defection of Burgess and Maclean – which was carried out under the very noses of MI5 – proved successful beyond the wildest dreams of its KGB organizers. Its prime objective, to shield the frightened and unstable Maclean from direct interrogation and thus safeguard the identity of his several Communist fellow-conspirators in British government service, was achieved overnight. Its many propaganda bonuses there-after stemmed largely from the ostrich-like response of the British authorities to the situation they then faced. Stubborn ministerial evasion in the face of repeated Press disclosures which clearly demonstrated the total unsuitability of either man to hold any position of trust in running the country's affairs, served only to heighten the public's suspicion of a cover-up. The failure over many years by the security service to spot even the most glaringly obvious character defect in either man – and they were legion – or to pick up so much as a whisper of their publicly expressed radical left-wing views, likewise provided much food for scandal in the climate of anger and recrimination which followed the news of their defection. And it was not only political reputations which suffered. The status of MI5 and MI6 sank to an all-time low, causing considerable, and perhaps permanent, damage to the Anglo-US 'special relationship'. The KGB themselves could not have planned it better.

When Guy Francis de Moncy Burgess, then aged forty, and his Cambridge contemporary, Donald Duart Maclean, fled from Southampton at midnight on Friday, 25 May 1951, aboard the cross-Channel steamer *Falaise*, the cold war between Soviet Russia and the West was at its height. The mere fact that both men were from the Foreign Office – that storehouse of secrets, at the time possibly the most respected of all British institutions after the monarchy – was enough in itself to send shivers down the nation's spine. Equally, the mystery of the disappearance seemed all the more sinister because – on the surface at least –

there appeared to be nothing in their make-up to fit the conventional Red spy image.

Here were two young men of impeccable family background and public-school education. Maclean, who was Head of the American Department of the Foreign Office in London, and the son of a former Cabinet Minister, was married with two children. He had vanished on his thirty-eighth birthday, at a time when his American-born wife Melinda was shortly expecting their third child (a daughter, born three weeks later). Old Etonian Guy Burgess, a single man, was a wartime (Special Operations Executive) secret serviceman and son of a Royal Navy officer. He had been appointed Second Secretary at the British embassy in Washington less than a year earlier and his Foreign Office career included a two-year spell as Assistant Personal Private Secretary to the Minister of State, Hector McNeil.

That any two members of the diplomatic service should flee the country together, for any reason, was cause enough for alarm: and there was infinitely worse to come. Their joint defection, sensational and unprecedented though it was, proved to be only the tip of the iceberg. Its true significance lay in the fact that it provided the security authorities with their first inkling of a conspiracy for treason within the ranks of the Establishment itself.

From the beginning it was apparent that the conspiracy had to involve not only Burgess and Maclean but also one other traitor at least; one so highly placed, moreover, that he had immediate access to the country's most sensitive intelligence material. That much was self-evident, from the timing and circumstances preceding the disappearance. Maclean had long been regarded by many colleagues as the 'white hope' of the British diplomatic service. What none of his admirers knew was that '*Operation Bride*', a US Intelligence inquiry into the wartime leakage of top-secret political and scientific information to Moscow from Washington – where Maclean had served as First Secretary in the British embassy – had identified him as the principal suspect. This information had now been relayed to London and the fateful decision to set an early date for Maclean's interrogation was taken at a special meeting, chaired by Foreign Secretary Herbert Morrison and with only the most senior security and intelligence officers present, a matter of hours before Burgess and Maclean fled the country. Clearly, someone within – or who was party to the decisions reached by – that august band was guilty either of monumental indiscretion . . . or treachery.

Terrifying though that prospect was, there were also clear indications of even deeper penetration of the security/intelligence network. Although Burgess had been under no suspicion until the night he adopted an assumed name ('Roger Styles') and disappeared with Maclean, it was straining credulity too far to accept that he might have returned coincidentally from Washington to London less than three weeks beforehand. Equally, it was inconceivable that the findings of '*Operation Bride*', reached after more than two years of secret US intelligence inquiry, would have been made known at Second Secretary level in the British embassy. Clearly someone in Washington too had been guilty of indiscretion – or deliberate betrayal.

The fact that the first announcement of the double defection – by then a fortnight-old *fait accompli* – should have come not from the Prime Minister (whose duty it was as head of all security and intelligence services) to the House, but from the Press, served only to exacerbate the inevitable public reaction of shock and outrage. This blunder was compounded by the fact that while every effort thereafter by the British Secret Service over the next four years failed to locate the missing diplomats, the man in the street had little doubt from the beginning where they would be found – in Moscow. Nor was that based on blind guesswork. Within days of the first newspaper accounts of their midnight flight, former friends revealed that both had spouted Marxist sentiments from undergraduate days. Within a year the nation learned how both had openly admitted, long before they disappeared, to being Russian spies: Burgess before the outbreak of World War II (and his acceptance into the Secret Service), Maclean in the winter of 1950. The lame excuse that none of this had been reported to the authorities did little to allay the sense of anger and frustration these disclosures aroused. Why, it was asked, had such elementary facts not emerged in the course of routine security vetting?

And if the failure to trace them was not scandalous enough, lurid details of both Burgess and Maclean's myriad character defects had likewise long since come to light. Although they had apparently escaped the notice of both security officers and Foreign Office mandarins alike over the years, these details came into the possession of inquiring reporters after the defection as easily – and plentifully – as windfall apples. They included homosexuality (then a criminal offence, thus leaving both men open to blackmail), habitual drunkenness and a bent for brawling in public both in London and abroad. Moral standards were stricter in the 1950s than in today's permissive society and eyewitness accounts of such conduct by serving British diplomats fuelled the fires of scandal every bit as much as the thought of the political damage they might have done. As a result, each new Press disclosure gravely embarrassed a whole succession of governments, Ministers and ex-Ministers, by showing them to be either sadly misinformed, grossly inefficient, guilty of a deliberate cover-up – or even, perhaps, all three.

Four days after Clement Attlee's Socialist government of 1951 confirmed that Burgess and Maclean were indeed missing, former Tory Foreign Secretary Anthony Eden said of Donald Maclean's alleged 'breakdown through overwork' in Cairo in 1950, 'May I be allowed to say, as Mr Maclean was serving under me at the time that in all the reports I received the work he did there was very good indeed.' Alas for Mr Eden, he had never been in office during Maclean's service in Cairo: all of it had been spent under a Socialist administration.

Following that remarkable gaffe, Lord Reading, the joint Under Secretary for Foreign Affairs, said in 1952 that, 'Mr Maclean . . . performed his official duties satisfactorily up to the date of his disappearance.' This was more than a year after the security authorities had been warned by the Americans that Maclean was a likely traitor. And both ministerial views of Maclean's conduct – on duty or off – were in sharp contrast to those of author Cyril Connolly, who told *Sunday Times* readers, also in 1952, about his behaviour both in Cairo and London.

He revealed how in one drunken escapade in Cairo, before an audience of twenty people (including his wife), Maclean had seized an Egyptian guard's rifle and assaulted a fellow British diplomat, breaking the man's leg in the scuffle. Later, said Connolly, after treatment from a woman psychoanalyst for his 'breakdown' in Cairo – and promotion to Head of the American Department in the bargain – Maclean openly confessed to a friend that he was a Communist agent.

Of Burgess, Foreign Secretary Herbert Morrison told the Commons on 18 July 1951, 'Mr Burgess was appointed to the office of the Minister of State on 31 December 1946. He was transferred to the Far Eastern Department on 1 November 1948. The transfer took place in the normal course of routine and was intended to give Mr Burgess experience in a political department . . . At that time there was nothing adverse, as far as we were aware, against Mr Burgess.'

Only a month earlier the poet Wystan Auden, an old friend of Burgess, had revealed that, 'Burgess . . . was an open Communist in the late 1930s. In New York, where I spend six months of the year, we met several times. While he was at the embassy in Washington, he was still pro-Communist. We met last in March this year. We talked about Fuchs and Nunn May, who was a close friend of Burgess.' (Physicists Klaus Fuchs and Allan Nunn May were both serving prison sentences at the time for betraying atom secrets to Russia.) 'I asked him if he had been screened and Burgess spoke of diplomatic immunity.' A week after that interview appeared in the *Daily Express*, Kenneth Younger, who was Minister of State at the Foreign Office under Herbert Morrison, informed the House that, '. . . a security check was made on Mr Burgess some time ago and it was negative in its result.'

It was small wonder that the public was left to debate who to believe and how efficient such security checks could be. For three days before Mr Morrison addressed the House, an official of a London firm of solicitors representing the owners of the New Bond Street flat rented by Burgess, told the *Sunday Dispatch*,

Soon after Burgess moved in there were complaints from other tenants of rowdy parties, shouts, screams, and fights throughout the night in the Burgess flat. He seemed to have a considerable number of parties, and they were always all-male affairs. Whenever I saw him, he seemed to have some part of his body in bandages. I told him about the complaints and he promised to be quieter in future. For a while things were quiet. Then one of our tenants in the flat above rang us in a panic. Early one Sunday morning she had been awakened by her baby girl, who was in tears and trembling. The noise from the flat below was almost indescribable. Soon afterwards an ambulance drew up and Burgess, with his head and arm bandaged, was taken to hospital on a stretcher. Quite obviously there had been a first-class fight. I rang the hospital and was told that he had a fractured skull, a broken jaw and arm injuries and was on the danger list.

Later an ex-ballet dancer and homosexual called Jack Hewitt, who lived with Burgess at the time, explained that, 'Guy was thrown down the stairs by a fellow diplomat,' adding, 'It was not Maclean.'

That happened early in 1949. Later the same year, while on holiday in Tangier and Gibraltar, Burgess was officially reported to the Foreign Office by the security authorities for 'indiscreet talk about secret matters of which he had official knowledge'. According to the government White Paper on the defection, published in 1955, Burgess had been 'severely reprimanded' for that blatant security lapse. How or why the details had not been given to the House earlier was not explained. In the same way the security check made on Burgess, which proved 'negative in its result', was made to look even more remarkable in the light of Cyril Connolly's account of an incident involving Burgess as far back as 1937. 'Burgess and a great friend of his', wrote Connolly in *The Sunday Times* 'would sometimes stay with a talented and beautiful novelist . . . One day Burgess's friend came to her, shaken and yet impressed. Guy had confided to him that he was not only a member but a secret agent of the Communist Party, and he had then invited him . . . to join in the work.'

To most ordinary people, officialdom's reluctance to open up this Pandora's box of self-confessed treachery seemed every bit as scandalous as its apparent lack of knowledge of the dangerous unsuitability of either man to work for the Foreign Office. On 10 July 1952 Mr Anthony Nutting, Under Secretary at the Foreign Office, was asked by Conservative MP Colonel Alan Gomme-Duncan if 'he would recommend the appointment of a Royal Commission, or appoint a suitable fact-finding body to inquiry fully into the disappearance of Burgess and Maclean and all the circumstances connected therewith.'

Mr Nutting refused, saying that, 'a full inquiry' had already been made by the security authorities, in conjunction with the Foreign Office departments concerned. 'I am satisfied,' he declared, 'that nothing further would be gained by the appointment of a Royal Commission or other fact-finding body . . .' Four months later he told the House that no action was to be taken against the (unnamed) official who had appointed Burgess and Maclean to their Foreign Office posts. 'I am not prepared to lend myself to a witch-hunt of this character,' he said. Three years later the government – and the British people – learned from newspaper articles written by Russian defector Vladimir Petrov, formerly head of the KGB in Australia, that both men were in Russia and had been from the start. Among other things, Petrov revealed that Burgess had supplied 'whole briefcases' full of secret documents to his Soviet control in London between 1945 and 1948.

In the Lords debate which followed publication of the government White Paper – some of it based on Petrov's admissions – Lord Astor, a member of *The Observer* newspaper board, said, 'It was particularly unfortunate that (Nutting) should have used the phrase "witch-hunt" of those who were trying to find the truth. Trying to uncover treason is as much a duty as to prevent burglary . . . We have got to recognize that for the first time since the reign of the first Queen Elizabeth, we have a Fifth Column in this country that has penetrated the highest ranks of the Civil Service, and apparently scientists – even the church.'

He said that after Maclean returned from Cairo to London, 'He used to go in the evening and get disgustingly drunk in a certain club. He twice engaged in drunken brawls with some Left-wing friends, in one of which they were rolling on the floor. In each case the attack was that they had betrayed their former Left-wing opinions. This was the Head of the American Department!' He also described Burgess as 'drunken, dirty, and sexually indecent. Ever since school he made no pretence about it, in his conversation or his conduct.' Everyone, it seemed, knew about the Communist beliefs and appalling conduct of these two long-term spies – except the authorities and their security advisers.

For the British security/intelligence network it was a matter of utter humiliation. From the outset the Americans had been sharply critical of Britain's failure to act sooner and more firmly on the evidence uncovered by '*Operation Bride*'. MI5 had been savaged by the home Press for its failure to confront Maclean and search his home – or even maintain surveillance on him there – for fear of upsetting his pregnant wife. The failure of both intelligence and security to note and act upon the glaring character defects shown by both men for so many years was a scandal in itself. Now it was the turn of the Russians to rub salt into British wounds. In February 1956 – almost five years after the two diplomats had disappeared and with MI6 unable to offer a shred of evidence as to their whereabouts – Burgess and Maclean were produced like rabbits out of a hat to correspondents gathered in the National Hotel off Gorky Street, in the very heart of Moscow. Everything was stage managed. No questions were allowed. The pair simply issued written statements claiming that they quit England 'to work for peace', after witnessing at first hand western preparations for another war. As a propaganda coup, however, it was a brilliant success: just to see the renegade pair in the flesh again was enough to bring the scandal to the boil once more in Britain.

From then on until their death – both died in exile in Moscow: Burgess in 1963 and Maclean twenty years later – their value to the Russians, as both working defectors and propaganda symbols, progressively declined. With so many questions about their flight left unanswered, however, each of the several related scandals which followed their 1951 defection proved almost as damaging. The first involved Mrs Maclean and the three Maclean children.

Mrs Maclean, who did not appear at the 1956 'press conference', committed no crime when she slipped out of Geneva three years beforehand to rejoin her husband. The scandal of that wholly foreseeable development lay rather in the failure of Britain's counter-espionage departments to mount a watch on her, in intelligent anticipation of gaining the first positive clue to her traitor husband's whereabouts. It was an omission which seemed all the more scandalous when Mrs Maclean then vanished with her children, destination unknown – for Donald Maclean had already demonstrated his ability to contact her through an intermediary in Switzerland.

On 3 August 1951 – ten weeks after Maclean disappeared with Burgess – Swiss bankers' drafts worth £2,000 intended for Mrs Maclean were sent to her mother, Mrs Dunbar, then living with her in Surrey. Mrs Dunbar reported the arrival of the money to MI5 and it was subsequently paid into an account opened with the authority of the Foreign Office. News of the payment (which was proof that Maclean was in the pay of a foreign power) was withheld from the public by the authorities in Britain but discovered and published by the *Daily Express* on 2 June 1953. Since the previous summer, complaints had been made that Mrs Maclean and the children were being 'hounded' by the Press and by the Express newspaper group in particular which had proved increasingly effective. The campaign was waged largely through the correspondence columns of *The Times* under the heading 'The ethics of journalism'. Public sympathy was naturally on the side of the apparently abandoned young family, and so successful was the campaign that no one from Britain – newspaperman or secret agent – dared to follow when Mrs Maclean left London in July 1952 with her children to live first in Paris and later in Geneva. Officialdom's reaction was spelled out by Foreign Secretary Anthony Eden (the British Secret Service is directly responsible to the Foreign Secretary) after Mrs Maclean's own disappearance behind the Iron Curtain. He told the Commons, 'She was a free agent and no form of surveillance would have been . . . either feasible or proper.'

It was as if the 'Great Game' was being played by the rules of cricket. Proper or not, it enabled Donald Maclean to re-establish contact with her (with help from the KGB) and the family to rejoin him within a year. On 11 September 1953 Mrs Maclean deceived her mother, now staying with her in Geneva, by pretending that she had accepted an invitation from a 'Robin Muir' – supposedly a friend from Cairo days – to visit him and his wife at their villa near Montreux, taking the children with her. 'Robin Muir' did not exist: instead Mrs Maclean drove with the children to Lausanne, where they boarded a train to Zurich and then changed on to an Austria-bound express. They were met next morning by a chauffeur-driven car at Schwarzach St Viet, near Salzburg, and taken to the Russian zone of occupation whence they flew to Moscow. Copies of the children's passport photographs, which Mrs Maclean had ordered under a false name, were later found in her Geneva flat. The date showed that her flight had been planned weeks beforehand.

Too late, two British security officers were sent to Switzerland to conduct inquiries. Two years and four months after the Burgess-Maclean defection, the KGB had notched another propaganda victory; and the great British spy scandal rumbled on.

Long before Mrs Maclean vanished, the search was on within the Establishment to try to identify the 'Third Man' believed to have engineered her husband's escape. The White Paper of 1955 revealed that, 'searching inquiries involving individual interrogations were made', but admitted that, 'insufficient evidence was available to form a definite conclusion, or to warrant a prosecution.' The main target for that individual interrogation had been Harold Adrian Russell ('Kim') Philby, First Secretary at the British embassy in Washington at the time of the defection and liaison officer to the CIA and FBI.

Philby fell under immediate suspicion for two reasons: because Burgess, his friend from undergraduate days, had stayed with him throughout his posting as Second Secretary at the embassy, and more importantly because Philby – as linkman with the CIA – had been among the first to know that Maclean was suspected of treason by the US intelligence team conducting '*Operation Bride*'.

Eleven years later, a KGB officer named Anatoli Golitsin defected to the CIA from the Soviet embassy in Helsinki. Among the information he passed on was a warning that Moscow Centre, or spy headquarters, had for many years controlled a group of high-level traitors in Britain known as 'The Ring of Five'. All had been recruited, said Golitsin, during their undergraduate days in the 1930s at Cambridge University. He knew Burgess and Maclean (then in Moscow) to be two of the five and although he was unable to name the others, some of the clues he gave pointed the finger at Philby as one of them.

'Kim' Philby was a former Westminster public schoolboy and son of the distinguished Arabist, Harry St John Philby. He went to Trinity College, Cambridge, in 1929 – the same year as Burgess – and later wrote in his book *My Silent War*: 'I left university with a degree (in 1933) and with the conviction that my life must be devoted to Communism.'

If much of the book was propaganda, that was certainly true. Why the Russians selected Cambridge as their main recruiting centre was explained by Andrew Boyle in his *The Climate of Treason*. 'The fact that a nucleus of perhaps a dozen Communists existed among the Fellows made Cambridge a natural choice. Although Clemens Palme Dutt nominally proposed it, there can be no doubt that the initiative came from the West European Bureau of the Committee, acting on instructions issued by Maxim Litvinov, Karl Radek and other leading policy makers in Moscow.'

Philby then spent his apprentice service as Communist agent in Austria, during the Nazi rise to power. It was there he married his first wife, a Communist named Litzi Friedman who herself became a Soviet agent. (He married three times altogether.) After his return to London, he pretended a conversion to the Right and later served as foreign correspondent for *The Times* during the Spanish civil war, with the Franco forces. On the outbreak of World War II he was sent to France as war correspondent with the British Expeditionary Force. Following the evacuation in 1940 he left Fleet Street to join the British Secret Service – sponsored by his Cambridge recruiter and fellow-spy in 'The Ring of Five', Guy Burgess. No mention of his 1934 marriage to Litzi Friedman was made until his second marriage, in 1946: even then it brought no repercussion. He won an OBE for his wartime intelligence service, yet spied for the Russians throughout, his value growing with each promotion. As head of the Iberian section he blocked reports suggesting that Admiral Canaris, chief of the Abwehr (German military intelligence), was willing to negotiate a separate peace with the Western Allies after the overthrow of Hitler – the Communist reasoning being that the longer the war lasted, the greater would be Russia's post-war influence in Europe. In 1945, Philby betrayed a would-be Russian defector in Istanbul named Volkov, who possessed information which could have identified 'The Ring of Five' spy group, himself included. Later, as head of station in Washington, he had access to the most sensitive information. Among other acts of treachery, he gave the Russians advance warning of Anglo-US plans to parachute Albanian nationalists into that country to topple the Hoxha regime; all were intercepted and shot.

As liaison officer to the CIA, he was ideally placed to save Maclean. After first informing Moscow that Maclean's wartime treason had been uncovered by '*Operation Bride*', he was instructed to send Burgess back to London to warn him. Burgess then arranged to have himself sent home for 'misconduct' – a series of wild driving offences: not once was he suspected of espionage – where in the natural course of events he reported to Maclean in his role as Head of the American Department. When the CIA demanded Philby's own recall from Washington a month later, all the British authorities could do – in the absence of proof against Philby – was to make him resign. Several of his colleagues continued to believe in his innocence. Much later, after he had been publicly named in an American newspaper as the 'Third Man', no British newspaper dared follow suit because of the libel laws. As a result 'Kim' Philby's name remained unknown to the public at home until 25 October 1955, when Socialist MP Colonel Marcus Lipton asked the then Prime Minister, Anthony Eden, 'Have you made up your mind to cover up at all costs the dubious "Third Man" activities of Mr Harold Philby, who was First Secretary at the Washington embassy a while ago?'

Sir Anthony made no reply; Philby declined to comment from his home in Sussex. Then in the Commons debate which followed shortly afterwards, Foreign Secretary Harold

Macmillan took it upon himself to clear Philby with this statement,

> Mr Philby had been a friend of Burgess from the time when they were fellow undergraduates at Trinity College, Cambridge. Burgess had been accommodated with Philby and his family at the latter's home in Washington from August 1950 to April 1951 . . . and, of course, it will be remembered that at no time before he fled was Burgess under suspicion. It is now known that Mr Philby had Communist associates during and after his university days. In view of the circumstances, he was asked in July 1951 to resign from the Foreign Service. Since that date his case has been the subject of close investigation. No evidence has been found . . . to show that he was responsible for warning Burgess or Maclean. While in government service he carried out his duties ably and conscientiously, and I have no reason to conclude that Mr Philby has at any time betrayed the interests of his country, or to identify him with the so-called 'Third Man', if indeed there was one.

No Minister before or since, in all the long-running spy scandal, has been proved more hopelessly wrong in his judgment. In *Their Trade is Treachery* Mr Chapman Pincher, who discussed the issue with Mr Macmillan, revealed that, 'He . . . was told by the Law Officers that Philby was almost certainly guilty but was unprepared, in the interests of individual liberty, to use the privilege of Parliament even to suggest an unproven situation regarding Philby, as MI5 wanted. He was not prepared to say in Parliament what he knew he would not dare to say outside.'

As Marshal Bosquet observed of The Charge of the Light Brigade, '*C'est magnifique, mais ce n'est pas la guerre.*' At once Philby took full advantage of Macmillan's gullibility. Whitewashed by the Foreign Secretary, secure in the knowledge that MI5 had no evidence against him, and aware that such an unsolicited character reference – coming whence it did – would effectively muzzle the newspapers too, he promptly called a press conference. He used it both to lie about his past ('I have never been a Communist') and to call Colonel Lipton's bluff, by challenging him to repeat his remarks outside the House. Typically, he was to complain later that, 'Lipton had shattered my dream . . . of extracting a very large sum (in libel damages) from a Beaverbrook newspaper.'

Next, discreet lobbying of influential friends led to his re-employment as a foreign correspondent in the Middle East, based on Beirut. At the same time the Secret Service – hoodwinked yet again – used the appointment to reinstate Philby as a freelance agent in the area, under his journalistic cover. Incredible though it now sounds, he thereupon served as both British agent and Russian spy for a further seven years, until Golitsin's debriefing in 1962 reinforced all the old suspicions against him. Finally, after new evidence had come from an independent source, suspicion that he had been a traitor all along hardened into certainty. In 1963 he was questioned once more, in Beirut, when he finally confessed that he had been a Russian spy since 1934. Knowing that his MI6 investigator had no powers to order him home, Philby played for time by pretending to 'consider' an offer of immunity from prosecution if he returned voluntarily to face more detailed interrogation. Instead, he promptly defected in his turn, almost certainly via a Russian freighter which left Beirut harbour on the night of 23 January 1963. To some, it seemed poetic justice that he should have done so during Harold Macmillan's premiership. Perhaps not surprisingly, Philby's defection – like that of Burgess and Maclean twelve years earlier – was attended by an almost deafening official silence right to the end. It was five months before the government admitted that he was indeed the original 'Third Man' – and the great spy scandal boiled up all over again.

The ubiquitous Philby even provided a whiff of scandal for the Kremlin Establishment, as well as the 'Grey Brigade' in Moscow (the Western defectors and fellow-travellers living out their dull if privileged lives in the Soviet capital), by conducting an affair with Donald Maclean's wife, Melinda. It became common gossip in diplomatic circles and was well-publicized in the West while Philby's third wife, Eleanor, who had twice joined him in Russia – at his request – left him and returned home.

Art historian Anthony Blunt, born in 1907 and a fourth member of 'The Ring of Five', was the son of a London vicar who became British embassy chaplain in Paris at the time of World War I. He won a scholarship from Marlborough College to Trinity College, Cambridge, in 1926 and stayed eleven years, latterly as a don. He was recruited to Marxism by his friend and fellow-homosexual Guy Burgess; after Burgess left, Blunt took over as Red 'talent spotter' at Cambridge. Thanks to lax security vetting later, he joined MI5 in 1940 (after first being rejected as a security risk) via the Army Intelligence Corps, whereupon he gave the Russians every scrap of classified information that came his way during the war. No great skill or courage was needed. He and Burgess shared a flat in Bentinck Street, in London's West End, and turned it into a haven of drink and plenty for their friends in security and intelligence, as well as for homosexuals and fellow-travellers – a veritable Tom Tiddler's ground for espionage. They then took their notes and stolen secret papers to Blunt's quarters at the Courtauld Institute, where they were photographed for delivery to the Soviet embassy in Kensington Palace Gardens. Neither came under suspicion at any time. In *Their Trade is Treachery* Chapman Pincher described Blunt as: '. . . one of the most damaging spies ever to operate in Britain, contrary to the common belief that, compared with Philby or Maclean, he was in the second division. His crimes against his country, dragged out of him during hundreds of hours of taped interrogations, are such an indictment of wartime security that every effort has been made to cover them from public knowledge.' Blackmail was carried out at Bentinck Street too. In *The Climate of Treason* Andrew Boyle revealed: 'Just to demonstrate that blackmail could be an unpleasantly two-sided affair, he [Burgess] invited his Foreign Office friend [Maclean] to a stage-managed orgy at Bentinck Street. Some choice erotic photographs of Donald lying naked and oblivious in the arms of another man were duly added, Burgess later told Maclean, to his private collection.'

After he left MI5 in 1945, Blunt remained in close touch with Burgess. On 7 May 1951 he met Burgess off the *Queen Mary* at Southampton and learned that he was under KGB orders (via Philby) to warn Maclean the net was closing round him. Blunt himself came under suspicion almost immediately after the defection, both as a friend of Burgess and because the security authorities had learned for the first time how Burgess had admitted to being a Comintern agent in 1937, naming Blunt as a fellow-conspirator. However, he bluffed his way through every interrogation until his confession in 1964. He confessed then only after new evidence against him came from American sources – and on promises of immunity from prosecution. His part in the Burgess-Maclean affair was encapsulated by Mrs Thatcher, who said that while he had no (official) access to secret information after leaving MI5 in 1945, Blunt 'used his old contact with the Russians to assist in the arrangements for the defection of Burgess and Maclean.'

Her carefully worded reference to Blunt's role in their defection leaves open to doubt the identity of the 'Fourth Man' in the conspiracy. In his book Andrew Boyle named Blunt as the one who rang Burgess during the afternoon of 25 May 1951, to pass on the precise date on which MI5 planned to interrogate Maclean (Monday, 28 May), thus pre-empting their flight. (Burgess had previously arranged to leave for France on 25 May with a young, homosexual American; their cabins on the *Falaise* were already booked.) Others believe the final tip-off came from Philby in Washington. Chapman Pincher put forward another theory in his book. Blunt's denial that he warned Burgess was confirmed by his own sources, said Pincher, adding: 'But there seems to be no firm evidence that Philby was told this date. He certainly did not pass it on to the CIA or FBI, where officers complained later of being kept in the dark. As I have indicated, there was an alternative source nearer at hand – the Soviet penetration agent within MI5.'

Within the framework of Mrs Thatcher's statement, both authors could be right. The original leak had to come either from someone who attended the conference on 25 May at which tne date to interrogate Maclean was set, or who straightaway learned the date through indiscretion, or – much more likely – was told in order to take part in the interrogation. Direct contact with Burgess or Maclean would have placed such a penetration agent at maximum risk, so that a decision may have been taken to use the more expendable Blunt as go-between. However, it was not Blunt's role that sparked off the storm which broke after he had been unmasked as a Russian spy. The scandal was not that he had got away with it for so long, but rather that he had remained in the Queen's service after his confession – at the request of the security authorities. And the question which had to be answered was – did Her Majesty know he was a spy, or had she been deceived by MI5 in order to score off the KGB?

Mrs Thatcher's statement to the commons in November 1979 answered that question only in part. She said,

It was considered important to gain [Blunt's] cooperation in the continuing investigations by the security authorities, following the defections of Burgess, Maclean and Philby, into Soviet penetration of the security and intelligence services and other public services during and after the war. Accordingly the Attorney-General authorized the offer of immunity to Blunt if he confessed . . . The Queen's Private Secretary was informed both of Blunt's confession and of the immunity from prosecution, on the basis of which it had been made. Blunt was not required to resign his appointment in the Royal Household, which was unpaid. It carried with it no access to classified information and no risk to security and the security authorities thought it desirable not to put at risk his cooperation.

It was not until 1981 that Chapman Pincher revealed that Sir Michael Adeane, the Queen's Private Secretary, '. . . asked what action the authorities would like the Queen to take regarding Blunt's Royal appointment if Blunt agreed to confess. He was told that it would be advisable for the Queen to take no action whatsoever because, otherwise, traitors to whom Blunt might point could take evasive action . . . Normally writers do not really know what the Queen does or says but, because of a fluke circumstance, I *know* the Queen was properly alerted to the Blunt situation by Adeane as soon as he had received the brief of the confession. She merely asked what the official advice was, and on being told agreed to accept it in the national interest.'

Remarkably, that decision in 1964 to grant immunity to Blunt – taken by Attorney-General Sir John Hobson (a Minister, although not a member of the Cabinet) – was withheld from the Prime Minister, Sir Alec Douglas-Home. When the facts were finally made known by Mrs Thatcher – fifteen years later – Lord Home's insistence that he had never been told, completely borne out by the record, served only to add to the smell of a cover-up which had attended this long, sorry, spy scandal from the start. And scandal it most certainly was, all over again. It was one thing for the nation to learn that the Queen had become involved, in the interests of national security – that was something all could understand, if not approve – but what added insult to injury was the realization that honours galore had been conferred on the traitor Blunt since he was first interrogated on suspicion of being a spy back in 1951.

Although the authorities had failed to unearth corroborant evidence against him, as they had similarly failed in the case of Philby, Blunt had remained a firm suspect since he was first reported to them. Indeed, he had been subjected to no less than eleven interrogations before he finally confessed in 1964. Yet not only had he retained his Palace appointment, he had also received a knighthood along the way and he continued to have further honours bestowed upon him after he confessed to being a spy. To the man in the street it was an 'Alice in Wonderland' situation. Already appointed Surveyor of the King's Pictures after leaving MI5 at the end of the war, Blunt later became Surveyor of the Queen's Pictures in 1952, a year after his interrogation had begun; he was also made a Knight Commander of the Royal Victorian Order in 1956 – an honour which led in turn to the prestigious appointment as Slade Professor of Fine Art, at both Oxford and Cambridge Universities, to honorary degrees from the universities of Bristol, Durham, Oxford and Paris, and an honorary Fellowship of his old college, Trinity. In 1972, the year he survived an operation for cancer – eight years after he had confessed to being a Soviet spy – he was appointed Adviser of the Queen's Pictures and Drawings, a position he held until his retirement in 1978. He remained Director of the Courtauld Institute, the scene of his wartime spy photography, until 1974.

Even after he was stripped of his knighthood, following his denouncement by Mrs Thatcher in the Commons, he continued to be treated in some quarters with respect bordering almost on obsequiousness. The 'press conference' to which he assented five days later was stage managed and restricted to journalists from *The Times* and *The Guardian*. Two television crews were allotted ten minutes apiece for questions before Blunt disappeared into the *Times'* boardroom for a lunch of trout and white wine. Its one enduring achievement was to perpetuate the belief that he still had much to hide.

The *Daily Express*, which first broke the spy-scandal story twenty-eight years earlier, growled that: 'Professor Blunt would not have been offered so much as a stale kipper in the *Express* offices . . . In the event (the "conference") failed to produce a single satisfactory answer to the questions that matter.' Former Prime Minister James Callaghan observed: 'I am bound to say that I think . . . there has been a tendency to treat Mr Blunt with kid gloves. That is not my view with hindsight; I expressed it as Prime Minister, and was minuted to that effect.'

What the security authorities gained from their feather-bed treatment of this long-term traitor is open to doubt. Chapman Pincher's verdict was that: 'It was concluded that during his interrogations he had lied and misled MI5 over some of his dealings with the Russians. It was suspected that he had met with his Russian friends on more occasions after the war than he had admitted. Further, he had not changed ideologically and was proud of what he had done.'

True to form, the cynical Blunt continued to profit from his immunity guarantee until his death in 1983. Even though he had been publicly disgraced, he still preferred the life of a wealthy recluse in the West rather than join Philby & Co. in proletarian Moscow.

In the thirty-three years following Burgess's and Maclean's defection to Moscow, by 1984 only four of the five Cambridge undergraduates who became members of 'The Ring of Five' were officially named by the British authorities – Burgess, Maclean, Philby and Blunt. The 'Fifth Man' remains a mystery figure, although the two authors who have done most to fit together the pieces of the jigsaw, Boyle and Pincher, have each offered their separate clues to his possible identity.

In *The Climate of Treason* Boyle named him only as 'Basil'. He described him as an English physicist, now a naturalized

American citizen, who worked hand-in-glove in Washington first with Donald Maclean and later with Philby – on the orders of a high-ranking US intelligence agent who had 'turned' him, without the knowledge of the British Secret Service. According to Boyle, he was 'turned with ease, and on practical rather than ideological grounds. He was not a strong character. He proved cooperative because he knew which side his bread was buttered on.' Thereafter he pretended to work with Maclean for the Russians by '. . . advising him which nuclear-programme files, and which items in those files, should be extracted from the US Atomic Energy Commission's headquarters, where the First Secretary used his special unauthorized pass to gain entry unattended. The information thus obtained was carefully monitored by the Americans before "Basil" handed it to Maclean for transmission to the Russians.'

According to Chapman Pincher in *Their Trade is Treachery* the 'Fifth Man' was 'a defence scientist in a most sensitive position in the Government service. This person is not Dr Basil Mann, the atomic scientist living in the US and recently named as the "Fifth Man", and against whom I am assured there is no evidence . . . The man in question has no connection with atomic science.' Pincher also said that, 'As long as Hollis remained head of MI5 he refused to allow the Blunt case officers to interview the scientist.' After Hollis retired in 1965, the man's telephone was tapped and he was interrogated over a period of six weeks. He then admitted that, 'he was still a committed Communist and had breached the Civil Service security rules by failing to admit it on his positive vetting form.' He further admitted to having met the early Russian controller of 'The Ring of Five' while he himself was at Cambridge, and other members of the Soviet-embassy staff later, although he flatly denied that he had ever given them classified information. He further ignored an offer of immunity from prosecution if he 'cooperated', said Pincher, and 'as he was quite close to retirement – and perhaps to cover up the suspicion which could have serious consequences for the Anglo-American exchange of defence secrets – he was allowed to retire early for "personal reasons" and on full pension.'

On 22 July 1984 *The Sunday Times* printed a list of twenty-one names, which it claimed had been 'drawn up by senior MI5 officers and suspected by them of having been spies for the Soviet Union . . . The list is a top-secret MI5 assessment of the suspected extent of Soviet penetration of senior Whitehall positions.' It was split into four groups, under the headings: Known Defectors; Partially Confessed; Confessed; Unresolved. Heading the list of names in Group 2 (Partially Confessed) was 'Alister Watson, scientist, dead.' The newspaper identified Watson as the scientist Chapman Pincher had described but not named in his book. The name at the top of Group 4 (Unresolved) was that of 'Sir Roger Hollis, Head of MI5, dead.'

The newspaper also said that the list was 'drawn up partly by Peter Wright, a former MI5 officer who now lives in Australia. Wright represents a faction of retired MI5 officers who were closely involved in the hunt for moles within the British governing Establishment and who believe there was a cover-up to protect the guilty . . .'

Today, the long list of spy trials held over the four decades from the mid-1940s onward tells its own story of the extent and depth of the Soviet conspiracy against Britain. The early post-war trials, involving the so-called 'atom spies' – all of whom were traced from documents and information provided by Igor Gouzenko, the Russian cipher clerk who defected in Ottawa, Canada, on 5 September 1945 – aroused no great public outcry: the memories of Russia's wartime losses were too green for that. The scandal that grew out of a combination of government complacency, intelligence and security inefficiency, and Soviet penetration, was a gradual process brought to a head by the 'Cold War'.

The fact that physicist Allan Nunn May, who was sentenced to ten years' imprisonment in 1946 for betraying atomic secrets to Moscow, had been a contemporary of Burgess, Maclean, Blunt and Philby at Cambridge University, appeared to hold no significance then. After his arrest Nunn May stubbornly refused to identify his contacts, or to assist his interrogators in their counter-espionage inquiries, so that no one knew when or where he had been recruited. Like Burgess and the rest, however, he held strong left-wing views in his undergraduate days, and like Burgess and Blunt he, too, had made a pilgrimage to Russia in the 1930s. None of it affected his scientific career and he became one of a select band of traitors whose combined perfidy changed the balance of world power.

During World War II he worked on 'Tube Alloys' (the cover name for British atomic research) and was in close contact with the KGB by the spring of 1945, by which time he was working at the experimental atomic research stations in North America. He gave the Russians their first separated uranium isotopes, as well as the most advanced information on atomic research, for which he accepted token payment in whisky and a few hundred dollars. His controller in Canada made arrangements for him to re-establish contact with agents from the Soviet embassy on his return to London, where he was finally arrested in March 1946. His counsel said at his trial that Nunn May felt 'full of indignation that promises of communication of technical assistance, which had been given to one wartime ally, should have been made the monopoly of another. Shortly after the trial, the Association of Scientific Workers in Britain called for a reduction of the 'extremely harsh' sentence passed on him.

Next came Klaus Fuchs, the German-born physicist who fled to Britain in 1933 – not because he was Jewish (his family was Protestant) but because he was wanted by the Gestapo as a member of the outlawed Communist Party. This was later reported to the security authorities in London, but no action was taken because – then as now – Party membership is not an offence in Britain. In May 1940 Fuchs was interned as an 'enemy alien' and subsequently transported to Canada, but returned to Britain on his release in January 1941. Four months later he joined 'Tube Alloys' in Birmingham, with security clearance. Soon afterwards he voluntarily contacted the Soviet embassy in London and was already handing over top-secret information when he took the oath of allegiance as a naturalized British citizen on 7 August 1942. After the successful test explosion of the first atomic bomb in the United States in July 1945, he gave the Russians (via the American traitor, Harry

Gold) details of its size, component parts, construction and trigger mechanism.

He returned to Britain in 1946 (a dormant period in his espionage career) and was posted to Harwell, the British centre for atomic research, where routine security checks – conducted over five months, without his knowledge – proved negative. The following year Fuchs resumed contact with the Soviet embassy in London, apparently on his own initiative. He came under suspicion in 1949 for the first time, following a warning from US intelligence that there had been further leaks of atomic information to the Russians, possibly from a British scientist. Fuchs later confessed after interrogation by MI5 and pleaded guilty at his trial early in 1950 to four counts of espionage. He was then sentenced to fourteen years' imprisonment and was warned by Lord Chief Justice Goddard that the crime he had committed differed only by a technicality from 'high treason' (for which he could have been hanged but under English law, high treason can only be brought against a traitor who assists an 'enemy'. Fuchs had passed his information to an 'ally').

In his book *The Traitors* Alan Moorehead observed that: 'This time no one came forward to protest against the sentence, as they had done in the case of Allan Nunn May. It was not just a question of the prisoner Fuchs, or the intriguing duality of the Communist mind . . . The whole question of British security was involved. How far had security slipped? How many other Fuchses were running around in the British and American laboratories? How was it possible that a traitor could walk through all the security barriers in England and America, and for years, without anyone being the wiser?'

The one possibility which appears to have occurred to no one at the time was long-term Soviet penetration of the security/intelligence network. Scarcely had the dust settled on the Fuchs case when a third atomic scientist, naturalized Briton Bruno Pontecorvo, a senior Harwell man of Jewish-Italian parentage, defected to Moscow with his family on 2 September 1950. Why he went and what secrets he may have passed to the Russians – if any – is not known.

Bruno Pontecorvo was born in Pisa on 22 August 1913, one

of a family of eight children. Four of them left for England before the outbreak of World War II, because of Mussolini's repression of the Jews. A fifth went to America. One other brother crossed into France in November 1939. He was a Communist and joined the French underground after the German occupation. Another sister stayed in Italy and later married an agricultural scientist, also a Communist.

Pontecorvo's own political views were unknown to his British colleagues at Harwell, where this tall and handsome man – a fine tennis player as well as an able scientist – was much-liked and respected. He gained his Doctorate in Physics at Rome University in 1934, where he studied under Enrico Fermi. In 1936 he left for Paris to study in the Laboratory of Nuclear Chemistry at the Collège de France and stayed on after the outbreak of World War II. In January 1940 he married Marianne Nordblom, a Swedish girl. They fled south with their infant child after the German invasion and made their way to America, via Spain and Portugal. Early in 1943 – at the same time as Nunn May left Britain for Canada – Pontecorvo also joined the Anglo-Canadian atomic research team. His name was known to Fermi, who was then in America, and Pontecorvo was sent first to Montreal and later to Chalk River, where he and his family remained for six years.

He was vetted three times before he was granted British nationality in 1948 – the first time before he entered Canada – and was finally promoted to a senior appointment at Harwell in 1949. At the time of the Fuchs trial in 1950, Pontecorvo volunteered the information to the Harwell security authorities that his brother Gilberto was a Communist. By then, a trace in Sweden revealed that Bruno Pontecorvo and his wife Marianne were also suspected Communists and a watch was placed on him by Harwell security. He did nothing to arouse suspicion, although Chapman Pincher revealed that as soon as Pontecorvo left to join the British atomic research team in Canada in 1943, his home in the US had been searched by the FBI. They found 'documentary evidence that both he and his wife were Communists and intensely anti-American, and sent a warning report to the British embassy.' It went to the senior SIS man in Washington – 'Kim' Philby – who promptly hid it away (it was found, years later, in the files). Worse still, there was also a misunderstanding between MI5 and Canadian security over Pontecorvo: each thought the other had cleared him. 'Had (the report Philby intercepted) been forwarded to London as the FBI expected, it is likely that Pontecorvo would have been refused permission to work at Harwell when he came to Britain after the war . . . Instead a Canadian security clearance, which had never taken place, was accepted by MI5.

Whether Pontecorvo realized that he was under surveillance at Harwell in 1950, or was warned, is not known but he defected a few months later. On 25 July he set off by car with his wife and three children for a touring holiday on the Continent, which was scheduled to include a reunion with his parents at Chamonix in France and with his brother and sister in Italy. He finally reached Rome on 27 August, where he stayed with his married sister. On 30 August he paid in US $100 bills for five air tickets from Rome to Stockholm. Initially, all five were one-way: after an animated discussion with his wife (which the sales clerk later recalled) Pontecorvo changed his own from single to return, presumably to allay suspicion in the event of a query from London. They left Rome on 31 August and arrived in Stockholm via Munich and Copenhagen in the late evening of 1 September. Marianne Pontecorvo made no attempt to contact her parents, who lived near the airport; instead the Pontecorvos spent their one night on Swedish soil in a house owned by the Soviet embassy, according to unconfirmed reports. Next day they flew on to Helsinki, giving 'tourism' as the alleged reason for their visit. They were met at the airport there by an unidentified man and woman and left in a car with them – to surface again later in Moscow.

Like Marianne's parents in Stockholm, Bruno Pontecorvo's relatives in Italy insisted they knew nothing of his flight to Moscow. As far as is known, no evidence was found that he had spied for Russia either in Canada or at Harwell. Chapman Pincher's explanation for his sudden departure is that Pontecorvo 'was needed in connection with the crash development of the Soviet H-bomb. He was one of the few scientists in the world with knowledge of the type of nuclear reactor required to make the essential component of the H-bomb called lithium deuteride.'

In addition to Nunn May, Fuchs, Pontecorvo, Burgess, Maclean, Philby and Blunt, the long list of traitors in British service who either defected, confessed their guilt but were granted immunity, or were caught and brought to trial between 1946 and 1984 included George Blake, John Cairncross, William Vassall, Frank Bossard, William Martin Marshall, Harry Houghton, Ethel Gee, Geoffrey Prime and Michael Bettaney, among others. George Blake (né Behar, of Dutch-Jewish parentage), another SIS officer, fought in the Dutch Resistance early in World War II and escaped to England, where he volunteered for the Royal Navy. He first served as interpreter at SHAEF (Supreme Allied Headquarters) and later with naval intelligence in Hamburg. In 1947 he attended a Russian languages course at Cambridge University and joined the Secret Service the following year. His first foreign service appointment, as vice-consul in Seoul, ended with his capture by northern forces during the Korean war: it is not known whether he was recruited in prison camp or at Cambridge. During his subsequent service in London, Berlin and Beirut, Blake betrayed such damaging information to the Russians that he was sentenced to an unprecedented forty-two-year imprisonment at his trial in 1961. He first came under suspicion from information given by a Polish intelligence agent who defected to the CIA. All the evidence at his Old Bailey trial was heard *in camera* but press reports claimed that he received a year in jail for each Western agent he had sent to his death.

Chapman Pincher said in *Their Trade is Treachery* that: 'Much of the effort made by Macmillan and his government to blanket the horrific details of Blake's treachery was to conceal from the British public the inefficiency which had allowed such a spy to operate for so long inside the Secret Service. The main objective, however, was to conceal the facts from the US Congress, after the Fuchs and Maclean cases had already done so much damage to the reputation of Britain as a safe ally with whom to share secrets.' It was also one more chapter in the continuing great spy scandal. Another was added six years later when, with the help of ex-prisoner Seamus Bourke, Blake escaped from his cell in Wormwood Scrubs and made his way safely to Moscow. He now leads a privileged life there, like Philby, courtesy of the KGB.

John Cairncross, one-time diplomat, wartime Secret Service-man, Treasury official and long-term Russian spy, was finally betrayed by papers abandoned in 1951 by his erstwhile friend and Cambridge contemporary, Guy Burgess. Like so many others who were netted during the Soviet trawl of the 1930s to enlist potential long-term spies, Cairncross was recruited as an undergraduate at Cambridge. His recruiter was a fellow undergraduate named James Klugman, a schoolfriend of Donald Maclean and now also a close associate of Burgess, Blunt and Philby. Klugman later introduced Cairncross to the first Soviet agent in London who controlled 'The Ring of Five'; on his instructions Cairncross offically quit the Communist Party, successfully sought entry into the diplomatic service, and subsequently transferred to the Treasury. In 1942, he joined the Secret Service code and cypher school at Bletchley Park (forerunner of today's GCHQ), returning to the Treasury after World War II.

He spied for the Russians throughout but did not come under suspicion until after the Burgess-Maclean defection in 1951, when MI5 searched Burgess's New Bond Street flat. They found what were in effect pen portraits of a number of Whitehall officials, listing their political views, their personal circumstances and peccadilloes – all of it invaluable material for a potential spymaster – which were traced back to Cairncross. When confronted, he admitted authorship but flatly denied being a spy himself or knowing that Burgess was one. In the absence of corroborant evidence he was allowed to resign his post, whereupon he moved to Rome and worked for the UN. During later interrogation by MI5, he admitted to being a Soviet agent all along; he was not granted immunity, however, and remained abroad. Both his name and that of James Klugman appeared in the *Sunday Times* list of twenty-one persons said to be suspected by MI5 of having been Russian spies. Cairncross was placed in Group 3 (Confessed) and Klugman in Group 4 (Unresolved).

William Vassall spent three years as an RAF photographer in World War II before he was demobilized in 1946 and returned to his former job as Admiralty clerk. In 1953 he was posted to the British embassy in Moscow, as Writer on the naval attaché's staff. There the KGB discovered something the British authorities seemed to have missed, that Vassall was a practising homosexual; whereupon they first compromised and then blackmailed him into passing over secret documents. At no time did he come under suspicion of espionage. On his return to London in 1956 Vassall served successively in the Naval Intelligence Division at the Admiralty, the office of the Civil Lord of the Admiralty, and secretariat of the Naval Staff before his arrest in 1962. In that time, although lowly in rank, he had access to a wealth of top-secret defence material which he photographed and passed on to his Soviet control. The cash he received for his treachery enabled him to live in an exclusive Dolphin Square flat, although his official pay was only £15 a week: still he came under no suspicion.

Ronald Seth said in his *Encyclopedia of Espionage* that: 'British security was extremely lax throughout the whole of the time that Vassall worked for the Admiralty. It apparently had not known that he was a homosexual when they had passed him: now they did not discover the comparative opulence in which he lived. Some of his colleagues knew about the apartment and the kind of genteel grace with which he conducted his life, but knowing his background [he was a clergyman's son] his hints that he had received one or two small legacies from dear old ladies they regarded . . . as a satisfactory explanation.'

He was caught in the autumn of 1962, following recommendations by the Radcliffe Committee to improve security in the wake of the George Blake case. Once the proper attention was paid to his life-style, Vassall was placed under surveillance. A search of his flat revealed numerous Admiralty documents together with his spy-camera equipment; caught red-handed, he made a full confession. At his Old Bailey trial Vassall was sentenced to eighteen years' imprisonment.

Press reports arising from the Vassall case led to an official Tribunal of Inquiry, through which two respected Fleet Street journalists were themselves imprisoned for refusing to name their sources. Whatever that hard punishment may have done to smooth ruffled Establishment feathers, it did nothing to repair the damage done, or to lessen the public alarm caused by, the long-laid Soviet conspiracy.

On the instructions of his Soviet controller in London Vassall lay doggo throughout 1961, the year of yet another espionage drama which ended in the 'Portland Spy Ring' trial. All five spies involved – ringleader Konon Trofimovich Molody (alias 'Gordon Lonsdale', and a professional KGB operative), Morris and Lorna Cohen (alias 'Peter and Helen Kroger', two Soviet agents sought by the FBI for their involvement in the Rosenberg atom spy conspiracy eight years earlier), and two more British traitors, Harry Houghton and Ethel Gee – received long prison sentences. Houghton, a former master-at-arms in the Royal Navy and now an Admiralty clerk employed at the top-secret Underwater Weapons Base at Portland, Dorset, had (like Vassall) also served earlier as a Writer and spy in a British embassy behind the Iron Curtain; in his case in Warsaw. Houghton, a heavy drinker with domestic problems, was sent back to England when the authorities became aware of his circumstances but he was not suspected of treason. Instead, he was posted to the hush-hush Underwater Weapons Establishment at Portland. There he separated from his wife (they were later divorced) and with the help of his mistress Ethel Gee – a filing clerk at the base – Houghton carried on spying by selling the Navy's nuclear-submarine secrets to the KGB. The papers were smuggled out to Lonsdale, who passed them on to the Krogers for microdot radio transmission to Moscow – from the loft of their rented suburban home in Cranley Drive, Ruislip, Middlesex.

Houghton was positively identified as a traitor from statements made by the same Polish defector who betrayed George Blake. He was kept under surveillance over a long period by MI5 and Special Branch officers, when the trail led to the arrest and imprisonment of all five members of the spy ring. Houghton and Gee were sentenced to fifteen years apiece. Lonsdale received twenty-five years, the Krogers twenty years each. But these sentences proved to be academic; all three were later exchanged in East-West spy swaps.

Frank Clifton Bossard, who was born at Driffield, Yorkshire, in 1912 was a radio enthusiast who built his first receiver at the age of sixteen. He served two short prison sentences in the 1930s, one for a cheque offence, the other for non-payment of a hotel bill in Austria; joined the RAF in 1940, and rose to Flight-Lieutenant in a radar unit by the time he was demobilized in 1946. He then joined the Ministry of Civil Aviation and by 1951 was serving as an intelligence officer in Germany. In 1956 he was transferred to Ministry of Defence intelligence, with the rank of attaché at the British embassy in Bonn. He drank heavily and ran short of money to become an easy KGB target and was eventually recruited in London. From 1961 to 1965 he handed over guided-missile secrets to the Russians for cash payments totalling £15,000, then a very considerable sum, and was sentenced in May 1965 to twenty-one years' imprisonment.

William Martin Marshall, a former Royal Corps of Signals private soldier and small-time spy, was recruited by the KGB while serving as radio operator at the British embassy in Moscow in 1951. He was arrested in a London park on his return to Britain the following year, as he kept a rendezvous with Second Secretary Pavel Kuznetsov from the Soviet embassy. Kuznetsov claimed diplomatic immunity, Marshall was sentenced to five years' imprisonment. Much was made of his arrest, which occurred at the height of the Burgess-Maclean spy scandal. Thirty years later, Chapman Pincher revealed, that far from being a counter-espionage triumph, it had been 'an absolute fluke'. Marshall was followed home and placed under surveillance, said Pincher, only because an off-duty MI5 officer stepping down from a bus in London happened to see him in conversation with someone he recognized as a KGB agent.

Certainly Britain's counter-espionage units played no part in the unmasking in 1982 of Geoffrey Prime, the GCHQ linguist described by the Lord Chief Justice, Lord Lane, as a 'ruthless and rationally motivated spy', whose fourteen years of undetected treachery caused immense harm to Britain and the Western alliance.

Prime was arrested in April 1982 not for spying, but for indecently assaulting young girls. When he arrived home and told his wife what had happened, he further confessed to being a Soviet agent. Not surprisingly, her reaction was one of 'total shock'. Three weeks later, however, when her husband was in custody on the sex charges, she found a plastic bag under the bed containing the mini-camera he used to photograph secret documents, pads specially designed to carry coded messages, a powerful radio receiver and a tape recorder to help him decipher coded transmissions. Mrs Prime, who was commended by Lord Lane as 'a woman of great character, sympathy and humanity', consulted her solicitor, family doctor and parents before taking the ultimate step of reporting her find – and her husband's 'confession' – to the police. Only then were the counter-espionage departments called in.

Prime's counsel claimed that the GCHQ traitor had been turned into a 'sexual and social misfit' by an unhappy childhood. He made his first approach to the Russians while serving with the RAF in Berlin in 1968, by leaving a message at one of the East-West checkpoints. The KGB response arrived via a metal cylinder magnetically attached to his car. First his controllers taught him how to use microdots, one-time pads and other standard spy apparatus. On their instructions he then applied, successfully, for entry to GCHQ, the government secret communications centre at Cheltenham, in Gloucestershire. So valuable was he to the Russians in this Aladdin's Cave of secrets that in 1976 his controllers promised him that if ever he defected, he would be rewarded by the rank of colonel with an equivalent pension. They paid him more than £7,000 and he travelled to Berlin, Vienna and even on a Danube pleasure-cruiser to contact his spy-masters. In his final year alone at Cheltenham, he took fifteen rolls of film (five hundred photographs) of classified information. Yet the two 'positive vetting' security checks carried out during his service proved negative and not once had he come under suspicion.

Prime himself decided to quit his GCHQ job and the double life that went with it in 1977 – a year after his marriage and 'playing the part of a loving father' to his wife's three sons. He became a taxi driver, but the Russians refused to let him go without first obtaining their pound of flesh. He still possessed secrets they coveted, so at their behest he flew to Vienna to hand over photostat copies of GCHQ files and to Berlin for direct interrogation. Meanwhile, back in Cheltenham he led another kind of double life, indecently assaulting little girls and drawing up a card-index of more than 2,000 potential young victims. After sentencing Prime to thirty-five years' imprisonment for spying, plus a concurrent three years for indecent assault, the Lord Chief Justice told him, 'You have done incalculable harm to the interests and security of this country, and the interests and security of our friends and allies.' And once again the Press expressed public concern both for the national security and the effect of Prime's treachery on the 'Special Relationship'.

Ironically, MI5 officer Michael Bettaney – one of the men responsible for keeping watch on KGB activity in Britain, but who secretly aspired to become a Soviet agent himself – made his first attempt to contact the Russians only a year after Prime had been jailed.

At midnight on 3 April 1983, he personally delivered a letter to the Holland Park home of Soviet-embassy official and KGB suspect Arkady Vasilyevich Gouk, offering his services as double-agent. Already he had squirrelled away a hoard of secret documents and canisters of film at his own home in Coulsdon, Surrey, in anticipation of his acceptance. It proved to be the first of three unsuccessful attempts by Bettaney to betray his country before he was arrested.

Twice he personally delivered letters to Gouk's home, each containing a 'sweetener' of intelligence information to establish his bona fides and suggestions for different sites to be used as 'dead letter-box' contacts. Fearing a trap, the Russians made no response. Finally Bettaney rang Gouk's ex-directory telephone number direct, at a given time; this, too, was left unanswered. How Bettaney was caught has not been revealed, but he was arrested by Special Branch officers on 16 September 1983 – the day he planned to fly to Vienna to make personal contact with known KGB officers there. When his house in Victoria Road, Coulsdon, was searched later it was found to contain handwritten notes of secret information hidden in the bottom of a box of glasses; typewritten notes stuffed inside the cushion of a sitting-room sofa; canisters of film in the laundry cupboard, index cards in the dining-room, a list of KGB agents in Vienna inside the electric-shaver box, and photographic equipment together with a developing tank inside a suitcase in the cellar.

Bettaney, a working-class boy from Stoke-on-Trent who once planned to become a priest, won a scholarship to Oxford in 1969. After graduating in 1972 he took a teaching job in Germany and was accepted into MI5 three years later. At his trial in April 1984 the Lord Chief Justice, Lord Lane, described him as 'puerile' but 'self-opinionated and dangerous' and sentenced him to twenty-three years' imprisonment. 'It was after careful consideration you made treachery your chosen course of action,' he said. 'It was small thanks to you that the Russians rebuffed your advances.'

Press criticism was directed more at the security authorities. Under the heading Senior Heads Of MI5 Must Roll, *The Daily Telegraph* Old Bailey correspondent, Mr Ian Henry, declared: 'An alarming scandal of apparent complacency at the heart of the West's counter-espionage network allowed Michael Bettaney to try to become a traitor. Astounding errors of judgment by Bettaney's security service superiors . . . have infuriated Mrs Thatcher, who has demanded an urgent Security Commission investigation into the case. Intelligence sources are speculating that senior heads must roll within MI5. Others are insisting that a complete overhaul is needed.'

Mr Henry pointed out that – as in the case of Guy Burgess, thirty-three years earlier – clear signs of Bettaney's impending treachery were evident before his arrest, yet his superiors turned a blind eye to them. On 12 October 1982 Bettaney appeared at Marlborough Street magistrates' court charged with drunkenness and was fined £12. Ian Henry said, 'He had apparently been arrested in a babbling state, boasting "I am a spy, I am a spy."' Within days the secret serviceman, known for his pompous, bordering on arrogant, nature was back in court for failing to pay his rail fare. Embarrassed MI5 chiefs successfully managed to have the criminal convictions suppressed during the public session of Bettaney's trial.

'Bettaney, who confesses that by that time he had decided to

turn traitor, was so obviously at a crisis crossroads in his
personal and political life, but the signs were ignored . . . The
story has striking parallels to that of MI6 traitor Guy Burgess,
who also boasted of his treachery during bouts of drunkenness.
In Bettaney's case it was two months later, December 1982,
that he was promoted to an MI5 post . . . in control of the
ultra-sensitive Russian desk.'

Bettaney himself claimed a conversion to Communism in
1982. According to Ian Henry, 'Other Intelligence sceptics
suspect his violent switch of allegiance dates back further, to
his (MI5) days in Ulster and later, in Dublin. The Bettaney
scandal is already being seen in Intelligence circles as the most
powerful argument yet for the introduction into the Security
Services of the polygraph lie detector tests, already on trial at
GCHQ in Cheltenham.'

The Attorney-General, Sir Michael Havers, said at the trial
that Bettaney's motive was ideological. The 34-year-old would-
be traitor said nothing in his own defence. Instead he issued a
defiant statement, which was read out later by his solicitor. It
consisted of an attack on 'The Establishment', accusing the
Thatcher government of 'slavish adherence to the aggressive
and maverick policy of the Reagan administration', as well as
oppression of the poor, workless, sick and old, and concluded:
'As my last political act I call on comrades everywhere to
renew their determination and redouble their efforts in pursuit
of a victory which is historically inevitable.'

It sounded like a ghostly echo from the 1930s when the
original 'Ring of Five' was recruited. On 9 May 1985, Prime
Minister Mrs Thatcher told the Commons of 'serious errors of
judgment' by MI5 in the Bettaney case, and announced a
number of procedural changes which included stricter 'positive
vetting' of all future recruits.

Her statement followed an inquiry by the Security Commission, which found that 'insufficient importance' had been
placed on Bettaney's known character defects by his superior
officers in the Security Service. They included heavy drinking,
convictions for petty offences such as drunkenness and travelling on trains without first paying a fare, and of making wild
utterances at parties ('I'm working for the wrong side', 'Come

and see me in my dacha when I retire', and 'I'm sure the East Germans would look after me better'). To some observers it must have sounded like a re-run of events in 1951, when similar revealing statements by Donald Maclean and Guy Burgess were similarly ignored by their superiors.

The Commission's 29-page report revealed that Bettaney had been judged a suitable candidate for MI5 *after* he had been turned down by the Civil Service Selection Board because of doubts about his 'intellectual abilities'. Those doubts, said the Commissioners, pointedly, 'were not regarded as sufficient to warrant rejecting him as a potential intelligence officer . . .' Instead Bettaney was positively vetted and accepted by MI5 in 1975, although he then had one conviction (as an undergraduate, for travelling on British Rail without paying his fare). Even after his subsequent work in MI5's counter-terrorism section was regarded as 'only a qualified success', in 1982 he was transferred to the section studying the KGB's 'order of battle' in Britain – and this despite his drink problem, which then included a recent conviction for drunkenness. (He was found sitting on the pavement in the West End of London, too drunk to stand, and was fined £10 by Marlborough Street magistrates. His offer to resign from MI5 was not accepted. One week later he was caught travelling on a train without a ticket, and fined £40 plus costs). It was while he served with this ultra-sensitive security section that Bettaney started to memorize and photograph top-secret material with which he attempted to persuade the Russians to enlist him as a 'mole'.

Ironically, this disclosure of the Commission's findings came almost a year after Mr Peter Wright, a former senior MI5 officer now retired and living in Australia (*see p. 49*), told the *Observer* newspaper that he was prepared to break the Official Secrets Act if need be to try to bring about a full inquiry into the failings of the Security Service. In its report on Bettaney, the Security Commission stated, 'We feel bound to record our impression that the ethos of the Security Service in the past has tended to be insufficiently alert to the potential security risks of excessive drinking among members of the service.' The commissioners felt that Bettaney should have been suspended following his conviction for drunkenness in 1982, and queried the decision to transfer him instead to the counter-espionage section.

On his positive vetting test in 1981 they commented, 'We believe that this review was both superficial and inadequate, not least because of the failure to consult those who had supervised Bettaney during the previous five years. The Security Service . . . justify their decision not to call for special reports on the grounds that their review process is effectively coordinated. We disagree.' While they found that Bettaney's drink problem in itself played no part in causing his treachery, they observed, 'We do consider that the extent of his drinking, and the occasions of extreme drunkenness which became known to his superiors, provided the most significant pointer to his instability of character, to which insufficient importance was attached.'

In her report to the Commons, Mrs Thatcher agreed that such an inquiry into Bettaney's lifestyle '. . . would probably have led to a cessation of his employment in the Security Service', but still insisted: 'It remains the case, however, that Bettaney's attempts to get himself recruited as an agent of the Russian intelligence service were not successful. The Security Service's investigation which led to Bettaney's eventual conviction was effective and conclusive. Although in the course of his attempts to get himself recruited Bettaney did communicate some secret information to the Russians, he was arrested before he was able to pass over the major proportion of the secret information he had collected, and the grave damage that would have ensued by such communication was averted.'

Not all MPs felt inclined to take such a generous view of MI5's belated success. Opposition Leader Neil Kinnock retorted acidly: 'No man could have tried harder to get himself recruited to the Russian secret service, and his fortunate incompetence is not sufficient reassurance . . .' SDP (Social Democrat) leader and former Foreign Secretary Dr David Owen, MP, called for a 'complaints Ombudsman' for the Intelligence and Security Services, and said it was time Britain followed the example of America's CIA and FBI by forming an all-Party Select Committee to which both services should be answerable. Mr John Browne, Tory MP for Winchester, said,

'Some of us feel that infiltrations at a very senior level, and a continued catalogue of errors, must call into question not just the management but the actual operations of the Security Service. In order for credibility to be restored nothing short of forming a new service will suffice', while Jonathan Aitken (Tory, Thanet South) asked Mrs Thatcher bluntly: 'Will you be a little more sensitive to views held in all parts of the House that some form of Privy Counsellors' Committee or Ombudsman would reassure public opinion?'

While she showed some sympathy with another suggestion, that a Complaints Committee might be appointed to deal with complaints from officers within the Security Service, the Prime Minister remained adamant, 'I do not think it would be helpful to the Security Service to have their operations and their management exposed, and cross-examination in this House would be highly damaging to it.'

BYRON, Lord
'Mad, Bad and Dangerous to Know'

Not long after the death of Lord Byron in Greece in April 1824, two of his closest friends – Tom Moore and John Cam Hobhouse – met at the office of his publisher John Murray to decide what ought to be done with the poet's memoirs. The vote went against Moore, who wanted to preserve them, and they were consigned to the office fire.

What was in them that shocked Murray and Hobhouse so much? It may have been the admission that he had slept with at least two hundred whores, or that he had committed incest with his half-sister and fathered her child, or that he had sodomized his wife, or simply that he found boys as sexually enjoyable as girls. But although the memoirs are lost to us, the researches of biographers have uncovered most of Byron's scandalous secrets.

Byron's father, 'Mad Jack', was a notorious rake and gambler; he ran away with a married woman, the Marchioness of Carmarthen, who died six years later after presenting him with three children, two of whom died young. Then 'Mad Jack' married a plump and plain Scottish heiress, Catherine Gordon, who (like the Marchioness) was at first able to keep him in the style to which he was accustomed. But he soon spent her £23,000. On 28 January 1788, the poet George Gordon, Lord Byron, was born. 'Mad Jack' deserted his wife soon after and died in France three years later, possibly by committing suicide.

The boy's childhood was miserable; he had a deformed right foot and his schoolfriends made fun of his limp. The attempts of various doctors to 'cure' it caused him a great deal of agony but made no difference whatever. Even his mother sometimes jeered at him as a 'lame brat' – she seems to have been subject to violent changes of mood, which laid the foundation of his lifelong mistrust of women. He took refuge from reality in books, preferring history and stories of the Mediterranean. When he was nine he had his first sexual experience with a young servant girl named Mary Gray. She seems to have been a nymphomaniac: when she was not introducing the shy boy to the delights of nakedness, she was giving herself to a succession of lovers, often with Byron looking on. It seems doubtful that he lost his virginity with her but she made him aware that he was attractive to women. Mary threatened him with hellfire if he told anyone their secret – as his biographer Frederick Raphael remarks: 'Cant and cunt revealed their proximity very early in Byron's life.'

Byron became next in line for the title when he was six and his cousin was killed in battle. He inherited on the death of his grandfather, when he was ten, and he and his mother moved to the decrepit and gloomy Newstead Abbey, near Nottingham, a picturesque ruin that was the ideal setting for a romantic poet. For the next four years he attended Harrow School and was probably introduced to homosexuality. He was in love with his cousin Mary Parker, and also with a neighbour, Mary Chaworth – but this feeling turned to hatred when he heard Mary Chaworth ask her maid, 'What, do you think I could feel anything for that lame boy?' His mother meanwhile had been forced to rent Newstead to a certain Lord Grey de Ruthyn, a 23-year-old rake who pursued Byron's mother and even made homosexual advances to Byron himself when he was home during the holidays. (Byron fled in terror – his own homosexual inclinations were always directed towards those younger than himself.)

Byron's real sexual initiation began when he went to Cambridge in 1805, where he began to frequent prostitutes with such vigour that even a French procuress had to advise him to season ardour with delicacy (i.e. be less rough). He also renewed his acquaintance with his half-sister Augusta, who had married a Colonel George Leigh and had a fine house near Cambridge. Byron fell in love with a choirboy named Edleston, whom he saved from drowning, but he later insisted that this friendship was 'pure' – a clear hint that others of the same type were not. He began to put on weight; he had always been inclined to fleshiness, and soon weighed sixteen stones. For a man of his vanity this was intolerable and he starved himself and played cricket wearing half a dozen waistcoats to induce perspiration.

At this time he published his earliest poems but they were reviewed so unfavourably that he thought for a while of killing himself. However, instead he wrote a satire in the manner of Pope called *English Bards and Scotch Reviewers*, which gave him a certain reputation. Before leaving Cambridge, Byron had acquired his first mistress, a girl called Caroline, whom he liked to dress in boy's clothes and pass off as a male.

At the age of twenty-one, he went off on his first tour of the Mediterranean with his friend Hobhouse, who was planning a book called *Sodomy Simplified, or Pederasty Proved to be Praiseworthy*. They visited Greece, Albania, Turkey and Spain, and when Hobhouse left him alone in Greece, Byron took the opportunity to enjoy a sentimental and impure friendship with a boy named Nicolo, who was fifteen. He also spent a great deal of money on prostitutes. One day his curiosity was aroused by a cart containing a sack that was wriggling; he bribed the driver to open it and found that it was a woman who had been condemned to be thrown into the sea for infidelity to her husband. Byron is said to have recognized her as one of the women he had slept with. He succeeded in smuggling her out of harm's way.

Back in England in 1812, Byron was deeply moved by the death of his mother. He later made his maiden speech in the House of Lords, supporting the Nottingham weavers who had smashed the mechanical frames that were putting them out of work. A few weeks later, John Murray published the poem that Byron had written during his period abroad: *Childe Harold's Pilgrimage*. This gloomy and romantic piece of work, about a young man who has tasted every forbidden pleasure in his early twenties and finds life an intolerable bore, made him famous overnight. Suddenly, Byron was the social success of the season. Young girls regarded him with adoration; young men imitated his brooding silence, his melancholy frowns, even his limp.

One of the women who learned *Childe Harold* by heart was

a beautiful and wilful young married woman named Lady Caroline Lamb, the wife of the politician William Lamb (later Lord Melbourne). She declared in her journal that Byron was 'mad, bad and dangerous to know', and added: 'That beautiful pale face is my fate.' Soon, Byron was a regular visitor at Melbourne House and the two became lovers. But his attitude towards her remained detached and ironical, and he greatly preferred her mother-in-law, Lady Melbourne, who became a close friend. Byron's indifference drove Lady Caroline to desperation; on one occasion, she disguised herself as a page boy and hid in Byron's carriage. Such exploits amused him but he grew increasingly tired of her waywardness and of a certain lack of prudishness – on one occasion she sent him some of her pubic hairs as a keepsake. When – with the help of Lady Melbourne – he broke off the affair, she burned his image in effigy. Byron fled to Cambridge and his half-sister Augusta, whose husband was away hunting. No doubt seduced by the idea of incest as much as by Augusta's attractions, Byron began an affair with her. He had also allowed himself to be seduced by the promiscuous Lady Oxford, whose children were known as the Harleian Miscellany because of their doubtful paternity (her husband's family name was Harley). After an abortive affair with the wife of a friend – whom he decided to spare at the last moment – he and Augusta went to Newstead and she became pregnant. By way of flaunting his triumph, he inserted the incest theme into his latest novel in verse, *The Bride of Abydos*.

Byron, having been the darling of London society, was now its chief source of malicious gossip. Caroline Lamb was still pursuing him and the affair with Augusta had become known largely through the lack of discretion of both parties. He decided that it was time to silence the gossip by marrying. Lady Melbourne's niece, an heiress named Annabella Milbanke, had already turned him down once, wounding his vanity; she was prim, serious-minded and demure. Rather to Byron's dismay, she accepted him the second time he proposed.

A character as spoiled and undisciplined as Byron was bound to be thrown into torments of ambivalence by marriage. In the carriage, on the way to their honeymoon (or 'treacle-moon', as

Byron preferred to call it) he set out to make her miserable by assuring her that he was bound to hate anyone he married. But their first sexual experiment – on a settee before dinner – seems to have been successful. Annabella was totally inexperienced – it seems probable that she had never even been instructed in what lovers do in bed – and the evidence indicates that she came to accept sodomy as a perfectly normal variant of sexual intercourse. At first, Byron seems to have found marriage unexpectedly pleasant. But his natural gloom and self-pity, his determination to be unconventional, his obscure conviction that he was somehow 'accursed', made his temper uncertain. He flirted openly with his half-sister and he was frequently drunk. And Annabella's demure virtue irritated him. Soon she was pregnant and that must have increased his feeling of being trapped. They moved to London although this was an extravagance they could not afford and the bailiffs became frequent visitors. His attempts to keep his weight within normal limits increased his irritability; sexual abstention may also have played its part – although later gossip stated that he continued to sodomize his wife until late into her pregnancy. The birth of a daughter was a disappointment; Byron had wanted an heir. Exhausted by a laborious birth and by quarrels with her husband, Annabella decided to go home to mother to recuperate. The separation was probably not intended to be permanent – certainly not as far as she was concerned. The deciding factor was probably her admission to her mother that Byron enjoyed anal intercourse. Sir Ralph and Lady Milbanke were undoubtedly what would now be called 'squares', and once Annabella had admitted to an act of 'criminal perversion' with a man who was reputed to be his sister's lover, nothing would have induced them to allow her to return to him. (In fact, Byron made some attempts at reconciliation.)

It is still not clear why the end of Byron's marriage caused him to become suddenly the most vilified man in London – Regency London was not the most virtuous place in the world. The answer is probably a combination of rumour – about incest, sodomy and so on – and envy. The desire to see idols hurled violently from their pedestals is strong in all human beings. Byron had been one of the most successful literary men of all times; poems like *The Corsair*, *The Bride of Abydos*, *The Giaour*, were the nineteenth-century equivalents of best-sellers. He had a reputation as a seducer of other men's wives. He was too successful. So London hostesses decided that it was time the wicked Lord was ostracized. If Byron had remained in England and ignored the disapproval, his next successful poem would probably have made society change its mind. But he was too moody and self-centred to endure the least suspicion of a snub. If society despised him, he would show that he despised society. He ordered an elaborate coach, costing £500, had one last fling with a young girl called Claire Clairmont, the stepdaughter of the social philosopher William Godwin (whose daughter Mary was about to run away with another poet, Shelley), and in April 1816 left England for the last time. The casual one-night stand with Claire eventually resulted in the birth of a daughter.

Claire reappeared in Switzerland, together with Shelley and Mary. When Shelley mildly reproached Byron for seducing Claire, Byron replied that no one had been more carried off than 'poor dear me' – he had been ravished more often than anyone since the Trojan War. He really believed this.

In Venice, Byron took lodgings in the house of a draper and quickly seduced his wife Marianna, whose appetite was so strong that Byron had to make love three times a day. Then he met a pretty 22-year-old peasant, Margarita Cogni, when he was out riding, and had soon persuaded her into his bed. In January 1818 he was asked to escort a young married woman – recently out of a convent – Teresa Guiccioli, to an art exhibition; she also became his mistress. The sale of Newstead (for £94,500) enabled him once more to live in the style he enjoyed and he rented a palazzo and moved Margarita in. Then, in the words of Frederick Raphael, 'he embarked on an orgy to challenge even the Venetian capacity to remain unshocked'. The Palazzo Mocigeno became virtually a brothel. When Margarita began to learn to read so she could keep track of his amours through his letters, he decided to get rid of her. She threatened him with a knife and stabbed his hand, then threw herself into the canal. After that, Byron firmly put her out-of-doors and she returned to her husband.

Teresa, the girl he had taken to the art exhibition, was Byron's last great *affaire*. Even in his early thirties, he was growing fat and his hair was receding fast; he began to feel the need for a more relaxed and domesticated existence. Teresa was nineteen, her husband, Count Alessandro Guiccioli, fifty-eight. The Count was reputed to be a dangerous man who had poisoned his first wife and murdered the novelist Manzoni. But it was tacitly understood that when a teenager from a convent marries a man nearly forty years her senior, he cannot expect permanent fidelity; in fact, one lover – or *cavaliere servente* – was thoroughly respectable. When, at one point, her husband protested about Byron, she replied indignantly: 'It is hard that I should be the only woman in Romagna who is not to have her *amico*.' The problem was that Teresa was nearly as indiscreet as Caroline Lamb and Byron was tactless enough to get mixed up in Italian politics. Eventually, the Count and Countess separated; Byron found, to his disgust, that he was expected to be a substitute husband rather than an *amico*. She even ordered him to cease working on *Don Juan* which she detested. But he was getting older and no longer so disposed to revolt against anything that looked like conventionality. A flash of the old Byron appeared when he told Hobhouse apropos Teresa, 'Cain was right to kill Abel, that he might not have the bore of passing two hundred years with him.' The death of his daughter (with Claire Clairmont) Allegra – from fever – and the death of Shelley by drowning made Byron feel that he needed a change from Italy. And so, with the accompaniment of noisy tears from Teresa, he set off for Greece where, instead of fighting for freedom, as he had intended, he succumbed to a combination of boredom, non-stop rain and fever, and died in his thirty-seventh year.

CALVI, Roberto
The 'Suicide' of God's Banker

On the morning of Friday, 18 June 1982, a postal clerk walking across Blackfriars Bridge in London looked down and saw a body dangling by the neck from the scaffolding. When the police arrived, they cut down the corpse of a paunchy man of about sixty, with large bricks stuffed into his pockets, and about $15,000, in various currencies, in his wallet. His passport identified him as Gian Roberto Calvini, but a check with the Italian authorities revealed that he was, in fact, Roberto Calvi, chairman and managing director of the Banco Ambrosiano in Milan.

In the previous year, Calvi had been sentenced to four years in prison for illegally importing $20 million in lire; he had been released pending his appeal. He had also been connected with a sinister order of Freemasons known as P2 – Propaganda Due – which was now under police investigation for various forms of bribery and corruption. A week before his body was found Calvi had vanished from his Rome apartment.

On 23 July a coroner's jury in London decided that Calvi had committed suicide. But long before that it had become clear that Calvi had been involved in an incredible fraud involving many fake international companies and that there was a hole of about $1.4 billion in the Banco Ambrosiano accounts. He had also been involved with the crooked financier Michele Sindona and with the pope's bodyguard and financial adviser, Archbishop Paul Marcinkus. Marcinkus's response to the increasing scandal was to take refuge in the Vatican – a sovereign state beyond the reach of Italian law – and decline to answer questions. Sindona was already in prison in the United States.

The full story behind Calvi's death – now generally accepted as murder – has never emerged but there are enough fragments of information to present a reasonably clear picture.

Roberto Calvi had joined the Ambrosiano Bank in 1946, at the age of twenty-six. It was a Catholic bank – anyone who wished to open an account there had to produce a baptismal certificate. Calvi was a fine linguist and played an active part in its international dealings. Within ten years he had become joint manager and within twenty years, its 'central manager'. The 1950s were the time of Italy's 'economic miracle' and some of Calvi's brilliant schemes made the bank a great deal of money. He was a quiet, introspective man, regarded by some as cold and ruthless – although his wife insists he was merely shy. In spite of his success he was, in banking terms, a small-time operator. Then, in the late sixties, he made the most important – and fateful – contact of his career, with Michele Sindona, one of Italy's most successful financiers. Sindona owed his success to two of Italy's most respected institutions: the Vatican and the Mafia.

Sindona was a Sicilian. Born in 1920, he had taken a law degree in 1942 and built up the basis of his fortune by trading in the Black Market at the end of World War II. In 1957, Mafia families in New York and Sicily asked Sindona to invest for them some of the immense profits made from the traffic in heroin. Sindona 'laundered' their money and reinvested it. In 1959 he made an influential friend and ally when he raised over $2 million for an old people's home at the request of the Archbishop of Milan, Cardinal Montini. When the Cardinal was elected pope in 1963, Sindona gained the free right of entry into the Vatican; he became an *uomo di fiducia*, a trusted adviser of the Vatican's own bank.

Why the Vatican should have a bank was a question that had been raised by various anti-clerical newspapers. It had been founded with the $80 million that Mussolini had paid the Vatican in 1929, when he annexed the Papal States. It was known under the initials IOR – Istituto per le Opere di Religione – Institute of Religious Works. The money had been well invested and the bank had prospered. But owning vast sums of money placed the Vatican in an embarrassing position. For the Vatican was part-owner of many companies and businesses. This meant that the Vatican had to do business with Communist trade-union leaders. While this might sound amusing in the Don Camillo stories, it was altogether more difficult and painful in reality. How could the pope, for example, close down a loss-making plant, when charity is supposed to be a Christian duty? The answer, of course, was that he couldn't – not as long as the Vatican was clearly responsible for the closure. But if the ownership could be transferred elsewhere, into the hands of an *uomo di fiducia*, then the Vatican was absolved of responsibility. This is why Michele Sindona was so useful. He could take over inconvenient holdings – like the Banca Unione in Milan, whose board included Communists – and substitute overseas holdings that were less embarrassing. (A Vatican company built the Watergate complex in Washington.) Says one commentator (Nino Lo Bello): 'It was never altogether clear, whenever Sindona completed one of his spectacular business deals in Italy, whether the deal was Vatican business or Sindona business, or both.'

Sindona's closest associate in the Vatican was the secretary – future president – of the Vatican bank, Bishop (later Archbishop) Paul Marcinkus, a beefy American, born in Al Capone's Cicero, who was also the pope's bodyguard. Marcinkus was a pragmatist who had once remarked: 'The Church can't be run on Hail Marys.' He and Sindona made excellent allies: Sindona, described in London banking circles as 'the greatest banker in the world', and Marcinkus, head of a bank that belonged to a sovereign state – the Vatican – and, therefore, not subject to Italian banking laws. (It had been called 'the best offshore bank in the world.')

When Sindona met Calvi in the late 1960s, he recognized a man after his own heart: a 'man of trust' and tremendous ambition. Calvi was not satisfied to be the manager of a sleepy little Milan bank; he wanted to expand. That meant trading on the stock market and owning companies. There was only one small problem: in Italy, banks were forbidden to own companies in case they were tempted to use customers' money to finance their deals. Sindona, who owned many banks, had found a way around that problem. He set up companies in 'fiscal paradises' like Luxembourg and Liechtenstein and did his Italian share dealing through these. One of the first results of the cooperation between Calvi and Sindona was a deal by which the Ambrosiano Bank bought a Luxembourg company (called Compendium) from Sindona. This was the beginning of the massive overseas operations that eventually brought about Calvi's downfall and death. When Calvi opened a bank in South America, the Italian banking authorities only learned about it through the newspapers. Calvi became an empire builder – outside Italy.

When, in 1971, Calvi bought control of an Italian finance company, La Centrale Finanziara, many people expected the Bank of Italy to put its foot down, for the deal was plainly in contravention of the law that banks should not own businesses. But once again Calvi somehow got away with it.

The Centrale Finanziara deal was, in fact, a small part of Sindona's 'grand design' to take over another major industrial holding company – Bastogi – as well as the National Agricultural Bank, and merge them with Centrale Finanziara, forming one of the most powerful financial concentrations in Europe. This time the Bank of Italy objected. Business interests and government officials ganged up on Sindona and prevented the takeover. The deal collapsed. Sindona, his pride and reputation damaged, retired to America to lick his wounds. But he continued to do business for the Vatican, buying shares in Standard Oil, Chase Manhattan, Unilever, Westinghouse and other giants. Sindona also acquired for himself a controlling share in the Franklin National Bank for $40 million. This was a bold gamble; he was paying almost 25 per cent more than the shares were worth and the bank was in a far from healthy state. Sindona seems to have hoped to change all that with immense foreign exchange dealings. But the Arab oil crisis of 1973 caused shock waves in the financial world and Sindona suddenly found himself struggling to prevent a massive collapse. Rumours reached two of his banks in Italy – the Banca Unione and the Banca Privata Finanziara in Milan – and their depositors began to panic. When it was learned that Sindona had lost $39 million in his foreign currency deals, the Franklin Bank collapsed – the biggest American bank failure of all time.

The Banca Privata had already gone into liquidation. The Italian authorities demanded Sindona's extradition on the grounds that he had illegally removed money from his Italian bank and faked the balance sheet to cover up the deal. Sindona was also charged with various violations of the American banking rules. The Vatican was rumoured to have lost $60 million; Marcinkus hastily declared he hardly knew Sindona.

But while Sindona's empire was tottering, his protégé in Italy was flourishing. Calvi completed the Centrale Finanziara deal and bought various banks and insurance companies. He also replaced Sindona at the Vatican as an *uomo di fiducia* and bought a Catholic bank, Banca Cattolica del Veneto, from the Vatican bank, doing this through 'offshore' companies that enabled them to leave large sums of money overseas.

One man did strongly object to the sale of the Veneto Bank – Albino Luciani, Cardinal Patriarch of Venice. He is said to have protested to Marcinkus but without success. Six years later, Luciani became Pope John Paul I, a position that would have enabled him to put an end to the close relations between Calvi and the Vatican bank. He was to die after only a month in office. One writer – David Yallop – has argued that John Paul I was yet another murder victim in the complicated Ambrosiano story.

Meanwhile, Calvi began to acquire a formidable reputation in the Italian financial world; he became known as a 'coup-maker'. Through his foreign companies, he was smuggling millions of lire out of Italy by the simple expedient of selling shares to one of his companies, then buying them back at an inflated price. His activities were far from popular, since he caused 'waves' in the market and many smaller operators were drowned by them. The Italian finance minister, Ugo La Malfa, did a great deal to clip Calvi's wings by raising the interest rate and cutting off the supply of easy money. Calvi was inconvenienced but not seriously threatened.

In 1974, when Sindona's Franklin investment crashed, Calvi scented danger. The Italian Communist Party was gaining support; the Church had suffered a humiliating defeat in a referendum on divorce. Calvi had two aims: to become owner of the Banco Ambrosiano and to establish a vast financial power-base abroad, a power-base that could resist any political shocks in Italy. The method was to set up 'ghost companies' abroad and to get them to buy Ambrosiano shares, using money borrowed from international banks. Within a short time, Calvi was the *de facto* owner of the Banco Ambrosiano. In 1975 he became chairman of the bank.

At this point, another important name entered the story of Calvi's rise and downfall: that of Licio Gelli, the head of the Freemason's lodge known as P2. Gelli is still a man of mystery; one writer on the case – Larry Gurwin – says: 'No one has been able to explain fully how he obtained his power or to what ends he used it.' Born in 1919, Gelli had fought for Franco in Spain in 1937 but, during World War II, he had formed links with left-wing members of the Resistance. At the end of the war he came close to being executed as a Nazi collaborator but was spared on the intervention of the Communists. Whether Gelli was a Communist or a double agent or simply an opportunist is not known. In Rome after the war he became assistant to a member of parliament and learned something about the 'corridors of power' and the *sottogoverno* or 'undergovernment' – the secret forces that influence governments. He became a Freemason in 1963 and grew to be so well-liked and trusted that he eventually obtained permission to form his own lodge – or sub-lodge – of men of power and influence. His rise over the next few years was as extraordinary as that of Sindona or Calvi, but far less public. In effect, Gelli became a super-Mafia boss, with so many friends in business, finance and government that he was in a position to dispense favours to the most powerful in the land.

Calvi had one great weakness: a kind of superstition about the 'undergovernment'. He had the conspiracy mentality; if he had been told that all the wars of the past five centuries had been organized by some sinister secret society, he would have believed it. He thought that Mario Puzzo's *The Godfather* was a great work of fiction because it showed how power really operated – it is said that he always travelled with a copy in his briefcase, like a Bible.

If Calvi thought *The Godfather* was an accurate picture of the 'corridors of power' – with gangsters hand in glove with politicians and policemen – then it is no surprise that he swiftly accepted Gelli's offer to become a member of Propaganda Two. (Propaganda was the name of a well known lodge of the nineteenth century.) He joined on 23 August 1975. Calvi was a devout Catholic and the Church has always regarded Free-masonry as the incarnation of evil. But from Calvi's point of view, it was a necessity for any international businessman, like a wallet full of credit cards. P2 included in its membership forty-three members of parliament, including three cabinet ministers, the heads of every branch of the armed services, and the heads of Military Intelligence and Civilian Intelligence. This amazing network gave Gelli the power to 'dig up the dirt' on practically anybody. It also meant that he could exert pressure to cause embarrassing investigations to be abandoned. The basic assumption of Propaganda Two was that anybody could be bought.

This was not quite accurate. There were a number of honest magistrates and government officials who became aware of the existence of P2 through their investigations into terrorism. In the 1970s terrorism in Italy had become a growth industry. Most of the terrorists belonged to various 'red brigades', extreme leftist groups, but there were also a number of neo-fascist groups. A magistrate named Vittorio Occorsio became aware of the existence of links between a fascist group called National Vanguard and P2, and instituted an investigation. On 10 July 1976, he was murdered by a burst of machine gun fire. Another fascist group called New Order claimed responsibility. But the investigation into P2 was dropped.

Calvi was feeling the need for political protection at about this time. His old ally Michele Sindona had turned against him. As Calvi's fortunes had improved Sindona's had deteriorated. Sindona was also a member of P2 but since he was in New York, Gelli was not able to offer much help. After the crash of the Franklin Bank, Calvi had also become unwilling to throw good money after bad (he had provided $40 million that Sindona had used to purchase control of the bank). A Sindona henchman named Luigi Cavallo was given the job of harassing Calvi, hiring students to paint anti-Calvi slogans on walls and to plaster the walls of the Banco Ambrosiano with posters accusing Calvi of financial swindles. In 1977, Cavallo wrote a long letter to the Bank of Italy denouncing Calvi. As a result, the Governor of the Bank, Paolo Baffi, ordered his head of banking surveillance to investigate the Banco Ambrosiano. When interviewed in April 1978, Calvi's replies were evasive. The result of the investigation was a lengthy document, the Padolino Report, which contained some strong criticisms of the Ambrosiano Bank and raised the suspicion that Calvi was violating Italy's exchange control laws by exporting billions of lire abroad. The report also stated that the Banco Ambrosiano was involved in many 'questionable' deals with the Vatican bank. If the exchange-control accusations proved to be true, it could mean a jail sentence for Calvi.

There was an even greater threat on the horizon than the Bank of Italy. In August 1978, Pope Paul VI died – the man through whom Sindona had obtained his entrée to the Vatican. The man who was appointed pope in his place was Albino Luciani – the Cardinal who had raised strong objections to the Banco Veneto deal and whose objections had been – allegedly – overruled by Marcinkus. The new pope showed no disposition to be merely a 'rubber stamp' who allowed his advisers to run the Vatican. Luciani was the son of a Socialist and his views were distinctly to the left (as, of course, were those of Jesus). When he received a circular from the Office of Exchange Control about the illegal export of vast sums of money from Italy – an export that was increasing the unemployment problem – his immediate reaction was a determination to curb this particular activity of the Vatican bank. According to the investigative journalist David Yallop (whose book *In God's Name* contains the results of three years of research at the Vatican) there were immediate rumours that the end of Marcinkus's presidency of the bank was in sight. The new broom was apparently going to sweep the money changers out of the temple.

It was not to be. On the morning of 29 September 1978, the new pope was found dead in his bed. He had been in office only thirty-three days. Doctors gave the cause of death as a heart attack but the Vatican resisted an inquest. Cardinal Jean Villot, the Vatican Secretary of State, hastened to the pope's bedroom and, according to Yallop, removed the medicine he had been taking for low blood pressure and various notes about transfers and appointments that the pope was still holding. (Villot was himself due to be replaced.) None of the missing items ever reappeared. In spite of demands for an autopsy, the body was embalmed (which would have made it more difficult to determine the cause of death) and interred a few days later. Yallop argues convincingly that the death of Pope John Paul I was due to poison. Whether this is true or not, Calvi must have undoubtedly heaved a sigh of relief.

He still had the Bank of Italy investigation to worry about. But in 1979, this also began to recede. In March, a right-wing magistrate indicted the Governor of the Bank, Paolo Baffi, together with his investigator Sarcinelli, on a charge of failing to pass on to the legal authorities information about possible crimes committed by banks under their jurisdiction. The charges later proved to be totally groundless but Baffi resigned and Sarcinelli was suspended from his job for a year.

By a fortunate coincidence, another threat to Calvi had been removed in January 1979, when a man who was investigating the Padolini Report, Judge Emilio Alessandrini, was assassinated by a group that later claimed to be 'left-wing terrorists'. He was shot when sitting in his car at a set of traffic lights.

The Bank of Italy, already demoralized by the arrest of its governor and chief investigator, received another unmistakable warning in July 1979. The lawyer who was liquidating Sindona's Banca Privata in Milan, Giorgio Ambrosoli, was making some interesting discoveries about Calvi and his deals – including his deals with the Vatican. Death threats were made by underworld characters but Ambrosoli ignored them. Sindona's trial began on 9 July 1979, in New York. In Milan, Ambrosoli was making a deposition about Sindona's affairs. On 10 July he described how, when the Banca Veneto had changed hands, a brokerage fee of $6.5 million had been paid to 'a Milanese banker and an American archbishop'. That evening he spoke to the writer Gianfranco Modolo and admitted that the banker was Calvi and the archbishop was Marcinkus. The following day, about to enter his apartment around midnight, a man approached him and shot him dead.

The Bank of Italy took the hint. The investigation into Calvi was not dropped but it was slowed down to a snail's pace.

Killing Ambrosoli was not the solution to Sindona's problems. Neither was the murder of Lieutenant-Colonel Antonio Varisco, head of the Rome security service, which took place forty-eight hours later – Varisco and Ambrosoli had been collaborating in an investigation of P2. Neither was the murder of the Palermo police chief, Boris Giuliano, on 21 July in a Palermo café – Giuliano was investigating the way that Sindona recycled heroin proceeds through the Vatican bank. Sindona was in America, not Italy, and his only hope lay in killing the Assistant District Attorney John Kenney, who was probing his affairs. Sindona's Mafia associates had put out a $100,000 contract on Kenney's life but, even at this price, no one could be found to kill him. In America, murdering a law official would be counterproductive. In August 1979, Sindona decided that his only hope lay in returning to Italy and exerting a little pressure on various associates. He was on bail so the difficulties were not insurmountable but, obviously, jumping bail would prejudice the results of his trial. His solution was to arrange a fake kidnapping. He vanished from New York on 2 August 1979 and several ransom demands were duly received by various people. On 16 October Sindona reappeared in New York, limping from a bullet wound in the thigh and claiming that he had been tortured by his kidnappers. In fact, he had been in Palermo contacting Gelli, Calvi and other old friends to try to rally support. His chief defence was that the charges against him were all part of a Communist plot and he felt that if enough politicians and clerics supported his story, the American court would be bound to believe it. In fact, Marcinkus and some other prelates in the Vatican gave videotaped interviews to be used by Sindona's defence lawyers but the Vatican Secretary of State stepped in and ordered that they should not be used. In March 1980, Sindona was convicted on sixty-five counts of fraud and sentenced to twenty-five years in jail.

Calvi, meanwhile, was finding out that even his membership of P2 could not guarantee a quiet life. In return for favours received, he was expected to do favours in return, and some of these made heavy demands on his bank. For example, the Rizzoli publishing company, one of the largest in Italy, urgently needed an infusion of new cash. It owned one of Italy's most influential newspapers, the *Corriere della Sera* (*Evening Courier*) and such a newspaper could be extremely useful to P2 and to Calvi. Andrea Rizzoli, the owner, was told that if he joined P2, assistance would be forthcoming, but he decided against it. However, his son Angelo saw no objection to mutual aid; he and various other board members joined P2 and Gelli's second-in-command, Umberto Ortolani, was appointed to the board of Rizzoli. The result was a loan of $184 million for Rizzoli from the Ambrosiano Bank. When another masonic 'brother' wanted to borrow $5 million from Ambrosiano, Calvi's deputy Roberto Rosone turned him down but Calvi himself countermanded the refusal. 'Give him twenty million.' It was a bad decision; the 'brother' – Mario Genghino, head of a construction company – went bankrupt. The deputy, Rosone, was himself to be the victim of an assassination attempt.

But even the mighty Gelli, the Grand Master of P2, was not invulnerable. One of the members of P2 was a journalist called Mino Pecorelli who ran a scandal sheet – a kind of Italian version of *Private Eye* – called *O.P.* The information published by *O.P.* was usually alarmingly accurate – as might be expected from someone with access to huge files of secret information. Then Pecorelli stumbled on an interesting scandal about the sale of diesel oil. The diesel used for heating homes is taxed at a far lower rate than that used in vehicles and is dyed so it can be recognized. Gelli, with the help of an oil magnate and the head of the Finance Police – both members of P2 – found a way to sell domestic diesel as fuel for vehicles and so made $2.5 billion. Through Sindona, this was funnelled abroad via the Vatican bank.

Pecorelli stumbled on this scandal, without being aware of all its implications and began to publish titbits of information about it. He was swiftly 'bought off' by a deputation that included a judge, a general and a senator. This was a mistake. Pecorelli realized he could make vast sums of money by blackmailing the masons and he published an article revealing that Gelli had spied for the Communists during the war, and dropping strong hints about P2 and its activities. Within hours of publishing this article on 20 March 1979, Pecorelli climbed into his car and was shot twice in the mouth.

But Pecorelli had named many P2 members, including Cardinal Jean Villot, the man who had removed the medicine and papers from the pope's room after his death. His accusations added more fuel to the investigations into P2. In 1981, two magistrates who were investigating Sindona's ties with the Mafia went to Palermo where Sindona had hidden during his fake kidnapping. There they interviewed a man who was known to have helped Sindona and who had also made a sudden visit to Arezzo while Sindona was in Palermo. After long interrogation, this man admitted that he had gone to Arezzo to see Licio Gelli who lived there. The magistrates immediately ordered a search of Gelli's home in Arezzo. In a safe, they found masses of files which revealed that the membership of Propaganda Two included many of the most influential men in Italy. At first, the investigators suspected that Gelli was planning a *coup d'état*, then they realized that this was unnecessary. P2 was already a kind of *coup d'état*. It was virtually a state within a state.

Gelli fled from Italy. When the P2 scandal erupted, a few weeks later, it brought down the government of Prime Minister Arnaldo Forlani. It also led to the arrest of Roberto Calvi whose name had been found on one of the files. Two share deals in which Calvi had been involved had led to the illegal export of billions of lire.

As far as Calvi is concerned, the arrest on 20 May 1981, was the beginning of the end. For years he had been surrounded by bodyguards, living in fear of his life. Now his 'protector', Gelli, was on the run and he himself was in a prison cell. He told his wife and son, who visited him in jail, that the share deals had been done on behalf of the Vatican bank and asked them to approach Marcinkus and ask for his help. He also asked them to lobby politicians. They were totally inexperienced in such matters but were assisted by a new ally, a young man named Francesco Pazienza, who had been hired two months before as a consultant to Ambrosiano at a salary of $½ million a year. Carlo Calvi flew to the Bahamas where he found papers verifying his father's claim that the share deals had been done on behalf of the Vatican bank. He telephoned Marcinkus but was told 'Ambrosiano's problems are yours, not mine.'

Calvi seemed to be a broken man who had lost the power to think for himself. In court he told the magistrates: 'You must get me out of here', and offering to make compromising disclosures about the diesel scandal and his secret payments to the Rizzoli group and the Socialist Party. The magistrates replied that they had no power to release him. On 9 July 1981, Calvi failed to appear in court and his lawyer announced that he had attempted suicide by taking an overdose of barbiturates and slashing one of his wrists. Whether the suicide attempt was genuine is doubtful; at all events, it earned Calvi much sympathy and support. Politicians began to speak up for him, including the Socialist Bettino Craxi, who told Parliament that the trial was being conducted in an atmosphere of 'intimidatory violence'. When judgment was finally given, on 20 July 1981, Calvi and three other members of the Ambrosiano group were found guilty of illegal export of currency and Calvi was sentenced to four years in prison and fined sixteen billion lire. But on payment of the fine, he was released and given leave to appeal against conviction. Within a few days, Calvi was confirmed in his position as chairman of the Ambrosiano Bank. Only Roberto Rosone, the general manager, objected. He appealed to the Bank of Italy to replace Calvi as chairman but the bank refused. On 27 April 1982, Rosone was approaching the bank when a man began to shoot at him. A bank guard shot the man dead; Rosone was only wounded in the legs. Calvi hurried to Rosone's bedside exclaiming, 'Madonna! What a world of madmen.' But his friend Flavio Carboni paid a member of the Roman underworld, Ernesto Diotavelli, $530,000 the next day; Diotavelli was a close associate of the dead assassin, Danilo Abbruciati.

Calvi was in trouble but he still had vast holdings abroad, particularly in South America. There were no less than seventeen subsidiaries of the Banco Ambrosiano, mostly owned by a Luxembourg company which, in turn, was owned by the Vatican bank. When the directors of the companies in Peru and Nicaragua wanted more guarantees to cover their loans,

Marcinkus issued the necessary documents; known as 'letters of comfort', they admitted that the Vatican bank controlled, directly or indirectly, eight of Ambrosiano's subsidiaries abroad. The implication was that the debts would be the responsibility of the Vatican. These letters were, says one commentator, almost the last indulgences dispensed by the Vatican.

Calvi attempted to restore the Banco Ambrosiano's image of respectability by persuading the chief executive of the Olivetti company, Carlo De Benedetti, to buy into the bank and become deputy chairman. Benedetti accepted but offer but was to regret it. Whenever he tried to find out more about the bank's overseas affairs, he encountered a 'wall of rubber'; he was given excuses, but not information. He sent someone to look at the Ambrosiano Bank in Peru, whose loan portfolio stood at $800 million, and was disturbed to find that it was not a bank but a kind of finance company specializing in overseas business. Calvi assured him that 'the guarantees are fine' – meaning the letters of comfort. (As guarantees these were, in fact, worthless.) In January 1982, Benedetti decided he had had enough and resigned. His comments on the reason for his dissatisfaction led to a demand in Parliament to dissolve the Ambrosiano board and send in special commissioners. Calvi's ship was slowly sinking.

Calvi had one important new ally, a Sardinian businessman named Flavio Carboni, to whom he had been introduced by Pazienza in the previous August, after the trial. Carboni owned a magnificent yacht and seemed to have many influential friends in the political world. It was also to be alleged that he had many contacts in the underworld. As Calvi's relations with Pazienza became strained – Calvi's daughter says Pazienza was always demanding money – the relationship with Carboni became closer. Calvi lent Carboni five billion lire for a construction project; Carboni lobbied for Calvi among his influential friends.

Calvi needed help. The Bank of Italy was probing his South American companies, while a new stock exchange organization, CONSOB, formed to prevent corruption, tried to force Calvi to disclose more information to shareholders.

Calvi's increasing anxiety is easy to understand. He knew about the $1.4 billion 'hole' in the Ambrosiano accounts and that, if his jail sentence was confirmed, nothing could prevent this from becoming known – in which case he might well end by being sentenced to twenty-five years, like Sindona. Pazienza was deputed to try and find a buyer for about 12 per cent of Ambrosiano stock, mostly that owned by the 'ghost companies' abroad. (In fact, after Calvi's death, Pazienza claimed he had succeeded in setting up such a deal.) This was only one of many plans. Calvi was becoming frantic; Carboni describes him as sobbing and sounding delirious. Marcinkus had told Calvi angrily that he could stop looking for help from the Vatican; Calvi seems to have tried to blackmail him by threatening to reveal that the Vatican was giving money to the banned Polish trade union, Solidarity.

In early June 1982, the Bank of Italy demanded details of the $1.4 billion in loans made by the Ambrosiano's ghost companies abroad. Calvi realized this could be the end. He told his board about the demand; the new deputy chairman, Orazio Bagnasco, asked to see the documents about the ghost companies and to take them home to study them. Calvi flatly refused and for the first time in its history, the board voted against Calvi by four to ten. So far, Calvi had never had any difficulty dominating the board. On 10 June Calvi met his lawyers to discuss his appeal against conviction. On the morning of 11 June he disappeared from his Rome apartment.

Calvi's wife Clara and his son Carlo were in Washington. Calvi had told his daughter Anna that she was in danger and must leave Italy. Pazienza rang Clara Calvi to tell her of her husband's disappearance. When the news leaked out in Italy, Ambrosiano shares dropped by 12 per cent.

Why did Calvi decide to 'disappear'? The answer is still not fully known but it seems likely that he was hoping to accumulate materials for his defence. What is known about the last week of his life is that he drove halfway across Europe, then flew to London from Innsbruck. On the day of his disappearance, a Friday (11 June 1982), he telephoned a smuggler named Silvano Vittor in Trieste and asked him to meet him – Calvi had met Vittor through Carboni. Carboni also came to Trieste by private plane. With him was Ernesto Diotavelli, reputed to be a member of the Roman underworld. He was carrying a fake passport in the name of Gian Roberto Calvini. Calvi's real passport, of course, had been impounded in case he tried to leave Italy while on 'bail'. In fact, Calvi drove all night to Klagenfurt, in Austria, where he was to meet Carboni at the house of two sisters, Michaela and Manuela Kleinszig. He appeared to be much more relaxed now and telephoned his daughter Anna in Switzerland to say he was safe and that he felt things were improving. Anna in turn telephoned Clara Calvi in Washington to say Calvi was safe. Carboni and Vittor arrived. On Sunday evening, Vittor drove Calvi to Innsbruck. Carboni flew to Zurich and from his hotel room made calls to America, the Vatican, London, Austria and Czechoslovakia. Later that day, Calvi and Vittor drove to Bregenz, in Austria, where they were joined by Carboni and a Swiss businessman named Hans Kunz, who had agreed to make arrangements for Calvi and Vittor to go to London.

Through a London solicitor, Kunz made arrangements for Calvi and Vittor to stay in a kind of students' hostel called the Chelsea Cloisters. On the following day, Tuesday, Calvi and Vittor flew by hired plane from Innsbruck to Gatwick. They checked in at the Chelsea Cloisters, which Calvi found thoroughly depressing – he had been accustomed to expensive hotels. He seemed nervous and irritable. On Wednesday evening he rang his wife and revealed that he had high hopes of a solution to the bank's problems. 'A crazy, marvellous thing is about to explode which could even help my appeal.' But he added the curiously ominous information, 'I don't trust the people I'm with any more.' By this time, Carboni had arrived in London. He was staying at a block of council flats near Heathrow with a man called William Morris. For a millionaire, this was almost as curious a choice as the Chelsea Cloisters. Morris's Italian wife was the aunt of Carboni's mistress.

Calvi may have been optimistic about his prospects, but his fellow directors at the bank were not. On Thursday, 17 June 1982, there was a meeting of the Ambrosiano directors, at which many of them for the first time heard the truth about the ghost companies and about the refusal of the Vatican to offer further help. It was decided to sack Calvi as chairman; Rosone was appointed in his place. At about seven that evening, Calvi's secretary, Graziella Corrocher, died as a result of a fall from a window in the building. On her desk there was a note that seemed to confirm that this was suicide and which said that Calvi should be 'twice damned' for the damage he had done to the group.

Calvi's death was also only a few hours away. That afternoon he had been nervous and tense and did not take his usual rest. He told Vittor that if he went out, he was to telephone every twenty minutes; Vittor had to give a special knock to identify himself when he returned. Evidently Calvi was expecting unwelcome visitors.

That evening, according to Vittor (in a BBC interview), Carboni came to the hotel at a late hour and asked Calvi and Vittor to go down to see him. Calvi was nervous and refused so Vittor went alone. When Vittor returned to the room, Calvi was no longer there. The man who had been afraid to leave the flat had suddenly left on his own. He was found dead under Blackfriars Bridge a few hours later.

What did Vittor and Carboni do? Vittor left London and returned to Italy before Calvi's body was identified, Carboni decided to return to Rome. But although he was close to Heathrow, from which there were many flights to Rome, he preferred to travel down to Gatwick, from which there were no flights to Rome. From there he flew to Edinburgh, then took a private jet back to Zurich.

A BBC team, reconstructing Calvi's death, established that on the previous day, Carboni's brother booked into a hotel in Geneva. On the evening after Calvi's death, a private plane flew from Geneva to Gatwick. It spent only ninety minutes at Gatwick and when it flew back to Geneva it had a briefcase on board. Calvi never travelled without his briefcase but it was not found in his room or at the scene of the 'suicide'. The briefcase, according to the BBC, contained papers about his deals with the Vatican and P2. It has never been found.

In August 1982, the Banco Ambrosiano was declared insolvent. The Vatican bank had refused to act in accordance with the spirit of the 'letters of comfort' and make good the vast sum that had vanished through Calvi's ghost companies.

Licio Gelli, the head of Propaganda Two, had fled to South America. He was lured back to Geneva in September 1982; apparently to clear up some problem with his bank, into which Calvi had transferred $100 million, and was arrested. He was held in a maximum security prison, Champ Dollon. But a multi-millionaire cannot be expected to remain in prison for long. In August 1983, he vanished from his cell; smears of blood on the floor seemed to indicate that he had been abducted forcibly. Soon after, a prison guard was charged with having arranged his escape for a fee of 20,000 Swiss francs. Most writers on the case have expressed extreme scepticism that only one man could have been involved.

Flavio Carboni was extradited back to Italy in the autumn of 1982. In April 1983, he was charged – together with underworld leader Ernesto Diotavelli – of involvement in the murder plot on Roberto Rosone, Calvi's deputy. He was also charged with many other offences, including fraud, laundering money from kidnap ransoms, robberies and drug trafficking. At the time of this writing, the case has still not come to trial.

Who, then, did kill Roberto Calvi and why? The problem in answering that question is that many people must have felt relieved to hear of his death. David Yallop quotes Calvi's wife as saying she is convinced that the Vatican was behind the murder. Yallop speaks openly of the 'swindles' perpetrated by Calvi and Marcinkus together. But Marcinkus remains behind the walls of the sovereign state of the Vatican, beyond the reach of the police officers who would like to question him about his dealing with Calvi. The view disseminated by the Vatican is that Marcinkus was simply too naïve and trusting in his dealings with Calvi.

A more widely held view is that Propaganda Two was responsible for Calvi's death. In February 1984, the Prime Minister, Bettino Craxi, went on record as saying that he believed that Calvi was murdered and that his death could probably be traced to 'criminals connected with the Lodge'. Craxi believes that Gelli was not the leader of P2, but merely a general secretary. If true, this could support the view that P2 was responsible for Calvi's death, the aim being to prevent him 'making a deal' to save his own skin at his second trial by telling all he knew about the Banco Ambrosiano's illegal dealings.

The problem with all the theories is that there are altogether too many suspects, a point underlined by one of Yallop's disclosures: 'Until the end of his life he was laundering money for the Mafia . . . He was also recycling money for P2. These functions were carried out with the assistance of the Vatican Bank . . . He laundered money from kidnapping, drug sales, arms deals, bank raids, hold-ups, thefts of jewelry and works of art. His criminal contacts ranged from what is known as High Mafia to ordinary run-of-the-mill murderers, through to right-wing terrorist organizations.' (According to Yallop, the Bologna Station bomb outrage, in which eighty-five people died, was organized by P2, in order to direct outrage towards the Italian Communists.)

All this leaves an impressive list of suspects for the murder.

In June 1983, a second inquest on Calvi in London preferred to return an open verdict, meaning that murder was now recognized as a possibility. That decision meant that insurance companies had to pay Calvi's widow about $3 million.

Professor Keith Simpson, who originally returned the verdict of suicide on Calvi, admitted that Calvi could easily have been rendered unconscious by some drug that leaves no trace – like curare – then taken by boat or car to Blackfriars Bridge. It would have been easy to remove an unconscious man from the Chelsea Cloisters in the early hours of the morning; unlike the kind of hotels Calvi was accustomed to there was no doorman or desk clerk to keep watch.

Calvi's bodyguard, Silvano Vittor, was asked by the BBC reporter whether it was not highly convenient that he happened to be downstairs talking to Carboni when Calvi vanished from his room. His reply: 'I cannot answer that question, because whatever reply I give will be the wrong one.'

One thing seems clear: that the view held by Calvi's family, that he was the victim of 'countless injustices' in those final years, is one that is hard to sustain.

However, as a postscript to this, the *Financial Times* reported the following on 26 May 1984:

The final settlement on the long-running Banco Ambrosiano affair, expected to total as much as $539 million, was signed yesterday in Geneva by more than fifty representatives of the Vatican bank, foreign bank creditors and the liquidators of the late Senor Roberto Calvi's failed Milan bank . . .

The settlement reached after nearly two years of tortuous negotiations, involves the payment by the Vatican bank of close to $250 million 'in recognition of moral involvement'.

The Vatican bank, directly and indirectly, owns 10 per cent of the dummy overseas companies to which Ambrosiano lent $1.2 billion.

Despite the agreement by creditors to drop financial claims against the Vatican bank, Archbishop Paul Marcinkus, Vatican bank chairman, is still under investigation for fraud in connection with the collapse of Ambrosiano.

CAROLINE, Queen

The Only British Queen to be Tried for Adultery

It is something of a mystery why the Prince of Wales, the son of King George III, agreed to marry the fat, ugly and tactless Caroline of Brunswick. It is true that he did it largely to persuade parliament to pay his enormous debts. But he could have married the Queen's niece, the beautiful and talented Louise of Mecklenburg-Strelitz. His marriage to Caroline was a disaster for everyone.

George Augustus Frederick, the Prince of Wales, was born in August 1762. Determined that his son would grow up virtuous and serious-minded, George III had him brought up far from the court according to a strict academic and physical regime. It had the opposite effect: the Prince became a rebel, a spendthrift and a waster. At the age of seventeen he embarked on an affair with an actress, Mary Robinson, and his letters to her had to be bought back eventually for £5,000. The Prince became a member of a hard-drinking, hard-gambling set, which included the Whig politician Charles James Fox – one of his father's chief enemies – and the playwright Sheridan. He began to run up vast debts. He voted for Fox – and against his father – when Fox's India Bill came before parliament but the Whig politician lost and was dismissed. When he was twenty-three, the Prince fell in love with the beautiful Catholic, Mrs Fitzherbert, and although she fled to France to escape his attentions, he finally persuaded her to go through a secret marriage. But constancy was not one of his strong points and he soon took another mistress, Lady Jersey.

By the time he was thirty, the Prince was an embarrassment to his father and intensely unpopular with the British public. His debts now amounted to £630,000 – many millions in

present-day terms – and Pitt's administration showed no eagerness to find the money. So when it was suggested by his father
that he should marry and furnish an heir, he agreed on
condition that parliament paid his debts.

Caroline of Brunswick was short, plump and ugly, and she
suffered from body odour – probably as a result of infrequent
washing. Lady Jersey, the Prince's current mistress, may have
pushed him into marrying Caroline rather than the beautiful
Louise of Mecklenburg-Strelitz as she would be less of a rival.
On 5 April 1795, at St James's Palace, the Prince was introduced to Caroline; he was shattered. He staggered to the far
end of the room and called for a brandy. He went on drinking
brandy for three days until the marriage ceremony. On the
honeymoon – with Lady Jersey also in attendance – he seems
to have done his duty as a husband for Caroline discovered
she was pregnant soon thereafter. But the Prince found her
unbearable and stayed as far away from her as possible; in the
following year, he wrote her a letter saying that, 'our inclinations are not in our power', but that being polite to one
another was. When she received the letter, Queen Caroline
was with the politician George Canning and asked him what he
thought it meant; Canning replied that it seemed to give her
permission to do as she liked. Whereupon Queen Caroline
proceeded to do just that with Canning.

What no one realized at the time was that the royal line of
Hanover suffered from the disease known as porphyria, the
'royal disease', a genetic disorder in which, due to an enzyme
defect, the body accumulates large quantities of porphyrins
(precursors of red blood pigment). The disease affects the
digestive tract, the nervous system, the circulatory system and
the skin; it caused psychotic disorders and epilepsy. George III
had several attacks of it and died insane. The Prince of Wales
was also subject to it and so was Caroline – two of her brothers
were imbeciles, probably due to porphyria. It may explain
Caroline's utter lack of self-control and her tendency to behave
outrageously which led many to suspect she was insane.

Rejected by her husband she retired to a house in Blackheath
and behaved in a manner that led Lady Hester Stanhope to
call her 'a downright whore'. She had a Chinese clockwork

figure in her room which, when wound up, performed gross
sexual movements; she was also given to dancing around in a
manner that exposed a great deal of her person.

In 1806, rumours that a four-year-old child in her entourage,
William Austin, was her illegitimate son led to what became
known as 'the Delicate Investigation'. A Royal Commission
repudiated the charge and found Lady Douglas, who had
started the rumour, guilty of perjury. But years later, Caroline
told her lawyer's brother that the child was the natural son of
Prince Louis Ferdinand of Prussia, who had always been her
love. Mrs Fitzherbert was to state later that Caroline had
secretly married Prince Louis before she married the Prince of
Wales.

Finally, in August 1814, Caroline decided to leave England.
In Geneva, at a ball given in her honour, she shocked her
hosts by dancing naked to the waist. In Naples she became the
mistress of King Joachim, Napoleon's brother-in-law. When
she left Naples – at the time Napoleon escaped from Elba –
she had with her Napoleon's courier, a coarsely handsome
Italian named Bartolomeo Bergami, a former quartermaster in
a regiment of hussars. This swarthy, bearded, intensely masculine character looked like a brigand from a Drury Lane play.
He travelled with her to Munich, Tunis, Athens, Constantinople and Jerusalem, and when they settled in her villa near
Pesaro they behaved as man and wife.

James Brougham, her lawyer's brother, now wrote to
England suggesting that the prince – he was now Prince Regent
(his father having become insane) – should obtain a legal
separation from Caroline so she could never become queen of
England. But the prince wanted divorce or nothing. So nothing
came of this suggestion.

George III finally died in January 1820 and his son became
George IV. Caroline of Brunswick was now Queen Caroline.
The government quickly offered her £50,000 a year if she
would agree not to return to England. In a fury, Caroline
hurried across the Channel. Her husband was one of the most
unpopular men in the country and on that count many people
espoused her cause. To the intense embarrassment of the

government, she settled at Brandenburg House, in Hammersmith. And on 17 August the government took the offensive by hauling her in front of the House of Lords. Its aim was to dissolve the marriage on the grounds that Caroline had engaged in 'a most unbecoming and degrading intimacy' with Bergami, 'a foreigner of low station'. But the government had bitten off more than it could chew. Noisy mobs demonstrated in favour of Caroline and the House of Lords had to be surrounded by two strong timber fences. The queen's coach was always surrounded by a cheering crowd. After fifty-two days the divorce clause was carried. But the oratory of Henry Brougham caused a turn in the tide and when the Bill was given its final reading, it had only a pathetic majority of nine. The Lords decided to drop it.

The coronation was scheduled for 29 April 1821. The queen wrote to the Prime Minister, Lord Liverpool, to ask what kind of a dress she ought to wear for the coronation. He replied that she could 'form no part of that ceremony'. But when George was crowned, Caroline arrived at the Abbey dressed in a muslin slip and demanded to be admitted. When she shouted, 'The queen – open!', pages opened the doors. She continued with 'I am the queen of England.' An official roared, 'Do your duty, shut the Hall door', and the door was slammed in her face. Undaunted, Caroline drove back to Brandenburg House and sent a note to the king asking for a coronation 'next Monday'.

She died two weeks later, on 7 August 1821 – so suddenly that it was widely rumoured that she had been poisoned. When her body was on its way to the ship that would take it back to Brunswick, there were riots at Kensington Church, bricks were thrown, and two men were shot by the Life Guards. Caroline was buried in Brunswick Cathedral, with an inscription on her coffin: The Injured Queen of England.

George IV remained intensely unpopular. He lived on for only nine years after the death of Caroline. The major issue of the time was Roman Catholic emancipation. (England had been anti-Catholic since the time of Elizabeth I, and George I had come to the throne of England from Hanover because of the Act that prevented a Catholic from becoming king of

England.) As Prince of Wales, George had been in favour of Wellington who, as Prime Minister, carried the act of parliament that finally achieved Catholic emancipation (although Wellington was himself basically opposed to it, believing it would finally destroy English rule in Ireland – as it did.) George IV became hysterical about the issue and threatened to use the royal veto. But the throne no longer held the political power it had under George III, and he was reluctantly forced to accept Catholic emancipation. After that, the king's health deteriorated swiftly and he died on 26 June 1830. He had a portrait of Mrs Fitzherbert round his neck on his death bed. But the two had been estranged for many years – ever since, at a dinner in honour of Louis XVIII in 1803, he had made sure there was no fixed place for her at table, so she must sit 'according to her rank'. After that insult, she had retired from the court.

CASTANEDA, Carlos
The Don Juan Hoax

In 1968, the University of California Press published a book called *The Teachings of Don Juan: A Yacqui Way of Knowledge*, by Carlos Castaneda. Castaneda had entered the University of California – UCLA – as an undergraduate in 1959, and had received a BA in anthropology in 1962. The University of California Press accepted *The Teachings of Don Juan* as an authentic account of Castaneda's 'field work' in Mexico. The book told how, when he was an anthropology student, in 1960, Castaneda made several trips to the southwest to collect information on medical plants used by the Indians. At a Greyhound bus station, he was introduced to a white-haired old Indian who apparently knew all about peyote, the hallucinogenic plant. Although this first meeting was abortive – Castaneda tells with touching honesty how he 'talked nonsense' to Don Juan – Castaneda made a point of finding out where Don Juan lived and was finally accepted by the old *brujo* (medicine man or magician) as a pupil, a sorcerer's apprentice. The teaching begins with an episode in which Don Juan tells Castaneda to look for his 'spot', a place where he will feel more comfortable and at ease than anywhere else; he told Castaneda that there was such a spot within the confines of the porch. Castaneda describes how he spent all night trying different spots, lying in them, but felt no difference. Don Juan told him he ought to use his eyes. After this, he began to distinguish various colours in the darkness: purple, green and verdigris. When he finally chose one of these, he felt sick and had a sensation of panic. Exhausted, he lay by the wall and fell asleep. When he woke up, Don Juan told him that he had found his 'spot' – where he had fallen asleep. The other spot was bad for him, the 'enemy'.

This episode helps to explain the subsequent popularity of the book which was published in paperback by Ballantine Books and sold 300,000 copies. Don Juan is a teacher, a man of knowledge – the kind of person that every undergraduate dreams of finding – and he introduces Castaneda to the most astonishing experiences. When Castaneda first eats a peyote button, he experiences amazing sensations and plays with a mescalito dog whose mind he can read. On a later occasion he sees the mescalito dog himself as a green man with a pointed head. When Don Juan teaches him how to make a paste from the *datura* plant – Jimson weed – he anoints himself with it and has a sensation of flying through the air at a great speed. (In their book *The Searches for Abraxas*, Stephen Skinner and Neville Drury speculate that witches of the Middle Ages used a similar concoction and that this explains how they 'flew' to Witches' Sabbaths.) He wakes up to find himself half a mile from Don Juan's house.

During the period when the book was published every young American was smoking pot and experimenting with 'psychedelic drugs' like mescalin and LSD, and Timothy Leary was advising American youth to 'Turn on, tune in, drop out.' This apparently factual account of semi-magical experiences became as popular as Tolkien's *Lord of the Rings* and for much the same reason: it was escapist literature, but, more important, it claimed to be true.

Reviews were excellent. Anthropologists and scientists took the book seriously – the psychologist Carl Rogers called it 'one of the most vividly convincing documents I have read'. The philosopher Joseph Margolis said that either Castaneda was recording an encounter with a master or he was himself a master.

This was clearly a success that had to be followed up. *A Separate Reality* described how Castaneda had returned to Don Juan in 1968. A giant gnat, 100 feet high, circles round him; he rides on a bubble; he has a semi-mystical experience in which he hears extraordinary sounds and sees the sorcerer's 'ally', who shows him a 'spirit catcher'.

The demand for more about Don Juan remained strong but Castaneda had a problem. *A Separate Reality* came to an end in 1970 and was published in 1971; for the time being he had used up his Don Juan material. But not quite. He explained in his next book, *Journey to Ixtlan* (1973), that he had made the erroneous assumption that the glimpses of reality that Don Juan had given him could only be obtained through drugs. Now he realized he was mistaken. In fact, Don Juan had told him many other things during his years as a sorcerer's apprentice, but although he had written these non-drug revelations in his 'field notes', he had failed to see their significance. Now, looking back over his notes, he realized that he had a vast amount of material that showed that drugs were not necessary for achieving unusual states of consciousness. So *Journey to Ixtlan* goes back to 1960 and recounts still more astonishing adventures: he has strange visions, mountains move, and Castaneda describes his encounter with a sinister but beautiful sorceress named Catalina.

In retrospect, it seems that Castaneda made his first major error in writing *Ixtlan* (although it was one that, according to his agent, made him $1 million). The 'lost' field notes sound just a little too convenient. Yet, oddly enough, scholars continued to take him seriously. Mary Douglas, a professor of social anthropology, wrote an article about the first three books called 'The Authenticity of Castaneda', which concluded: 'From these ideas we are likely to get advances in anthropology.' Moreover, UCL granted Castaneda his Ph.D for *Ixtlan* and he lectured on anthropology on the Irvine campus.

If reviewers would swallow *Ixtlan* they would clearly swallow anything. Now that enough time had elapsed since his last visit to Sonora, Castaneda could renew his acquaintance with Don Juan and bring his revelations up to date. But *Tales of Power* (1974) seems to indicate that either Castaneda or his publisher felt that the game would soon be up. The dust jacket declares that this is the 'culmination of Castaneda's extraordinary initiation into the mysteries of sorcery'. At last, it declares, Castaneda completes his long journey into the world of magic and the book ends with a 'deeply moving farewell'. In many ways *Tales of Power* – covering a period of a few days in 1971 – is more rewarding than the earlier Don Juan books because it attempts to present a philosophical theory about reality, in terms of two concepts which Don Juan calls the *tonal* and the *nagual*. The *tonal* is 'everything we are', while the *nagual* is pure potentiality. The *tonal* is the pair of Kantian spectacles through which we see the world and impose meaning on it; it consists mainly of linguistic concepts and preconceptions. These conceptions are illustrated with the usual tales of magical experiences: Don Juan shows him a squirrel wearing spectacles which swells until it is enormous and then disappears; Carlos walks a few steps and finds he has travelled one and a half miles.

It was at this point, after publication of *Tales of Power*, that a teacher of psychology named Richard De Mille was persuaded by his niece to read all four Don Juan books one after the other. ('You have to take the whole trip.') *The Teachings* struck him as authentic and factual. *A Separate Reality* raised doubts; it was better written but somehow not so 'factual'. And the character of Don Juan had changed; he seemed more 'joky', while in the first book he had been grimly serious. Of course, Castaneda himself had already mentioned this. 'He clowned during the truly crucial moments of the second cycle.' But when he came to *Ixtlan*, De Mille was puzzled to find that the Don Juan of the notes made as early as 1960 was as much of a humorist and a clown as the later Don Juan. Made suspicious by this inconsistency, he began to study the books more closely and soon found contradictions. A friend pointed out one obvious inconsistency: in October 1968 Castaneda leaves his car and walks for two days to the shack of Don Juan's fellow sorcerer Don Genaro but when they walk out of the shack they climb straight into the car. De Mille discovered a similar contradiction. In *Ixtlan*, Castaneda goes looking for a certain bush on Don Juan's instructions and finds it has vanished; then Don Juan leads him to the far side of the hill, where he finds the bush he thought he had seen earlier on the other side. Later Don Juan tells him, 'This morning you *saw*', giving the word special emphasis. Yet six years later, in 1968, Castaneda is represented (in *A Separate Reality*) as asking Don Juan what is *seeing* and Don Juan tells him that in order to find out, Castaneda must *see* for himself. He seems to have forgotten that Castaneda had an experience of *seeing* six years earlier.

And while it is understandable that Don Juan should forget, it is quite incomprehensible that Castaneda should.

These and many similar inconsistencies convinced De Mille that one of the two books had to be fiction, or that, more probably, they both were. He published his results in a book called *Castaneda's Journey* in 1976 and it led many anthropologists who had taken Don Juan seriously to change their views. Joseph K. Long felt 'betrayed by Castaneda'. Marcello Truzzi, on the other hand, admitted that he had felt aghast at the initial reactions of the scientific community to Castaneda's books and that he was equally outraged by the lack of serious reaction now De Mille had exposed them as frauds.

Castaneda's admirers were mostly infuriated. Their feeling was that even if Castaneda had invented Don Juan, the books were full of genuine knowledge and wisdom, and should be gratefully accepted as works of genius. One lady wrote to De Mille saying she was convinced he didn't exist and asking him to prove it. De Mille had, in fact, accepted that the Don Juan books had a certain merit, both as literature and as 'occult teaching'. But when, in 1980, he edited a large volume of essays on the 'Castaneda hoax' called *The Don Juan Papers* his admiration had visibly dwindled. Some of the essays present an even more devastating exposure of Castaneda than De Mille's original volume; for example, Hans Sebald, an anthropologist who had spent a great deal of time in the southwestern desert, pointed out that it was so hot from June to September that no one with any sense ventures into it; dehydration and exhaustion follow within hours. Yet according to Castaneda, he and Don Juan wandered around the desert for days, engaged in conversation and ignoring the heat. Sebald goes on to demolish Castaneda's animal lore: 'Where . . . are the nine-inch centipedes, the tarantulas big as saucers? Where are the king snakes, scarlet racers, chuckawallas, horned toads, gila monsters . . .' A lengthy appendix to *The Don Juan Papers* cites hundreds of parallel passages from the Castaneda books and from other works on anthropology and mysticism that bear a close resemblance. The book establishes, beyond all possible doubt, that the Castaneda books are a fraud.

Richard De Mille's own researches revealed that Carlos

Arana was born in 1925 (not 1935, as he has told an interviewer) in Cajamarca, Peru, and came to San Francisco in 1951, leaving behind a Chinese-Peruvian wife who was pregnant. In 1955 he met Damon Runyan's distant cousin Margaret and married her; they separated after six months. In 1959 he became an undergraduate at UCLA and the Don Juan story begins . . .

Castaneda himself has proved to be an extremely elusive individual, as *Time* discovered when it sent a reporter to interview him in 1973. In the light of De Mille's discoveries this is easy to understand. Castaneda's career can be compared to that of the Shakespeare forger, William Ireland (*see* page 238), who began by forging a few Shakespeare signatures to gain his father's attention and found himself forced to continue until he had concocted a whole new Shakespeare play, which brought about his discovery and downfall. Castaneda presumably produced the original *Teachings of Don Juan* as a mild form of hoax. The publication by Ballantine launched him, whether he liked it or not, on the career of a trickster and confidence man. It would, perhaps, have been wiser to stop after *Ixtlan*, or possibly *Tales of Power*. But the demand for more Don Juan books has presumably overcome his caution. In fact, the fifth, *The Second Ring of Power*, reads so obviously as fiction that it raises the suspicion that Castaneda wanted to explode his own legend. But he shows caution in offering no dates, no doubt to escape De Mille's vigilant eye. Castaneda tells how he went back to Mexico looking for Don Juan and instead encountered one of his disciples, a sorcerer named Madame Solitude. Last time he saw her she was fat and ugly and in her fifties; now she is young, slim and vital, and within a few pages, she has torn off her skirt and invited him to make love to her – an invitation he wisely resists. Then Castaneda somehow invokes his own double out of his head – not a mild-mannered scholar but a super-male authority who hits Madame Solitude on the head and almost kills her. Then four lady disciples arrive and make more assaults on Castaneda, which he overcomes, after which they all encounter other-worldly beings . . .

In his sixth book, *The Eagle's Nest*, Castaneda returns to

Mexico as 'a sorcerous leader and figure in his own right' (as the blurb says) and enters into a closer relationship with one of the female sorcerers of the previous book, La Gorda. The two of them develop the ability to dream in unison. It is clear that, since writing the earlier book, Castaneda has come across split-brain psychology and now we hear a great deal about the right and left sides of a human being, the left being the *nagual* and the right the *tonal*. De Mille had pointed out that the Don Juan books seem to chart Castaneda's literary and philosophical discoveries over the years and this book confirms it. For those who read it with the certainty that the previous books were a hoax, it seems an insult to the intelligence. But it seems to demonstrate that Castaneda can continue indefinitely spinning fantasies for whose who regard him as the greatest of modern gurus.

CHATTERTON, Thomas
The Rowley Forgeries

The story of Thomas Chatterton is one of the saddest in the history of English literature. He committed suicide at the age of seventeen, when his mind was unbalanced by starvation.

Chatterton's father died three months before Thomas was born – on 20 November 1752 – in Bristol. His mother supported the family by needlework. Chatterton was a quiet boy, slow in learning to read, and his sister thought him stupid. But he was a dominant child who bullied his companions. At the age of seven (a crucial year in the lives of most children) his character changed; he began to read and write, and became an incorrigible daydreamer. He spent a great deal of time in the nearby church of St Mary Redcliffe, whose sexton was his uncle. The past seemed to fascinate him and he spent hours reading inscriptions on tombstones. In his seventh year he was sent to a charity school, Colston's Hospital, but found it boring. Chatterton's problem, throughout his life, was that he was far more mentally active than those around him and was accordingly in a perpetual state of rebellion.

He was an obsessive reader – he was able to obtain books through a local circulating library – and before he was eleven he was already writing verse. His family noticed that he became far less sullen and withdrawn after he had started to write.

There was only one teacher Chatterton liked and respected, a young apprentice usher called Thomas Phillips. It was apparently to impress Phillips that Chatterton produced his first forgery, a poem called 'Elinoure and Juga', a dialogue between two girls, who lament the death of their lovers in the Wars of the Roses and end by drowning themselves. It is a remarkable work for a boy in his early teens, simple, deeply felt and curiously restrained. Chatterton claimed that he had found this and other documents, in a parish monument chest in the church of St Mary Redcliffe. Indeed, there was such a chest and it contained documents and manuscripts from the fifteenth century. Chatterton used pieces of this parchment for his forgeries, writing in brown ink, with a spidery, almost indecipherable hand. The author of the poem, according to Chatterton, was one 'Thomas Rowley, secular priest'. Rowley had, in fact, lived in Bristol at that period.

The forgery gained him what he wanted – the attention of Phillips and the respect of his schoolfriends. Thereafter, Chatterton often amused them by writing satirical poems at the expense of the masters.

His next major excursion into forgery took place in the spring of 1767, when he was fourteen. He had met a local self-made man, a manufacturer of pewter named Henry Burgum. Burgum was anxious to trace his family tree. Chatterton 'discovered' old parchments in the Redcliffe church which included the de Bergham coat of arms and a family tree tracing the Burgums back to the Norman Conquest. He also 'found' a poem by Rowley that mentioned a knight called Johan de Berghamme. For good measure, Chatterton included a branch of his own family that had intermarried with the de Berghams. Burgum rewarded Chatterton with five shillings – a weekly labourer's wage at the time.

There can be no doubt that Chatterton descended gently and almost imperceptibly into the habit of deception. The Reverend Walter Skeat says in his introduction to the collected poems: 'It can scarcely be denied that a system of concealment, though commenced with no guilty end in view, must gradually have produced a habit of deception, and tended more and more to blunt all moral feelings on this point.' In fact, Chatterton was too young to have very strong moral feelings; his strongest desire was to 'become known'. At about the same time, Chatterton met a well-known surgeon called William Barrett, who was compiling a work on the history of Bristol. Chatterton had soon endeared himself to Barrett by discovering in the old chest various old parchments and plans about Bristol. He and Barrett spent long hours in earnest discussion and Barrett was impressed by the young man's brilliance. Chatterton was, at this time, writing various poems which he acknowledged as his own, so it is hard to understand why he felt it necessary to take in Barrett with various ballads by Thomas Rowley: perhaps, as Skeat says, the habit of deception was becoming second nature.

Chatterton left school a few months before his sixteenth birthday and went to work for a solicitor, John Lambert. The job bored him and he detested Lambert. But he continued writing and one of his forgeries, a description of the opening of the old stone bridge over the Avon, was printed in a local newspaper on the day a new bridge was opened and excited some attention. Pressed about his source, Chatterton explained that the description came from an old parchment found in a chest in the church of St Mary Redcliffe. But he admitted to a friend, John Rudhall, that he was the author of the description.

Burgum's partner, George Catcott, also came to admire Chatterton and was also the recipient of various poems by Thomas Rowley. Friends like Burgum, Catcott and Barrett made Chatterton feel that success was just around the corner and his optimism was strengthened when a number of magazines accepted pieces by him in 1769. He tried to interest a publisher in the Rowley poems without success. Then he decided to try Horace Walpole, the author of the romance *Castle of Otranto* – after all, Walpole had originally claimed that his novel was a translation of an ancient manuscript. Walpole was greatly interested by a *History of Painting in England* (or rather, *The Ryse of Peyncteyne yn Englande* wroten by T. Rowleie). To Chatterton's delight, Walpole said he would like to publish the Rowley manuscripts but when Chatterton hinted that he was in need of money, Walpole was chilled. After two friends had given their opinion that the manuscripts were forgeries, he wrote to Chatterton advising him to stick to becoming a lawyer before trying to make a name as a writer. The relationship became notably cool.

Like most teenagers, Chatterton was capable of extravagant self-pity and self-dramatization. On 17 April 1770, he wrote a 'last will and testament', hinting that he intended to kill himself the next day. Then, having persuaded his employer to release him with four years of his apprenticeship still to run, he left Bristol to seek his fortune in London.

His new life began well enough; he lodged with a cousin, Mrs Ballance, in Shoreditch, became friendly with various writers and politicians, including the radical John Wilkes, and contributed to the Whig journals. His satirical verses impressed his new friends. But soon after his arrival in London, he committed a major error when he wrote a satirical poem called 'The Exhibition', in which he pilloried most of the acquaintances he had left behind in Bristol. It alienated his former friend Barrett. Chatterton's fortunes declined when the Whig journals fell foul of the government and were forced to choose between pursuing a more cautious line and suspending publication. Payments became few and far between. His cousin infuriated him by suggesting that he ought to look for an office job until things improved and he moved into an attic room in Brooke Street, Holborn. He wrote to Barrett begging for help, but Barrett refused. Loneliness and hunger plunged Chatterton into self-pity. On 24 August 1770, he tore all his manuscripts to shreds, then took a dose of arsenic – bought to poison the rats with which his attic was infested – and died in agony. It may well be that the balance of his mind was disturbed for there was insanity in his family.

It was only after his death that the 'Chatterton scandal' erupted. The poems were handed about and the mystery of their authorship discussed by scholars. To begin with this was confined to Bristol but it soon spread to London. In the year after Chatterton's death, Horace Walpole was at a banquet of the Royal Academy when, to his surprise, he heard Oliver Goldsmith praising some ancient poems that had been found in Bristol. For the first time, Walpole learned that Chatterton had killed himself. He was upset and concerned but certainly felt by no means responsible for Chatterton's death. He had no way of knowing that within a year or two he would widely be regarded as Chatterton's murderer and that this myth – that he had scornfully rejected a young man of genius and caused his suicide – would pursue him for the rest of his life.

In 1777, the Rowley poems were published by Thomas Tyrwhitt, who left open the question of their authorship. Immediately, the literary world divided into those who believed they were forgeries and those who believed they were genuine.

Chatterton's former friend Catcott attacked Walpole for discouraging the poet; Walpole replied angrily and published his reply as a pamphlet in 1779. In the following year, Herbert Croft's novel *Love and Madness*, based on the murder of Martha Ray, the mistress of the Earl of Sandwich, by a lovesick clergyman named Hackman, created a sensation: it contained a long account of the life of Chatterton and made him a household name. (A young man named William Ireland (*see* page 238) was probably inspired to become a forger by Croft's novel.) The argument dragged on for years, until internal evidence finally convinced scholars that the poems were not the work of a fifteenth-century priest but of a phenomenally gifted Bristol teenager. Then, at last, Chatterton received the acclaim he had always longed for.

CLEVELAND STREET SCANDAL
The 'Sex-for-Sale' Telegraph Boys

In early July 1886, there was a theft of money from a room in the General Post Office in St Martin's-Le-Grand, in the City of London. A telegraph messenger boy named Charles Thomas Swinscow came under suspicion and, when he was searched, he proved to have eighteen shillings on him – a far larger sum than he was likely to save up from his wages. On 4 July 1886, a police constable named Hanks questioned the boy, who told him that he had obtained the money for doing some 'private work' for a gentleman named Hammond, who lived at 19 Cleveland Street, just north of Soho. Finally, he admitted that he had been taken to the house by a post office clerk named Henry Newlove – who, like Swinscow, was fifteen. Newlove, it seemed, had earlier persuaded Swinscow to go with him to a lavatory in the basement of the Post Office where he had 'behaved indecently'. Then Newlove had suggested that Swinscow might like to earn a little money by doing the same thing with a gentleman. At the house in Cleveland Street, Swinscow had got into bed with a gentleman who, in the language of the police report, 'put his person between my legs and an emission took place'. The gentleman then gave him half a sovereign, which Swinscow handed to the landlord of the house, Hammond. Hammond had given him back four shillings. The same thing had apparently happened on a subsequent occasion.

Swinscow mentioned two other telegraph boys who had gone to Cleveland Street: seventeen-year-olds George Wright and Charles Thickbroom. Wright admitted that he and Newlove had gone to the basement lavatory and 'Newlove put his person into me . . . and something came away from him.' Wright went with Newlove to the Cleveland Street house where he went to a bedroom with a 'foreign looking chap'. They undressed and got into bed. 'He told me to suck him. I did so. He then had a go between my legs and that was all.' Wright also received four shillings. Thickbroom told how Newlove had persuaded him to go to Cleveland Street, where he went to bed with a gentleman and they 'played with one another. He did not put his person into me.' He also received four shillings.

Newlove admitted the truth of the statements. The next morning he hastened to 19 Cleveland Street and warned Hammond. Charles Hammond, a 32-year-old male prostitute, married to a French prostitute known as 'Madame Caroline' – on whom he had fathered two sons – lost no time in fleeing. So did another homosexual, George Veck, who liked to pose as a clergyman. Veck moved to lodgings nearby under a false name, while Hammond fled to France.

Chief Inspector Frederick Abberline of the CID applied for warrants for the arrest of Hammond and Newlove on a charge of criminal conspiracy. But when the police arrived at Cleveland Street the next day the house was shut up.

On his way to the police station, Newlove commented that it was hard that he should be arrested when men in high positions should be allowed to walk free. Asked what he meant, he replied, 'Lord Arthur Somerset goes regularly to the house in Cleveland Street. So does the Earl of Euston and Colonel Jervois.'

Lord Arthur Somerset, the son of the Duke of Beaufort, was a major in the Royal Horse Guards, and superintendent of the stables of the Prince of Wales, Queen Victoria's son, whose name was to be associated with many scandals (including the Tranby Croft card scandal: *see* page 22). When Lord Arthur – known as 'Podge' – was identified by the two telegraph boys Swinscow and Thickbroom as the man who had climbed into bed with them, 'Podge' hastily obtained four months leave of absence and vanished to the Continent. His elder brother Henry had been deserted by his wife because of his homosexual inclinations.

Veck was also arrested and he and Newlove were committed for trial at the Old Bailey. But by that time, the press had got hold of the story. The *Pall Mall Gazette* published a paragraph deploring the 'disgraceful nature' of the charge against Veck and Newlove and asking whether the 'two noble lords and other notable persons in society' were going to be allowed to get away with it. It obviously had the makings of a first-class scandal. It may have been at this point that Arthur Newton, 'Podge's' solicitor, breathed another name that made the Director of Public Prosecutions raise his eyebrows: that of 'Eddy', the Duke of Clarence, son of the Prince of Wales. Eddy, according to rumour, had also visited the Cleveland Street brothel. Meanwhile, 'Podge' was in more trouble; another teenager, Algernon Allies, had been interviewed by the police and admitted that he had been intimately involved with Lord Arthur Somerset, whom he called 'Mr Brown'. 'The prosecution wishes to avoid putting any witness in the box who refers to "Mr Brown",' wrote the Director of Public Prosecutions, Sir Augustus Stephenson to the Attorney-General.

It was no surprise to anyone when the case came up at Bow Street on 18 September 1886 and lasted a mere half-hour. Veck and Newlove both pleaded guilty and were both given light sentences: Veck nine months' hard labour and Newlove four months'. That, it seemed, was the end of the case.

But the Press was not willing to allow it to rest there. There were many crusading editors in London, like W. T. Stead of the *Pall Mall Gazette*, Henry Labouchere of *Truth*, and Ernest Parke of the *North London Press*. It was Parke who put the cat among the pigeons. On 16 November 1889 – three years after the case – Parke identified the aristocrats whose names had been so carefully suppressed at the time of the trial: Lord Arthur Somerset and the Earl of Euston. (These names, we may recall, had been mentioned to Abberline by Newlove when he was arrested.) Parke also commented that 'a far more distinguished and more highly placed personage . . . was inculpated in these disgusting crimes.'

The Earl of Euston, Henry James Fitzroy, was thirty-eight years old at the time of the Cleveland Street trial. He immediately instructed his solicitor to sue for libel. Parke's trial opened at the Old Bailey on 15 January 1890. One of the most serious points against Parke was his allegation that the Earl of Euston had fled to Peru; Euston had done nothing of the sort. (It had been unnecessary, for his name had never entered the case after Newlove mentioned it to Abberline.)

Euston admitted that he had been to 19 Cleveland Street. But, he said, it had been a misunderstanding. He had, he said, been in Piccadilly in May or June 1886, when someone had put an advertising card into his hand. It said '*Poses plastiques*', and gave the address of 19 Cleveland Street. *Poses plastiques* meant naked girls posing in Grecian attitudes. So, according to Lord Euston, he hurried to 19 Cleveland Street. He was admitted by a man who told him there were no women there but left no doubt about what the house had to offer. 'You infernal scoundrel, if you don't let me out I'll knock you down,' said Lord Euston and rushed out.

The defence called several witnesses who said they had seen Lord Euston going in or out of Cleveland Street. The final defence witness was a male prostitute named John Saul. He claimed to have been picked up by Lord Euston and took him back to Cleveland Street where they went to bed. *The Times* declined to report what Saul claimed then took place but we can reconstruct what he said from a comment Saul had made to Ernest Parke about Euston: 'He is not an actual sodomite. He likes to play with you and then "spend" on your belly.'

The judge emphasized the contradictions in the statements of witnesses, and described Saul as a 'loathsome object'. The strongest point against Parke was his statement that Euston had fled to Peru. The jury found Parke guilty of libel without justification. He was sentenced to a year in prison without hard labour. The sentence was not regarded as severe by the Press.

The case was still not quite over. In December 1889, 'Podge's' solicitor, Arthur Newton, was accused of conspiring to defeat the course of justice. The charges said that he had tried to get an interview with Algernon Allies – the youth who had admitted being 'Podge's' lover – and had collected three of the accused telegraph boys after they had left police custody and sent them to a lodging house while he arranged for them to leave the country. Newton's defence was that his clerk Frederick Taylorson, who was charged with him, had met Allies by accident and exchanged a few words with him. And as to the second charge, it was true that he had sent the three boys to a lodging house overnight, telling them that they ought to go abroad, but that this was because 'Podge's' father, the Duke of Beaufort, wanted to interview them to see if they had been bullied by the police. The Duke had subsequently changed his mind. Newton was, he admitted, therefore technically guilty of conspiracy. The judge took a light view of it and sentenced him to six weeks in prison. Taylorson, who pleaded not guilty, was acquitted.

Hammond, the man who ran the brothel, had fled from France to America and was never tried. 'Podge' spent the rest of his life living abroad, under an assumed name, and died in Hyères, on the French Riviera, in 1926. The scandal undoubtedly ruined his life. In his book *The Cleveland Street Scandal*, H. Montgomery Hyde suggests that he would have been wise to return and 'face the music'; a good solicitor could also certainly have secured his acquittal, as in the case of Lord Euston. (The evidence suggests that Euston was a regular visitor at Cleveland Street.) Euston's trial certainly did him no harm; at the time of the Cleveland Street case he was a prominent Freemason, the Provincial Grand Master of Northamptonshire and Huntingdonshire, and subsequently became Grand Master of the Mark Masons. He was also appointed an aide-de-camp by King Edward VII in the coronation year, 1901. He died of dropsy in 1912.

Ernest Parke became a Justice of the Peace after he retired as a newspaper editor. But the subsequent career of Arthur Newton, who went to prison for conspiracy, was less fortunate. In 1910 he defended the murderer Crippen and received much favourable publicity. But he then conceived the idea of forging a Crippen 'confession' and selling it to a newspaper: *The Evening Times* bought it for £500, the writer Edgar Wallace acting as a go-between. Although Newton got cold feet at the last moment, the newspaper forced him to deliver the promised confession and sold a million copies as a result. Newton was suspended from practice by the Law Society for unprofessional conduct. In 1913 he was charged with being involved in a Canadian timber fraud, sentenced to three years in jail, and struck off the rolls as a solicitor.

COE, Frederick 'Kevin'

The Strange Case of the Spokane Rapist and his Mother

In the spring of 1981, the small conservative city of Spokane, in Washington State, USA, was rocked by the biggest scandal in its respectable history. The son of one of its most reputable families had been arrested and charged with being a multiple rapist.

The rapes had started in the summer of 1978. The attacker was a tall, well-spoken young man with an expensive haircut and a smell of aftershave. But if his smell was agreeable his manners were atrocious; his method was to ram a gloved hand down his victim's throat and to punch and kick her if she resisted. As the rapist became a one-man crime wave, a large reward was offered for his capture and the Spokane newspapers demanded vigorous action; the *Chronicle*, edited by Gordon Coe, offered a reward of its own.

It seemed clear that the rapist was psychologically sick and that the assaults sprang from a hatred of women rather than a compulsive sex urge. He liked to utter obscenities, 'You cunt! You whore! I'm going to fuck your cunt. You bitch!' Yet in a large proportion of the three or four dozen rapes, he failed to achieve an erection and was forced to masturbate himself to orgasm. He liked to ask his victims intimate details of their sex lives – when they last had sex, whether they made love with boyfriends, whether they masturbated. After the orgasm, he often became tearfully apologetic.

The first victim had been a young married woman, walking home alone from a restaurant after a quarrel with her husband; she was thrown to the ground by a man who seemed to be a jogger. After the rape, she suffered long periods of depression. But in due course, this victim would positively identify the rapist after his arrest.

In November 1978, a man approached a woman on a lonely street and grabbed her breasts. A car approached and he ran away; he was seen to jump into a silver-grey Pontiac. The other car followed him to a nearby pizza house and the police were called. But by the time they arrived, he had left. A witness had noted down his licence number and the police were able to identify the owner of the Pontiac as Frederick Harlan Coe, born 2 February 1947, who lived in the expensive neighbourhood called South Hill. At sixteen he had been mentioned in connection with damaging a swimming pool and two years later was accused of 'carnal knowledge'. In the following year he was listed for 'possible assault'. In 1971 he had been charged with indecent liberties and burglary but the charge had been dropped. In 1977, he was charged with 'disorderly conduct' – peeping over the wall of a ladies' lavatory in a restaurant and remarking to the occupant, 'You sure have a nice cunt.' This charge had also been dropped.

But by the time the police had read Coe's 'record', they were unable to locate the victim. So the case was dropped.

The 'near miss' seems to have made the rapist cautious. The next case occurred in June the following year, 1979. A man entered a 'massage parlour' called the Tiger's Den, tied up two of the girls at knife point and performed an uncompleted act of rape on one of them; after his orgasm he became apologetic. In August, he grabbed the breasts of a female jogger but the woman escaped; the following evening, a woman was raped a mile away. On 9 September 1979, a 21-year-old female disc jockey was attacked in the parking lot of the radio station. She was ordered to urinate on him and to masturbate herself; finally, the man achieved orgasm.

By the end of the year, the rapist was clearly becoming more confident; in late November and early December there were six rapes. In one case, he made the victim empty her bowels on his chest but his attempts at rectal and vaginal intercourse were both unsuccessful. One girl was unfortunate enough to be raped twice in the following year; in March and again in July. The rapist was much gentler with her on the second occasion and was startled when she asked him if he had done this to her before. He had to achieve his climax by masturbation. The girl decided not to report the second rape – she felt the police examination was worse than the assault.

One woman avoided rape by using psychology. When the attacker told her he wanted to take her into the bushes 'to lick your pussy', she disconcerted him by telling him that she wanted to perform fellatio on him first. When he forced her hand on to his penis, she said, 'This excites me so much I can't be responsible for what I do.' Placed in this position of the potential 'rapee', the rapist told her he wanted to be her friend and even gave her his business card: it contained the name 'Kevin Coe' and gave his occupation as 'realtor' (estate agent). He escorted her to her front door. When he saw her a week later in the same park he sprinted away at top speed. The woman decided not to go to the police.

Now, in 1981, the citizens of Spokane were finally aware that a young man (most victims thought he was in his early twenties) in jogging uniform had committed dozens of rapes over the past three years. Gun shops sold out of handguns and hundreds of canisters of chemical spray were purchased. Karate and kung-fu studios did record business. Female joggers carried police whistles. There had been a new and disturbing development; the rapist was pulling open his fly as if to expose himself and revealing a rubber dildo. Evidently this was his solution to his frequent failure to achieve penetration. Catching him became more urgent than ever before.

The first break in the case occurred early in 1981. A school caretaker noticed an expensive sports car, A Citation Chevrolet, parked in a spot reserved for the school bus; he noted the colour and model. Shortly afterwards, a woman jogger was raped nearby. By seven that morning, the car had gone from the school-bus park. When the rape was reported in the newspapers, the caretaker finally mentioned the Citation to the police.

The police began to check on all Citation owners. One by one, they were eliminated from the investigation. Among the few that remained was Gordon H. Coe, editor of the Spokane *Chronicle*. Since he was sixty-four, he was also eliminated. But a detective felt the name was vaguely familiar. Could Coe have a son who sometimes drove the car? A check revealed Fred

Coe's police file. Yet this also seemed unlikely. Coe was now thirty-four and most victims thought the rapist was in his twenties. Nevertheless, the detective obtained Fred Coe's picture and sent it to a couple of policemen with instructions to show it to the last rape victim – the jogger who had been attacked near the school. She immediately identified Fred Coe as her attacker.

The identification had come just in time: because of its lack of success, the special rape squad was about to be disbanded.

Other victims quickly identified Coe as the rapist. The police decided to keep Coe under close surveillance in the hope of catching him in the act. But when the rapist again 'exposed' himself to a woman and revealed a dildo, they decided that it was becoming too dangerous. On Tuesday, 10 March 1981, the police arrested Frederick Harlan Coe at the realty office where he worked. He was charged with the rape of the woman near the school. In a police line-up, several of his victims – ranging from schoolgirls to middle-aged women – identified him.

Fred Coe, it soon transpired, had been a problem child from the beginning. Ever since his schooldays he had been a fantasist who was convinced that he was destined for world fame but he had no very clear idea of how to achieve it. He was a spoiled brat who lacked all self-discipline. The main problem was his mother, Ruth Coe, one of those assertive, domineering, high-powered American matrons who behaved as if she was a combination of Queen Victoria and Elizabeth Taylor. She adored her son and never ceased to interfere in his life; the slightest attempt to get away from her apron strings aroused frantic resistance. Her meddling had wrecked his marriage – on one occasion she had raked her nails down the cheek of his wife leaving a permanent scar. But her overprotectiveness made Fred Coe totally irresponsible; he was unable to hold down any job and reacted to heavy debts by going out and buying a new car. Fred's father, Gordon Coe, was treated by his wife as a cipher. Fred's attitude towards his mother was ambivalent and the sadism of the rapes seemed an indication of a deep-seated resentment of women in general.

Fred's closest friend was Jay Williams, a mobile-home salesman and a devout Christian. Williams and Coe had been at school together and Williams had immense admiration for his friend's remarkable flights of fantasy and for his conviction that he was going to be a great man. 'He boasted about the fortune he was going to earn and the beauties he was going to seduce,' Williams told Jack Olsen, the author of *Son*, a detailed study of the Fred Coe case. But although he was apparently highly sexed and described endless love affairs, he seemed oddly inhibited with women, particularly those of his own social station. He seemed drawn to pathetic, submissive women. When his first marriage broke up – his wife became an alcoholic – he started a relationship with a girl he found working in a laundromat.

From being a rather morose teenager, Coe developed into a man of immense plausibility and charm; with his immaculate clothes and expensive haircut he looked like the typical 'all-American boy'. He had no difficulty finding jobs – his employers were always convinced they had a virile 'go-getter', until it slowly became clear that his activity was all confined to talk: he never really did anything. Coe was convinced he was a literary genius: he wrote three novels and a satirical work called *Sex in the White House*, full of puns like 'cuntree' and 'unwashed-ington', and uninhibited scenes like the one describing 'Richyard Obb Noxious' masturbating in the Oval Office of the White House. This last work was published at his father's expense, but no distributor would handle it and the copies remained in a warehouse.

When Jay Williams went to visit Fred Coe in jail, Coe pencilled a note saying: 'Go to police . . . Tell them you and I were trying to catch the South Hill rapist.' Another note read: 'I have a dildo and sweater that have to be disposed of.' Williams was finally persuaded to go to the house – formerly occupied by Coe and his girlfriend – and make an excuse to the present tenants which enabled him to escape with the incriminating articles. But he declined to tell the various lies that Coe suggested to prove that, far from being the rapist, he was involved in a one-man campaign to catch him.

Released on a $3,500 bond (his father sold the family car to raise the money) a month after his arrest, Coe continued his attempts to persuade Jay Williams to provide him with alibis and excuses.

John Nyberg, another schoolfriend, was also approached by a friend of the family with a request to provide a false alibi. The person who approached Nyberg insisted, 'We both know Fred's innocent.' But Nyberg knew nothing of the sort. He had known Fred Coe intimately and knew that he was a peeping Tom who broke into apartments and led a distinctly perverse sex life.

The trial began on 15 July 1981. The rape victims testified, many of them admitting that they could not be certain about the rapist's identity, since it was dark. Gini Perham, the girl with whom Coe had lived during most of the rapes, described his peculiar sex habits – practising cunnilingus on her while he masturbated – and how he walked around naked holding a dildo in front of him. Coe's defence was one of blanket denial and he insisted that he had alibis for most of the rapes. He showed considerable aplomb in the witness box and seemed to be enjoying himself. But he made a bad impression by talking too much and splitting hairs. After a sixteen-day trial, he was found guilty on four counts of rape and sentenced to 'life' for each.

In November 1981, four months after the trial, Spokane police heard a rumour that Ruth Coe was trying to hire a 'hit man' to kill someone. A policeman rang her and said that he'd heard she had a job she wanted performing discreetly. '*Very* discreetly', said Mrs Coe. Her son had been used as a scape-goat, she explained, so she wanted to have the judge and the prosecutor 'removed'. The bogus 'hit man' finally agreed to do this for $4,000. The following day, the policeman called on her and was given $500 on account – she promised the rest when the two men were killed. As they talked, the police arrived. 'I thought so!' said Mrs Coe with disgust.

Gordon Coe declared that this was a clear case of entrapment and raised $30,000 to bail his wife out.

Ruth Coe's defence was based on what the prosecution called 'psychobabble'. She suffered from 'disordered sexual functions'. Her psychiatrist testified that she was depressive and neurasthenic; her daughter Kathleen testified that she had raved that the judge in the case was the Devil. Ruth Coe was found guilty but a twenty-year sentence was suspended; she was to serve one year in the county jail of her choice. Ruth Coe chose a pleasant, quiet jail in Washington's north woods, where she was the only woman prisoner and was allowed to wear her own clothes.

In a note accompanying review copies of his book *Son, A Psychopath and his Victims* (1948), Jack Olsen mentions that since he wrote the book, he has been harassed by Mrs Coe and has had to hire armed guards to protect him. Fred Coe himself, as breezy and plausible as ever, has convinced his fellow inmates that he is innocent and continues to issue press releases to that effect. It seems clear that no reality can ever break through into the fantasy world inside his head.

CROWHURST, Donald
The Round-the-World Yacht Race Scandal

On 31 October 1968 Donald Crowhurst, from Bridgwater, Somerset, a 36-year-old electronic engineer and married man with four children, set sail aboard the trimaran ketch *Teignmouth Electron* in a bid to win the the prestigious *Sunday Times* Golden Globe single-handed round-the-world yacht race. He was towed over the bar at Teignmouth, in Devon, only nine hours before the entry deadline expired, amid all the last-minute confusion automatically created by such a close call. Such was the disorganization, that old salts ashore predicted he would get no further than the neighbouring port of Brixham, a few miles to the south. Some felt he was personally unsuited for what was clearly going to be a supreme test of character, as much as the navigational skills and seamanship involved. In addition, his boat was new and untried; her hatch-covers let in water on the maiden voyage from her Norfolk yards to Devon, yet in the rush to beat the deadline Donald Crowhurst sailed without the vital length of piping he needed to pump out the numerous 'watertight' compartments. Nor was that all. Any entrant who was forced to accept outside help during the voyage faced instant disqualification – yet he had also left his box of essential spares behind him on the quay.

He went ahead as planned for a variety of reasons. Personal pride was almost certainly the most compelling: to turn back at the eleventh hour would have made him a laughing-stock, since it was only his own, near-paranoid belief in his ability to out-sail such boating giants as Sir Francis Chichester and Sir Alec Rose which led him to enter in the first place. Prize money was another, although he longed almost as much for the kudos victory would bring. For months past he had cajoled and persuaded others to back him financially so that he could have a boat built to compete in this toughest of all single-handed races, in the belief that he could win honourably. Two months at sea, however, with their attendant terrors and numbing loneliness were enough to convince him that he was wrong. So he decided to cheat, by marking time in the green wastes of the South Atlantic instead of rounding the Horn, and by keeping a false log so as to deceive his family, his friends, his own publicity agent, the race organizers and the British public into believing that he had triumphed over every adversity to win the Golden Globe race by his natural ability and sheer, dauntless courage.

Donald Crowhurst started too late to have any real hope of winning the Golden Globe trophy itself, which was to go to the first man home. His aim was to repay his backers by winning the £5,000 prize awarded for the fastest passage, together with the glamour and spin-off benefits that went with it. Then months later, just when it seemed he had got away with fraud and the 'fastest passage' prize money looked a near-certainty, he realized that the obligatory log-book inspection on arrival would inevitably expose him as an imposter. He, therefore, decided to bide his time and arrive a close second (thus avoiding an official log-book inspection), forgoing the prize-money but winning nationwide acclaim in being such a gallant loser. Unfortunately, his luck ran out and even this was denied him: his only rival for the £5,000 award sank on the homeward stretch, leaving Donald Crowhurst the winner anyhow, as long as he kept going. His nerve failed him then, or perhaps his conscience, as the first congratulatory radio messages started to come through. After recognizing that he was hoist with his own petard, he went mad and committed suicide. At first, when his abandoned ketch was found by a passing vessel, Crowhurst's dramatic disappearance on the eve of what seemed certain victory appeared to rank with the greatest of all sea mysteries, the riddle of the *Mary Celeste*. The truth was eventually uncovered by two *Sunday Times* reporters, the late Nicholas Tomalin and Ron Hall, who with the help of Donald Crowhurst's agent Rodney Hallworth, recovered the log books which revealed the whole fraudulent, sad story.

* * *

Donald Crowhurst was born in British India in 1932, the son of a railway superintendent and a schoolteacher. He came to Britain with his parents after independence in 1947, and went to live in Tilehurst, near Reading. His father died a year later, after a heart attack. Donald Crowhurst served in the RAF for six years, only to resign his commission after a foolish escapade (never properly explained; according to one version, he rode a powerful motorbike through a barrack room full of sleeping men). He thereupon joined the Army and was again commissioned, only to resign his commission a second time. On this occasion he was caught trying to steal a car – for a bet and after a night's drinking. Back in civilian life he held a number of jobs as a promising electronics engineer, and married at the age of twenty-five. It was about this time, in 1957, that he bought his first boat, a 20-foot sloop named, significantly perhaps, *Pot of Gold*. While at Bridgwater he invented a radio direction-finding device for boats, which he called the Navicator. His mother, who had been ill and was living in a home for elderly people, agreed to sell her house at Tilehurst and invest some of the money to help him launch his own business, and market the Navicator. Donald Crowhurst was eventually bought out for £8,500 by Pye Radio. Some time later, businessman Mr Stanley Best – who had previously loaned him money to tide the firm through a difficult period – agreed to sponsor him in his bid to win the Golden Globe race and put up the bulk of the capital he required.

Marathon single-handed voyages gripped the public imagination as never before in 1967, when Francis Chichester was knighted by the Queen at Greenwich after circumnavigating the globe (with only one enforced stop, at Sydney) in his yacht *Gypsy Moth IV*. The *Sunday Times* race was a natural sequel, with two prizes on offer. The Golden Globe trophy would go to the first home. But since not all entrants could start together, there was an 'elapsed time' clause to give a separate prize of £5,000 for the fastest passage. To qualify for either, all voyages had to be completed without the lone yachtsman putting into harbour *en route* or accepting outside assistance. Starting dates were between 1 June and 31 October 1968; to qualify for the fastest-passage award, voyages had to begin and end in the British Isles.

Donald Crowhurst convinced himself he could win and after several fruitless attempts to borrow Sir Francis Chichester's *Gipsy Moth IV*, finally persuaded Mr Best to sponsor him in a specification-built trimaran. After talks with agent Mr Rodney Hallworth, who handled public relations for Teignmouth, the ketch was named *Teignmouth Electron* – the second half for his firm, Electron Utilisation, makers of the Navicator. He carried one aboard in the round-the-world race. It was Donald Crowhurst's own choice to opt for a multi-hull boat: one of the disadvantages of this was that although she was fast, the lack of a keel created problems to windward. It was a problem that faced the most experienced of crews, never mind a comparative novice. *Teignmouth Electron*'s maiden voyage from Norfolk to Teignmouth took him two weeks instead of the estimated three days and this with the aid of various volunteer crew members. One of them, experienced sailor Lieutenant-Commander Peter Eden, who found that the ketch vibrated so badly at speed it gave him toothache, reported that while Donald Crowhurst's sailing techniques were good, his navigation tended to be 'a mite slapdash'. Those two weeks spent on the maiden voyage left only sixteen days to prepare in all respects for the round-the-world 31 October deadline, a nightmare task. In addition, Donald Crowhurst faced some formidable opposition.

Final entrants included Captain John Ridgway and ex-Sergeant Chay Blyth, now one of the world's premier yachtsmen: these two former paratroopers had already achieved fame by rowing the Atlantic in a cockleshell craft. There were also Robin Knox-Johnston, the eventual winner, in his 32-foot ketch *Suhaili*; two very able Frenchmen, Bernard Moitessier and Loick Fougeron; Bill Leslie King in *Galway Blazer II*; Commander Nigel Tetley in another trimaran and Alex Carozzo, in a big 66-foot ketch. A ninth entrant, the Australian-born dentist 'Tahiti Bill' Howell who earlier finished fifth in the *Observer* trans-Atlantic single-handed race, withdrew; but it was a field of such quality that Donald Crowhurst ranked as the biggest outsider.

In his optimistic pre-race calculations, he estimated that it would take him 243 days to circumnavigate the world. In practice, he encountered trouble from the start. Excessive vibration at speed caused him to shed two screws from his self-steering gear by the time he was off the Lizard, and, since he had no spares aboard, he had to make good by denuding less essential equipment. His port bow float filled with water. Without the vital length of hose, he had to bale it out by hand. Unfavourable winds which forced him to tack his keel-less trimaran reduced the distance sailed by almost half; at one time it took him a week to progress 210 miles. After a fortnight at sea he found his cockpit hatch – which housed his Onan generator – flooded, and he wrote in his log: 'With so much wrong with the boat in so many respects – it would perhaps be foolish or at any rate a subjective decision to continue. I will try to get the generator working, and think about the alternatives open to me . . .'

The BBC was another of his sponsors, so that he carried a camera and tape recorder aboard. To the tape recorder he promised, 'I will sail this boat as though she were a clipper ship, and I will stick to the traditional clipper ship routes [in search of favourable winds] if it takes me a month longer . . .' But to his log he confided, on 15 November: 'Racked by the growing awareness that I must soon decide whether or not I can go on in the face of the actual situation . . .' The 1,300 miles he had logged by then represented only eight hundred in terms of race progress, an average of fifty miles per day. He was never going to win anything at that rate, while his inability to pump out the leaking hatches worried him incessantly. 'It would be crazy to go into the 40's [the Roaring Forties] with present pumping arrangements . . .' Furthermore, the flooded generator meant that, in addition to all his other worries, he was temporarily without radio communication, lights and the services of his chronometer.

Events showed it was some time during the first week of December that Donald Crowhurst made up his mind to cheat his way to 'victory'. On 10 December he claimed to have sailed 243 miles in a day, which if true meant that he would have set a new world record for any lone sailor. The story was given much publicity at home, where he was quoted as saying: 'It took a pretty strong nerve. I have never sailed so fast in my life, and I could only manage speeds of up to 15 knots because the sea was never higher than 10 feet . . .' Coincidentally, the field had narrowed now to only four, including himself (Robin Knox-Johnston, Bernard Moitessier and Commander Nigel Tetley were the other three), while because of his amazing burst of speed, some newspaper observers were already talking of Donald Crowhurst as a possible winner. By 12 December he was keeping a second, fictitious, log book (a genuine log was needed for accurate navigation). As his plan, to hide in the wastes of the South Atlantic while reporting speedy progress round the world, took shape he began to note down Cape Town Radio weather reports to match the false entries in this second log. But to keep up the pretence without being caught out, he first had to explain away some forthcoming long radio silences. So on 19 January he sent a fraudulent message to agent Rodney Hallworth, which read: '100 [miles] south-east Gough [Gough Island, in the Roaring Forties]. 1086 [miles sailed in the past week]. Generator hatch sealed [which meant an enforced temporary radio silence]. Transmissions when possible especially 80 East 140 West [an indication that radio stations in that area, far removed from his real position, should listen out for any transmissions he might send].' Then, after sending three other brief personal messages, he made no radio transmission for the next three months – even though he was receiving perfectly and knew that his silence was causing great anxiety at home.

On 16 March 1969 he broke more race rules by putting ashore in Argentina for repairs to his damaged starboard float. Although his arrival and departure were logged by the local coastguard unit, they were not passed on to HQ in Buenos Aires and the outside world. After setting a northeasterly course to fool the local coastguard that he was heading for Britain, he then headed south again to continue the deception. His radio told him that the landing in Argentina had gone unreported. Thereafter he monitored New Zealand radio to keep abreast of race developments, while he filmed the white-caps of the Roaring Forties for subsequent BBC consumption.

By now there were only three competitors left in the Golden

Globe race; Moitessier had opted out and set off round the world a second time; Robin Knox-Johnston, who had been genuinely out of radio contact for four months, was sighted homeward bound on 6 April by a passing tanker, and was clearly set to win the Golden Globe trophy as first man home. However, his monohull boat was slower than either of the trimarans, so both Nigel Tetley (round the Horn by 20 March and already well into the Atlantic) and Donald Crowhurst, supposedly hot on Tetley's heels, were both well placed to beat him for the fastest-passage prize. Crowhurst broke his self-imposed radio silence on 9 April – a deliberately vague transmission aimed at heightening the apparent drama – which led Fleet Street to believe that he, too, was round the Horn and pressing hard. However, Sir Francis Chichester, who was chairman of the race judges and had nursed doubts about his progress throughout, now voiced them openly to his fellow judges who were waiting with him at Falmouth to welcome Robin Knox-Johnston home.

Donald Crowhurst, who knew nothing of this, broke radio silence next on 30 April to report himself off the Falklands. On 4 May he recommenced sailing in earnest so that he could claim a faster time home than Nigel Tetley. He was brought up with a start by a message from his agent who joyfully reported: 'Teignmouth agog at your wonders. Whole town planning huge welcome.' It was now that he realized he would have to fake a photo-finish, because he would have to face the obligatory examination of his log as winner. On 16 May he radioed: 'No chance overtake Tetley now. Probably very close result.' It seemed the perfect way out – until on 21 May Commander Nigel Tetley, RN, who had overcome far worse problems than Crowhurst to push his leaking trimaran into a winning position, had to abandon ship as she sank under him with only 1,200 miles to go.

There was no logical way in which Donald Crowhurst could fail to win the £5,000 prize for 'fastest passage' now, and in the agonizing month that followed, he broke under the strain and went mad: the entries found in the log which was later recovered left no room for doubt about that. There was also no doubt by this time that, had he sailed on and tried to brazen it out, his fraud would have been exposed. Sir Francis Chichester had written to the *Sunday Times* race secretary asking for certain checks to be made; in particular, for Donald Crowhurst to explain his radio silence from the Cape of Good Hope to the Horn and the ensuing twelve-day silence until he 'arrived' off the Falklands.

The last words he wrote, which to his deranged mind were addressed to God, read: 'It is time for your move to begin   I have not need to prolong the game   It has been a good game that must be ended at the   I will play this game when I choose   I will resign the game 11 20 40   There is no reason for harmful   ' Then, carrying the chronometer (which read 20 minutes and 40 seconds precisely past 11 o'clock on 1 July 1969, the date of his last entry) and the lying logbook, he is presumed to have leapt overboard and waited to drown in the Sargasso Sea. His body was never found. In his 243 days at sea, by remarkable coincidence the same number he had predicted it would take him to circumnavigate the world, he had sailed more than 16,000 nautical miles: most of them to live a lie.

On 10 July the Royal Mail ship *Picardy*, outward bound for the Caribbean, found the *Teignmouth Electron* drifting in mid-Atlantic. A boarding party found three log books waiting on the chart table, which told their own story of the voyage. The life raft was properly secured, there were adequate supplies of food and water – but no Donald Crowhurst, no chronometer, and no fourth log. The trimaran was hauled aboard the *Picardy* and after a search of the area Captain Box put into Santo Domingo with his find. When the truth was finally established and published by *The Sunday Times*, Robin Knox-Johnston, now undisputed winner of both the Golden Globe trophy and fastest-passage prize, promptly handed the £5,000 to the Appeal Fund established for Donald Crowhurst's widow and four young children. 'None of us should judge him too harshly,' he said. By his unrivalled act of generosity, the winner of the Golden Globe race made his rival's fraud seem more of a tragedy than a scandal.

DAVIDSON, the Reverend Harold

'The Prostitute's Padre'

The curious affair of the rector of Stiffkey sounds like high comedy – the vicar who spent his life pursuing ladies of easy virtue and ended by being eaten by a lion. Even the name of the village has an air of *double entendre*. But for the central character and his family, it was a bleak tragedy.

Harold Francis Davidson, born in 1875, was the son of the vicar of Sholing, a suburb of Southampton. His father decided from the beginning that Harold should enter holy orders, so he was brought up with Victorian strictness, as befitted a future clergyman, and not allowed to play with rough boys. At the age of fourteen, he was placed in the charge of two maiden aunts who lived in Croydon. There, at the Whitgift School, he became friendly with a boy named Leon Quartermaine, who wanted to become an actor; Harold was also bitten by the theatre bug. In a school entertainment Harold recited comic monologues of George Grossmith and decided that he preferred the stage to the pulpit. When he was nineteen he made his debut as a comedian at Steinway Hall in London and was successful enough to decide to defy his father and make the stage a career. He became a 'drawing-room entertainer', a kind of stand-up comedian of the sort who plays modern clubs – except that his repertoire was strictly proper. He was a hit in a touring production of *Charley's Aunt*, in the title role.

However, the church was in his blood and when on tour he made a habit of calling on vicars and finding out if any of their ageing parishioners would like to hear the Bible read aloud. On one occasion he was just in time to save a sixteen-year-old girl from jumping into the Thames one foggy night; he gave her the money to return to her home and seems to have acquired a lifelong taste for helping young ladies who had fallen or were about to fall.

By the time he was twenty-two he had decided he preferred the church to the stage after all and with the help of the Reverend Basil Wilberforce, chaplain of the House of Commons, he was able to secure a scholarship to Exeter College, Oxford, to study for holy orders. Although he was always late for exams and took five years instead of the usual three to obtain his degree, he finally gained his first curacy at Holy Trinity, Windsor. In 1905 he was transferred to St-Martin-in-the-Fields in London. Through the patronage of the Marquis of Townshend, whom he joined in wedlock to a company promoter's daughter, he was finally awarded the living of the little Norfolk village of Stiffkey – worth over £500 per annum and later increased to £800, an excellent salary in 1906. (His own father had only been paid £120 a year.) He was able to marry a pretty Irish actress whom he had met at Oxford and to whom he had been engaged for six years. During the next eight years she presented him with four children. But she seems to have possessed a violent temper and to have disliked being a vicar's wife for she never called on the parishioners. Soon her husband took to spending most of the week in London, returning only at weekends (he was usually so late for the service that most of the congregation had gone home by the time he arrived). He was working with underprivileged boys in the East End and helped to found the London Dockland Settlement. His zeal was tremendous and attracted the attention of Queen Mary. Then he became chaplain to the Actor's Church Union and began to frequent the dressing rooms of actresses. Bert Ross, a theatrical historian who knew him, records that he would ogle the girls as they stripped for a quick change and was finally barred from some theatres.

During World War I he became a chaplain in the Royal Navy and soon acquired himself a name as an utter nuisance for holding church parades at inconvenient times. It seems clear that he greatly enjoyed his authority and when captains objected, he appealed over their heads to Vice-Admiral Tupper, known as 'Holy Reggie'. During the war, he was arrested in a police raid on a Cairo brothel – he explained he was tracking down a diseased whore who was infecting his men.

When he came back from the war, he was shocked to find his wife about to give birth to a child – he later told someone it was the child of a colonel, for at the time one of his old friends, a colonel, was living in the vicarage. It was the end of the marriage; Davidson applied to go to India as a chaplain and even hired a locum tenens to take over in Stiffkey. The India appointment failed to materialize and Davidson returned to his habit of spending most of his time in London.

One late night in September 1920, Davidson was standing in Leicester Square when he saw a slim, poorly clad girl who looked as if she needed a good meal. He asked her what she was doing in that notorious area and she said she had no money and nowhere to sleep. Davidson gave her fifteen shillings for a room and arranged to meet her in a Lyons teashop a few days later. Meanwhile he went home to take the services in two local churches. The girl's name was Rose Ellis and she was twenty years old, she had just become a prostitute but was not particularly successful. She became one of Davidson's protégées; he found lodgings for her and tried to find her jobs. Rose Ellis was one of the first of a long string of young ladies that Davidson attempted to 'help' during the next ten years – he himself later admitted that he picked up between one hundred and fifty and two hundred girls a year.

The rector's usual method was to approach a waitress in a teashop – they were known as 'nippies' – and to tell her that she looked like a film star and ought not to be working in such a place. He became a great nuisance and was forbidden entry to certain tea shops. His greatest asset was undoubtedly that he looked so inoffensive. He was a tiny man with a high-pitched voice, and a chirpy manner and a great deal of charm. He seemed to be a father figure. The girls usually felt there could be no possible harm in taking tea with him; after all, he might, as he promised, be able to get them on to the stage. (In fact, he did succeed, at one point, in getting Rose Ellis a job with a touring company.)

Typical of these relationships was the one that developed with an attractive girl named Barbara Harris. In August 1930,

Barbara, who was sixteen, was walking out of Marble Arch tube station when Davidson approached her with the words: 'Excuse me, Miss, but has anyone told you how much you look like Mary Brian, the movie actress?' Barbara was a shop girl who spent her days reading movie magazines. Without hesitation, she agreed to accompany the bright-eyed little man to the nearest Lyons Corner House, where she listened, fascinated, as he flattered her and told her she ought to be on the stage.

Barbara Harris had no father and her mother was in an asylum for the insane. She had been seduced at fifteen by an Indian who had infected her with gonorrhoea – the seducer had been sent to jail – then been taken in charge by the church army. She had been in Holloway prison for stealing and had already taken up prostitution when Davidson met her. He gave her small sums of money, tried to help her find jobs – although she preferred to lie in bed all day reading fan magazines – and tried hard to persuade her to yield to him. Like many of Davidson's 'protégées', Barbara was invited down to Stiffkey – she went with Rose Ellis – but when she discovered that Mrs Davidson expected her to work in the kitchen, she left.

According to Barbara, Davidson kissed her at every opportunity and put his hands 'all over her'. The judge asked 'Where?', and she repeated: 'All over.' At one point when she was penniless and out of work, Davidson told her she could move into his lodgings while he stayed with his sister at Ealing. But after a week, he sneaked into her room, saying he had missed his train. That night he slept in a chair. Then he moved on to the bed sleeping on top of the bedclothes until he eventually got into the bed wearing only a pyjama top. But Barbara firmly declined to allow him to make love to her. On another occasion he came in and found her in her pyjamas; he pushed her back on to the bed. A few days later, he sat beside her on the bed and again tried to possess her: this time he undid his trousers and as a result of his excitement, 'made a mess' of his trousers. According to Barbara, he 'made a mess two or three times'.

By the mid-1920s, Davidson's habits were getting him into trouble. To begin with, he became acquainted with a Canadian confidence man called Arthur John Gordon, who claimed to have vast sums of money tied up in Australian mining interests. Davidson invested £5,000 in Gordon's dubious schemes and predictably lost it. But instead of breaking with Gordon, he introduced him to other potential clients and did his best to persuade them to invest money. Some of these lost thousands of pounds. Davidson began to borrow money from money-lenders at 250 per cent interest and in 1925 had to declare himself bankrupt, with debts of £3,000. Half his living was earmarked to satisfy his creditors – £400 a year – so his family and his various 'lame dogs' (his wife called them 'lame cats') had to live on the remaining £400 a year. In 1925 that was still an adequate income and the rector of Stiffkey continued to part with ten-shilling notes to fallen women and to promising-looking shopgirls.

Nemesis was approaching in the form of a magistrate called Major Philip Hammond who lived in the village of Morston – also included in the rector's parish. Most Sunday mornings, Davidson arrived late for the service at Morston. Hammond felt this was deplorably 'slack'. When he heard that various young ladies were staying in the vicarage at Stiffkey and that, as a result, villagers were likely to stumble over couples closely intertwined in ditches, he became indignant. A clerical cousin told him that he could make a formal complaint about Davidson to his bishop, Dr Pollock, the Lord Bishop of Norwich, under Article 2 of the Clergy Discipline Act. This Act stated that a clergyman could be brought to trial before a consistory court if charged with moral offences.

Now it so happened that the bishop knew all about the vicar of Stiffkey. Davidson was a born nuisance who often plagued the bishop with his problems. But although Dr Pollock knew about Davidson's interest in fallen women, he had never had the slightest doubt that it was solely an interest in their spiritual welfare. So when he received the complaint, his first reaction was to defend Davidson. Then he gave it more thought and decided that there would be no harm hiring a private-detective agency to look into the rector's activities. In June 1931, Charles Arrow, a retired CID officer began to follow Davidson around

London. Davidson seemed to scurry like a rabbit from appointment to appointment. He spent much time in the company of various young ladies – although these did include his own daughter. He certainly seemed to make no secret of his 'charitable' activities. In December 1931, Davidson was finally summoned before the bishop to account for himself. Under the impression that the bishop was interested in his financial dealings, he took his friend Arthur Gordon along. But Gordon was sent away and Bishop Pollock explained that Davidson was under investigation. Davidson already knew this for, in the previous November, Rose Ellis had come to him in a state of tearful remorse and told him that a detective had taken her out for a drink, given her a great many ports (Rose had a drink problem) encouraging her to speak at length about her relationship with Davidson. She had subsequently signed a long statement and had been given forty shillings. Davidson apparently treated this betrayal as a joke and told her that she had done better than Judas, who only got thirty pieces of silver.

The bishop's proposal was that Davidson should resign his living to avoid a scandal; in exchange, the bishop would promise that he should not be defrocked. They discussed it again at a meeting at the Athenaeum Club the following January. The bishop was anxious to avoid a public scandal and Davidson saw this as his strongest card. His wife Molly, not unnaturally, also had the strongest objection to his being deprived of his living – it would leave her destitute. She advised her husband to defy the bishop and to threaten to give full details of the whole unsavoury affair to the Press if he persisted in trying to make Davidson resign.

The bishop persisted. The result was that on 1 February 1932, when the bishop arrived in London intending to make Davidson a new offer of substituting a lesser charge of 'indiscipline', he was shocked to see newspaper placards announcing: Rector To His Accusers: I Will Fight To The Bitter End.

From that moment onward, Davidson was front-page news. The notion of an amorous vicar, endlessly pursuing teashop waitresses, tickled the humour of the British public. For the first time since he had been ordained, Davidson preached to a packed church. He was extremely popular in Stiffkey; although his parishioners only saw him at weekends, they liked him and found him charitable, good-humoured and hardworking. They simply declined to believe any evil of him – they still felt the same nearly half a century later when the writer, Tom Cullen, went to Stiffkey to collect material for his book *The Prostitute's Padre*.

The trial – an ecclesiastical affair – opened on 29 March 1932, at Church House. On his arrival Davidson was cheered by admirers, including some parishioners, as he climbed out of a taxi. Roland Oliver was counsel for the prosecution; Davidson was defended by Richard F. Levy. The judge was F. Keppel North, chancellor of the diocese of Norwich. The prosecution opened the proceedings by explaining that this case was about sex and that for years Davidson had been systematically misbehaving with young women.

The first witness for the prosecution was Barbara Harris. She had written voluntarily to the Bishop of Norwich to tell him about the Reverend Harold Davidson. Barbara told the court how Davidson had picked her up outside March Arch tube station, telling her she looked like a film star. She went on to reveal how Davidson had tried to persuade her to give herself to him and had 'relieved himself' in the process of trying to rape her. It emerged that Barbara had had many lovers and that it would not have been inaccurate to describe her as a prostitute. However, her evidence made it clear that she was sexually frigid. After Barbara Harris, a number of waitresses testified that Davidson had 'pestered' them. He seems to have invited most of them down to the rectory at Stiffkey for the weekend and many had accepted.

The trial dragged on through April and into May. On 20 May 1932, Davidson himself went into the witness box. He was not a good witness. He was inclined to talk too much, and his occasional facetiousness or impertinence was detrimental to his case. Asked if he had put his arm round a certain young lady in a car, he replied that it would have been uncomfortable. The judge pointed out that he seemed to be saying that if it had been more comfortable, he might well have put his arm round her. He failed to take advantage of the hint and insisted that, in spite of his landlady's evidence to the contrary, he 'couldn't have' had his arm round the girl's waist. There were times when he seemed to be trying to irritate the judge: at one point, he claimed to be ignorant of the meaning of the word 'buttock'. Evidence about his finances revealed that he was a habitual begging-letter writer; he tried to borrow £500 from the Duchess of Devonshire, telling her that his wife and children were starving, when he was taking actresses out to dinner and the theatre. His openness often damaged his own case – such as when he admitted that he had not realized that Barbara Harris's gonorrhoea was catching. His own counsel had earlier established a point in his favour when he induced Barbara to admit that she was suffering from VD while Davidson was doing his best to make love to her and that Davidson knew this: now Davidson had undone all the good work.

Yet the most incredible example of Davidson's capacity to do himself harm came towards the end of his cross examination. It seemed that an actress named Mae Douglas had a great liking for Davidson and in an interview with the *Daily Herald* she had declared that she had often left her fifteen-year-old daughter in his charge when she was working at the theatre. Mae Douglas had also asked Davidson to arrange a photographic session for her daughter, Estelle. On Palm Sunday 1932, Estelle and three other girls went down to the vicarage, where a freelance photographer took photographs of them in pyjamas on the lawn. The photographer ran out of plates and some photographs of Estelle in a bathing costume had to be postponed until Easter Monday. On the evening of Easter Monday, Davidson escaped from his son Nugent and his fiancée, hurried to Mae Douglas's flat and posed for some photographs with Estelle. When the prosecution asked Davidson whether the photographer had taken a picture of Estelle in the nude, he said no. Then, with a flourish, Oliver produced a photograph. It showed Estelle with her back to the camera, naked except for a shawl draped only on her right shoulder and across the front of her body. Davidson faced her with one hand on her right shoulder.

Davidson looked shocked and incredulous, and suggested

that the photograph was faked or touched up. Then he explained that the shawl had slipped out of his hand 'accidentally without my knowledge'. He went on to tell the court that someone was conspiring against him. Only a few weeks earlier he had been warned not to go to a certain house because a lady of title would slip off her dress and reveal herself to be wearing nothing underneath and two detectives would step out of hiding. Presumably he was hinting that the Bishop of Norwich was trying to entrap him in this way. As to the photograph of Estelle, he said later that she had originally been wearing a bathing costume under the shawl, but that the strap had been showing so she went up to the bedroom to adjust it. He had not known that when she reappeared she was naked underneath the shawl. He was asking the judge to believe that, confronted by a girl who was obviously not wearing a bathing costume, he had not even noticed that she had removed it.

The newspaper headlines proclaimed: Nude Photo Bombshell. Anyone who thought about it for a moment must have seen that Davidson could hardly have been engaged in seduction in a room with two photographers. (As it happened, his son Nugent and his fiancée had charged into the room a moment after the photograph was taken and the session ended.) But as far as the public was concerned, the photograph was the final proof of Davidson's guilt.

After a nine-week trial, the case was adjourned for a month to give the chancellor time to consider his verdict. On 8 July 1932, he gave it: Davidson was guilty on all five counts of immoral conduct. Davidson's testimony, said the judge, had been a tissue of falsehoods; he preferred to believe Barbara Harris. The judge ended by ordering Davidson to pay costs. But why had Davidson refused to call three vital witnesses: Rose Ellis, his wife, and his crooked friend Gordon?

Davidson continued to protest his innocence, pointing out that Christ had consorted with sinners.

Ten days after his trial he appeared in a variety act in Wimbledon. Leave to appeal was refused at the end of July. On 9 August he was ejected from a nudist camp at Harrogate and told reporters that he was thinking of establishing something of the sort at Stiffkey. Finally, on 21 October 1932, he arrived late for his defrocking ceremony at Norwich Cathedral and interrupted the proceedings with the assertion that it was the church that was on trial, not himself.

Deprived of his living, Davidson decided to accept an offer from Luke Gannon, the 'Showman King of Blackpool', to exhibit himself in a sideshow in a barrel. He and Gannon came into conflict because Davidson wanted to harangue his audience about the wickedness of the church authorities, while Gannon wanted the crowds to move on as fast as possible. Davidson spent five years at Blackpool during the summer seasons and it is estimated he earned between £5,000 and £20,000.

He tried hard to get his case reopened. When his right to appeal was turned down, he wrote a pamphlet called *I Accuse* and distributed it to anyone who would take it. He jumped up in the Church Assembly in Westminster Hall in 1936 and tried to interrupt the proceedings – he was chased out by stewards. He continued to get into trouble and appeared in front of Blackpool magistrates on several occasions for obstruction of the public footpath. He went to prison for nine days for rent arrears owing to his London landlady. And in November 1936 he demonstrated that his problems with the law had not blunted his taste for young girls: on Victoria station he accosted two sixteen-year-old girls and told them he was looking for an actress to play a leading role in a West End play and offered them £5 to audition for the part. They made an appointment with him for the next day but when he arrived, the railway police arrested him. He was fined forty shillings.

His appeal as a sideshow was diminishing as the public forgot the scandal. He had undertaken a thirty-five-day fast in 1935 and, when arrested and charged with unlawfully trying to commit suicide by starvation, had successfully sued Blackpool Corporation and won £382 in damages. But a rumour spread that food and drink were smuggled into his cabinet at night and the suggestion that he was an old fake as well as a hypocrite made the public cynical. When his Blackpool contract was not renewed, he signed an agreement with a menagerie owner in Skegness to appear in a cage with two lions, billed as

'A Modern Daniel in the Lion's Den'. It was a courageous decision since he was terrified of animals.

The act consisted of a talk by Davidson about his case after which he would enter the cage for a few minutes. The lions were apparently very tame but in case of trouble a lion tamer stood outside the cage with a pole. On 28 July 1937, Davidson was a little too self-confident, snapping his whip at the lions and ordering them to 'get a move on'. Suddenly, the male lion, Freddy, reared up and struck Davidson with his fore paws, knocking him down. The audience roared with laughter. Then Freddy picked up Davidson by the neck, like a mouse, and began to carry him round the cage. While one man tried to poke the lion with a stick, a sixteen-year-old girl named Irene Somner rushed into the cage and grabbed Freddy by the mane, trying to make him let go. Freddy dropped the rector and the lioness immediately tried to jump on him. Irene dragged him out of the cage and slammed the door.

Davidson was taken to the Skegness Cottage Hospital. It is reported that he opened his eyes as he was pulled out of the cage and gasped, 'Telephone the London newspapers – we still have time to make the first editions.' In fact, he was more or less in a coma when admitted to hospital – he was found to have a broken bone in the neck and he died two days later.

The most baffling part of the story is why Davidson behaved as he did. Was he, as many suggested, slightly insane? Or just an incorrigible publicity seeker? Or a dirty old man?

In *The Prostitute's Padre* (1975) Tom Cullen quotes Davidson's lifelong friend J. Rowland Sales, who was convinced that Davidson was a classic case of 'multiple personality'. Cullen cites the look of total incredulity that appeared on the rector's face when he was shown the picture of the naked Estelle Douglas in court as evidence that, up until that moment, he had no memory whatever of the photograph being taken. Sales believes that Davidson was at least three totally distinct persons: 'Uncle Harold', the respectable clergyman, 'Little Jimmy', a mischievous child who loved getting Uncle Harold into trouble, and 'the Bunco Kid', an incorrigible confidence swindler. Cullen cites the famous case of 'Sally Beauchamp', recorded by Dr Morton Prince, to show that in many ways

Davidson conforms to the medical picture of a multiple personality. The objection to this view is that nearly all cases of multiple personality are people who have had horrifying or traumatic experiences in childhood. Davidson's childhood, while rather Victorian and depressing, was quite unremarkable.

The clue to the real explanation probably lies in a remark made by Molly, Davidson's wife. She commented about his conviction that he was always right, 'It is useless to tell a lunatic who says he is a poached egg that he is not one, for he will exhaust your logic and outstrip your reasoning powers.' The clue to Davidson is his refusal to admit, under any circumstances, that he was ever in the wrong. The writer A. E. Van Vogt has called such types 'Right Men'. The Right Man's ego is as hard as a rock and is based on the conviction that he cannot be wrong. Van Vogt makes another interesting observation when he explains that the Right Man will have affairs with other women, but if his wife so much as looks at another man, he becomes almost insane with jealousy. This is borne out by Davidson's reaction to discovering that Molly was pregnant by another man. This shock seems to have started him on his career of 'pestering' young girls.

Davidson's conduct during World War I shows a man of immense self-importance and conceit. His own counsel in court admitted that he was a 'troublesome busybody'. For such men, eccentricity is a way of asserting their uniqueness. His son described an occasion when Davidson spent the afternoon with himself and his wife: when it was time to catch the last train, he rushed out to the Rayner's Lane tube station but a few minutes later they heard him rushing back up five flights of stairs. He burst into the room, gasped, 'Your clock is three minutes fast by the station clock', and rushed out again. Nugent Davidson's comment was, 'Mad, utterly mad, that was father.' But one may be forgiven for suspecting that Davidson loved being thought 'mad' and that the effect of rushing back – when he was already late – to shout that his son's clock was fast was intended to be dramatic and memorable – the kind of story his son would tell again and again.

Oddly enough, Davidson still has his warm defenders – Ray Gosling proved to be among their number when he presented a programme about the rector of Stiffkey on the BBC. They believed that Davidson was, as he inisted, only interested in helping fallen women and that he was telling the truth in court when he insisted that any suggestion of sex would have shocked him. Davidson's supporters believe that Barbara Harris was lying when she claimed Davidson wanted to seduce her – Davidson's own version of the story was that she tried to seduce him, thrusting her tongue into his mouth and wrapping her legs around him and he claimed he threw her on to the bed. Cullen even quotes a senior Health Officer who treated Barbara Harris and Rose Ellis for syphilis as saying that Davidson was impotent but this hardly seems to be borne out, either by the size of his family, or by Barbara Harris's story that he 'relieved' himself against her.

The truth is probably that, like most 'Right Men', Davidson was an incurable self-deceiver and an obsessive seducer – some of the thousand or so women must have been more obliging than Barbara Harris. He lived in a dream and firmly refused to wake up. It is his family that deserves our pity.

THE DREYFUS AFFAIR
The Political Scandal that Shook France

The Dreyfus scandal, usually known simply as 'the affair', is probably the most famous *cause célèbre* of all time. It divided France, caused unprecedented bitterness, and finally became an international scandal that tarnished the reputation of France.

On the morning of 26 September 1894, Major Hubert-Joseph Henry, a French intelligence officer, summoned a number of War Office colleagues and showed them a handwritten document written on onion-skin paper. It was unsigned, but its last sentence: 'I am just going on manoeuvres', made it clear that it had been written by an officer. The writer said that he was sending five documents and then listed them: a note on an army field gun, on artillery formations, and similar items. It had been recovered from the waste-paper basket of Colonel Max von Schwarzkoppen, the Germany military attaché in Paris and it indicated unmistakably that a French officer was betraying his country by spying for Germany. After the Franco-Prussian war of 1870–1, the French general staff suffered an understandable phobia about Germany and no one doubted that the two countries would soon be at war again. This is why the unsigned letter – the *bordereau* (list) as it came to be known – caused so much fury and dismay. Colonel Jean-Conrad Sandherr, Henry's immediate superior, had the letter photographed and copies circulated to all departments of the War Office, asking if anyone recognized the handwriting. A certain Captain Alfred Dreyfus soon came under suspicion. He was not much liked, partly because he was a Jew – there was much anti-Semitism in the French army – and partly because he was inclined to be critical of his superiors. A sample of Dreyfus's handwriting was compared with the *bordereau* and there was a general agreement that they were identical.

There were obvious reasons for doubting that Dreyfus could be a spy. To begin with, he was rich – his family owned a cotton-spinning mill in Mulhouse – and secondly, he came of an intensely patriotic family who, when the Germans seized Alsace, had preferred to emigrate rather than adopt German citizenship. But the evidence of the handwriting struck Sandherr as conclusive. Dreyfus was summoned to the War Office and asked to write down words that would be indicated by a certain Major Du Paty de Clam. The major dictated the words of the *bordereau*, then suddenly grabbed Dreyfus by the shoulder and shouted, 'Captain Dreyfus, in the name of the law I arrest you . . .' The bewildered Dreyfus retorted, 'I'm going mad!'

Long before his trial, the French Press – known as the most irresponsible and corrupt in Europe – had convicted him. France was in political turmoil with mass unemployment, falling prices, widespread hunger, and the wine industry ruined by a curse known as phylloxera; the Dreyfus scandal was exactly what was needed to distract the public from these miseries. One newspaper reported that Dreyfus was a gambler who had been losing thousands of francs a night; another declared that he had confessed to his treachery. Major Henry kept the Press fed with rumours. And when the trial opened, on 19 December 1894, no one had the slightest doubt that Alfred Dreyfus was a traitor. The defence protested at the decision to hold the trial *in camera*, arguing that it would surround Dreyfus with a wall of secrecy. The protest was overruled. Major Henry declared on oath that an 'honourable person' had told him that there was a traitor in the war ministry, then pointed at Dreyfus and declared, 'There is the traitor.' When Dreyfus demanded the name of his accuser, Henry replied, 'There are secrets in an officer's head which must not even be revealed to his *képi* [his cap].' Asked to swear on his honour that an 'honourable person' had named Dreyfus as a traitor, Henry declared in his stentorian voice, 'I swear it!' The famous criminologist Bertillon testified that the handwriting of the *bordereau* bore a strong resemblance to that of Dreyfus. The members of the court were also shown a letter – intercepted by the French Secret Service – from the Italian to the German attaché, referring contemptuously to *ce canaille de D–* (that scum D) who had passed on certain secret plans to him. Still, the evidence was thin and Dreyfus had no doubt he would be acquitted. He was stunned when, on the third day of the trial, he was found guilty and sentenced to deportation. On 5 January 1895, Dreyfus was publicly stripped of his rank and his sword was broken. Then he was shipped off to Devil's Island, off French Guiana, a former leper colony, where he was incarcerated in a tiny hut; at night, his ankles were chained to his bed. There he was to remain in solitary confinement for more than four years.

Dreyfus's problem was that he was a victim of France's political conflicts. The economic problems were spawning revolutionaries. In 1891, troops had fired on a crowd of demonstrating workers, killing women and children – it became known as the massacre of Fourmies. Anarchist bombs exploded in public places – in December 1893 an anarchist named Auguste Vaillant detonated a bomb in the Chamber of Deputies. Only three months before Dreyfus's arrest, President Carnot was stabbed to death in Lyons. The Trade Union Congress at Nantes adopted the principle of the general strike. The middle classes expected bloody revolution any day. The Church, the monarchists and the army stood shoulder to shoulder to hold back the tide of destruction. As a Jew, Dreyfus was hated by the right; his natural allies and supporters were the left. It was the right-wing Press that clamoured for his conviction and celebrated his downfall with howls of triumph. Dreyfus became a kind of political football; whether he was really guilty was almost an irrelevance. It was liberalism that was on trial, not Dreyfus.

For the prisoner on Devil's Island – who was now prematurely aged – help was to come from an unexpected quarter. In 1895, Sandherr – head of the Statistical Section which had been responsible for Dreyfus's arrest – became paralysed and his place was taken by Major Marie-Georges Picquart. Picquart was asked to continue to find conclusive evidence of Dreyfus's guilt and accordingly had all letters to and from Devil's Island intercepted. Another source of information was a cleaning woman called Bastian who worked for the German attaché

Schwarzkoppen and regularly sifted the contents of his waste-paper basket – she was probably the source of the original *bordereau*. On 15 March 1896, Madame Bastian handed over the latest consignment of discarded scraps of paper, among which was a postcard known as a *petit bleu*. It had been torn into fragments but was painstakingly reconstructed by one of Picquart's subordinates. It was addressed to a certain Major Marie-Charles-Ferdinand Walsin-Esterhazy and the message was cryptic and incomprehensible. But it was obvious that it meant something sinister – which in turn meant that Esterhazy was probably a spy for the Germans.

Esterhazy was a ne'er-do-well who spent as little time as possible with his regiment; he preferred women and gambling. As a result, he was always heavily in debt. Picquart instituted cautious enquiries; he soon discovered that a number of Esterhazy's brother officers were fully aware that the major had a curious thirst for classified information about gunnery. Then Picquart received two letters from Esterhazy himself requesting a transfer to the War Office. He recognized the handwriting immediately; it was that of the infamous *bordereau*. Picquart was a man of courage and honesty; he went to his superior, General Boisdeffre, and told him that he was convinced Dreyfus was innocent and that the real culprit was Esterhazy. Boisdeffre pulled a face and told Picquart to go and see General Gonse, who had been intimately involved in the Dreyfus investigation. Gonse said, 'So it looks as though a mistake has been made?' Then, after further reflection, he added, 'Keep the two cases separate.' In other words, forget Dreyfus, and concentrate on investigating Esterhazy. To Picquart, this was preposterous; if Esterhazy was the real spy, then the two cases could not be separated. 'But Dreyfus is innocent!' Gonse shook his head. 'If you keep silent, no one need know.' Picquart was outraged. 'What you say is abominable! I shall not carry this secret to my grave.'

Even darker depths were being revealed. It turned out that Major Henry, who had first announced the existence of the *bordereau*, had been a friend of Esterhazy's for years – although he claimed he had not seen him for a long time. It began to look as if Henry might have recognized his friend's handwriting on the *bordereau* from the beginning. He might well have decided to destroy it had not another subordinate seen it first.

Picquart's inconvenient streak of honesty pained his superiors. In November 1896, Picquart was summoned before three generals, rebuked for 'lack of discretion', and told that he was being removed from his job and posted to the frontier of Tunisia, where the Arabs were giving trouble.

If Picquart had died in Tunisia, as Boisdeffre obviously hoped he would, the Dreyfus affair would have been over. But Picquart was not killed and he continued to brood about Dreyfus. He even wrote a long letter to the President of the Republic, stating his belief in Dreyfus's innocence and stating his reasons but he did not mail it. Instead, he handed it over to a lawyer friend, agreeing that its details could be secretly 'leaked' to certain sympathetic members of Parliament. The lawyer, Louis Leblois, began cautiously to circulate the truth about Dreyfus and Esterhazy.

Dreyfus's brother Mathieu had never ceased his efforts to have the case reopened. Now he began to find powerful allies, among them Georges Clemenceau, a radical Republican and editor of *L'Aurore*. Clemenceau opened his columns to the 'Dreyfusards' – as they were now called – and the conservative government began to realize that it had a scandal of immense proportions on its hands. Mathieu Dreyfus provoked the next major development by publicly demanding Esterhazy as the author of the *bordereau*. Esterhazy had already been retired on half pay, after quarrelling with his former ally Henry. (Oddly enough, neither he nor Schwarzkoppen had realized they were the cause of Dreyfus's downfall as the trial had been held *in camera* – Esterhazy only found out when the *bordereau* was finally leaked to a newspaper.) Now Esterhazy was forced to try to clear himself by demanding to be court-martialled. It was granted and on 11 January 1898, it took the judges only three minutes to acquit him. Crowds cheered him in the streets, shouting 'Long live Esterhazy!' and 'Death to the Jews.' But anyone who believed that was the end of the affair was being naïve. Two days later, *L'Aurore* exploded a bombshell – a long open letter to the President of the Republic by the novelist Emile Zola. In a flash of inspiration, Clemenceau called it

'*J'accuse*'. It denounced the trial as a frame-up and named various officers, including Paty de Clam, of having ordered the acquittal of Esterhazy. He ended by daring the government to prosecute him for libel.

The government had no alternative. Zola's trial, in February, lasted two weeks. The charge was simply that Zola had accused the army of ordering Esterhazy's acquittal; the government was still trying hard not to reopen the Dreyfus case. After a fortnight of tumult, Zola was found guilty; he was fined the maximum 3,000 francs and sentenced to a year in jail. The mob screamed, 'Death to Zola', and tried to lynch him. The Chamber of Deputies passed a resolution ordering the 'energetic repression' of people who wanted to rehabilitate the traitor Dreyfus. Picquart was dismissed from the army and his friend Leblois was suspended from the bar for six months for his part in circulating the story of Esterhazy's guilt.

Now came the dramatic climax of the astonishing affair. The new war minister, Godefroy Cavaignac, announced in the Chamber that the army now had irrefutable proof of Dreyfus's guilt, in the form of three letters that had passed between the Italian attaché Panizzardi, and the German attaché, Schwarz-koppen. One referred to *ce canaille de D–*, while another named Dreyfus as a traitor. The whole Chamber cheered wildly and voted to have the speech posted on official billboards all over France. This, certainly, looked like the final end of the *affaire Dreyfus*.

Then Picquart dropped his own bombshell. In a letter to *L'Aurore*, he declared that he was in a position to establish before a court that one of the letters was a forgery and the other two did not refer to Dreyfus at all. The War Minister reacted with fury and ordered Picquart's arrest. Esterhazy was also arrested for 'conduct unbecoming to an officer'.

A young officer on the general staff, Captain Louis Cuignet, was appointed to re-examine the Dreyfus file with a view to refuting Picquart's charge. To everyone's dismay, Cuignet quickly realized that the three letters revealed that Picquart was telling the truth. The one that named Dreyfus was an obvious forgery. The likeliest culprit was Henry – now a colonel – and in the presence of the war minister he confessed to the forgery.

What had happened, it seemed, was that French Intelligence had intercepted a letter from the Italian attaché asking the German attaché to dine. A letter implicating Dreyfus was then forged on a blank sheet of paper by a petty crook named Lemercier-Picard; this was carefully glued on to the invitation that contained the Italian attaché's signature. On closer examination, Cuignet could see at once that the letter had been fabricated. (His motive was not a desire for justice – he spent the rest of his life denouncing Dreyfus as a traitor and trying to atone for causing his superiors so much embarrassment.)

Colonel Henry was arrested and General Boisdeffre resigned. The next morning, Henry was found dead in his prison cell; he had cut his throat with a razor. His accomplice Lemercier-Picard hanged himself. The War Minister Cavaignac also resigned. The government was further embarrassed when more of Henry's forgeries were later published – seven letters from Dreyfus to the German kaiser and a reply from the kaiser. The *affaire* was now thoroughly out of hand. France was now virtually in a state of civil war with mobs of Dreyfusards and anti-Dreyfusards clashing in the streets. The Dreyfusards were still very much a minority, regarded as dangerous left-wingers and hated by most 'decent' Frenchmen. When the High Court of Appeals agreed to review the case, one right-wing journalist suggested that the judges should have their eyes put out – the only way to handle traitors. In spite of its defeats, the right still seemed so much in charge that the pretender to the throne, the Duc D'Orleans, held himself in readiness at the Belgian border to take over the throne. (The last French king had abdicated as a result of the 1848 revolution.)

On 16 February 1899, the President, Felix Faure, died of a stroke – probably in the act of making love to the pretty young wife of a painter, who was hastily spirited away. Faure had been the chief obstacle to the reopening of the Dreyfus case, a die-hard conservative. The new President, Emile Loubet, was a moderate and he agreed to a retrial. There was an almost successful *coup d'état* by right wingers but when it failed, the judges summoned their courage and, on 3 June 1899, annulled Dreyfus's conviction and ordered a retrial before a military court. Picquart was released after almost a year in prison, Zola returned from exile in England, and Dreyfus was finally brought back from Devil's Island. (Ironically, most of his supporters found him a disappointing little man – dull, prosaic and rather irritating.)

It might seem that now was the time to right the injustice and put an end to the *affaire*; after all, Henry had confessed to forgery and Paty de Clam was in prison on a charge of forging documents in the case. But France was still full of hysteria. Anti-Dreyfusards were demanding that Dreyfus should now be sentenced to death. In August 1899, Dreyfus's court martial took place in Rennes. Dreyfus, who was only thirty-nine years old, had a white beard and looked like an old man. The trial lasted four weeks and the generals who entered the witness box rehashed all the old evidence, including the forgeries, and insisted on Dreyfus's guilt. Incredibly, the court ended by finding Dreyfus guilty of treason and sentencing him to ten years in prison.

There was talk of pardoning Dreyfus; the Dreyfusards objected strenuously, saying that this would be an admission of guilt. Dreyfus himself had a nervous breakdown – he had been absolutely certain that he would be vindicated. Finally, worn out by suffering, he agreed to accept the pardon and, on 19 September 1899, became a free man again.

The left, naturally, had no intention of allowing matters to rest there. They could see that they had the enemy on the run. The army was now thoroughly discredited. As a result of the *affaire*, socialism had gained enormous ground in France. The Church was also on the run. In France, the Catholic Church had always held enormous power – much as it still does in Spain or Ireland. In 1801, Napoleon had concluded a Concordat with the Pope; the French clergy were to be paid by the government. The Dreyfus affair led to such powerful anti-clerical feeling that it finally brought about the separation of the Church and the state in 1904, and the takeover of Church property by private corporations. In effect, Catholicism ceased to be the official state religion of France. One writer on the *affaire* (Guy Chapman) has called this the 'Dreyfusian revolution'.

Meanwhile, the Dreyfusards continued their attempt to clear Dreyfus's name. The Socialist leader Jean Jaurès lent his support. In 1903, Dreyfus himself requested a new enquiry. A search of War Office records revealed new evidence supporting his innocence and Esterhazy's guilt. The Minister of Justice agreed to allow the Rennes verdict to go to the Court of Criminal Appeal. Baudouin, the Procureur-Général, studied all the documents expecting to find at least some reasonable ground for the Rennes verdict and was shocked to realize that there were none whatever. Finally, on 12 July 1906, a court decided that not a fragment of the original evidence against Dreyfus was valid. The verdict of the Rennes court martial was finally annulled. Dreyfus was reinstated in the army with the rank of major; Picquart was made a Brigadier-General. Dreyfus was also decorated with the Legion of Honour. Picquart later became War Minister and eventually died in January 1914 after a fall from a horse. He seems to have shown a certain small-minded resentment of anti-Dreyfusards among army colleagues and obstructed certain promotions. Dreyfus himself served honourably in World War I, commanding an ammunition column. He died at the age of seventy-six, in 1935. An amusing story is told of these final years. A companion of Dreyfus's at bridge remarked that a certain person had been arrested for espionage, then, realizing that this sounded tactless, added hastily 'I daresay there's nothing in it.' 'Oh, I don't know,' said Dreyfus placidly, 'there's no smoke without fire.'

Esterhazy had been forced to flee the country and moved to London. Accused by his cousin of embezzlement, he was sentenced to three years in prison in his absence and so decided never to return to France. He later changed his name to Fitzgerald and became a journalist, writing anti-British articles for a French newspaper. Later still, he called himself the Comte Jean-Marie de Voilemont, moved to Harpenden and lived by selling tinned foods. He died in May 1923.

On Sunday, 28 September 1902, Emile Zola and his wife Alexandrine returned to their house in Paris and told the servants to light a fire in the bedroom stove. The next morning, both were found lying in their bedroom: Zola was dead and his wife was only just breathing. The cause of death was carbon dioxide poisoning, due to a blocked chimney. Yet when a fire was lit in the bedroom by two investigators and guinea pigs were locked in for the night, the animals were unharmed. It has been plausibly argued that the chimney was stopped up deliberately by anti-Dreyfusards and the blockage removed the next day.

L'affaire has been written about extensively, both in fiction and non-fiction. It figures prominently in Proust's novel *A la recherche du temps perdu* – Proust (who was half-Jewish) was understandably a Dreyfusard. Zola fictionalized the affair in his novel *Truth* and Roger Martin du Gard wrote about it in his novel *Jean Barois*. Perhaps the most amusing account is to be found in Anatole France's *Penguin Island*, where Dreyfus figures as Peyrot, accused of stealing 80,000 trusses of hay intended for the cavalry. France's satire on the case occupies many pages and tends to strike the modern reader as long-winded and heavy-handed; yet anyone who reads it after studying the affair itself will realize that, far from being heavy-handed, it understates the realities of the Dreyfus affair. The facts of the case, and the emotions to which it gave rise, are so extreme that they defy all attempts to fictionalize them.

FAGAN, Michael

The Intruder who Broke into the Queen's Bedroom

Twice within a month in the summer of 1982 human fly Michael Fagan, a 32-year-old Cockney from Islington in North London, successfully evaded the armed sentries and policemen on duty to break into Buckingham Palace. On the second occasion he entered the Queen's bedroom as she lay sleeping. When she awoke and her alarm calls went unanswered, he sat on the royal bed chatting for ten minutes before help arrived – a security scandal without precedent in the long history of the Royal Family.

His first break-in, at half-past eleven on the night of 7 June was spectacular enough. He scaled the high iron railings around the Palace grounds to enter Ambassadors Court, shinned 50 feet up a drainpipe and peered into Room 151 as he clung to the wall above a sheer drop to the yard below. Housemaid Sarah Jane Carter, who was in bed reading with the curtains open, thought she was seeing things as a face appeared at the window. However, she got up and reported what had happened, while Fagan continued his climb and crawled across a flat roof to break into the royal residence. Once inside, he went walkabout: pausing occasionally to sit on the Throne, to admire the portraits in the Picture Gallery, and note the names on various royal bedrooms before entering Room 108, the Post Room. By this time he felt thirsty, so he helped himself to a half-bottle of Californian white wine (intended for the Prince and Princess of Wales) and settled down to await what he assumed would be his inevitable interception and arrest. But somehow all the Queen's men remained blissfully unaware of the intruder in their midst and Fagan was able to make his way out, and home, undetected.

On the night of 9 July he drank (on his own admission) nine

or ten whiskies before setting off on the repeat break-in of what most people imagined to be the best-guarded home in Britain. This time he made his way into the Queen's bedroom, so that she awoke to find an unknown intruder sitting on her bed, dripping blood from one hand (which he had cut when accidentally breaking a royal ash-tray). What followed next must have been an even more harrowing experience. She immediately rang her Night Alarm bell – but no one came. Unknown to her, her police guard had already gone off duty. Her footman was outside in the grounds exercising the royal dogs. The housemaid was busily working in another room. The Queen, therefore, made a house telephone call, to try to alert the Palace police guard-room: but they, too, failed to respond promptly. So, with enviable self-control – and no little personal courage – she kept Fagan talking until a new opportunity arrived to summon help, when he asked for a cigarette. Instead, footman Paul Whybrew came hurrying in. Fagan told him he merely wished to talk to the Queen, 'my Queen' as he called her. 'All right,' said the young unarmed Whybrew. 'But let her get dressed first' – and with the help of a maid, ushered Fagan into a pantry where the police finally arrested him.

Almost astonishingly, no charges could be preferred against Fagan for breaking into the Queen's home and her bedroom. (Under English law, it is not a criminal offence to enter someone's home as long as there is no intention to commit an offence.) Instead, after Fagan had admitted the previous break-in, he was charged with stealing the half-bottle of wine, valued at £3. 'Burglary contrary to Section 9 (1) of the Theft Act, 1968, the particulars being that between the sixth day and ninth day of June, 1982, he entered Buckingham Palace as a trespasser and stole therein a quantity of wine.' Fagan denied the charge, claiming that he had entered the Palace only to show how lax security was.

The scandal of the apparently non-existent royal security was revealed by the *Daily Express* on 12 July. In one of the greatest of all scoops, it proclaimed in banner headlines: 'Intruder At The Queen's Bedside. Storm over new Palace security breach. She kept him talking for 10 minutes . . . then a footman came to her aid.' If the accompanying details seemed difficult to believe, they were quickly confirmed in a statement to the Commons by a shaken Mr William Whitelaw, then Home Secretary. He admitted there had been 'a most serious failure' of Palace security and blamed it on a combination of human and technical errors. An immediate inquiry was conducted by Scotland Yard's Assistant Commissioner John Dellow. His detailed account of the incident led to a thorough overhaul of all security precautions designed to protect the Royal Family, as well as changes in police security personnel.

On 19 July Fagan appeared at Bow Street Court and was committed for trial at the Old Bailey on three charges. As well as the alleged theft of the wine, he faced two unrelated charges: one of taking a car without the owner's consent on 16 June (to which he pleaded guilty), and another of assaulting his fourteen-year-old stepson on 26 June, causing bodily harm (to which he pleaded not guilty and of which he was subsequently acquitted). It took the Old Bailey jury of seven men and five women less than twenty minutes to find him not guilty of stealing Prince Charles's wine. Fagan told the court he entered the Palace merely to show how poor security was there. 'I done the Queen a favour,' he said. 'I proved that her security was not a hundred up [100 per cent].'

Some of the proceedings sounded more like a passage from the fictional court of newspaper satirist *Beachcomber*'s Mr Justice Cocklecarrot than solemn Old Bailey procedure. 'It wasn't your drink, was it?' asked Mrs Barbara Mills, prosecuting. 'It wasn't my Palace either,' replied Fagan, 'I'd done a hard day's work for the Queen, showing how to break her security.'

Since no charges could be brought arising from 'the intrusion into the Queen's bedchamber', evidence was confined to the first break-in. Fagan said, 'I'd gone round there with the children, and noticed the security was a bit lax. I wanted to prove the Queen was not too safe . . . I could have been a rapist, or something . . . I walked past a couple of rooms. One said it was a prince's, Mark Phillips . . . so I decided not to disturb him. "Prince Philip" was on another door, but they were out. So, to say I could break the security system, I went into the room where the wine was . . . After half an hour, I realized no one was going to pinch me. I might have been doing the Queen a favour. No one had seen me and I had been half an hour in the Palace. I even sat on the Throne.'

He told the court he thought security would have improved after the first break-in. 'It didn't, did it?' He went on to say that on the second occasion, he found the Queen's bedroom by accident. Although he was found not guilty of stealing the wine, he was remanded in custody to face the further charges on 4 October. For driving away the car without the owner's consent, he was then ordered to be detained in a mental hospital. Judge James Miskin, QC, made the order under Section 60 of the Mental Health Act, saying, 'I express confidence that the skilled members of the medical profession, in whose charge he will be, are admirably suited to determine the moment when he is safe to be released.'

Earlier, Dr Edgar Unwin, the medical director of Broadmoor, had described Fagan as 'potentially dangerous to any member of the public, and to one person in particular . . .' which was interpeted as a direct reference to the Queen. Under Section 60 of the Act, Fagan had the right to appeal for release within six months. The Recorder rejected a suggestion by three doctors that Fagan should be detained without a time limit under a Section 65 Order, which would have meant his release could have been sanctioned only with the approval of the Home Secretary.

On 19 January 1983 Michael Fagan was freed from the top-security Park Lane mental hospital at Liverpool, even though his cure was not complete. The decision to release him followed his appeal to the Mental Health Tribunal of the Mersey region, consisting of a lawyer, psychiatrist and one lay member. They had the power to order his release on two grounds: if he was not considered to be mentally disturbed, or if his disorder posed no danger to the public. The hearing lasted seven hours, during which a Park Lane doctor submitted medical grounds for Fagan's continued detention, while an independent psychiatrist argued in favour of his release. The Tribunal chairman said in a statement that Fagan was 'not fully recovered', adding, 'He remains vulnerable to pressure, and it is eminently desirable that he should be left alone to re-establish himself in society, and should not be subject to approaches from the media.' Inevitably, his release sparked off more controversy and questions were tabled in the House of Commons.

GESUALDO, Carlo
Composer of Genius and Murderer

The Prince of Venosa, who died virtually insane, was known to his contemporaries as the man who murdered his wife when he caught her in bed with her lover. For posterity, he is one of the greatest of all composers of madrigals.

Gesualdo's grandfather was made a prince in 1560 when his son married a niece of the pope. His grandson Carlo was born a year later. Gesualdo's father, Fabrizio, kept his own band of musicians. His son became a close friend of the paranoid poet Tasso, who wrote several poems about the tragic events which ended in murder.

In 1586, Fabrizio arranged a betrothal for his son, Carlo, with his cousin, a beautiful young girl named Maria d'Avalos. At the age of twenty-five, she had already been widowed twice. The wedding in Naples was followed by magnificent celebrations that lasted for days. In due course a son, Don Emmanuelle, was born. For four years, they lived 'more like lovers than man and wife' says a *chronique scandaleuse* of the period. But it seems that the lady became bored with her intellectual husband, whose greatest enthusiasm was for music. One of the visitors to their palazzo in Naples was a handsome young cavalier named Don Fabrizio Carafa, the Duke of Andria, described as 'perhaps the most handsome and graceful cavaliere in the city [of Naples], vigorous and flourishing and not yet thirty years of age.' The Duke was already married to a lady of religious inclinations, on whom he had fathered five children.

Donna Maria – who is depicted in a painting as a typically plump Italian beauty – seems to have been a woman of irresistible charm, so much so that Gesualdo's uncle, Don Giulio, fell in love with her and, 'not heeding the fact that she was the wife of his nephew', left no stone unturned to persuade her into his bed. She turned him down with sharp words, threatening to tell her husband if he did not stop pestering her.

Don Giulio was thrown into a passion of jealousy when he observed that his niece-in-law was obviously fascinated by the handsome Duke of Andria, Fabrizio. 'The first messages of their desires were their glances which, with the tongue of the heart, betrayed the fire that burnt in each other's breast. From glances of love they proceeded to written messages . . .' When husband and wife were on a visit to the house of a friend, Don Garzia of Toledo, in the town of Chiaia, the Duke hid in a pavilion in the garden, and bribed the wife of the gardener to help him. Donna Maria walked in the garden with her maid and some gentlemen, which must have struck her husband as safe enough, then she pretended she had a pain and persuaded the others to go in. The gardener's wife led her to the pavilion, where the Duke took her in his arms 'and kissed her a thousand times, as she did him, and with the greatest ardour they were moved to enjoy together the ultimate amorous delight.' After this, they used the house of Don Garzia for secret rendezvous and sometimes even in Donna Maria's own bedroom, with the maid acting as sentinel.

When Gesualdo's lecherous uncle heard the news he rushed to tell the Prince, who was 'more dead than alive' after receiving this unpleasant piece of information. Being an artist and an intellectual, he was not the type to challenge the Duke to a duel (besides which, the Duke had a reputation as a formidable swordsman). But the Duke soon divined – probably from his scowls – that the secret was out and told Donna Maria that it would be safer to end the affair, or at least suspend it until Gesualdo had ceased to be suspicious. Donna Maria's response was to pour scorn on him and tell him that if he loved her as much as she loved him, he would not be afraid of anyone. The Duke's pride was stung and he told her that if she felt like that, then he was willing to die with her.

According to one chronicler, Gesualdo announced that he intended to go hunting and would not be back until the following day. This does not accord with the testimony of Gesualdo's valet, who states that Gesualdo had supper in his room at his usual time, 'three hours of the night' (probably about nine o'clock). Donna Maria had supper at 'four hours of the night' – evidence that they led separate lives. Then she went to bed and was undressed by her two maidservants, Silvia Albana and Laura Scala. The maids seem to have slept in an ante-room between the bedroom and the corridor – and from which a flight of stairs led down to the mezzanine where Don Carlo had his bedroom. An hour later, Donna Maria called Silvia and asked her to bring some clothes; she had heard the Duke whistling in the street below and wanted to go out on to the balcony. Silvia brought her a skirt and shawl and Maria opened the window. Presumably her lover then climbed up on to the balcony and joined her. Not long after, Donna Maria called Silvia again and asked to be undressed and also asked for another nightdress, claiming that hers was damp with perspiration. It is not clear where the Duke was hiding during these proceedings. Silvia brought her a nightdress with ruffs of black silk and fringes at the bottom, then went back to her own room where she sat dressed on the bed and read a book until she dozed off to sleep.

She was awakened by the sound of her door opening. Opposite the door was the spiral staircase leading down to Gesualdo's room. Three men came into the room, one carrying a halberd. They went straight into the bedroom of Donna Maria. Silvia heard two shots. A moment later, Gesualdo came into the room, followed by his valet, who was carrying two torches. Gesualdo snarled at Silvia, 'Traitress, I shall kill you', and ordered his manservant not to let her escape. Gesualdo strode into his wife's bedroom, whereupon Silvia escaped into the bedroom of Donna Maria's small son and hid under the bed. Meanwhile, Gesualdo was heard to shout, 'Kill that scoundrel, along with this harlot. Shall a Gesualdo be made a cuckold?' There were sounds of a struggle. Then the three men came out, followed by Gesualdo, whose hands were covered with blood. Gesualdo said, 'I don't believe they are dead', and went back into the bedroom. His valet looked into the room and saw a man, wearing a woman's bloodstained nightdress, lying near the door. Gesualdo went back to the bed, where his wife was lying, and stabbed her several times more – according to one chronicler 'especially in those parts which most ought to be kept honest'. Gesualdo then ordered the two bodies to be dragged out on to the spiral staircase, and the same chronicler alleges that 'while the said cadavers were lying on the said staircase, a monk of San Domenico used the said Donna Maria even though she was dead.' But this chronicler is suspect; he is the one who tells the story of Gesualdo pretending to go hunting, which seems to be embroidery; he also states that when the Duke entered Donna Maria's bedroom, they 'gave each other solace several times', when it is obvious that there were no witnesses, so he could not possibly have known.

Gesualdo knew that his life was now in danger from Donna Maria's kinsmen and fled from Naples to his castle, destroying the surrounding woodland so that enemies could not take him by surprise. The Duke's wife, Donna Maria Carafa, retreated to a convent; there was a widespread rumour that she had suddenly experienced the conviction that her husband was about to die as she knelt in prayer a few hours before his death.

In the retirement of his castle, Gesualdo began to suffer from melancholia. He also began to write madrigals; his first two books were published in 1594 and made him a reputation as a fine composer. Until then he had been regarded as an aristocratic amateur. In 1594 he also married again, this time Leonora d'Este, a member of a rich and artistic family. But his second marriage was no happier than the first. Leonora was bored with her composer husband and with the castle at Gesualdo; she preferred to spend much of her time at Modena with her brother. Between Gesualdo's marriage and his death in 1613, there was a steady deterioration in his mental state. A son by Leonora died in 1600, and his eldest son by Donna Maria died only a few weeks before Gesualdo himself.

The first two books of madrigals are relatively conventional in style. Thereafter, Gesualdo's work became increasingly difficult and complex, full of dissonances and chromaticism. Most of his contemporaries regarded these peculiarities as a sign of his madness. It is only in the twentieth century that his genius has been appreciated.

GREGORY, Maundy
The 'Honours for Sale' Scandal

Maundy Gregory was an amiable con-man who was selected by Lloyd George as his chief broker in the sale of honours – knighthoods, baronetcies, and so on – to replenish the coffers of the Liberal Party. It has also been plausibly suggested that he was guilty of two murders.

Arthur John Peter Michael Maundy Gregory was born on 1 July 1877, at Southampton, the son of the vicar of St Michael's. He was a boyhood friend of Harold Davidson, later notorious as the Rector of Stiffkey (*see* page 151). Gregory's father was an unpopular vicar, for he had imbibed the High Anglican principles of Newman's Oxford Movement and his Low Church parishioners objected furiously to what they felt was an attempt to introduce popery. This may partly explain why Gregory was also unpopular at his prep school, Banister Court, where the boys were inclined to jeer at him and call him 'bum cheeks' (in reference to his rosy cheeks). Another cause may have been a certain effiminacy in his manner – he was a lifelong homosexual.

His great love was the theatre. At Oxford, he organized amateur theatricals. He also practised ventriloquism, and (like Davidson) recited comic monologues. Gregory's father was poor and Gregory was a non-collegiate student. When his father died in 1899, he left Oxford without a degree. What happened next is unclear but in a theatrical *Who's Who* of 1907 he is described as a theatrical manager and playwright who had first appeared as a drawing-room entertainer, then manager of the Prince of Wales Theatre, Southampton, and later toured in various dramas and farces. He now called himself J. Maundy-Gregory. In 1903 he became a manager of Frank Benson's touring Shakespeare company at £5 a week but was sacked for dipping his hand in the till. In 1908, Gregory and Harold Davidson went into a kind of partnership. By now, Davidson had many acquaintances among the aristocracy, through his charitable activities. Davidson's role was to direct his aristocratic friends towards Gregory, who would persuade them to buy shares in a syndicate whose purpose was to bring over successful Broadway shows from America to tour the provinces in England. Partly due to bad timing – Gregory tried to launch a revival of *Dorothy* just before Christmas, when there were dozens of pantomimes to compete with it – this partnership collapsed in 1909.

As a theatrical manager, Gregory had given a benefit performance of *Dorothy* for the Messina earthquake victims and was astonished at how many rich patrons he could entice to the theatre. He had a feeling that snobbery could somehow be utilized to make him a fortune. He launched a magazine called *Mayfair*, and persuaded rich industrialists to pay well for the privilege of having their portraits sandwiched between those of the aristocracy. He also launched a kind of unofficial detective agency to keep note of distinguished guests who registered at the major hotels of London and Paris, and to establish their credit ratings. Many hotels, restaurants and jewellers paid him a fee for his information. When the beginning of World War I put an end to these activities, Gregory used his ability as an information gatherer by becoming a member of MI5, the British Secret Service. He claimed to have impersonated Winston Churchill, then First Lord of the Admiralty, at a public banquet when Churchill was in danger of assassination.

In December 1918, the Prime Minister, David Lloyd George – the 'Welsh Wizard' – was head of a coalition government consisting mainly of Conservatives, with less than a quarter of the Members of the House belonging to his own Liberal Party. He urgently needed at least £4 million as a campaign fund. The solution lay in the sale of honours. 'You and I know that the sale of honours is the cleanest way of raising money for a political party,' he once confided to J. C. C. Davidson. Knighthoods could be sold for £10,000 each; baronetcies – since they could be inherited – were £40,000 each. Lloyd George needed a reliable man to act as his chief salesman –

someone who could be trusted not to embarrass him by doing it too openly. Maundy Gregory seems to have been recommended by Lord Murray of Elibank, the Liberal Chief Whip (who had been involved in the Marconi scandal before the war). Gregory's first step towards becoming an honours broker was to launch another magazine, *The Whitehall Gazette*, as a cover for his activities. The aim of the *Gazette*, he said, was to conduct a campaign against Bolshevism and Communism. A henchman named J. Douglas Moffat, who had himself been in the 'honours for sale' business before Lloyd George decided to go into mass production, would keep his ear to the ground and approach likely prospects – such as a Justice of the Peace or Master of Foxhounds who would be willing to pay £10,000 for a knighthood, or a rich war profiteer who was anxious for a baronetcy or even a peerage. A meeting with Gregory would be arranged. And in due course, Gregory would receive his cut – probably 10 per cent of the price paid. Maundy Gregory is credited with suggesting that Lloyd George should originate a new honour, the Order of the British Empire (OBE) that might be sold cheap – at about £100. Lloyd George created 25,000 of them in a few years. He also created ninety-one new peers – double the number that either of his two predecessors had created.

Maundy Gregory was soon a very rich man, and he loved the role. He was always beautifully dressed, changing his suit at least twice a day. He bought a house at No 10 Hyde Park Terrace – he could then tell his staff to say that he was 'over at No 10' if anyone rang up while he was out – the impression being that he was at 10 Downing Street with the Prime Minister. He also owned a bungalow on Ditton Island, on the Thames, a flat at Brighton, and the Ambassador Club in London.

Gregory was by no means a vulgar confidence man. He was a collector of first editions and had a genuine love of literature. He seems to have been a likeable and generous man, who loved to give presents. There is a story that he bought the Ambassador Club as a present for a handsome 23-year-old waiter named Peter Mazzina, who became manager there.

Mazzina was one of the few who did not desert Gregory at the time of his later disgrace.

One writer, Donald McCormick, has connected Maundy Gregory with one of the most baffling mysteries of the twentieth century: the total disappearance of the Labour Member of Parliament Victor Grayson. Grayson was a fire-eating socialist, who was elected to Westminster in 1907 at the age of twenty-six as Member for Colne Valley. He was a charismatic personality and a magnificent orator, his only major weakness being his love of drink. Before World War I, his political career seemed to be at an end because of his inability to appear sober on a platform. But at the beginning of the war he went to Australia and New Zealand to lecture on socialism and to proclaim the virtues of fighting for one's country – a new departure for Grayson. He joined the New Zealand Expeditionary Force and fought in France, where he received war wounds. Back in England after the war, he was placed under surveillance by MI5 as a possible agitator who might try to link up with the Russian communists or the Irish rebels. Grayson's biographer Reg Groves states: 'Somehow Victor Grayson became concerned at the sale of honours and found out about Gregory's part in it. Gregory was keeping tabs on Grayson and Grayson was led into finding out what Gregory was doing.' Grayson was, of course, precisely the person who might blow the honours conspiracy sky high.

On an evening in September 1920, Grayson was in the bar of a London restaurant, the Georgian, when the receptionist told him that she had just received a telephone call saying that some luggage of Grayson's had been delivered to the Queen's Hotel, Leicester Square, by mistake. The restaurant was in Chandos Place, just behind the Strand. Grayson apparently remarked, 'Don't let anybody touch my whisky – I'll be back in a moment.' He walked out and was never seen again.

Since Grayson was now an obscure figure, living 'in the shadows', his disappearance was not noticed for some time – so long that the precise date is not even certain. (There is even some doubt about whether Grayson was in the Georgian Restaurant or in some hotel in the Strand.) The acquaintance with whom he had been drinking, E. K. Donovan, telephoned the Queen's Hotel to ask if Grayson had collected his luggage, only to be told they knew nothing whatever about it – they had not made the call to the restaurant receptionist.

A short time later, a painter named George Flemwell was standing on the Middlesex bank of the Thames painting a watercolour on the afternoon of 28 September when he saw an 'electric canoe' with two men in it, crossing to Ditton Island. He recognized one of the men as Grayson, whom he had known for some time. The boat stopped at the island and Grayson and the man walked into the bungalow. Since Flemwell wanted to see Grayson, he took a ferryboat to Ditton Island and knocked on the door, asking for him; a middle-aged woman answered and door and irritably denied all knowledge of Grayson. Shortly thereafter, Flemwell returned to Switzerland, where he lived, not even aware that Grayson had vanished.

It is conceivable, of course, that Flemwell was mistaken – after Grayson's disappearance became known, many people were convinced that they had seen him. (My old friend, Sidney Campion, who knew Grayson well, was absolutely convinced that he saw him on the London Underground in 1939 – C.W.) One of the likeliest theories is that he embarked for Russia, but never reached his destination. It is certainly hard to imagine the amiable Gregory – who had more in common with Oscar Wilde than Bill Sykes – murdering a man who must have known he had every reason to distrust him. But it is conceivable that, with the connivance of Lloyd George and the Secret Service, he lured Grayson into a trap. (A still-unpublished book by David Clark, Labour MP for South Shields, suggests: 'Quite simply, Grayson contrived his own disappearance, and lived out his life in North England under a different name.' Clark claims to have made the discovery that Grayson was homosexual, and that his decision to 'disappear' was due to the mental strain of his growing alcoholism and the emergence of his old homosexual tendencies.)

The irritable middle-aged woman who answered the door may have been Gregory's second murder victim, and here the evidence is altogether stronger. She was Edith Marion Rosse, the tenant of the bungalow named 'Vanity Fair' and perhaps

Gregory's closest friend. She had been on the stage under the name of Vivienne Pierpont and had married Frederick Rosse, a composer and director closely associated with Gregory's abortive theatrical ventures. The three of them seemed to be inseparable and spent a great deal of time exploring the Thames which they all loved. It seems reasonably certain that Gregory was not having an affair either with Mrs Rosse or her husband. In 1910, Gregory rented 'Vanity Fair' and Edith Rosse moved in as his tenant and hostess. From 1921 to 1923, the three were still together; then – for reasons unknown – Rosse and his wife decided to separate. Gregory and Mrs Rosse continued to be inseparable. She was an alibi for his homosexual activities.

Throughout the 1920s, Gregory's wealth increased, in spite of the Honours (Prevention of Abuses) Act, passed by Parliament in 1925. He spent lavishly, on the Ambassador Club, on his *Whitehall Gazette*, and on his friends. There were, however, times when he needed cash urgently. One amusing story tells how he asked one of his clients for payment in advance on a peerage. The man agreed but post-dated the cheque and signed it with the title he had chosen.

It seems reasonably certain that Gregory was being blackmailed in the late 1920s, not for his part in the sale of honours but because of his homosexuality. There is a fine irony in the notion that the man who often resorted to blackmail should himself become a victim. Then there was another blow. A man who had paid out £30,000 in expectation of a title died before he received it and his executors – pointing out that they had no further use for the title – demanded the money back. Gregory refused to pay but when they started court proceedings against him was forced to avert disaster by repaying the cash in three instalments.

On 19 August 1932, Mrs Rosse complained to the housekeeper at the Ditton bungalow that she felt unwell. At the time, Gregory was lunching with his friend King George of Greece but he received a message that made him hurry back. The doctor had diagnosed Bright's Disease. In the presence of the housekeeper and the doctor, Edith Rosse said she wanted to make her will and demanded paper. Gregory pulled a menu card out of his pocket. On this, she wrote that her goods were all to be left to Maundy Gregory; the doctor and housekeeper witnessed the will. By 1 September Mrs Rosse seemed quite well again and went for a drive with Gregory. Two days later, she had a relapse, with sickness and diarrhoea; she died on 14 September.

Gregory now behaved rather oddly. He said that Edith Rosse had expressed a desire to be buried near the river she loved so much. Thames Ditton graveyard would seem to have been the obvious choice but Gregory said that was not close enough. He went much further afield, to Bisham, where there was a burial charge of a hundred guineas to anyone not born in the parish. With some difficulty, Gregory obtained the necessary permission and paid the hundred guineas. The undertaker who asked if Gregory wanted the coffin soldered up was told that 'she wouldn't like that', and to simply allow the lid to rest on the coffin. In the graveyard, he told the gravediggers that she wanted to lie close to the surface so the grave was only eighteen inches below the surface.

Mrs Rosse had left £18,000 – she and Gregory had had some disagreement not long before because she refused to lend him some of it. Now he was able to use all of it to pay off his more urgent debts. But it was not enough. He decided that the answer lay in a few quick sales of honours. His 'scout', a man called Pengelley, reported that a certain Lieutenant-Commander Edward Whaney Billyard Leake, RN, was a possible candidate. Accordingly, Leake was cautiously approached by Gregory's tout, J. Douglas Moffat, who requested an interview, hinting that it would be to Leake's advantage. Leake wanted to know what it was all about but Moffat was evasive. Eventually, out of curiosity, he agreed to a meeting. On 23 January 1933, Moffat asked Leake if he wanted a knighthood; if so, it would cost him £12,000. (Lloyd George was no longer in power but Gregory apparently had powerful friends in the national coalition government under Ramsay MacDonald.) Leake said he was not interested. Moffat should have taken warning but instead he persuaded Leake to meet Maundy Gregory. They went to Gregory's house and there Gregory confirmed that, for somewhere between £10,000 and £12,000, Leake could be included in the June Birthday

Honours. There was a second meeting – Leake was now consumed with curiosity but he finally declined the offer. Gregory asked him to reconsider and asked for £2,000 'to keep the pot boiling'. After discussing it with a friend, Leake went to Scotland Yard and reported it.

Gregory behaved with extreme coolness when Chief Inspector Arthur Askew called on him and handed him a summons. No doubt he felt that it should be easy to use influential friends who would 'fix' it. When this proved unexpectedly difficult, Gregory blackmailed various previous recipients of honours for £2,000 each, to pay for his defence.

The case came up at Bow Street Court on 16 February 1933. Gregory had been persuaded to plead guilty so that it would not be necessary for the prosecution to produce damning evidence. Gregory was sentenced to two months' imprisonment – without hard labour – and fined £50.

While Gregory was in prison, a niece of Mrs Rosse, Ethel Marion Davis, consulted a solicitor to see whether she could contest the will. Then she went to the police and told them she thought her aunt's death was suspicious. A week after Gregory had been sentenced to prison, London newspapers announced that various relatives of Mrs Rosse had been questioned about her sudden death. While Gregory was working in the prison library and earning remission for good conduct, the police were applying for permission to exhume Mrs Rosse's body. Meanwhile, an auction was held at Gregory's Hyde Park Terrace house and his goods – including many beautiful antiques – were sold for a total of just over £300.

Gregory came out of prison on 11 April and was met by Peter Mazzina. He had a quiet lunch at the Ambassador Club, at which certain politicians were present; the result was that he took the first boat from Newhaven to Dieppe.

Two weeks later, Mrs Rosse's body was exhumed. As Dr Roche Lynch, the Home Office analyst, watched water pouring out of the coffin as it was raised he muttered, 'Not a chance.' He was right. If Mrs Rosse had been poisoned, as her niece suspected, the Thames had done its work and removed all trace of it from the badly decomposed body. The inquest made one thing quite certain: Mrs Rosse had not had Bright's Disease. No cause of death could be found.

Gregory retired to Paris, and took rooms at 8 rue d'Anjou. In spite of having been declared bankrupt, he never seemed short of money. His friend Peter Mazzina also prospered for a while, running the Bristol Grill and the Millionaire's Club but in 1943, he committed suicide by hanging himself at a house in Welbeck Street. He was heavily in debt. In the summer of 1940, after the German invasion of France, Gregory was hidden in a tiny room in a hotel in Châteauneuf-du-Faou, in Finistère, Brittany, for four months. He was captured in November and taken to a civilian internment camp at Drancy; he died on 28 September 1941, at the age of sixty-four. A fellow inmate told Gregory's biographer, Tom Cullen, that 'he died of lack of booze', the Germans having cut off his supply of whisky that he had smuggled in from Paris.

HOLLYWOOD

Scandal in the 'Dream Factory'

The history of Hollywood begins in 1886, when Mrs Deida Wilcox, the wife of a Kansas City estate agent, gave that name to a huge ranch not far from the small city of Los Angeles (population around 12,000), where they had decided to retire. But if by Hollywood we mean the motion-picture industry, then it is arguable that the history of Hollywood – and of Hollywood scandal – began twelve years earlier, on 17 October 1874, when the photographer Eadweard Muybridge murdered his wife's lover. On the afternoon of that day, Muybridge was at work on his photographic plates in San Francisco when he was interrupted by a lawyer who wished to discuss a debt of $100 that Muybridge owed to a midwife named Susan Smith. By way of inducing Muybridge to settle the debt, the lawyer hinted that Mrs Smith knew of a scandal concerning Mrs Muybridge and that she might spread the word unless she received her money. Muybridge rushed off to interview Mrs Smith. He had reason to be jealous, for his wife Flora was a pretty girl of twenty-three while Muybridge was an introverted and bad-tempered man of forty-seven. What Mrs Smith told him threw him into a frenzy. A certain Major Harry Larkin had brought Flora Muybridge to her house for the delivery of a baby and from the tender love scene that took place between them, it was to be inferred that Larkin was the baby's father. Mrs Muybridge was in Dalles, Oregon, far from her husband's rage, but the handsome and debonair Major Larkin, a San Francisco reporter, was closer at hand at the health resort Calistoga. Muybridge took a boat there, went to the house where Larkin was living and called out for him. Larkin came to the door. 'Here is a message from my wife', said Muybridge, and shot him in the heart.

In California in those days, shootings were commonplace and a man who had murdered from an outraged sense of honour aroused public sympathy. The defence pleaded temporary insanity, pointing out that Muybridge had received serious head injuries in 1860 in a runaway stage-coach accident. The Napa Court found him not guilty.

Mrs Muybridge had vanished after the trial, and Muybridge himself disappeared into obscurity. The drama had interrupted Muybridge's work on an interesting scientific enterprise – an attempt to photograph a horse in motion. In 1872, Governor Leland Stanford had bet a friend that when a horse is galloping at full speed, all its feet leave the ground for a brief moment. Stanford was a rich man – he owned a racing stable – and he was willing to spend money to back his assertion. Muybridge had been trying, without much success, to photograph a horse in motion; his plates showed little more than a blur. But when he emerged from his five years obscurity in 1880, photographic emulsion had improved so much that a mere fraction of a second was enough for a successful exposure. Stanford spent $40,000 equipping Muybridge with a whole row of cameras. Then a machine with a metal cylinder and projecting pins (like a music box) closed a series of electrical contacts, setting off the cameras one after the other, as the horse galloped past. Governor Stanford won his bet and Muybridge achieved a certain celebrity.

A friend of Muybridge, Wallace Levison, took the next major step when he evolved a method for moving photographic plates on a wheel behind a lens. And by 1888, Thomas Alva Edison had discovered how to take a series of pictures on a moving strip of film. From there, it was a short and very obvious step to projecting them on to a screen like slides. In 1889, his workmen had solved the problem of synchronizing a moving picture with sound. The first 'film' showed his engineer William Dickson stepping on to the screen, raising his hat, and saying 'Good morning, Mr Edison. I hope you are satisfied with the kinetophonograph.'

The Kinetoscope was basically a peep-show machine for use in fairgrounds. It showed such subjects as a man sneezing or girls dancing. But when the first dramatic motion picture, *The*

Passion Play, was presented at the Eden Musee on 30 January 1898, its producer Rich Hollaman knew he had taken an important step. He commented, 'I knew I had them when I saw the tears in the eyes of those Broadway sports.' This was, in fact, the most incredible thing about the film as a medium: its emotional impact. Today we take it for granted because we are familiar with television and cinema since childhood. It is difficult for us to grasp the overwhelming effect of the first films: the way they transported the audience into 'another world'. Edison was the first to make full use of this potential in a film of 1902 called *The Life of an American Fireman*. It showed a house on fire and a man being rescued from an upstairs window followed by a woman and child, coughing and staggering as they were overcome by smoke. The firemen dashed through the streets on their horse-drawn wagons. As the mother and child collapsed, unconscious, a fireman burst in through the door. He carried the unconscious mother to a ladder; she awoke and begged him to save her baby. He took her down, then went back for the child. Mother and child were united as the house blazed. At the first showing there was not a dry eye in the place; the film had lasted only a few minutes but people felt as if they had been through a crisis together – they smiled through their tears at their next-door neighbour.

It was this emotional impact that turned the film star into something far more renowned and illustrious than the great actors of the past. David Garrick, Edmund Kean, Henry Irving, all had 'set the town on fire' in their time. But their admirers were separated from them by the footlights. In the cinema, you were there, in the blazing bedroom, clinging to the upturned boat about to be swept over the waterfall, or clambering over the rooftops of the runaway train in an effort to reach the engine. It was ten times as real as the theatre. Furthermore, every woman in the audience was in the arms of the romantic hero as he swept her on to his horse and galloped away from the murderous ruffians hired by the villain; every male in the audience gazed into her adoring eyes. Of course, there had been plenty of romantic heroes in literature, from Byron's Childe Harold to Owen Wister's Virginian but they were for the literate. The screen brought romance, excitement and laughter to people who never read a newspaper. The result was that film stars achieved a degree of celebrity that had been unknown in the nineteenth century, even to popular idols like Dickens and Jenny Lind. Charlie Chaplin came to Hollywood in 1912 to make pictures for Mack Sennett at Keystone. He knew his films were popular because they made money. But when he took a trip to New York in 1915, he was staggered to be met by enormous crowds at every station; the telegraph operators, who had relayed a telegram announcing his arrival, had passed on the news to the Press. When he came to England in 1920 there was even greater excitement; telegrams began to arrive by the dozen when he was halfway across the Atlantic. Every time he stepped off a train he was met by the local mayor and a brass band.

It was because the film star was regarded as a kind of god that the slightest breath of scandal could be magnified into a tempest of opprobrium. The first great Hollywood scandal broke in 1920, when news arrived that the lovely and popular Olive Thomas had committed suicide with poison capsules in Paris. Hers had been the classic success story. As a teenager she had escaped from a Pennsylvania slum and an unhappy marriage to become a shop girl in New York. Then she entered a competition for 'the perfect artist's model' and won it. After that she became a Ziegfeld girl, then a Hollywood film star. She was married to another screen idol, Jack Pickford – Mary Pickford's brother, a clean-cut young man who was regarded as the all-American boy. But investigations into Olive Thomas's death revealed that she was not quite the charming innocent she played on the screen. Olive had arrived in Paris ahead of her husband and her perambulations included sleazy night clubs where she drank with members of the French underworld. Newspapers began to publish reports that she had been in these places trying to buy heroin for her husband who was an addict. Later still, an American government investigation revealed that she herself had been purchasing heroin and cocaine before her marriage to Pickford. The headlines declared: Olive Thomas, Dope Fiend. The American public had been prepared to believe that its idols were not angels – after all, Mary Pickford and Douglas Fairbanks had just divorced their respective mates in order to marry – but this was beyond belief. Olive Thomas's husband survived the scandal but made only a few more films.

The next scandal was greater still. In 1921, the comedian Fatty Arbuckle was charged with criminal responsibility in the death of Virginia Rappe (*see* page 17), who died of a ruptured bladder after being raped by him. Again, it seemed incredible, as if Santa Claus had turned out to be Jack the Ripper. The inference seemed to be that the inhabitants of the 'dream factory' were dope fiends or sex fiends.

Chaplin himself was lucky to escape the same fate as Arbuckle. When he came to Hollywood in 1912 (at the age of twenty-three), his love life had been minimal and he suffered from shyness and loneliness. His natural penchant was for very young women – in fact, for under-age girls. When he met Mildred Harris at a beach party in 1917 she was fifteen and looked younger. In the following year her announcement that she was pregnant led to her marriage to Chaplin but followed two years later by divorce. (Chaplin confided to Fairbanks that his wife was 'no mental heavyweight'.) He charged infidelity and she charged cruelty – a concept his admirers found hard to associate with the sentimental little tramp. It seemed to confirm the notion that Hollywood was the opposite of what it seemed and that the great film moguls – Adolph Zukor, Samuel Goldwyn, Jesse Lasky, Louis B. Mayer – were trying to deceive the public.

Chaplin's next major involvement was with a girl named Lillita McMurray – she preferred to spell it Lolita – whom he had met for the first time in April 1914 – her sixth birthday. When she was twelve, she appeared as a child angel in *The Kid*. Her mother was distinctly suspicious of Chaplin's intentions and kept a beady eye on him. Two years later, Lita was invited to play in *The Gold Rush*, which was filmed in Trukee, California. In her autobiography, *My Life With Chaplin*, Lita admits: 'I wanted to be his little girl – and yet I wanted him to put his tongue in my mouth. I knew I was playing with fire . . .' Chaplin's response to this teasing attitude was to leap on her in his red silk pyjamas. Lita was duly horrified at his 'animal movements' and fled. The next time, he tried the softly, softly approach. 'He was softer; even before he touched me I sensed I wouldn't have to struggle . . . With deft, still unhurried movements he peeled the bathing suit off me and sat back on his knees to look at me nude. Instinctively I began to cover with my hands the parts of me that no man had seen until this moment, but looking at him again, I saw the absence of lewdness in his eyes, and abruptly there was no shame. My hands fell to my sides.' At the last minute she changed her mind. '"No", I whimpered, shaking my head wildly, taking my arms from around him, trying to close my legs. "Oh, I can't, I can't!"' The next time he tried was in the back of a limousine. 'Wordlessly he found his way to the top of the elastic-banded underpants, and wordlessly he yanked them down; I murmured for him to stop, though without much force, for he was kissing me again. Then he was struggling with his own clothing and pulling me over on top of him.' Their position made it impossible, and again Chaplin gave up. Finally, he took her to his home in Beverly Hills and the long-awaited deflowering took place in the bathroom. 'The foglike mist billowed, grew thicker and thicker, finally filled every inch of the room. I couldn't see anything . . . What happened next was Charlie, lying beside me and teasing my neck with swift darting kisses . . . Then there was a sharp, piercing pain inside me and I cried out, but I did not release my grip. The pain blinded me far more than the encircling steam, but I writhed wildly, as though in ecstasy, to let him know I belonged to him – and then I received all of him.'

Chaplin disliked contraceptives and the result was that his child-mistress became pregnant. He had to marry in haste or face a charge of statutory rape. Chaplin and his fifteen-year-old bride tried to marry quietly in Mexico but were pursued by hordes of reporters. Chaplin is quoted as saying to his friends of the wedding party, 'Well, boys, this is better than the penitentiary, but it won't last.' Mrs McMurray moved in with the newly weds. Chaplin began to spend most of his time with old cronies while Lita and her clan took over the household. After two years, Chaplin fled to New York and Lita filed for divorce. While Chaplin was fighting off a nervous breakdown, the McMurray clan swooped on his home and studio. A pamphlet entitled *Complaint by Lita Grey* passed from hand to hand; it contained details of her allegations against Chaplin, including the accusation that he had tried to persuade her to perform the 'abnormal, against nature, perverted, degenerate and indecent act' called fellatio and that when she declined he had said, 'Relax, dear – all married people do it.' It went on to state that after their original lovemaking scene, they never had normal sex together. The newspapers made the most of the revelations and H. L. Mencken commented in the Baltimore *Sun*: 'The very morons who worshipped Charlie Chaplin six weeks ago now prepare to dance around the stake while he is burned.' When Lita's lawyers threatened to reveal in court the names of five prominent actresses with whom he had slept since his marriage, Chaplin capitulated and Lita was paid $625,000. Chaplin could afford it; his total estate was reckoned to be worth $16 million. He was so embittered about the episode that he does not even mention Lita Grey in his autobiography. But the divorce case did no permanent damage to his popularity and when his next film *The Circus* was released in 1928 it was as popular as ever.

The experience with Lita Grey made Chaplin secretive and when he married the twenty-year-old Paulette Goddard (at sea) in 1933, he kept it a secret for three years; Chaplin was forty-four at the time of the marriage. Before this marriage ended in divorce in 1942, Chaplin was the defendant in a paternity suit brought against him by a young actress named Joan Barry and he was also charged under the Mann Act – transporting a minor across state lines for immoral purposes. He was found not guilty of this charge but ruled to be the father of the child. A year later, in 1943, Chaplin married the eighteen-year-old daughter of playwright Eugene O'Neill, Oona; he was then fifty-four. They lived together happily until his death in 1977. The final scandal in which he was involved was not sexual but political. During the McCarthy era he was accused of being a communist and his film *Monsieur Verdoux* was widely boycotted in America. In 1952, he was in mid-Atlantic when he was told that the Attorney-General had decided to deny him re-entry into the United States unless he submitted to an enquiry into his 'moral worth'. He preferred to move to Vevey in Switzerland. He was knighted in 1975. A few months after his death two years later his body was 'kidnapped' from the graveyard in Vevey and demands for ransom were received – probably the only occasion on which the victim of a kidnapping has already been dead; his body was later recovered.

Chaplin's career epitomizes the basic problem of Hollywood. The famous always attract members of the opposite sex and since most famous people are naturally dominant they are also, in most cases, highly sexed. Where sex is offered casually, it will inevitably be accepted casually. Chaplin tells of a typical episode in his autobiography. In a hotel room in Los Angeles, he was undressing and humming a popular tune when a feminine voice from the next room took it up. He whistled it and again the girl hummed it. When he laughed the girl said, 'I beg your pardon.' Chaplin persuaded her to open her door and saw 'the most ravishing young blonde' dressed in a negligée. He introduced himself but it was unnecessary for the girl already knew who he was. They slept together that night, taking care not to acknowledge one another in public the next day. The next night, she tapped on his door and again they slept together. On the third night he was beginning to feel tired and his work was suffering. On the fourth night, he tiptoed into bed and ignored her when she tapped on the door. The next day, she passed him icily in the hotel lobby. But that night, the handle of his door turned – the door was locked – and she knocked impatiently. He decided it was time to check out of the hotel.

If this episode had been told in court or in the newspapers, it would have ruined his popularity as surely as the Virginia Rappe case ruined Arbuckle's. Everyone who watched the little tramp flirting awkwardly with some pretty maiden would have found themselves thinking about Chaplin's 'sex orgies' with a beautiful stranger in a negligée and the illusion would have been destroyed. Yet Hollywood was no more a Sodom and Gomorrah than Broadway or Shaftesbury Avenue in London were. And Chaplin's methods of seduction were endearingly innocent compared to the 'casting couch' method inaugurated by Lewis J. Seltznick about 1914, in which the corridor to his office was guarded by men whose job was to ensure his privacy, and any young actress who wanted a part was expected to remove her clothes and lie down. (The method was later imitated by Harry Cohn of Columbia – the film star Louise Brooks described how her refusal to lie on the couch led to the end of her career in films.)

The next major Hollywood scandal occurred before Fatty Arbuckle had been acquitted of killing Virginia Rappe. William Desmond Taylor, an Irish actor and film director, was head of one of the most successful of the early Hollywood film companies, Famous Players-Lasky. (The trio of Jesse Lasky, Cecil B. De Mille and Samuel Goldfish – who later changed his name to Goldwyn – had virtually founded Hollywood as a film colony in 1914, when De Mille rented an old barn and made *The Squaw Man* there.) In 1922, Taylor was forty-five years old; he had the kind of thin, keen face that would have made him ideal for the part of Sherlock Holmes. He looked and spoke like a typical English aristocrat. On 2 February 1922, his valet entered the living room at 7.30 in the morning to find his master lying dead on the floor, with two bullet holes in his back. Investigations revealed that the film star Mabel Normand, Chaplin's first leading lady in Keystone, had been with him for an hour the previous evening. Another Chaplin leading lady – and girlfriend – Edna Purviance, had rung his doorbell about an hour later but received no reply. It looked as if a killer had been waiting for Mabel Normand to leave. When the police began investigating Taylor's love life, they found that he seemed to have had affairs with half the beauties in Hollywood. Mabel Normand had written him passionate love letters; as had twenty-year-old Mary Miles Minter – and, in fact, her mother. Silken undergarments belonging to many different women were found in his bedroom – apparently left as mementoes by his mistresses. Mary Miles Minter played the same kind of 'little girl' parts as Mary Pickford and Olive Thomas, and was another symbol of girlhood innocence. When handkerchiefs with the monogram MMM were found in Taylor's bedroom and newspaper reporters revealed that she was not twenty but thirty, her career came to a sudden end. Taylor's murderer was never found but it seems likely that it was a woman. Many clues were destroyed when Zukor and other Famous Players executives descended on Taylor's home and incinerated love letters and other telling evidence. The police found pornographic photographs showing Taylor in the act of lovemaking with a number of female stars.

At the funeral, Mary Miles Minter kissed the corpse on the lips, then announced that the corpse had whispered, 'I shall always love you, Mary.'

A new dimension was added to the scandal by the discovery that Taylor's previous valet had been a homosexual (like his present one, Peavy), who had forged cheques in his name, smashed up his car, and burgled his home twice. Was Taylor a bisexual who was being blackmailed? This mystery was cleared up when it was discovered that the previous valet was Taylor's brother, an actor who had fallen on hard times.

Further shock was caused when it became evident that Taylor had been a drug addict. He also seems to have spent much of his time at parties where men dressed as women – the collection of underwear seemed to hint at transvestite tendencies.

The final blow to Mabel Normand's career came a year later, when her chauffeur shot one of her admirers. Cortland Dines, at the home of Edna Purviance. It was clear that she was having affairs with both men. An article in *Good Housekeeping* suggested that she was too 'adulterated' (perhaps a pun) for domestic consumption and her career foundered.

Startling new information came to light in 1967 when the director King Vidor decided it would be worth resurrecting the forty-five-year-old tragedy and turning it into a movie. His investigations revealed that the case was far more complicated than it looked. Vidor soon came to suspect that Taylor was not what he appeared to be; the evidence indicated that the insatiable Don Juan was, in fact, a homosexual – possibly with a taste for young boys procured by his valet. And at least one Hollywood journalist was able to tell him authoritatively that the killer was Mary Miles Minter's mother Charlotte, who like everyone else, was unaware of Taylor's true sexual inclinations. Charlotte was not only fixated on Taylor; she was also quite determined that her daughter – who was also her meal ticket –

would not get involved with any man. It seems that on the evening in question, Mary was having a tête-à-tête with Taylor when Mabel Normand turned up; so Mary fled into hiding. Her mother became increasingly irritable, and finally went looking for her with a pistol. She saw Mabel Normand emerge from Taylor's house, then peered in through the window and saw her daughter coming out of hiding. This was too much, and she stalked in and shot the dastardly seducer – in the back, having made him raise his arms.

So what about all the stories of underwear and pornographic pictures? These, apparently, were the work of the film studio's publicity department, which arrived at the house before the police, and promptly went into action to throw up a heavy smokescreen – according to Vidor, involving widespread bribery. Vidor was so upset by his discoveries that he hid his notes in a tin box in his garage, where they were discovered many years later by an investigative journalist, Sidney Kirkpatrick, who eventually told the full story in his book *A Cast of Killers*.

The newspapers of the millionaire tycoon William Randolph Hearst took every opportunity to thunder about the immorality of Hollywood; they continued to make the most of Fatty Arbuckle's problems even after he had been acquitted. Hollywood moguls felt that they had to do something quickly to improve the image of the film capital. An organization called the Motion Picture Producers and Distributors of America was formed and Will H. Hays, who was Postmaster-General in Harding's administration (*see* page 393), was appointed head of the organization and censor-in-chief at a salary of $100,000 a year. It was only later that it emerged that Hays himself was a man of dubious moral standards – he had accepted gifts and 'loans' of a quarter of a million dollars in exchange for his part in getting the unsuitable Harding into the White House. But at least his appointment averted censorship by the federal government. After Hays became Hollywood's conscience, a 'morality clause' was inserted into most contracts, stating that any action likely to result in public scandal would be a sufficient reason for rescinding the contract. But the double standard continued to prevail. Cecil B. De Mille insisted that his stars should regulate their personal life so that 'any degrading or besmirching' behaviour should be avoided. However, he himself was known to make full use of his position to sleep with female stars, while his religious films always included a sinful orgy and an undressing scene in the bath-house.

In the month Hays was appointed – March 1922 – Famous Players suffered another major blow when their popular leading man Wallace Reid was consigned by his wife to a private nursing home. The studio told the Press he was suffering from overwork, but Reid's wife Florence preferred honesty and admitted that her husband was a morphine addict. In 1919 Reid had suffered head injuries in a rail crash and had been given morphine to ease the pain; he became an addict and accelerated his breakdown with heavy drinking. He was in a padded cell for much of the time until his painful death in 1923.

Juanita Hansen, one of the original Mack Sennett comediennes, was a victim of the Reid scandal. Her name was discovered in a letter from a doctor from whom she had sought treatment, and she was arrested and held in jail for three days to determine whether she was still on drugs. In fact, she had been cured but her arrest destroyed her career. She later launched a foundation to help narcotics addicts.

Other drug scandals followed. In 1923, Barbara La Marr, the actress who had played the beautiful but villainous Lady de Winter opposite Douglas Fairbanks in *The Three Musketeers*, died of a drug overdose. The studio tried to blame her death on dieting but the truth soon came out. Alma Rubens, star of *East Lynne* and *Show Boat*, suffered a 'brainstorm' when her doctor tried to incarcerate her in a private sanatorium in 1929, and stabbed a gas station attendant. Released from an asylum for the insane, she announced her intention of making a comeback but was arrested for being in possession of forty cubes of morphine. She died two weeks later in January 1931.

Hollywood was treading a tightrope. America was enjoying the age of jazz and bootleg liquor, and the film audiences wanted to know all about it. The Hays office wanted 'virtue' but the public wanted sin. In 1921, a young unknown called Rudolph Valentino created a sensation by the manner in which he danced with Helen Domingues in *Four Horsemen of the*

Apocalypse – he made it look as though they were having sex or were about to vanish to the nearest bedroom. In his next film *The Sheik*, the lustful gleam in his eye as he lifted Agnes Ayres clear of the ground left no doubt whatever that she was about to be subjected to a long-drawn-out rape. But Valentino's private life was unhappy; both his wives proved to be lesbians – the first deserted him on their wedding night. A newspaper article calling him a 'pink powder puff' plunged him into gloom and he died from discouragement as much as from a perforated ulcer. Thousands of women mourned his death on 23 August 1926; some even committed suicide.

The female equivalent of Valentino was Clara Bow, who became a symbol of the jazz age in 1927 when she starred in Elinor Glyn's film *It*. Elinor Glyn was herself a symbol of liberated womanhood; her novel *Three Weeks* is about a young Englishman who has a three-week orgy with a princess before she marries a decrepit old king. The book sold five million copies in 1907. A popular rhyme of the time ran:

> Would you like to sin
> With Elinor Glyn
> On a tiger skin?
> Or would you prefer
> With her to err
> On some other fur?

No doubt this was a reference to the famous seduction scene on a tiger-skin rug. After *It*, Clara Bow became the 'It' girl – 'it' being some indefinable quality that made a woman irresistible. She became the archetypal 'flapper' – the zany young lady who rushed from party to party gulping cocktails and shrieking with laughter. ('Flapper' at first referred to any innocent teenager whose pigtail, tied with a bow, flapped as she ran about; by the 1920s it simply meant any unconventional young lady.) For the studio, the problem was that Clara's private life was a little too much like the roles she played on screen. She was the co-respondent in a divorce case, when the wife of her physician alleged that he found it necessary to remove all his own clothes before examining Clara. Clara was forced to pay $30,000 for alienating the doctor's affections. She was also the mistress of B. P. Schulberg, the man who launched her into stardom. He came to refer to her as 'crisis-a-day Clara'. There was the occasion when she wandered into a gaming casino at Lake Tahoe and played blackjack, then roulette. She was convinced that her chips were worth 50 cents each when they were, in fact, worth $100. She ended by signing a cheque for $24,000. The next day, on the advice of Schulberg, she stopped the cheque. Menacing bruisers called on her, then on Schulberg; but behind the curtains in Schulberg's office were two concealed policemen, who overheard a threat to throw sulphuric acid in Clara's face. The bruisers were placed in handcuffs. Schulberg and Clara needed police protection for some months after this incident. The newspaper stories portraying Clara as a bad loser tarnished her image as a 'bright young thing'.

Then came the Wall Street crash and bright young things ceased to be admired by families on the breadline. The advent of talkies further damaged Clara's image: the fans had imagined her as the kind of girl whose father owned a mansion on Long Island and the sound of a flat Brooklyn accent issuing from that inviting cupid's bow of a mouth was a disillusionment.

The final crisis came in the form of a lady named Daisy De Voe, who became a secretary-companion for three years standing between Clara and the world. A young actor named Rex Bell fell in love with Clara and became increasingly suspicious of Miss De Voe. After inducing Clara to fire her, he obtained a warrant to open Daisy's bank vault; it was found to be stuffed with Clara Bow's jewellery and records of endless transfers from Clara's special bank account into Miss De Voe's – Daisy had the power to sign cheques on Clara's account.

Threatened with the law, Miss De Voe tried to blackmail the studio for $125,000 in exchange for Clara's love letters from the numerous stars with whom she had had affairs – these included Gary Cooper, Eddie Cantor and Bela Lugosi. Since Clara's career had taken a downward turn, the studio felt she was not worth that much money. Miss De Voe was told to publish and be damned. The court case was a sensation; with so many irrelevant revelations about Clara's bedroom behaviour that the judge had to remind Daisy that it was she who was on trial, not Clara. She was found guilty and sentenced to eighteen months in jail. When she emerged, she took her revenge by selling a lengthy series on Clara's love life to a Hearst scandal sheet. It included such revelations as a description of the time Clara had given herself to a whole football team, including a young man called Marion Morrison (who became John Wayne). By mutual agreement, the 'It' girl and her studio tore up her contract. As a result Clara had a nervous breakdown – the first of many. She married her admirer Rex Bell and moved to a ranch in Nevada, where a combination of alcohol and sleeping pills induced a weight problem and more nervous breakdowns. She spent much of the rest of her life (she died in 1965) in sanatoriums. Her career had ended when she was twenty-six.

The star who replaced Clara Bow as Paramount's major attraction was twenty years Clara's senior and her sex life was just as uninhibited, if more private. Born about 1886, Mae West was billed as 'the Baby Vamp' before she was a teenager. In 1926, starring on Broadway in her own play *Sex*, she was jailed for ten days on obscenity charges. She followed it up with a play called *Drag* about homosexuals, which she decided not to risk on Broadway. She then scored an enormous success in her play *Diamond Lil*. In her first film, *Night After Night* (a typical Mae West title) she uttered one of her classic lines – when a hat check girl says 'Goodness, what beautiful diamonds!' she replies (in her sexy drawl), 'Goodness had nothing to do with it.' She had the gift of making sex funny. Middle-aged men and women chuckled when she sang, 'I like a man who takes his time'. After *She Done Him Wrong* (1933) she became identified with the line (addressed to Cary Grant), 'Come up and see me sometime.' (In fact, it was 'Come up sometime, see me.') Her films were a tremendous success and she saved Paramount (Zukor's company) from bankruptcy. But the innuendoes scandalized the Hays office and caused a tightening up of regulations. They refused to permit dialogue like:

MAE: I like sophisticated men to take me out.
MAN: I'm not really sophisticated.
MAE: You're not really out yet either.

When her film *It Ain't No Sin* was advertised on Broadway, a squad of priests marched up and down with a poster: Yes It Is. The title had to be changed to *Belle of the Nineties*. For her next film, Will Hays appointed a censor to stay on the set; despite this, she managed to get away with lines like, 'A man in the house is worth two in the street,' and 'It's better to be looked over than overlooked.' But in a later film, *Every Day's a Holiday*, she lost at least two of her best lines: 'I wouldn't even lift my veil for that guy' and 'I wouldn't let him touch me, even with a ten-foot pole.' Even so, lines like: 'Beulah, peel me a grape' and 'It's not the men in my life that count; it's the life in my men', entered the public domain. Finally driven to bowdlerize her material by a combination of the Hays office and the Hearst Press, she returned to the theatre. At the age of sixty-eight, a cabaret act, in which she was surrounded by musclemen, ran for three years.

The scandal caused by Mae West was all on the screen. She was known to love hulking, muscular males, but she was discreet about them. Hollywood's other sex image, Jean Harlow, had indiscretion thrust upon her by the suicide of her husband, Paul Bern, production assistant of 'wonder boy' Irving Thalberg at MGM. Bern was a soft-spoken intellectual who treated women as if they were ladies in King Arthur's court. He had been wildly and romantically in love with Barbara La Marr and was rumoured to have attempted suicide when she died of a drugs overdose. In 1932, after the highly successful première of *Grand Hotel*, Bern drove Jean Harlow to see his home and as they drank sherry by his swimming pool he talked at length about wine. Harlow later told her director why she liked Bern, 'He explains things and lets me know I've got a brain. He's different and doesn't talk fuck, fuck, fuck, all the time.' Two months later Bern and Harlow were married.

Jean Harlow was Hollywood's latest sex symbol, the 'blonde bombshell'. She attracted attention in a Laurel and Hardy film in which she lost her skirt when it caught in a door; she became famous in 1930 in Howard Hughes's *Hell's Angels*. Her conversation was laced with obscenities and she looked and sounded like a gangster's moll. In fact, she was intelligent (she wrote a more-than-passable novel), sensitive and a delightful comedienne.

Three months after the marriage, on 5 September 1932, Bern shot himself in the garden of his house in Benedict Canyon. He left a note saying:

Unfortunately this is the only way to make good the frightful wrong I have done you and to wipe out my frightful humiliation.
    Paul
PS. You understand last night was only a comedy.

On the previous evening, apparently, he had gone into their bedroom wearing an enormous artificial phallus. Harlow had burst into shrieks of laughter. Bern had laughed too and together they slashed the phallus to pieces with scissors and flushed it down the lavatory. Was this what Bern was referring to? If so, the implication was obviously that he was impotent and that he had intended to improve his wife's sex life with the dildo. But Harlow denied that Bern was impotent. Bern's brother Henry, however, was able to provide a more plausible explanation. For five years, Bern had lived in the Algonquin Hotel in New York with another attractive blonde, Dorothy Millette, who was known as Mrs Paul Bern. She had had a nervous breakdown and suffered amnesia; she was confined in a Connecticut sanatorium and doctors agreed her condition was incurable. But it was not. When Dorothy Millette came out of hospital, she learned that her 'husband' was now married to Jean Harlow. She wrote to him and told him she was coming to California.

On the evening before Bern's suicide, neighbours heard sounds of a quarrel near the swimming pool. A chauffeur-driven limousine with a veiled woman had been seen in the area. It seems probable that Dorothy Millette arrived at the house late at night and there was a quarrel. The 'wrong' Bern was referring to in his suicide note was probably the scandal that would be unleashed by Dorothy's public denunciations. (In America, a couple need to live together for five years to achieve a common-law marriage so Dorothy would have been able to bring a charge of bigamy.)

On the day after Bern blew his brains out, Dorothy Millette boarded the steamer that left San Francisco for Sacramento and threw herself overboard. In her hotel room were found a number of letters from Bern, typed by his secretary, all courteous but formal.

Oddly enough, what frightened the studio was not that Harlow's reputation would be ruined by the scandal, but that people might feel sorry for her, which would destroy her image as the hard-boiled blonde-on-the-make. But nothing of the sort happened, for Louis B. Mayer stopped the scandal before it began. Her love life continued to be unhappy; a marriage to cameraman Harold Rosson – sixteen years her senior – lasted only eight months. After that, she fell in love with her co-star William Powell – twenty years her senior. But their relationship was stormy, punctuated by quarrels, and he declined to marry her on the grounds that he had already been married to one blonde bombshell – Carole Lombard – and was too old to start again. On Saturday, 29 May 1937, she began feeling ill on the set of *Saratoga* and returned home. Her mother, who was a Christian Scientist, declined to call a doctor; she died a week later of uremic poisoning, at the age of twenty-six.

In 1960, the screen writer Ben Hecht provided an interesting footnote to the Bern case when he stated in *Playboy* that Bern had been murdered – almost certainly by Dorothy Millette – and that the studio had forged the suicide note.

Hollywood's most publicized scandal of the 1930s was the divorce of Mary Astor from her husband, Dr Franklyn Thorpe. Mary Astor had a sad, dark-eyed prettiness that made her look vulnerable. Appearances were deceptive: her diary revealed that she was a highly dominant lady who thoroughly enjoyed sex. The diary was found in her underwear drawer and when Dr Thorpe opened it, his eye fell on the words: '. . . remarkable staying power; I don't know how he does it.' The man referred to was the playwright George S. Kaufman, co-author of the Marx Brothers' film *A Night at the Opera* and (later) of *The Man Who Came to Dinner*. Mary's diary recorded how she 'fell like a ton of bricks when she first met Kaufman. He kissed her for the first time in a taxi on the way to the theatre and during the third act 'my hand wasn't in my own lap . . . It's been years since I felt up a man in public but I just got carried away.' The couple had then hastened back to George's flat and settled down to an all-night lovemaking session. 'Once George lays down his glasses he is *quite* a different man. His powers of recuperation are amazing, and we made love all night long . . . It all worked perfectly, and we shared the fourth climax at dawn.' She described how 'we went frequently to 73rd Street [Kaufman's flat] where he fucked the living daylights out of me.' When Kaufman came to Hollywood, Mary hastened to his hotel. 'He greeted me in pajamas and we flew into each other's arms. He was rampant in an instant, and in a few moments it was just like old times . . . he tore out of his pajamas and I never was undressed by anyone so fast in all my life . . . It was wonderful to fuck the entire sweet afternoon away.' And when they went to Palm Springs together, she recorded: 'Ah, desert night – with George's body plunging into mine, naked under the stars.'

Dr Thorpe's reaction was to beg his wife to break off the affair; with tears in his eyes he pleaded that he needed her. Mary's reaction was impatience; she was determined to continue to test George's staying power for the remainder of his stay in Hollywood. She moved out of her Beverly Hills mansion and Dr Thorpe proceeded to file for divorce. At the trial, in July 1936, the judge declined to allow the diary to be read aloud in court – he later ordered it to be burned – but the doctor's lawyers leaked extracts to the press, including the desert-night quotation, which were printed with asterisks in the appropriate places.

For a while, it looked as if Mary Astor's career was finished. It would have been if she had been identified with the kind of parts played by Mary Pickford but her screen image already had a touch of sin in it – she had played Dreiser's *Jenny Gerhardt* – and her fans found these revelations piquant rather than disgusting. Mary went on to play a number of ladies of doubtful morals, like Brigid O'Shaughnessy in *The Maltese Falcon*.

The effect of the divorce case on Kaufman is not known but Miss Astor's recommendations can scarcely have done his love life any harm.

In the last weeks of 1935, Hollywood had another murder mystery to rival the death of William Desmond Taylor. The lovely Thelma Todd had become Miss Massachusetts in 1921. She threw up a job as a schoolteacher to make her way to Hollywood and in due course showed her talents as a comedienne opposite the Marx Brothers – in *Monkey Business* and *Horse Feathers* – and Laurel and Hardy – in *Fra Diavolo*. In 1932 she married an agent named Di Cicco but divorced him two years later. In 1935, she had decided to give up films and go into the restaurant business and she and a director named Roland West co-managed Thelma Todd's Roadside Rest, on the Coast Highway. Thelma was living with West although he was already married. On Saturday, 14 December 1935, Stanley Lupino and his daughter Ida gave a party for Thelma at the Trocadero; Thelma's former husband Di Cicco turned up and there was a quarrel. In the early hours of Sunday morning, Thelma was driven back to her home in Santa Monica. More than twenty-four hours later, at 10.30 on Monday morning, she was found dead in her car in the garage above her beach restaurant. There was blood on her face but she had died of carbon-monoxide poisoning. Yet her evening slippers showed no sign of having climbed 270 rough concrete stairs to the garage. West finally admitted that he and Thelma had quarrelled violently after she returned home that Sunday morning and that he had pushed her out of the front door; neighbours had heard her kicking the door and shouting obscenities. The inference was that she had gone to the garage and switched on the ignition. But why, in that case, were her clothes so rumpled, as if in a struggle? And what of the witnesses, including West's wife, who claimed to have seen her alive on Sunday, driving a Packard with a dark, handsome man beside her?

The Grand Jury brought in a verdict of 'death due to carbon-monoxide poisoning'. Her lawyer insisted that she had been murdered on the orders of Lucky Luciano, who had tried to take over the upper storey of Thelma's Roadside Rest to set up a crooked gambling establishment; she had turned down his offer. But at the mention of Luciano's name, Thelma's director Hal Roach insisted he was perfectly satisfied with the suicide verdict. The police received a telegram from Ogden, Utah, stating that Thelma's killer was in a hotel there but they did nothing about it.

One theory of her death, noted by Kenneth Anger, in his delightful but inaccurate *Hollywood Babylon*, is that she was murdered by Roland West, who was getting tired of the relationship and of the financial problems associated with the restaurant. According to this theory, West persuaded a girlfriend to knock on the door and scream, while he knocked out Thelma inside before she was carried to the garage and left to die. West himself never made another film after Thelma's death, and died, forgotten, in 1952.

Whether she was killed by West or by a Luciano henchman, or by some unknown man who drove her into the garage and left the ignition running, there seems little doubt that Thelma Todd was murdered. Her death remains a mystery.

For the remainder of the 1930s, Hollywood managed to keep out of serious trouble. The moguls found it very hard to get used to the idea that scandal did not necessarily mean public outrage and the banning of films. It came to them as a pleasant surprise after Errol Flynn was found not guilty of rape in 1943. Flynn had become famous playing the swashbuckling lead in *Captain Blood* in 1935, and by 1942 he was one of Hollywood's most successful male actors. That he was sexually insatiable he admits himself in *My Wicked, Wicked Ways*. Director Vincent Sherman felt that Flynn had a basic urge to debase women and tells how Flynn brought two prostitutes on to the set. When he asked how he could find the energy after a hard day's work, Flynn explained, 'I just lie there reading the trade papers while they work on me.'

In *Bring on the Empty Horses*, David Niven tells an amusing story that indicates the swiftness of Flynn's technique. After suffering from one of Flynn's practical jokes, Niven planned revenge. A writer friend mentioned that his aunt and niece were coming from Ohio, and suggested bringing them to the establishment shared by Flynn and Niven for drinks. In fact, the 'aunt' was a 35-year-old prostitute, while the niece was a beautiful whore of seventeen. Aunt and niece were introduced to Flynn, then the telephone rang, and the writer announced that he had to return to the hotel to collect the girl's mother.

Niven, together with the writer and the 'aunt', watched outside the window as Flynn grabbed the girl without further ado, pushed her on to the settee and raised her skirts above her head. The girl had been instructed to hold on to her panties for a few minutes but Flynn overcame this obstacle within seconds. Shortly afterwards, the 'aunt' strode into the room and shrieked: 'Eunice, what are you doing?', and the girl peeped out from under Flynn and replied: 'I don't know, mom. Ask Mr Flynn.' The 'aunt' retorted: 'Mr Flynn, get off my daughter immediately and explain yourself . . .' Eunice was sent out of the room suitably discomfited, whereupon the 'aunt' made a grab for Flynn's flies, explaining: 'I sent Eunice out because I want a bit of that myself.'

On 27 September 1942, Flynn drove to a party in Bel Air. Towards dusk, a car with half a dozen teenagers arrived. Among these was a studio messenger boy named Armand Knapp and his seventeen-year-old girlfriend named Betty Hansen. Betty drank too much and at one point, flopped on to Flynn's lap, while he continued the conversation over her head. At dinner, she had to rush out of the room to be sick. Afterwards, Flynn suggested she should come up to the bathroom attached to his bedroom; there he told her he thought she should have a sleep. Acording to Betty, she lay on a bed and Flynn began to undress her, removing everything but her shoes. She explained that she thought he intended to tuck her up in bed. Then Flynn removed all his own clothes, except his shoes, and proceeded to make love to her for half an hour. One of the girls who had brought Betty to the party came upstairs to look for her; by this time Betty had douched herself in the bathroom and was back in bed while Flynn was taking a shower. The next day, Betty told her sister that Flynn had seduced her and was taken into protective custody in Juvenile Hall.

The District Attorney recalled that fourteen months earlier, another seventeen-year-old named Peggy Satterlee had claimed that she had been raped by Flynn on his yacht. Flynn later insisted that the DA was inspired by a determination to 'clean up' Hollywood and felt that this was his opportunity. On 11 January 1943, Flynn appeared in court. He was defended by the brilliant lawyer Jerry Giesler. Betty described how she had allowed Flynn to remove her tight jeans in the belief that he was putting her to bed. Giesler asked her whether she still believed this as Flynn removed her panties and she said yes. 'When did you first think about sexual intercourse?', asked Giesler. The court roared with laughter when she replied, 'When I had sexual intercourse with him.' Without much effort, Giesler induced her to contradict herself. She had told the juvenile officers that she had undressed herself; now she said Flynn had undressed her. She flatly denied that she had helped him, then admitted that she had given him some assistance in removing her shirt. Asked if she had helped remove her panties she said, 'I might have.' Finally, Giesler obliged her to admit that when she had been 'raped' by Flynn, she was already in trouble with the juvenile officers for twice committing an act of oral sex on Armand Knapp.

After this, Peggy Satterlee gave her evidence: how she had been on a trip on Flynn's yacht; how she had climbed into bed in her underskirt and panties and how Flynn had come into her cabin, got into bed with her and had intercourse with her. Flynn seems to have used the same technique as with 'Eunice', pushing her underskirt over her head, her panties down, then making love to her for half an hour. After this they went up on deck and he brought her a glass of milk. The following day she swam with him and they had pictures taken together for *Life*. That evening, he invited her to his state-room to look at the moon through a porthole. Still in some pain from the previous night – she had been a virgin – she tried to resist but Flynn insisted that, since he had possessed her once, he could see no reason why he shouldn't do so again. When he tried to remove her slacks, she fought so hard that the bed curtains were pulled down. Even when Flynn was inside her, she struggled so hard that his penis came out. This was damaging evidence. So was the testimony of a police doctor that Peggy's genitals were bruised and swollen and that the hymen was newly torn. But Giesler scored a point when he pointed out that Peggy could have seen the moon just as well from the deck and that in any case, she could not have looked at the moon through the porthole since it was on the other side of the yacht. He also managed to bring out in evidence the fact that, in the following year, Peggy Satterlee had had an abortion – then an illegal operation – and that the charge still hung over her. The implication was clear: that both girls were hoping for leniency from the police in exchange for their testimony against Flynn.

In the witness box, Flynn denied everything. If the girls had been older, he might have argued that the intercourse occurred with their consent but since they were both under age at the time of the offence, he could still have been convicted of statutory rape. So he perjured himself in the witness box. And in due course, the jury found him not guilty. A hysterical woman rushed over to him and kissed him on the lips. And to the unspeakable relief of Warner Brothers, the scandal actually seemed to increase his popularity: his films *Desperate Journey* and *Gentleman Jim* played to crowded cinemas.

Most writers on the case take the view that Flynn had been 'set up' by a couple of 'tramps'; but no one who studies the transcript of the case can take this simplistic attitude. Betty Hansen had just been violently sick, so she was probably telling the truth when she said that she objected to Flynn's lovemaking. Peggy Satterlee had been a virgin; she may or may not have been willing to surrender her virginity to Flynn in due course, but it seems clear that he did not give her the choice. And her story of her struggle to avoid a second bout of lovemaking when she was still sore from the first has a ring of truth.

In his autobiography *My Wicked, Wicked Ways*, Flynn admits having sex with Peggy Satterlee, insisting that he had no idea she was under eighteen. On the delicate question of Betty Hansen, he avoids difficult questions by simply omitting to mention her appearance on the witness stand.

This close brush with the law seems to have taught Flynn nothing about the dangers of having intercourse without first asking the girl's permission. During the trial he noticed a pretty girl serving behind the tobacco stand in the Hall of Justice. Her name was Nora Eddington. Flynn persuaded her to go out with him and discovered that she was an innocent virgin who regarded herself as engaged to a marine. He bided his time, took her out, and tried repeatedly and unsuccessfully to steer her towards the bedroom. One night, after drinking heavily (and, according to one biographer, taking cocaine) he took her back to his house, pushed her into the bedroom and tore off her clothes. Then he undressed and raped her. She testified, 'I didn't know what was happening. I was terrified. Suddenly he was thrusting into me. It was like a knife . . . There was blood everywhere.' Afterwards, Flynn wept and begged forgiveness; Nora married him but then, when she discovered he was incapable of staying faithful, divorced him.

Flynn's career went downhill in the fifties, largely as the result of heavy drinking that caused the once-handsome face to become fleshy and coarse. He died in 1959 of a heart attack at the age of fifty. In 1980, in a book called *Errol Flynn, The Untold Story*, a writer named Charles Higham accused Flynn of being bisexual and a German spy. It is impossible to tell whether there is any truth in the bisexuality charge – Higham alleges that Flynn's frequent trips to Mexico were spent in pursuit of teenage boys – but the spy charge certainly remains unproven. Flynn was apparently a close friend of a certain Dr Hermann Friedrich Erben, whom Higham describes as 'one of the most important and ingenious Nazi agents'. Flynn apparently met him on the island of New Britain, in the Pacific, after Flynn had been shipwrecked in 1933. Subsequently, Erben seems to have turned up frequently in Hollywood. But even if, as Higham insists, Flynn had Nazi sympathies, it is impossible to see how, as a film star, he had any opportunity to do espionage work for Erben. Higham tells a story of how Flynn and Erben went to Spain during the civil war, their intention being to interview Germans fighting for the loyalists, and to report their names to Berlin, so their families could be persecuted. But it hardly seems necessary to send a famous film star from America for this purpose as an ordinary German infiltrator would have served just as well. Higham's account of Erben makes it clear that, for an 'important and ingenious Nazi agent' he was unbelievably incompetent and regrettably accident-prone. The reaction of most reviewers to Higham's 'untold story' was one of understandable scepticism; they found it difficult to credit the hard-drinking, sexually insatiable Hollywood playboy with the firmness of purpose necessary for a spy. It is true that there have been such spies, but none of them made highly successful films in their spare time. Whatever the final judgment on his life and personality, Errol Flynn will continue to live on in folk memory for the satisfyingly descriptive catch-phrase 'In like Flynn'.

At the time Flynn was deflowering Peggy Satterlee on the *Sirocco*, Hollywood was contemplating another evolving scandal with a mixture of eagerness and alarm. Hollywood's two leading gossip columnists were Louella Parsons and Hedda Hopper; the former worked for the multi-millionaire newspaper magnate William Randolph Hearst, the inventor of 'yellow journalism' (i.e. stories of doubtful authenticity but high scandal value). Early in 1940, the young theatrical director Orson Welles had arrived in Hollywood and before the year was out, the town was full of rumours that he was making a film based on the life of a well-known newspaper publisher. The obvious candidate was Hearst, although no one was sure (since there was only one script and Welles slept with that under his pillow). Hearst was one of the most powerful men in Hollywood – in fact, in America – so there were expectations of an explosion. To Louella Parsons, Welles solemnly denied that his film was about her boss. But when he invited her rival Hedda Hopper to a private screening of *Citizen Kane*, she watched it with increasing dismay. It was not a matter of 'accidental resemblance' to Hearst; this was a carefully considered, deliberately unfair attack on the arch-capitalist tycoon. Hearst was an old friend of Hedda Hopper's. 'You won't get away with it', said Hedda. 'You want to bet?' said Welles.

In making *Citizen Kane* Welles had every intention of creating a scandal. He had, in a sense, built his career on scandal, and so far it had done him no harm. His acting career began at the age of sixteen with a touch of deceit. He had presented himself at the stage door of the Gate Theatre in Dublin and announced himself as a star of the New York Theatre Guild. The theatre's director, Hilton Edwards, was not entirely deceived but liked the young man's cheek, and offered him a part in *Jew Süss*. Three years later he made his Broadway debut in Shakespeare. In 1937, he and John Houseman set up the Mercury Theatre project in New York; it was an attempt to transplant the left-wing theatre of Brecht and Weill to America. In July 1937, Welles had an opportunity to demonstrate his genius for improvisation and also for making the headlines. The theatre project had scheduled the production of Marc Blitzstein's satirical operetta *The Cradle Will Rock*, a violent attack on capitalism and glorification of trade unionism. At the last minute, the government cancelled the production. It happened so late that a queue had already formed outside the theatre. Welles told some of his actors to entertain them, while he tried to find a theatre. Finally a little man who had been trying to see Welles all day – and whom Welles had been avoiding because he looked like a process-server – managed to explain that he owned a theatre nearby which they could use. The whole audience of two thousand was led up Broadway to the Venice Theatre. A piano on a truck followed them. An Equity (union) ban prevented actors from appearing on stage but there was nothing to stop the actors from standing up in the audience and playing their parts, while Blitzstein himself played the piano on stage. A spotlight picked out each actor as he stood up. The evening was a sensation. The next morning, Welles was deluged with offers from other theatrical managers to present *The Cradle Will Rock* in exactly the same manner.

In the following year, Welles began presenting Mercury Theatre projects on the radio; for the fourth show he chose H. G. Wells's *War of the Worlds*. On hearing the recording, Welles decided it was dull and that the only way to improve it was to make it more 'newsy' by presenting it as a series of newsflashes. After the introduction (read by Welles), an announcer explained that the programme would be continued from the dance floor of a hotel. Then the music was interrupted by a newsflash about explosions on the planet Mars. A second newsflash announced a meteorite in New Jersey that had killed many people. After that, more news bulletins and on-the-spot reports described the arrival of the Martians, horrible leathery slugs with murderous ray guns.

Many people who switched on after the beginning were thrown into a panic. Families rushed out of their houses and took to the roads; others went and camped in the open.

Meanwhile, on the radio, the voice of President Roosevelt – in reality an actor – begged the nation not to panic. Before the end of the broadcast, the mayor of a mid-Western town had rung up to say that there were terrified mobs in the streets. The New York police department received 2,000 calls in fifteen minutes. The CBS network had to make broadcasts every ten minutes for the next twenty-four hours, reassuring America that the Martians had not really landed. Welles had achieved overnight fame – or, at least, notoriety.

It was inevitable that he should be invited to Hollywood and equally inevitable that he should think of his first film there in terms of scandal or sensationalism. His leftist affiliations suggested capitalism as a target and a super-capitalist as its subject. He chose one whose income was $15 million a year.

William Randolph Hearst, born 1863, was the son of a multi-millionaire owner of silver mines. He used his inherited fortune to become a press baron. In 1917, at the age of fifty-four, he had fallen in love with a Ziegfeld Follies girl, Marion Davies, a delightful blonde with a stutter and a sense of humour. He had set out to turn her into another Mary Pickford. He spent millions on her films. (When a friend told him there was money in the movie business Hearst replied drily, 'Yes, mine.')

Inevitably, the Hearst newspapers – he owned about forty – hailed every new Marion Davies film as a triumph. Unfortunately, Marion was no Mary Pickford; her real talent lay in light comedy, not drama. All her films lost money and Hearst's aggressive publicity campaigns alienated the public. Hearst was discreet about his affair but it became public knowledge in 1923 when a crooked attorney named Fallon, charged with corruption, stated in court that Marion Davies was the mother of twins and Hearst was the father. (The whole story was an invention.)

Three months after the Fallon trial, in November 1924, Hearst and Marion Davies were the subject of even more scandalous gossip. On 15 November a group of Hollywood celebrities was invited on to Hearst's yacht *Oneida* for the birthday party of the pioneer Western director Thomas Ince. Ince became ill, apparently with acute indigestion, and was put on a train for his home in Los Angeles. He died two days later of a heart attack. His body was cremated. But there were persistent rumours that Ince had been shot by Hearst, who had caught him making love to Miss Davies. The rumours were so persistent that the District Attorney felt obliged to investigate them. He concluded that they had no foundation. But inevitably, this only led to rumours that Hearst had paid out thousands of dollars to suppress the truth. In *Hollywood Babylon*, Kenneth Anger describes how Charlie Chaplin and Marion Davies had slipped off together to the lower deck and that when Hearst went looking for them, he found them *in flagrante delicto*. Marion screamed, 'M-m-m-murder!', which brought other guests rushing to the spot as Hearst ran for his diamond-studded revolver; when Hearst fired, it was Ince who dropped dead with a bullet in his brain.

In his autobiography, Chaplin insists that he was not even present on Hearst's yacht and explains that the rumours about Ince's death were absurd because he and Hearst went to see Ince two weeks before his death: 'He was very happy to see . . . us and believed he would soon be well.' Since Ince died only four days after being taken off Hearst's yacht, this story hardly disproves the 'ugly rumours'. Even a standard reference work like Ephraim Katz's *International Film Encyclopedia* states that 'Thomas Harper Ince was mysteriously and fatally injured aboard William Randolph Hearst's yacht . . . He died before regaining consciousness.' So it is just conceivable that the death of Ince occurred under suspicious circumstances.

All this explains why there was alarm and fury in the Hearst encampment when Hedda Hopper telephoned to say that *Citizen Kane* was a thinly disguised portrait of Hearst, complete with scandal. Hearst's film columnist Louella Parsons was asked to arrange a private screening and to take some lawyers along. Welles was delighted to oblige – his fellow actor George Coulouris believes that he had been hoping to create a scandal. Louella Parsons left the screening looking shattered and rushed to tell Hearst that he was being portrayed as a ruthless capitalist exploiter. Hearst immediately sent a telegram to the film's producer at RKO demanding that the film should be withheld pending legal action. The producer, George Schaefer, defiantly refused. There was panic in Hollywood; it was generally felt that if Hearst was offended, then his newspapers would boycott Hollywood films which might lead to the bankruptcy of some studios. Louis B. Mayer offered to pay RKO $800,000 – the cost of the film – to destroy it; Schaefer refused. Louella Parsons proceeded to attack Welles in her column, which was syndicated all over America. Her rival Hedda Hopper thereupon announced that she would devote six of her radio programmes to a biography of the young genius Orson Welles. The nationwide furore was a publicity godsend. When *Citizen Kane* was finally shown in April 1941, it was an immense critical success, one critic declaring it to be 'the finest film of all time'. (The truth is that *Citizen Kane* is rather a silly film, with its presupposition that the wicked newspaper magnate – the man who never loved anybody – has a sentimental yearning for childhood innocence, symbolized by his sledge 'Rosebud'. In fact – as Welles knew – 'Rosebud' was Hearst's pet name for Miss Davies's private parts.)

The scandal that Welles envisaged in *Citizen Kane* ('Newspaper Boss Caught In Singer's Love Nest') had no foundation in fact; apart from their one brush with scandal in the Fallon case, Marion and Hearst lived together as placidly as an elderly married couple until Hearst's death, at the age of eighty-eight, in 1951. It is an ironical footnote to the story that *Citizen Kane* was a box-office failure.

The year 1943 saw the downfall of the actress Frances Farmer, a determined individualist who frequently confessed that the only thing she liked about Hollywood was the money. She had won a trip to the Soviet Union in an essay competition when she was a student; when she came to New York in the late thirties, she acted in the Group Theatre, which (like Welles's Mercury) had strong leftist tendencies; she also acted in Clifford Odets's *Golden Boy*. A few decades later, she would have fitted perfectly comfortably into the anti-Vietnam war movement but in Hollywood in the forties, she was a misfit. Her increasing exasperation with the triviality of her Hollywood films led her to alienate 'old timers' like Zukor and she began drinking too much. In October 1942 she was arrested for drunken driving on the Pacific Highway and screamed abuse at the cop who arrested her. She was put on probation.

Arrested again for failing to report to her parole officer, she hid in a bathroom and was carried off naked by the police. At police headquarters she signed her occupation as 'cocksucker'. In court, the judge asked her about her drinking and she screamed: 'Listen, I put liquor in my milk, liquor in my coffee and liquor in my orange juice. What do you want me to do – starve to death?' The judge stood up and shouted out a sentence of 180 days. She screamed back, 'Have you ever had a broken heart?' (alluding to her stormy affair with Clifford Odets). Then she hurled an ink pot at the judge's head and was carried out kicking.

Her mother told the Press that this was only a publicity stunt but nevertheless declared her a mental incompetent and signed committal papers. In hospital, she was subjected to insulin shock treatment. For the most part, Hollywood was delighted with her downfall. Director William Wyler commented, 'The nicest thing I can say about Frances Farmer is that she is unbearable.' She spent much of the remainder of the forties in mental homes and although she made one film, *The Party Crashers* in 1958, never succeeded in making a 'comeback'. She died of cancer at the age of fifty-seven in 1970.

Chaplin's paternity case, already mentioned, occupied the headlines through much of 1943. He had suddenly lost his popularity when he appeared at a rally in New York demanding that the Allies open a second front to help the Russians. He records in his autobiography that after this, he suddenly ceased to be invited to the houseparties of the rich. The final verdict in the paternity case was paradoxical in that he was adjudged the father of Joan Barry's daughter although a blood test proved conclusively that it was impossible. Since he had admitted that he had been 'intimate' with Miss Barry, the court no doubt felt that he deserved to be the father.

In 1944, Chaplin was acquitted of transporting Miss Barry over state lines for immoral purposes and that year saw the suicide of one of Hollywood's most tempestuous actresses, Lupe Velez, at the age of thirty-six. Born in Mexico and educated in a Texas convent, she made her name starring opposite Douglas Fairbanks in *The Gaucho* in 1926. In 1929, she played in *Wolf Song* opposite Gary Cooper and had an affair with him. (Cooper's sex life seems to have been very nearly as eventful as Errol Flynn's – he made a habit of sleeping with his leading ladies; but since he was discreet about it and everyone liked him he managed to stay out of the gossip columns.) Cooper found her fiery temper too much for him and she transferred her affections to Johnny Weismuller, the Olympic swimmer who played Tarzan. Their married life was stormy – according to Kenneth Anger, 'She couldn't understand why Johnny would get mad when she'd flash her charms at Hollywood parties by flinging her dress over her head – she was always innocent of lingerie.' After her divorce from Weismuller, her love affairs became legendary – Anger calls her a 'man-addict'. Finally, heavily in debt, pregnant by her latest boyfriend (and barred from abortion by her Catholic upbringing), she swallowed seventy-five Seconal tablets and was found lying on her bed with her hands crossed on her breasts in the position of a sleeping madonna.

The news sensation of the summer of 1947 was the murder of the gangster Bugsy Siegel in the home of his mistress Virginia Hill, at 810 Linden Drive, Beverly Hills. Siegel was one of the major figures of Murder Incorporated, the Mafia organization headed by Luciano, and had the dubious distinction of turning Las Vegas into the gambling capital of the United States. Benjamin Siegel – known as 'Bugsy' because he appeared to become insane when he lost his temper – had been involved in many murders since he had shot Lucky Luciano's boss Joe Masseria – one of the old-fashioned style of gangster – to oblige Luciano. By the time he was twenty-five he had his own suite in the Waldorf-Astoria in New York – Luciano lived two floors above him. He was sent out to California as an emissary of Murder Inc., chosen, perhaps, because he was a friend of actor George Raft, whom he had known since childhood in Brooklyn. Soon the handsome, charming Siegel had forced his way into the drugs racket in California and had gained control of the movie extras and bit-part players. His sex life was also rumoured to be extremely active among the starlets – he had a reputation as a rapist in New York. His wife and family had moved west with him but Siegel always behaved like a bachelor. In November 1939,

Siegel and two more gangsters – Frankie Carbo and Whitey Krakower – were ordered to kill Harry ('Big Greenie') Greenberg, a New York mobster who had fled to California and was threatening to 'sing' to the DA. Greenberg was found dead outside his Los Angeles home late at night. In the following August, another member of Murder Inc., Allie Tannenbaum, had reason to believe that he was also on the death list and began to 'sing' to the DA of King County, New York, and implicated Siegel in the murder of 'Greenie'. In January 1942, Siegel and Carbo finally went on trial for the murder of Greenberg. They were defended by that Hollywood veteran Jerry Giesler, who was able to discredit Tannenbaum's testimony so effectively that Siegel was 'sprung'.

Siegel had been driving through the quiet little town of Las Vegas in 1945 when it struck him that this would be the ideal place for a gambling casino. He raised $6 million from the 'Syndicate', and built the Flamingo Hotel – his girlfriend, Virginia Hill's, nickname.

Luciano was deported from America in 1946. One year later, he called a meeting of members of the Syndicate in Havana, Cuba, whose crime was controlled by the Syndicate's 'accountant' Meyer Lansky. When Siegel was asked about repayment of $3 million, he lost his temper and stormed out of the room. Lansky was asked to talk sense into him but Siegel still refused to talk about repayment, no doubt pointing to the vast sums of money he had syphoned into Murder Inc. from the drugs racket in California.

At about ten o'clock in the evening of 20 June 1947, Siegel and some friends drove back from a Santa Monica seafood restaurant to Virginia Hill's home – she was away in Europe at the time. (She was a Syndicate courier.) As Siegel sat reading the *Los Angeles Times* on the settee, there was a sound of breaking glass and then the deafening roar of gunfire. Siegel had his nose shot off, his eyes blown out, and his vertebrae smashed; one eye was found on the other side of the room. At almost the same moment, a Syndicate member named Little Moey Sedway walked into the Flamingo Hotel in Las Vegas and shouted, 'We're taking over.' Few people attended Siegel's funeral and Jerry Giesler reflected that if he had not 'sprung'

Siegel five years earlier, the gangster would probably have still been alive.

In 1947, Hollywood had more serious problems than the occasional gang murder. The cold war had brought a wave of anti-communism. Senator Joseph McCarthy had not yet arrived on the scene – that would take another three years – but what would later become known as McCarthyism was already causing deep divisions in Hollywood.

In retrospect, it is easy to blame the Americans for over-reacting. But in the cold war climate of 1946, it seemed obvious that the Russians were hoping to take advantage of the chaos in Europe to implant communism from France to the Balkans. In due course, America would combat the growing threat with Marshall aid, which revitalized the economies of Europe. In the meantime, it struck many Americans that an enormous number of refugees who had fled from the Nazis were members of the communist party, and that they had implanted a communist 'fifth column' in their own country. The House Un-American Activities Committee, founded in 1938, was given a new lease of life in 1946. In Hollywood, the Motion Picture Alliance for the Preservation of American Ideals came into existence under the presidency of John Wayne. (He was followed by Hedda Hopper.) This was a direct result of a 'Reds under the bed' scare campaign initiated by New Hampshire congressman J. Parnell Thomas, who set out to prove that the communists had infiltrated the film industry.

Hollywood's problem had always been a certain tendency to view things simplistically, in terms of goodies and baddies. Its domination by a few powerful cliques also bred the conspiratorial mentality. In fact, very few actors or directors were deeply interested in politics. The problem was that those who were interested were usually the more intelligent ones and since many of them had been involved in the anti-fascist movement of the 1930s, it followed that their views were distinctly towards the left.

Thomas and his committee subpoenaed many actors and writers. Ten of the writers refused to tell the committee whether they had ever been communists and were sent to jail – they became known as 'The Hollywood Ten'. (Ironically, one of the ten, Dalton Trumbo, was to meet J. Parnell Thomas in jail – he had been sentenced for sharp practice concerning the payroll.) The thriller writer Dashiel Hammett was later sentenced to six months in jail for refusing to reveal names and all his books were allowed to go out of print. Charlie Chaplin was excused from appearing before the committee when he explained that he was simply a 'peace monger', but attacks on him in the Press led to the widespread banning of his latest film, *Monsieur Verdoux*. Many careers were ruined: John Garfield, Gale Sondergaard, Larry Parks (who had played the title role in *The Jolson Story*); many others – like Joseph Losey and Jules Dassin – found themselves unemployable in Hollywood and had to move abroad.

Humphrey Bogart, who was an individualist and a libertarian without having the slightest communist tendency, organized a protest group called The Committee for the First Amendment, which included Lionel Barrymore, John Ford, Gregory Peck, John Huston, Billy Wilder, Ira Gershwin, Gene Kelly, June Havoc and Danny Kaye. On 24 October 1947, a planeload of stars and directors, led by Bogart (acompanied by Lauren Bacall), flew to Washington, with press conferences *en route* at St Louis, Kansas City and Chicago. It was not a good idea. 'We went in there green and they beat our brains out', said Bogart later. 'In the shuffle we became adopted by the communists, and I ended up with my picture on the front page of the *Daily Worker* . . . That the trip was ill-advised and even foolish I am ready to admit . . .' Bogart was fortunate; he was the studio's biggest star. But many other of the three hundred members of his protest committee found themselves on a permanent blacklist that ended their careers in Hollywood.

The irony was that there were no real villains in this particular drama. The names who supported the Un-American Activities Committee – Ronald Reagan, John Wayne, Gary Cooper, Robert Taylor, Charles Coburn, Adolphe Menjou, George Murphy, Walt Disney, Howard Hughes – were equally sincere and well-meaning; they also regarded themselves as libertarians. It was basically a problem in communication – an art, paradoxically, in which Hollywood has never been skilled. The political scandal of 1947 was really a storm in a teacup, yet it came closer to destroying Hollywood than twenty-five years of sexual scandal.

In 1948, twenty-nine-year-old Carole Landis, star of the original version of *A Star is Born*, and described as having 'the best legs in town', told *Photoplay*, 'Every girl in the world wants to find the right man, someone who is sympathetic and understanding and helpful and strong, someone she can love madly. Actresses are no exception.' For Carole, the man who fitted these specifications was the English actor Rex Harrison, who was already married to Lilli Palmer. On 4 July 1948, in a fit of depression, Carole Landis took an overdose of sleeping tablets. One of the underlying causes of her depression may have been the fact that, although talented, she had never succeeded in starring in anything but second-rate B pictures.

A few weeks later, the studios had their biggest publicity headache since the Errol Flynn rape case. Late on the evening of 31 August 1948, Robert Mitchum, the idol of the 'bobby soxers', arrived at a party at the house of his friend Lila Leeds in Laurel Canyon, where everyone was smoking pot. Mitchum had only just lit up when the door burst open and two policemen rushed in. Mitchum was the major catch. RKO executives bit their nails at the thought of the moral outrage of American parents at the revelation that the hero of the teen-agers was a 'dope fiend'. Mitchum declined to worry. As a teenager he had been a convict in a Georgia chain gang, on a vagrancy charge, and had escaped; later he worked as a drop-hammer operator. He got into films by accident, as a result of wandering on to a 'Hopalong Cassidy' set, and the sleepy-eyed, menacing expression – the look of a born rebel – soon made him, together with Frank Sinatra, the dream-man of every underage girl. He had frequently remarked that acting was not a suitable job for a grown man; the thought of losing his public was, therefore, not entirely alarming.

He hired Jerry Giesler – it cost him $50,000 that he didn't possess – whose advice was not to enter a plea, either of guilty or not guilty. If he pleaded not guilty, it meant a lengthy trial and many revelations about pot-smoking in Hollywood that would be bad for the film industry in general. The minor disadvantage was that Mitchum would almost certainly draw a prison sentence. He decided to take the risk and the Press ground its collective teeth when Giesler announced in court that he would waive a jury trial. There was one bad moment for Mitchum when the judge announced that the sentence would be two years, followed by considerable relief when this was reduced to sixty days, with the rest on probation. Mitchum served his two months without complaint and had it shortened by a day for good behaviour. It emerged later that the whole thing had been set up by the police. The friend who had taken Mitchum to the party had been trying to persuade him to go all day. The police had hidden a microphone in the room and informed the Press in advance that they expected to arrest a major film star; they waited for Mitchum's arrival before bursting in.

The main question was how the fans would take it. In fact, it made no obvious difference to Mitchum's popularity – and neither did a great deal of bad publicity during the next decade about public brawls and a tendency to rip telephones off walls. It underlined the point that the public has no objection to stars behaving in private as they behave on the screen; the baddie who behaves like a baddie upsets no one. It is when the goodie behaves like a baddie that the fans ask for their money back.

As this recognition sank in, the whole concept of scandal became increasingly blurred in Hollywood. If 'bad behaviour' can, under the right circumstances, improve a star's image, then clearly it may be a waste of time to be good. In any case, the notion of what constituted a film star was changing. From 1920 onward, the women were expected to be glamorous and the men handsome and sophisticated. When twenty-three-year-old Marlon Brando created a sensation as the brutish working-class lout in *A Streetcar Named Desire* in 1947, the male image began to change. Brando talked in a mumble – a technique known as 'the Method' (which meant acting natural) – and slouched around with no attempt at athletic grace. In Hollywood he dressed in a rumpled T shirt and jeans and ate cherries out of a bag. His admirer James Dean improved on this image to the extent of taking out his penis on the set to urinate.

The public now seemed to expect its stars to behave scandalously and in 1952 a publisher named Robert Harrison decided to satisfy their expectations by launching a magazine called *Confidential*, whose first issue sold a quarter of a million copies. Its aim, quite simply, was to dig out the dirt on the stars – who was a nympho, who was a drug addict, who was sharing her boyfriend with her daughter, who was a homosexual or a lesbian. The financial success of the magazine was so enormous that Harrison could afford to pay spies considerable sums of money for a gossip-column item. The concealed tape recorder and the mini-camera took the place of the prying reporter whose manner invited a snub. What Harrison soon realized was that most stars prefer to minimize the danger by ignoring the attack – the principle utilized by Jerry Giesler in the case of Mitchum's arrest for pot-smoking. But finally, one of the victims decided the risk was worth it; after an article alleging nudist romps in a forest, Dorothy Dandridge sued *Confidential* for $2 million. Other stars followed suit. The movie chiefs realized that this could end as an unprecedented series of revelations about the private life of the stars and some of the more vulnerable – including Clark Gable – were hastily despatched on vacations to distant parts. All attempts by Hollywood moguls to hush up the scandal failed and the case came to court in August 1957. Dorothy Dandridge had dropped her charge, in exchange for a substantial out-of-court settlement. Maureen O'Hara moved into the front line. She sued *Confidential* because they had accused her of various indecent intimacies with a handsome South American in Grauman's Chinese Theatre. Her defence was that she had been in Spain on the date of the alleged indecencies and she was awarded $5,000. Liberace received an out-of-court settlement of $40,000. (Two years later, in England, he sued the *Daily Mirror* for implying he was a homosexual and received £8,000.) So many other stars received settlements that Harrison decided to call it quits and sold *Confidential* soon afterwards. Polly Gould, a member of his editorial staff, committed suicide the day before she was due to give evidence and it emerged later that she was virtually a 'double agent' selling the magazine's secrets to the DA and passing on the DA's secrets to the magazine.

After *Confidential*, the age of Hollywood scandal was virtually over. Stars realized that nothing short of murder was likely to cause adverse public reaction. Errol Flynn was one of the first to cash in with his autobiography *My Wicked, Wicked Ways*, and other stars followed suit. The next major Hollywood scandal did involve a murder. On 4 April, Good Friday, 1958, Jerry Giesler was summoned to the home of Lana Turner at 730 North Bedford Drive, where a corpse was lying on the floor, the stomach stained with blood. It was her gangster boyfriend, Johnny Stompanato. He had been fatally stabbed by Lana Turner's daughter, fourteen-year-old Cheryl, after hearing Stompanato threaten to painfully disfigure her mother.

Lana Turner's career had started at about the same age when she was playing truant from school, and sipping a milk shake in a drugstore on Sunset Boulevard, wearing a tight sweater. A journalist approached her and asked if she had ever thought of getting into the movies. Through an agent friend of the journalist, Lana (real name Mildred) achieved a bit-part in a film called *They Won't Forget* in which she was raped and murdered at an early stage. As 'the sweater girl' she achieved fame during World War II and became a favourite pin-up of American servicemen. Her first marriage to band-leader, Artie Shaw, lasted two months and caused her to have a nervous breakdown. The second husband, a young executive named Stephen Crane, asked her to dance for a bet, and married her nine days later; he was the father of Cheryl. Her third marriage was to a millionaire, Bob Topping; the fourth to the screen Tarzan, Lex Barker. There were also a number of well-publicized romances, with Frank Sinatra, Howard Hughes, Tyrone Power and Fernando Lamas, the Argentinian star. By the mid-1950s, her sweater-girl image had been outgrown and her careeer was foundering. It was after the break up of the marriage to Lex Barker that Johnny Stompanato, former bodyguard of gangster Mickey Cohen, telephoned her out of the blue – for a bet – and invited her out on a blind date. Stompanato was a muscular, hairy-chested specimen who was nick-named Oscar, apparently because a vital part of his anatomy was about the height of a Hollywood Oscar when upright. Like most dominating females, Lana apparently liked her men athletic and rough. On one occasion Stompanato told her, 'When I say hop, you'll hop; when I say jump, you'll jump.' Lana was not averse to obeying orders but when her own latent dominance surfaced, there were explosions.

It seems clear that there was a mutual obsession. When she came to England to star with Sean Connery, Stompanato followed her, and attempts to strangle her and threats to slash her with a razor led the police to have him deported. Back in America, she and Stompanato went on holiday to Acapulco, and then she returned in time to receive her academy award for her part in *Peyton Place*, a welcome upswing in her career.

On Good Friday 1958, Stompanato and Lana went to her home in Beverly Hills in a state of violent disagreement. The quarrel was so noisy that Cheryl was afraid he was about to attack her mother; she removed a carving knife from the kitchen drawer. The quarrel continued in Lana's bedroom and Cheryl looked in to see what was happening; her mother asked her to go away. But when her mother began to scream, Cheryl again looked in and saw Stompanato swinging at her mother with a coat on a coathanger. This time Cheryl rushed at him and, apparently, hit him in the stomach. Stompanato groaned, clutched at his stomach and collapsed. At this point, Lana Turner saw the carving knife in her daughter's hand.

A doctor was sent for and administered Adrenalin, while Lana tried the kiss of life. It was useless. Shortly afterwards, Stompanato's heart stopped.

The case made all the front pages and fuel was added to the flames when Stompanato's former boss Mickey Cohen handed over a dozen of Lana Turner's love letters to the Press. The scandal sheets hastened to print them in facsimile. They certainly revealed that she was hopelessly infatuated with Stompanato. In court, Lana and Cheryl had all the sympathy of the jury, which arrived at a verdict of justifiable homocide.

The dead man's brother filed a suit for $800,000 damages against Cheryl's parents, alleging parental neglect. It was settled for $20,000.

This time the studios had no doubt that their star would not survive; murder was surely going too far? But to everyone's astonishment, the scandal had the opposite effect; Lana Turner's declining career revived triumphantly. During the showing of *Another Time, Another Place* – the film she had made with Sean Connery – members of the audience shouted: 'We're with you, Lana.' And her career once more prospered as it had in the early 1940s. The scandal had proved to be the best kind of publicity.

The Stompanato scandal could be regarded as a watershed in the history of Hollywood. For it meant, in effect, that the age of scandal was over. A scandal is not a scandal unless people are shocked – or at least, pleasantly titillated. When, in 1958, the press discovered that Marlon Brando's latest wife, formerly Anna Kashfi, was not (as she claimed) an Indian actress but the daughter of a Welsh factory worker named Pat O'Callaghan, the news was splashed in the tabloids because it aroused malicious amusement. Brando, the great tamer of women, had been fooled by a scheming Welshwoman. But this was not true scandal, only gossip laced with spite. Real scandal, the kind that had destroyed Fatty Arbuckle in 1921 and almost destroyed Ingrid Bergman when she deserted her husband for the director Roberto Rossellini in 1947, was a thing of the past. In retrospect, it seems symbolic that the decade of the sixties opened with the publication of *Lady Chatterley's Lover* in England and America, followed shortly by Henry Miller's *Tropic of Cancer*. It meant that adultery and fornication had ceased to be shocking and had become only mildly reprehensible. And as far as Hollywood stars were concerned, it was taken for granted as part of their lifestyle. When Frank Sinatra came to Hollywood in the early 1940s, legend has it that he pinned on his dressing room door a list of the actresses he wanted to sleep with and crossed them off one by one as he achieved his object. A current joke had it that among Hollywood's hat-check girls, the definition of a square was someone who hadn't slept with Frank Sinatra. But the studio's publicity men were at pains not to allow this image to reach all those fans who adored Sinatra for the warm sincerity of his voice and the boyishly innocent smile. By the 1960s, a rock star was expected to prove his virility as a stud. Elvis Presley had been shocking the middle classes since the mid-1950s with his unashamedly sexual gyrations on stage. When he came out of the army in 1960, he brought a fourteen-year-old girl back with him from Germany and began to sleep with her immediately. Although he married Priscilla Beaulieu, he left her behind when he went to Hollywood in the early sixties, when his name was linked with a series of actresses. After his death from a drugs overdose in 1977, a cinema cashier described how Presley had made her his mistress fourteen years earlier. Before he married Priscilla, Presley had told his stepmother that he had slept with about a thousand girls. A biography published after his death describes how one of his lieutenants would go out to the gate of his Memphis mansion, select one of the mob of girls waiting outside and bring her in for Elvis. Even during his lifetime, no one was shocked by rumours like this; it was expected of a rock star.

Jimi Hendrix, the black 'rock demigod' of the sixties, deliberately tried to outdo Presley in open sexual movements so there were times when he looked as if he was sodomizing his guitar (which, typically, he called 'Electric Lady'). Often he ended his performance by smashing his guitar to pieces and on one occasion he set it on fire with lighter fluid. Surrounded permanently by 'groupies', Hendrix was able to 'use girls like some people smoke cigarettes', as one of his more permanent girlfriends put it. His virility was apparently extraordinary. Two groupies started an interesting project of taking plaster casts of the erect members of rock stars and other celebrities; one of them would induce the erection by fellatio. Hendrix was one of the few who could not only sustain his erection until the plaster dried but who made it impossible to remove the plaster because his penis refused to go limp. In 1970, at the age of twenty-seven Hendrix took too many sleeping pills one night and drowned inhaling his own vomit. He was mourned as wildly and intensely as Rudolph Valentino had been in the twenties.

Even the Beatles, whose public image was more seemly, made no real attempt to conceal active sex lives, aware that such revelations would do them no harm. Biographers Peter Brown and Steven Gaines in *The Love You Make* (1983) describe how, on the set of *A Hard Day's Night*, the Beatles hired a movie projector to watch porno movies, and, 'boys being boys, the young girls on the set being used as extras were discreetly lured into the trailers for quickies between takes.' Their two road managers had the task of keeping them supplied with sex when on tour. 'Mal wasn't above the "If you fuck me first I'll introduce you to *them*"' routine. The girls were screwed, blewed and tattooed, before Mal and Neil swept them out of the Beatles' suite at dawn. The girls left with an autographed picture, forged by Neil and Mal, and were told to keep their mouths shut. Miraculously, for no reason anyone can explain, the girls kept their mouths shut. In America, at least, there were no 'My Night with Paul' stories in their tabloids, nor were there paternity suits. It was no small wonder, either, since it was not uncommon to find fifteen girls waiting in line in Neil's and Mal's rooms, passing the time by ironing the Beatles' stage costumes.

All this, then, helps to explain why there have been so few Hollywood scandals since 1960. The nearest thing to the old 'shock headlines' of the twenties and thirties were the headlines announcing the killing of Sharon Tate and her three guests on 8 August 1969. Sharon, the star of *Valley of the Dolls* and wife of Polish film director Roman Polanski, had been entertaining her former lover, Jay Sebring, and coffee heiress Abigail Folger and her lover Wojtek Frykowski, in her house at Cielo Drive, Benedict Canyon, when three disciples of the drug addict Charles Manson burst into the lounge with knives and a revolver. Sharon and her guests were tied up and robbed, then murdered – Sharon Tate, who was pregnant, was stabbed in the stomach.

Polanski was in London when he received the news. Soon after, the rumours began. *Newsweek*'s reporter wrote: 'All week long the Hollywood gossip about the case was of drugs, mysticism and offbeat sex.' The first theory was that the murder was committed by drug peddlers; Frykowski was believed to be running a large 'drug operation', and there was speculation that he had been killed for hanging on to more than his share of the profits. There was also talk about black magic rites and kinky sex.

The evening after the Tate murders, Charles Manson himself led a gang of six, including four women, to the house of supermarket boss Leno LaBianca – chosen at random – where they murdered him and his wife Rosemary after tying them up in bed; to mislead the police into believing that the killers were Black Panthers, the words 'Death to Pigs' were scrawled in blood on the wall.

A few months later, in October 1969, a Manson gang-member named Kitty Lutesinger, in jail on a minor charge, named a girl called Susan Atkins as one of the killers of a musician named Gary Hinman, who had been murdered two weeks before Sharon Tate. Susan Atkins admitted to a cellmate that she had been involved in the Tate killings, and the cellmate reported it to the police. After one of the longest and most expensive trials in Los Angeles' legal history, Charles Manson and five members of his 'Family' (as he called the gang) were sentenced to death – commuted to life imprisonment. It became clear during the trial that the murder of Sharon Tate was virtually an accident – her house had been chosen because it had formerly been the home of a record producer named Terry Melcher, against whom Manson had a grudge. (Manson had hopes of becoming a pop star.)

In 1977, Polanski himself was to figure in the type of Hollywood scandal that seemed to date back to the 1920s. Polanski, who has openly admitted to having a penchant for underage girls, had suggested to *Vogue* that he might do an article with photographs of adolescent girls. As a result, he came to meet a thirteen-year-old girl who wanted to become a model and who had already appeared in a television advertisement. He went to the home of the girl's mother in the San Fernando Valley and was introduced to the nubile teenager. Subsequently he took her up the hill behind her home and photographed her in various costumes. Another session was arranged at the house of film star Jacqueline Bisset, but since the light was bad, they moved to another house across the way, belonging to Jack Nicholson. By this time the girl had confided that she had lost her virginity at the age of eight with a boy down the street, and described sex with her current boyfriend. After Polanski photographed the girl fully clothed, she undressed and climbed into the Jacuzzi. After taking a few pictures, Polanski stripped and joined her there. Then they got dried and after a few caresses, he led her to the couch. 'There could be no doubt about Sandra's experience and lack of inhibition', says Polanski in his autobiography *Roman* (1984). 'She spread herself and I entered her. She wasn't unresponsive. Yet when I asked her softly if she was liking it, she resorted to her favourite expression, "It's all right."'

Afterwards, Polanski drove her home and chatted amiably. He went into her home, shared a 'joint' with her mother and drove off to his hotel. The following day, a policeman approached him in the hotel lobby. 'Mr Polanski . . . I have a warrant for your arrest.' The charge was rape. He was released on a bail of $2,500. But it was obvious that former friends now regarded him with distaste. 'Overnight, I'd crossed the fine line between decent folk and scum.' People joked that his next film was to be called *Close Encounters With the Third Grade*. The case began in March. Sentencing was finally set for September. Meanwhile, Polanski was 'remanded in custody' for psychiatric observation. In spite of the scandal, producer Dino de Laurentiis had asked him to direct a film called *Hurricane* in Bora Bora. He spent his custody period in Chino prison in Southern California and was released at the end of January 1978, after forty-two days. The judge on the case was now hinting to the Press that he would expect Polanski to serve a further forty-eight days, to be followed by his deportation. Polanski reasoned that in that case, there was no point in returning to jail. He went to see Dino de Laurentiis, who handed him $5,000; then Polanski caught a flight to London. Up to the date of this writing, he has not returned to America.

Fifty years earlier, the scandal would have wrecked the career of any film director. In 1978, it was accepted with a shrug – an attitude that is undoubtedly healthier. Six years later, Polanski was able to publish an unprecedentedly candid autobiography, speaking in some detail of the various women he has slept with and telling the full story of the scandal that drove him back to Europe. *Roman* reveals clearly the immense change in sexual attitudes that has taken place since the 1920s – or even since the 1960s, when Errol Flynn's *My Wicked*,

Wicked Ways appeared. Flynn cheerfully admits to endless fornication but he omits the physical details. Polanski literally tells everything. He describes, for example, the promotion tour for his film *Repulsion* and what took place after its Vienna première. A female companion, provided by his host, led him into a box in the theatre, where the plush stools had been arranged into a makeshift couch.

'Then she sat me down, unzipped my fly, and without more ado, starting fellating me. In the midst of this unexpected proceeding, the curtains behind me were swept aside. Stricken with embarrassment, I simultaneously zipped myself up and rolled over into a fetal crouch. "Don't worry, *Liebling*," I was told, "it's only the waiter." After opening a bottle of champagne, the man withdrew.

My companion now removed her clothes, with the exception of her high-heeled shoes, black fishnet stockings, and garters, which made her look like a Kokoscha drawing. While she was undressing me, I glanced over the parapet. A remarkably dexterous conjuror was hard at work below. With similar dexterity, the girl produced a condom from nowhere and fitted me with it. Then having sluiced herself with champagne, she straddled me and engaged in some vigorous fornication. She later tossed the used rubber into the champagne bucket . . .'

When a man can describe his private life with such candour, the whole concept of scandal has clearly become obsolescent.

IRELAND, William

The Great Shakespeare Forgery

In the summer of 1793, a prosperous gentleman named Samuel Ireland went from London to Stratford-upon-Avon with his eighteen-year-old son William. Ireland, an architect and painter, the author of a number of popular illustrated travel books, was in search of relics of his idol Shakespeare; the Stratford tradesmen were delighted to oblige. They sold him a goblet carved from a mulberry tree planted by Shakespeare's own hand, a purse presented by Anne Hathaway to Shakespeare, and the oak chair on which the Bard sat in his courting days.

Samuel William Henry Ireland was his father's youngest child; he had two elder sisters. All three were bastards, for Samuel Ireland's 'wife' (he called her his housekeeper) was a cast-off mistress of the Earl of Sandwich, a notorious rake. The father was not particularly fond of his son; he considered him dull and lazy. As a child, William had been sent home from school with a note saying that it was a waste of money trying to instruct him. William craved affection but he received none. It is just conceivable that Samuel Ireland was not his real father.

William had been apprenticed to a conveyancer named Bingley, at New Inn. The Ireland family lived nearby, in Norfolk Street, off the Strand. In the evenings, Ireland senior often read aloud to his family from the works of Shakespeare. One evening, the conversation turned to the 'marvellous boy' Thomas Chatterton (*see* page 126), who had forged the poems of a fifteenth-century priest called Thomas Rowley. William was fascinated by the story. He read a novel called *Love and Madness* by Herbert Croft, in which a long passage is devoted to Chatterton's tragic life. William decided that he would try his own hand at forgery. Like Chatterton, he was an unappreciated poet; he would see whether he could put his own literary talent to good account.

He began cautiously. He had picked up cheaply a small quarto volume that had belonged to the library of Queen Elizabeth I; it had her arms on the cover. He wrote a 'dedicatory letter' from its author to the queen and inserted it in the end of the book. He took a bookseller friend into his confidence and asked if it looked convincing. A journeyman who overheard the conversation showed William how to mix an ink that looked ancient. William rewrote the 'dedicatory epistle', and took the book home to his father. Samuel Ireland received it with gratitude and William basked in his approval. He decided to try a more ambitious forgery. He found a terracotta relief head of Oliver Cromwell and wrote on old parchment a letter saying that it had been presented to John Bradshaw, president of the court that condemned Charles I to death, by Cromwell himself. Once again, his father was taken in. So were some of his knowledgeable friends; like young William, none of them was aware that a strong dislike existed between Cromwell and Bradshaw.

Now William was prepared for greater things. He told his father that he had met an aristocratic gentleman in a coffee house and had been invited to the man's chambers to look through a chest of old documents. The gentleman himself had no interest in antiquities and told William he could have anything he fancied. When Ireland finally availed himself of this invitation, he discovered a document signed by Shakespeare in the chest. The gentleman declared that he would keep his promise and that William could take the document away if he would first make a copy of it.

Samuel Ireland naturally wanted to know more about this generous aristocrat. That, William explained, was impossible. The man had made him swear a solemn oath not to reveal his identity. Samuel Ireland apparently found this perfectly acceptable for aristocrats were eccentric. All he now wanted to see was the document. Two weeks later, William brought it home – a deed of mortgage made between Michael Fraser and his wife, and John Heminge and William Shakespeare. When

William presented this to his father, Samuel Ireland impulsively handed him his library keys and told him to take any book he wanted. William refused but his father presented him with a three-guinea volume anyway. For William, with his impulsive, sentimental nature, his craving for affection, it must have been a moment of triumph.

All Ireland's literary and artistic friends gathered to examine the acquisition and were duly impressed. The forgery was convincing – on parchment of the right period, with the Shakespeare signature carefully traced from one of the few extant genuine ones. Even the seal seemed authentic – taken from some old document. Ireland's friend, Sir Frederick Eden unhesitatingly pronounced the document genuine.

Delighted with the attention he was receiving, William forged a short note, in which Shakespeare promised to pay his friend Heminge five guineas for some unspecified service, together with a receipt from Heminge dated a month later, to prove that Shakespeare had kept his word.

Samuel Ireland grew greedy; he wanted to know what else there was in the gentleman's chest. William's next forgery was of a letter by Shakespeare to his patron the Earl of Southampton and a reply from Southampton (written with the left hand in case the handwriting was too like the Bard's). William was deeply gratified when all his father's friends agreed that the style of Shakespeare's letter revealed that its author was a man of genius. The inference was obvious.

William had often heard his father raise the question of whether Shakespeare had been a Roman Catholic – a question that had been discussed by many scholars. William determined to scotch that rumour by producing nothing less than a profession of faith in Shakespeare's own hand. It was a document full of conventional piety, with a few echoes of Shakespeare's plays: 'O Manne whatte arte thou whye considereste thou thyselfe thus greatlye where are thye great thye boasted attrybutes buryed loste forre everre inne colde Deathe . . .' It is hard to understand why, for all his intelligence, William felt that the way to sound Elizabethan was to avoid punctuation and put an 'e' on the end of every word. Yet two eminent

ABOVE: Fatty Arbuckle

BELOW: Donald Maclean

ABOVE: Henry Ward Beecher

ABOVE: Melinda Maclean

BELOW: Guy Burgess

ABOVE: Harold 'Kim' Philby

ABOVE: Teresa Guiccioli

BELOW: Roberto Calvi

ABOVE: Lord Byron

Queen Caroline

OPPOSITE ABOVE AND CENTRE: The Reverend Harold Davidson
OPPOSITE FOOT: Captain Alfred Dreyfus

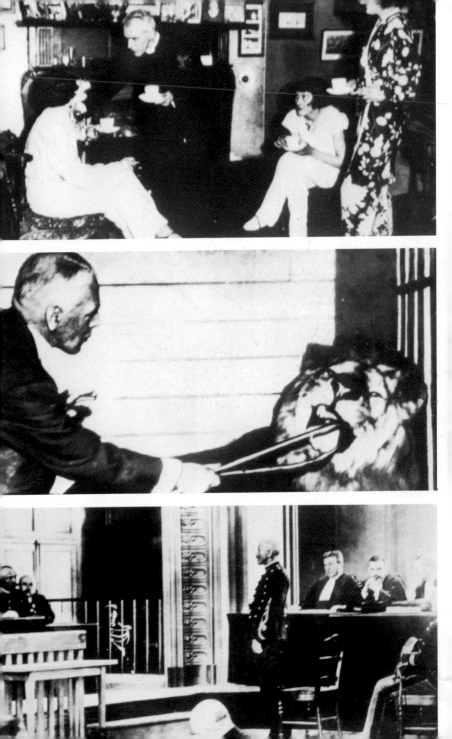

ABOVE: Charlie Chaplin

BELOW: Jean Harlow
with Clark Gable

ABOVE: Clara Bow

LEFT: Michael Fagan

RIGHT: 'Professor'
C E M Joad

Senator Edw
Kennedy and
his car in whi
body of Mar
Kopechne wa

Cecil Parkinson

Ivor Novello

Charles Stuart Parnell

ABOVE: Cynthia Payne

LEFT: John Profumo

BELOW: Mandy Rice-Davies (*left*) and Christine Keeler

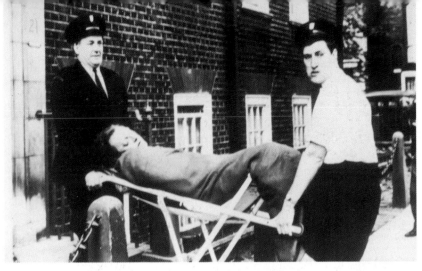

ABOVE: Dr Stephen Ward

RIGHT: Bertrand Russell

LEFT: Heinrich Schliemann

Daily Mirror

THE KING DECIDES: ABDICATION PLANS

DRAMATIC VISIT TO QUEEN MARY

THE KING HAS DECIDED.

His abdication unless he makes an eleventh hour change in his decision is regarded by the Cabinet as imminent.

His Majesty's decision will be announced by Mr. Baldwin in the House of Commons this afternoon. Lord Halifax will make a similar statement in the House of Lords.

Last night the Labour and Liberal Opposition leaders were informed by the Government of the latest moves in the crisis, and advised that there is little hope of a happy solution.

Over Rough-Track Roads

KING EDWARD VIII

DIARY OF THE DAY'S EVENTS

The Duke and
Duchess of Windsor

ABOVE: Mikhail Sholokhov

LEFT: Kakuei Tanaka

BELOW: Jeremy Thorpe

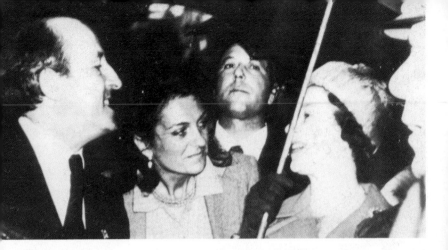

ABOVE: Commander Michael
Trestrail

RIGHT: Queen Victoria and
John Brown

BELOW: President Nixon
(*centre*) with Henry Kissinger
(*left*) and James Schlesinger

ABOVE: Carl Bernstein (*left*) and Bob Woodward of the *Washington Post*

RIGHT: H G Wells

LEFT: Oscar Wilde with Lord Alfred Douglas

Shakespeare scholars, Joseph Warton and Samuel Parr, both declared the Profession of Faith genuine.

William's trouble was that he was as greedy for his father's praise and approval as his father was for Shakespeare relics. He told his father he had seen a full-length portrait of Shakespeare and that the gentleman – now called 'Mr H' – had promised he could have it sooner or later. His father nagged him endlessly to produce it. He claimed he had seen Shakespeare's own edition of Holinshed's *Chronicles* – from which Shakespeare had taken much of his historical information; again, his father badgered him night and day to produce it. He managed to get hold of a number of Elizabethan books, which he annotated in Shakespeare's handwriting, and presented to his father as items from Shakespeare's library. But Samuel Ireland remained insatiable. He was like a spoiled child – nothing is more surprising than that William's admiration for his father remained undiminished.

Soon after this, William was caught at work. Fortunately, it was only by a fellow clerk, Montague Talbot – who had suspected all along that William was a forger. Talbot was so amused by the game that he was delighted to join in, supporting William's tales about the mysterious Mr H.

Driven by his father's greed, William now returned home almost every day with some new item: a drawing of Shakespeare's head executed by the Bard himself, a watercolour of Shakespeare in the role of Bassanio, a love letter from Shakespeare to Anne Hathaway, even a poem that began:

> Is there inne heavenne aught more rare
> Thanne thou sweete nymphe of Avon fayre
> Is there onne Earthe a Manne more trewe
> Thanne Willy Shakspeare is to you.

As usual William dispensed with punctuation, which had never been his strong point.

His next major discovery was a letter from Queen Elizabeth to Shakespeare, thanking him for some of his 'prettye Verses' and revealing that they had been on terms of easy intimacy. Here, once again, William came close to giving himself away;

he made the Queen refer to the Earl of Leicester, who died in 1588, when Shakespeare was only twenty-four. The letter was also addressed to the Globe Theatre which was not in existence in 1588. But no one noticed.

Understandably, Samuel Ireland longed to possess fragments of the plays in Shakespeare's own hand. William decided to go one better; he proceeded to copy out the whole text of *King Lear*, making his own alterations and expurgations as he went along. He had often heard his father say that he suspected the bawdy lines in Shakespeare had been inserted by hacks later; he now proved it by producing the original manuscript of *Lear* without a single word that might make a maiden blush.

The extraordinary spelling in the manuscript caused some hilarity in the press; the *Telegraph* parodied it in an invitation sent by Shakespeare to Ben Jonson which began: 'Tooo Missteeree Beenjaammiinnee Joohnnssonn, Deeree Sirree, Wille youe doee meee theee favvourree too dinnee Wythee mee onnn Fridaye nextte . . .'

Unabashed, William followed up the complete *Lear* with some selected pages of *Hamlet* – which he spelled *Hamblette* – in which Hamlet's bawdy pleasantries to Ophelia are expurgated and various other improvements made. When James Boswell came to examine the Shakespeare manuscripts, he fell on his knees and kissed them. Fortunately for Ireland, Dr Johnson had been dead ten years; the man who had unmasked 'Ossian' would have been a more formidable critic.

When one of his father's visitors raised the interesting legal question of whether these new Shakespeare papers should not belong to descendants of Shakespeare, William promptly produced a Deed of Gift from Shakespeare to a person called William Henry Ireland, who had saved him from drowning. That took care of that.

Now, finally, William took the step that led to his downfall. Convinced that his own talents were equal to Shakespeare's, he began to produce an 'original' Shakespeare play called *Vortigern and Rowena*. His father was now clamouring day and night for new Shakespeare material and William lacked the time to write out the whole play in Shakespeare's handwriting; instead, he wrote it in his own hand, explaining to his father

that he was copying it piecemeal. Theatrical managers immediately made offers to produce it; Richard Brinsley Sheridan, the
manager of the Drury Lane Theatre succeeded. Sheridan
decided that the play was genuine but that it belonged to
Shakespeare's earliest period, before his style had developed
its later subtlety. Delighted at the prospect of having his work
presented on the stage, William dashed off another play, *Henry
II* and began *William the Conqueror*. The following is an
extract in which Earl Edwyn meditates outside the Abbey:

> O my good Lord how lingering passed the time
> Whilse in yon porch I did wait your coming
> Yet as this Cloistral Arch, this bright heaven
> Doth shine upon the Emerald tipt wave
> And paints upon the deep each passing cloud
> E'eene so the smallest and most gentle Plant
> That waves fore the breath of thee sweet heaven
> To man gives food for contemplation.

It can be seen that Ireland's passion for terminal e's had been
curbed but his grasp of meter was still inadequate. *Henry II*
and *William the Conqueror* were to be part of a whole series of
Shakespeare histories, covering all those periods that Shakespeare had missed.

Sheridan had originally agreed to present *Vortigern* at Drury
Lane on 15 December 1795. (All the forgeries had been
produced in an incredibly short space of time, beginning in
December the previous year.) But the more he read the play,
the less happy he felt about it. Moreover, when Samuel Ireland
published the *Miscellaneous Papers of William Shakespeare*,
including the new version of *Lear* (but not *Vortigern*, which
had been found too late), the murmurs of critical dissent
became a chorus of mockery and ridicule. On the very day
when Samuel Ireland was invited to meet the Prince of Wales,
William came dangerously close to discovery. A neighbour of
his father's unearthed an authentic deed signed by John Heminge and pointed out that the signature bore no resemblance to
that on Ireland's deed. When William saw the authentic signature, he had to agree. He excused himself and said he had to
call on Mr H to find out what had happened. In fact, he went

to his employer's office, imitated the signature he had seen on a piece of old parchment, then wrote above it a receipt for some theatrical disbursement. He ran back to Mr Wallis's – the neighbour who had detected the fake – and showed him the new document; Mr Wallis had to agree that the signature was incredibly like the one on his own deed. William said Mr H had immediately produced the new document from his desk, explaining that there were two John Heminges, one at the Globe and one at the Curtain Theatre, and that Shakespeare had had dealings with both. Mr Wallis was convinced.

The actor-manager, John Kemble, had agreed to play Vortigern. His own view of the play may be guessed from the fact that he tried to put on the first performance on April Fools' Day but this was frustrated and the first night was announced for 2 April 1796. An immense queue formed. Ireland distributed copies of a handbill, defending the play against the 'malevolent and impotent attack' of the eminent Shakespeare critic, Edmond Malone; it was only one of many such attacks. Samuel Ireland was convinced that the play would silence these mockers once and for all.

The first act passed off well enough. In fact, actors like David Garrick had so often rewritten Shakespeare that Drury Lane audiences were used to a certain effect of absurdity. William had used various Shakespeare plays as his model, particularly *Macbeth*, so the situations had a certain pleasant familiarity. The second act rattled along at a good pace and was warmly applauded. It began to look as if William had got away with it. But, the third act began disastrously. An actor with a high tenor voice had to declaim:

> Nay, stop not there, but let them bellow on
> Till with their clamourous noise they shame the thunder . . .

He had the wrong voice for the lines and the house rocked with laughter. From then on, it found everything funny. A Member of Parliament who was present had to roar, 'Give the thing a fair trial.' Kemble had cast a comedian with an enormous nose to play a touching death scene; the curtain came down on his neck and as he struggled to free himself, the audience howled. Finally, Vortigern had to apostrophize death:

> O! then thou dost ope wide thy boney jaws
> And with rude laughter and fantastic tricks,
> Thou clapp'st thy rattling fingers to thy sides:
> And when this solemn mockery is ended . . .

That was as far as he got; the audience set up 'a most discordant howl', which continued for ten minutes. When they were quiet again, Kemble again delivered the same line with a lugubrious expression and continued:

> With icy hand thou tak'st him by the feet,
> And upward so, till thou dost reach his heart,
> And wrap him in the cloak of lasting night.

The actors managed to finish the play, in spite of laughter and catcalls, and the popular actress Mrs Jordan was even accorded an ovation when she took a curtain call. But when an actor announced that the play would be repeated the following night, his voice was drowned with yells of protest and fights broke out. It was undoubtedly the end of *Vortigern*.

The newspapers were derisive. But what hurt Samuel Ireland more than the jeers were the suggestions that he himself was the forger of the play. A committee of Ireland's friends was set up to investigate the matter but William was a thoroughly unsatisfactory witness, refusing to reveal Mr H's identity. His father became very angry, insisting that William had to divulge the identity – otherwise, he, Samuel Ireland, would remain under suspicion. William finally nerved himself to take the step he had always dreaded. He lacked the courage to confess to his father; instead, he told the full story to his sisters. They immediately passed it on to Samuel Ireland. Incredibly, Ireland refused to believe a word of it; he dismissed it outright as 'arrogance and vanity'. So William went to Mr Wallis, the man who had almost tripped him up on the subject of John Heminge, and confessed to him. Meanwhile, since his father declined to allow him to broach the subject of the plays, William soared into more absurd flights of fancy. He was about to marry a beautiful, rich girl who had fallen in love with him; Mr H had sent magnificent presents to all the actors involved in the fiasco; moreover, he had agreed to give William an allowance of £300 a year. The manager of Covent Garden had read *Henry II* and was anxious to present it next season. Samuel Ireland rushed to Covent Garden where the manager listened to him with a look of blank astonishment.

William drew up an advertisement, with Mr Wallis's help, which was placed in various newspapers. It stated that his father was innocent of all deception but stopped short of the admission that he, William Ireland, had forged the papers.

Finally, Samuel Ireland wrote his son a long, affecting letter, begging him to tell him the truth about the papers – making it quite clear that he was absolutely certain of their authenticity – and left for the country to give William time to reflect. William, deciding that this tangled web could be unravelled neither by honesty nor by new flights of fancy, fled from the house in Norfolk Street, never to return.

At Mr Wallis's instigation, he wrote his father a long, circumstantial letter describing his own part in the forgeries. It was no good; Samuel Ireland was too determined upon self-deception to take it seriously. He sent his son a furious reply, condemning his 'gross and deliberate impositions'. He was supported in this view by his wife-mistress, who was also totally convinced that her son was too dull to have written *Vortigern*.

So, at the age of twenty, William Ireland, the most gifted and audacious literary forger since Chatterton, found himself thrown out upon the world and obliged to support himself. The first thing he did was to marry a certain Miss Alice Crudge, a short, ugly girl about whom nothing else is known. He lived off small loans from friends of his father and on hopes of the production of *Henry II* but they came to nothing. Finally, he issued a pamphlet, an *Authentic Account of the Shakspearian Manuscripts*; this was so badly written that it only confirmed Samuel Ireland's view that his son was lying. Worse still, it confirmed the opinion of the newspapers that Samuel Ireland must have had a hand in the forgeries.

The scandal rumbled on for years. Samuel Ireland wrote a pamphlet defending himself and published *Vortigern* and *Henry II* to a new chorus of derision. For what was abundantly obvious was that Samuel Ireland was too unintelligent to see the difference between Shakespeare's confident precision of language and William's spirited but mediocre imitation. Samuel Ireland died in 1800, shaking his fist at the world.

William, who lived on for another thirty-five years, at least made some kind of career out of literature. In 1799 he published a three-volume novel called *The Abbess*, then went on to produce more than sixty titles, including a three-volume life of Napoleon. A full-length book describing the forgeries, the *Confessions* (1805), aroused rather less interest than it deserved because by then everyone had forgotten the affair. One of his more successful works was a long poem called *The Neglected Genius*, which contained an account of his hero, and model, Thomas Chatterton.

Ireland was undoubtedly a 'mythomaniac', for he lied for the sheer pleasure it gave him. What gives the case its psychological interest is that he would almost certainly never have written a word if it had not been for this 'Billy Liar' aspect of his personality. His father and mother cannot have been entirely mistaken to regard him as a dullard. Yet when he was driven by the need to invent convincing lies, he became a more-than-competent Shakespeare scholar and a writer of considerable talent. It is an interesting example of what can be accomplished by putting one's mind to it.

JOAD, 'Professor' C. E. M.
The Rail-Ticket Scandal

When 'Professor' Joad was caught out trying to dodge paying his rail fare in January 1948, he was a famous public figure, a writer and broadcaster whose favourite expression, 'It depends what you mean by . . .', had become a popular catch-phrase. The incident of the rail ticket brought his career to a premature close.

Cyril Edward Mitchinson Joad was born in Durham on 12 August 1891, the son of a school inspector. He was educated at Blundell's, the famous public school, and at Balliol College, Oxford. At twenty-three he was awarded the John Locke scholarship in mental philosophy and on coming down from Oxford, he became a civil servant in the Board of Trade. He later declared that he used his sixteen years as a civil servant mainly to write his books. By 1924, his *Introduction to Modern Philosophy* had underneath his name: 'Author of *Essays in Common Sense Philosophy, Common Sense Ethics, Common Sense Theology,* etc.' In his book on Shaw, Joad tells how he came to Oxford in 1910 and read simultaneously Wells's *Tono Bungay* and Shaw's *Candida*, and of the 'heady exhilaration' of this 'intoxicating intellectual brew'. A meeting with Shaw soon after that turned him into a 'Shaw-worshipper'. Joad himself had something in common both with Shaw and Wells: like Shaw, he was an incorrigible 'performer' who loved to propagate the myth of himself – even his titles reveal his obsessive self-preoccupation: *The Book of Joad, The Testament of Joad, The Pleasure of Being Oneself*; like Wells, he was an incurable philanderer. He once said that at the age of eleven he thought all women were solid from the waist down; his discovery that they were, so to speak, accessible seems to have resulted in a lifelong desire to prove that there were no exceptions to the rule. He also said once that he had no interest in speaking with a woman unless she was willing to sleep with him. He called all his mistresses Maureen, in case he made a slip of the tongue in addressing them. His wife, whom he married in 1915, seemed to accept his *affaires*.

Joad was one of the great popularizers; his *Guide to Philosophy* (1936) was as influential, in its way, as Wells's *Outline of History* or Hogben's *Mathematics for the Million*. But Joad was by no means an intellectual lightweight; his *Matter, Life and Value* (1929) is a brilliant and original exposition of the philosophy of 'vitalism'. He believed firmly in the reality of objective values and had no sympathy with the tendency of the logical positivists to dismiss metaphysics. He was, in his way, a religious man. But he was inclined to model himself on Shaw and to waste a great deal of his time in controversy to the detriment of his serious work. From the age of thirty-nine, he became head of the department of philosophy at Birkbeck College, London; but he was never, strictly speaking, a 'professor'.

In 1941, the British Broadcasting Corporation started a programme called 'The Brains Trust', broadcast on its 'Forces' wavelength. It was so popular that it was soon repeated on the Home Service. Soon it had become – together with Tommy Handley's comedy show ITMA – one of the most successful programmes of the war years. Joad had a rather precise, high-pitched voice, and sounded exactly like the popular idea of a university professor. *Punch* carried a cartoon of him saying to a waiter: 'It all depends on what you mean by (a) thick, and (b) clear.' He became so popular that police had to escort him through the crowds at public meetings, and the Ministry of Food launched a dish called 'Joad-in-the-Hole'. He loved his notoriety. 'He was an immensely vain individual', his BBC producer told Fenton Bresler, who devoted a chapter to Joad in his book *Scales of Justice*. The least suggestion of a snub could throw him into a towering rage but a soft answer – particularly if it was mixed with a judicious dose of flattery – had him cooing like a dove. He was not much liked at the BBC, partly because of a pathological meanness that made him dodge paying for his round of drinks whenever possible.

At 10.50 on the morning of 5 January 1948, Joad boarded the Atlantic Coast Express at Paddington, bound for Exeter in Devon; his secretary was with him. Both booked for the second sitting at lunch. When the ticket collector came to their table at lunch, his secretary held out her ticket but Joad explained: 'I haven't got one. I was late and the collector let me through. I got on at Salisbury.' The ticket collector gave him a return from Exeter to Salisbury. But the dining car attendant, who overheard the exchange, told the collector that there was something odd going on; Joad and his secretary had booked for lunch before the train reached Salisbury. The inspector went back to question Joad, who persisted in saying that he had boarded at Salisbury. It was only when the train stopped at Exeter that Joad admitted: 'I made a mistake. I did come from Paddington . . .' He had indeed made a mistake to admit his guilt. If Joad had kept silent, he would undoubtedly have heard the last of it. He made a further mistake by writing to the railway authorities and explaining that the problem had been a 'misunderstanding'.

What decided the authorities to take Joad to court was undoubtedly their discovery that this was not the first time and that he had made a habit of travelling without a ticket for years. On 12 April 1948, counsel on his behalf pleaded guilty at the Tower Bridge magistrates' court to 'unlawfully travelling on the railway without having previously paid his fare and with intent to avoid payment.' Joad was fined £2, with 25 guineas costs. That evening a newspaper carried the headline: Joad Fined For Common Ticket Fraud. Joad had tried to save himself 17s. 1d. On the same evening, Joad was on 'The Brains Trust' and seemed as jaunty and confident as ever. But in Parliament the following Friday, a Tory MP said, 'In the last week a public figure was convicted for telling lies and defrauding the public and he was hired the same evening by the BBC to entertain people.' On the evening of Joad's next scheduled appearance, he was dropped in favour of Commander King-Hall. He never again appeared on 'The Brains Trust'.

Joad continued to write books but he knew that, as a moral philosopher, his authority was gone. He became a practising

Christian and wrote books about his new religious belief. In 1953, at the age of sixty-two, he died of cancer.

Why did Joad do it? When he was asked this question by the 'Brains Trust' question master, Donald McCullough, he replied: '*Hubris*' – the Greek word for pride or conceit. Another motive was clearly his meanness. But his friend Hugh Schonfield, the Biblical scholar, has a different explanation. He told the present writer (CW) that Joad always had a need to 'kick over the traces'. Rebellion was a basic necessity of his nature – thumbing his nose at authority. So although he was 'Britain's foremost philosopher' (as he claimed at the head of his newspaper column) and a famous public figure, there was a need to reassure himself that he was still a rebel at heart by small acts of antisocial defiance.

KENNEDY, Senator Edward

The Enigma of Mary Jo Kopechne's Death on Chappaquiddick Island

Late on the night of Friday, 18 July 1969, Senator Edward Kennedy – aged thirty-seven, last of the four famous brothers and at that time, the only eligible presidential candidate in America's 'royal family' – turned right instead of left as he drove across Chappaquiddick Island, off the Massachusetts coast at Martha's Vineyard. It proved to be the turning point of his political career.

Travelling with the Senator was a blonde, twenty-eight-year-old girl named Mary Jo Kopechne. She had been secretary to his brother Robert, the former US Attorney-General assassinated one year earlier while running for President, in the footsteps of their murdered elder brother President John F. Kennedy. Miss Kopechne was one of six young women who had served on Bobby Kennedy's staff, either as secretaries or aides, during the fateful presidential campaign of 1968; now they had all gathered at Edgartown, in the Vineyard, for a Regatta Weekend reunion. On the Friday night they were invited to a barbecue party, given by Edward Kennedy together with five men friends, at a small, rented cottage on Chappaquiddick Island. The Senator left early to return to Edgartown, taking Mary Jo as passenger; but instead of turning left through Main Street, he turned right into Dyke Road and towards the beach. Shortly afterwards, as he crossed the eighty-five-foot-long wooden, hump-backed Dyke Bridge, his Oldsmobile car plunged over the side and into the strong currents of Poucha Pond.

What happened then may never be fully known, for the Senator's subsequent recollection of events was hazy. But whereas he somehow managed to scramble free, Mary Jo remained trapped inside and was drowned, even though – as the Senator clearly recalled later – he dived repeatedly to try to save her. Finally, exhausted and in a state of shock, instead of making for the nearest telephone to summon expert help, he walked back to the cottage (where the party was still in progress) and told two of his friends what had occurred. Nothing was said to any of Mary Jo's five women friends or to the other men there; and once again, no attempt was made to reach a telephone (there was none in the cottage) to report the accident to the police. Instead, the three men drove to Dyke Bridge, where they dived repeatedly to try to locate the missing girl, but without success.

According to his own account, Senator Kennedy was by this time so overcome by a variety of emotions – grief, fear, doubt and exhaustion among them – that he was unable to act rationally. In the event, he told his companions not to alarm Mary Jo's friends at the cottage but to drive him instead to the ferry crossing. When they got there, they found it closed for the night; whereupon the Senator dived in and began to swim across the 500-foot waterway. Although his two friends seemed to think he was in no difficulty (and made their own way back to the cottage), Kennedy himself said later that he had to struggle against a strong, northerly tide-race which threatened to sweep him out to sea. So strong was it, he said, that he almost drowned once again. As a result, he was so utterly spent when he did finally succeed in reaching the shore, that he was able only to make his way to his hotel room where he collapsed. No one at the Shiretown Inn saw him arrive in his wet clothing. He himself remembered getting up at one point to speak to the room clerk, but whatever was said, no alarm was raised. And it was not until the morning that he recovered sufficiently to try to ring a family lawyer and report the accident, belatedly, to the police.

By then they already knew that his car lay submerged in Poucha Pond. The abandoned Oldsmobile was first spotted by anglers Robert Samuel and Joe Capparella early on that morning of Saturday, 19 July. Local police chief Dominick Arena, a powerfully built man of six foot four inches and a good swimmer, drove to the bridge and personally dived in to investigate. The current proved too strong even for him, however, and another diver later found the body of Mary Jo Kopechne. She was dressed in white blouse and black slacks. A rear window of the car was shattered. The registration was quickly traced to Senator Kennedy but there was some confusion at first over the dead girl's identity. A handbag recovered from the car contained two keys to rooms at the Katama Shores Motor Inn, near Edgartown, and a US Senate pass in the name of Rosemary Keough. A police call established that Miss Keough was one of a party of six young women who had booked into three double rooms there, although none of the beds had been slept in overnight.

Local practitioner Dr Donald Mills examined the body and confirmed that death was due to drowning. Shortly afterwards police chief Arena rang his headquarters and was told that Senator Kennedy was there and wished to talk to him. The two men had a brief conversation; Arena then drove to Edgartown, where Edward Kennedy told him that the dead girl was Mary Jo Kopechne, not Rosemary Keough, and said that he had already informed her parents of the accident. He then volunteered a written statement. While it was being prepared, police chief Arena returned to Dyke Bridge where the search was continuing. His deputy, Christopher Look, told him that he had seen a car turn into Dyke Road at about 12.45 A.M. Look said there appeared to be a man and a woman sitting in the front, with someone (or something) in the back. When the car stopped, Look got out of his own vehicle and walked towards it, thinking the driver might be lost. When he was still about thirty feet away, the car left 'in a cloud of dust' in the direction of Dyke Bridge. In normal circumstances, the deputy would probably have followed but since this was Regatta Night, he went on his own way home. Now he wondered if the car lying in Poucha Pond was the same one he had seen earlier.

The police chief then returned to his office at Edgartown. Paul Markham, who sat at a desk writing while Senator Kennedy paced the floor, told him, 'It's coming along.' He later handed the written statement to Dominick Arena, who typed it out himself. It read:

On July 18 1969, at approximately 11.15 on Chappaquiddick Island, Martha's Vineyard, I was driving my car on Main Street on my way to get the ferry back to Edgartown.

I was unfamiliar with the road and turned onto Dyke Road instead of bearing left on Main Street. After proceeding for approximately a half mile on Dyke Road I descended a hill and came upon a narrow bridge. The car went off the side of the bridge. There was one passenger with me, Miss Kopechne, a former secretary of my brother Robert Kennedy. The car turned over and sank into the water and landed with the roof resting on the bottom. I attempted to open the door and window of the car but have no recollection of how I got out of the car. I came to the surface and then repeatedly dove down to the car in an attempt to see if the passenger was still in the car. I was unsuccessful in the attempt. I was exhausted and in a state of shock. I recall walking back to where my friends were eating. There was a car parked in front of the cottage and I climbed into the back seat. I then asked for someone to bring me back to Edgartown. I remember walking around for a period of time and then going back to my hotel room. When I fully realized what had happened this morning I immediately contacted the police.

It was a brief statement which left much unsaid, as might be expected in someone recovering from shock and exhaustion. Unfortunately by afternoon, the others who had been at the barbecue, including Mary Jo's five girl friends – all, in fact, who might conceivably have been able to shed additional light on events surrounding the tragedy while the details were fresh in their minds – had left the area. Mary Jo's body was flown to Pennsylvania that same afternoon, in an aircraft chartered by Senator Kennedy. He himself left for the family base at Hyannis Point, on a flight arranged by police chief Arena. While there he met with some eminent friends, including Robert McNamara, who had served his brother John F. Kennedy as Defence Secretary, Theodore Sorenson, the late President's speechwriter, and Professor Arthur Schlesinger, another of the former President's senior aides.

On 22 July, Senator Kennedy flew to Pennsylvania to attend Mary Jo's funeral, at St Vincent's Roman Catholic Church in Plymouth. He was accompanied by his wife Joan (who was three months pregnant) and his brother Bobby's widow, Ethel Kennedy. On this occasion only in public, he wore a neck-brace following the accident. The church was filled, reflecting the nationwide interest in the tragedy aroused by massive media coverage. On Friday, 25 July, Edward Kennedy returned to Martha's Vineyard to attend a court hearing. There he pleaded guilty to leaving the scene of the accident, a minor charge for which he was given a (suspended) two-month jail sentence and banned from driving for a year.

While the plea of guilty spared him the ordeal of testifying on other, still obscure, aspects surrounding the accident, it did little to halt the floodtide of rumour and innuendo which had followed in its wake. After the court rose, the Senator appeared the same night, at his own request, in a 'prime time' television broadcast which was carried by all the major American networks and channelled overseas. He used it as a platform to try to nail, once and for all, the rumours which had circulated both about the party on Chappaquiddick Island and his relationship with Miss Kopechne. He also gave a much fuller account of the accident and his subsequent conduct and spoke of the 'various inexplicable, inconsistent and inconclusive' things he had said and done on the night Mary Jo died.

My fellow citizens, I have requested this opportunity to talk to the people of Massachusetts about the tragedy which happened last Friday evening. This morning I entered a plea of guilty to the charge of leaving the scene of the accident. Prior to my appearance in court it would have been improper for me to comment on these matters. But tonight I am free to tell you what happened, and to say what it means to me.

On Chappaquiddick Island, off Martha's Vineyard, I attended on Friday evening, 18 July, a cook-out I had encouraged and helped sponsor for the devoted group of Kennedy campaign secretaries. When I left the party, around 11.15 P.M., I was accompanied by one of those girls, Miss Mary Jo Kopechne. Mary Jo was one of the most devoted members of the staff of Senator Robert Kennedy. For this reason, and because she was such a gentle, kind and idealistic person, all of us tried to help her feel that she had a home with the Kennedy family.

There is no truth, no truth whatsoever, to the widely circulated suspicions of immoral conduct that have been levelled at my behaviour and hers regarding that evening. There has never been a private relationship between us of any kind. I know nothing in Mary Jo's conduct on that or any other occasion – the same is true of the other girls at that party – that would lend any substance to such ugly speculation about their character. Nor was I driving under the influence of liquor.

Little over one mile away, the car I was driving on an unlit road went off a narrow bridge which had no guardrails and was built on a left angle to the road. The car overturned in a deep pond and immediately filled with water. I remember thinking as the cold water rushed in around my head that I was for certain drowning. Then water entered my lungs and I actually felt the sensation of drowning. But somehow I struggled to the surface alive. I made immediate and repeated efforts to save Mary Jo by diving into the strong and murky current but succeeded only in increasing my state of utter exhaustion and alarm.

My conduct and conversations during the next several hours to the extent that I can remember them makes no sense to me at all. Although my doctors informed me that I suffered a cerebral concussion as well as shock, I do not seek to escape responsibility for my actions by placing the blame either on the physical, emotional trauma brought on by the accident or on anyone else. I regard as indefensible the fact that I did not report the accident to the police immediately.

Instead of looking directly for a telephone number after lying exhausted in the grass for an undetermined time, I walked back to the cottage where the party was being held and requested the help of two friends, my cousin Joseph Gargan and Paul Markham, and directed them to return immediately to the scene with me – this was some time after midnight – in order to undertake a new effort to dive down and locate Miss Kopechne. Their strenuous efforts, undertaken at some risks to their own lives, also proved futile.

All kinds of scrambled thoughts – all of them confused, some of them irrational, many of them which I cannot recall and some which I would not have seriously entertained under normal circumstances – went through my mind during this period. They were reflected in the various inexplicable, inconsistent and inconclusive things I said and did, including such questions as whether the girl might still be alive somewhere out of that immediate area, whether some awful curse did actually hang over all the Kennedys, whether there was some justifiable reason for me to doubt what had happened and to delay my report, whether somehow the awful weight of this incredible incident might in some way pass from my shoulders. I was overcome, I'm frank to say, by a jumble of emotions – grief, fear, doubt, exhaustion, panic, confusion and shock.

Instructing Gargan and Markham not to alarm Mary Jo's friends that night, I had them take me to the ferry crossing. The ferry having shut down for the night, I suddenly jumped into the water and impulsively swam across, nearly drrowning once again in the effort, and returned to my hotel about 2 A.M. and collapsed in my room. I remember going out at one point and saying something to the room clerk. In the morning, with my mind somewhat more lucid, I made an effort to call a family legal adviser, Burke Marshall, from a public telephone on the Chappaquiddick side of the ferry and belatedly reported the accident to the Martha's Vineyard police.

Today, as I mentioned, I felt morally obligated to plead guilty to the charge of leaving the scene of the accident. No words on my part can possibly express the terrible pain and suffering I feel over this tragic incident. This last week has been an agonizing one for me and the members of my family, and the grief we feel over the loss of a wonderful friend will remain with us for the rest of our lives.

These events, the publicity, innuendo and whispers which have surrounded them and my admission of guilt this morning raise the question in my mind of whether my standing among the people of my state has been so impaired that I should resign my seat in the United States Senate.

If at any time the citizens of Massachusetts should lack confidence in their senator's character or his ability, with or without justification, he could not in my opinion adequately perform his duty and should not continue in office. The people of this state, the state which sent John Quincy Adams and Daniel Webster and Charles Sumner and Henry Cabot Lodge and John Kennedy to the United States Senate, are entitled to representation in that body of men by men who inspire their utmost confidence. For this reason, I would understand full well why some might think it right for me to resign. For me this will be a difficult decision to make. It has been seven years since my first election to the Senate. You and I share many memories – some of them have been glorious, some have been very sad. The opportunity to work with you and serve Massachusetts has made my life worthwhile. And so I ask you tonight, people of Massachusetts, to think this through with me. In facing this decision, I seek your advice and opinion. In making it, I seek your prayers. For this is a decision that I will have finally to make on my own.

It has been written that a man does what he must in spite of personal consequences, in spite of obstacles and dangers and pressures, and that is the basis of all human morality. Whatever may be the sacrifices he faces, if he follows his conscience – the loss of his friends, his fortune, his contentment, even the esteem of his fellow men – each man must decide for himself the course he will follow. The stories of past courage cannot supply courage itself. For this, each man must look into his own soul.

I pray that I can have the courage to make the right decision. Whatever is decided and whatever the future holds for me, I hope that I shall be able to put this most recent tragedy behind me and make some further contribution to our state and mankind, whether it be in public or private life. Thank you and good night.

America's reaction was mixed. The Senator received some 30,000 telegrams, most of them favourable. The Press weighed his words somewhat more coolly. *Life* magazine commented: 'He was simply hustling heart-strings, using words, cashing in on the family credibility.' If that seemed harsh, not even the most sympathetic viewer could deny that many pertinent questions had been left unanswered by the broadcast. He made no reference to taking the wrong turning, but merely said he drove on an unlit road and went off 'a narrow bridge which had no guardrails and was built on a left angle to the road . . .' Had he not picked it out in his headlights and slowed down accordingly? And again: given that the Senator himself had become too shocked and exhausted following the accident to think or act logically – why had his two companions not insisted on calling in expert help, once their own, desperate attempts to locate the missing girl had failed?

These and other questions which naturally sprang to mind despite the broadcast, meant that speculation was sure to continue. For the breath of scandal which had clung to the tragic, tangled skein of events from the outset was perhaps inevitable. The two principals were a pretty, blonde, unmarried secretary, now dead, and a handsome, charismatic US Senator – and much more than that, a potential presidential candidate and a Kennedy. Furthermore, deserved or not, like all the Kennedy menfolk he had a reputation as a womanizer. After the broadcast, speculation was fuelled afresh by other, related events; among them, the decision to exclude Press and public from the inquest on Mary Jo, while the transcript of proceedings was not published for a further three months after the inquest, at the end of April 1970.

Within those three months, the Duke's County Grand Jury on Martha's Vineyard had been convened in special session, after its foreman protested, 'A great deal of time has passed since the girl died, and it is time the public found out what happened.' However, since the members of the Jury were not given copies of the inquest transcript, they remained in ignorance both of the evidence and judge's conclusions, and disbanded. The judge had, in fact, concluded, among other things, that: '. . . a reasonable and probable explanation of the totality of the facts is that Kennedy and Kopechne did not intend to drive to the ferryslip and that his turn on Dyke Road was intentional.' Judge James Boyle also found that: '. . . there is probably cause to believe that Edward M. Kennedy operated his motor vehicle in a way or in a place to which the public have right of access, and that such operation appears to have contributed to the death of Mary Jo Kopechne . . .'

After the evidence was published, the Senator issued a statement rejecting the judge's conclusions, as was his right, and said he himself planned no further statement on 'this tragic affair'. He pulled out of the 1976 presidential campaign because of family troubles (his son Edward Kennedy Jr had a leg amputated in 1973 when he was found to be suffering from bone cancer, and there were other family accidents and illnesses). But in January 1980, when he was challenging Jimmy Carter for the Democratic nomination, *Time* magazine summarized what it described as 'new challenges' on Chappaquiddick, calling it 'The Campaign Issue That Will Not Go Away'. The article referred to separate stories which had appeared in the *Washington Star, Reader's Digest*, and the *New York Post*.

Time magazine said Senator Kennedy had himself revived public interest in the tragedy by his 'hesitant answers' to questions put to him in a CBS television interview the previous November by commentator Roger Mudd. During the interview (too long to report in full) he said: '. . . the problem is . . . from that night . . . I found the . . . the . . . the conduct and behaviour almost a sort of . . . beyond belief myself . . .' The *New York Post* in turn published an account of other parties the Senator was alleged to have thrown at Martha's Vineyard for his aides and various young women. *Reader's Digest* and the *Star* challenged his account of the strong current which he said had threatened to sweep him out to sea, and almost drowned him, as he swam the 500-foot passage to Edgartown.

The *Washington Star*, which published aerial photographs taken in May, July and November of the area, concluded that on the night of the barbecue, 18 July, the gap in the channel south of Chappaquiddick would have been too narrow and shallow to admit a northward tide-race of sufficient strength. *Reader's Digest* said bluntly that the Senator's story was 'false', maintaining that the tide would have helped rather than hindered him. It also published the findings of accidents expert Mr Raymond R. McHenry on the accident that led to the drowning. Senator Kennedy said at the inquest his speed on Dyke Road was 20 mph. Using the most modern techniques, including a computer, Mr McHenry put it at around 34 mph and concluded that the rented Oldsmobile skidded when the brakes were applied, somersaulted through the air off the hump-backed bridge and landed upside down in Poucha Pond. Said *Time* magazine: 'What more may be published, and when, is uncertain. But the issue has not left voters' minds . . .'

That verdict remains the one outcome of the tragedy at Chappaquiddick on which almost all political observers are agreed. It is an issue which refuses to go away – and is likely to ensure that the Senator will always find it difficult to be elected President of the United States and leader of the free world.

LAW, John

The Louisiana Scandal

John Law was a Scots adventurer whose brilliant but over-ambitious financial schemes brought France to ruin. He was born in Edinburgh in April 1671, the son of a goldsmith who made a fortune from moneylending. As a child, Law developed into a remarkable linguist and mathematician. He was tall, handsome and had enormous charm. His father died in 1685, leaving him two country estates. But Law's temperament was unsuited to country life; he wanted excitement and adventure. Besides, he was a born gambler. In London, he had a love affair with a certain Mrs Lawrence and fought a duel with another of her admirers, a man called Beau Wilson whom he killed in Bloomsbury Square. He was convicted of murder but managed to secure a royal pardon. But then Wilson's brother filed a suit against him and he was imprisoned; he escaped and fled to the Continent. He was twenty-six years old.

John Law was a gambler but he was fascinated by high finance, believing that it could be turned into a science. He studied banking in Amsterdam – then the financial centre of the world – and later in Venice. In 1700, he returned to Scotland and approached the government with a proposal which, he said, would relieve the poverty of the Scots. He proposed that a national bank should be founded and it should issue paper money instead of gold. This money was always to be instantly redeemable against gold in order to create confidence. Once confidence had been created, the government could then increase its wealth simply by printing more money. Nowadays, we are aware that this procedure creates an inflationary spiral but, to Law, it seemed foolproof. The Scots declined to try the scheme. And since a union with England was imminent, Law had to return to the Continent to avoid arrest. There he continued to live by gambling – being periodically moved on by the police as dejected losers reported their suspicion that he was cheating. He was also staggeringly successful in love in spite of the fact that he was married to the Earl of Banbury's daughter Catherine.

He continued to try to interest influential politicians in his scheme for a national bank without success. King Victor Amadeus of Sardinia told him, 'I am not wealthy enough to survive bankruptcy.'

In Paris in 1708, he was received into the innermost circles of the aristocracy and his skill – and luck – as a gambler became legendary. He ran a faro bank in the house of a famous actress, Madame Duclos, and had private counters made, each worth eighteen louis. There he met a man who took an immediate liking to him: the Duc D'Orleans. The duke was soon convinced that Law was a financial genius; he introduced Law to the Minister of Finance, Desmarets. Just as it seemed that the long-awaited turn in his fortunes had arrived, the Chief of Police, D'Argenson, ordered Law out of the country. Presumably D'Argenson must have had some evidence of illegal dealings otherwise Law could have appealed to his influential friends to countermand the order. As it was, he left France and spent the next five years travelling from capital to capital around Europe and amassing a fortune of £80,000 by gambling.

When he heard that Louis XIV had died in 1715 and that the Duc D'Orleans had become Regent (Louis XV being only five years old at the time), Law hastened back to Paris. He found that France was on the verge of bankruptcy, largely due to the extravagance of the 'Sun King'. Money, Law told the Duke, was the lifeblood of a country and credit is to business what the brain is to the human body. If a sound system of credit could be established, a merchant could embark on schemes that would normally be far too ambitious for his pocket. In this way, business would be stimulated and wealth increased.

The Regent was impressed but the Council of Finance was not and rejected the idea of a national bank. They agreed, however, to allow Law to set up a private bank. This he did, using his capital to start a bank in the Place Vendôme in Paris. His aim was to establish confidence. He sold shares in the bank at a price that attracted everyone who knew anything about finance: a quarter in gold and the rest in government bonds which were worth only one-fifth of their face value. At first, he lost money heavily but he created confidence. The government was impressed when he devised a dubious scheme which enabled it to make a 50 per cent profit on all bonds.

Law's problem was that he had issued sixty millions' worth of francs in notes and he only had 6 million francs in gold. If confidence ebbed, he would be bankrupt. He needed to find ways of increasing his capital until he could withstand any 'run' on the bank – some business that would expand and yield rich profits. He decided that the answer lay across the Atlantic, in Louisiana, which had been 'discovered' by the French. A businessman named Crozat had been granted a monopoly, but was finding that he lacked the capital to take advantage of it. Law persuaded the Duc to transfer the monopoly to him; Crozat seems to have been glad to get rid of it. From August 1717 Law's company became known as the Mississippi Company. It owned a piece of land 3,000 miles long and the company could plant colonies and develop it as it liked.

Law's first step was to organize 'propaganda'. He sent his agents all over the country, telling tales of the immense riches of the Mississippi basin, including whole rocks made of emeralds. He imported six dusky maidens from Louisiana and showed them off in Paris; one of them, who was described as the 'Daughter of the Sun', was married to a French sergeant with enormous publicity and the man sailed off to America with his royal bride. (Unfortunately, she exercised her royal prerogative of executing any husband who failed to please her and the marriage lasted only a few months.) The foundations of New Orleans were laid; Law himself started a German reservation in Arkansas. But there were still not enough colonists to provide the quick returns he wanted. Law took advantage of his privilege to raise his own troops – they were dressed in blue and silver and known as Law's Archers – and sent them round Paris collecting vagrants, ex-convicts and women of the streets, and packing them off to Louisiana.

When his troops began seizing ordinary men and women in the streets, there were riots; twenty Archers were killed, and the government hastily decided that powers of recruitment should be confined to criminals.

In spite of these setbacks, things looked promising. Law had been granted a monopoly of the Canadian fur trade and his profits were immense. He began to absorb other French colonial companies in the East Indies, China, Senegal and other regions. He even acquired a tobacco monopoly in Virginia.

For years, Law had been plotting to get his own back on the police chief D'Argenson for ordering him out of the country. In fact, he had made D'Argenson one of his chief lieutenants, to keep him out of mischief. In 1719, Law struck. D'Argenson and some business associates had made enormous profits by purchasing the right to collect taxes – the French government preferred ready cash. D'Argenson's group paid 48 million francs for this privilege. In 1719, Law stepped in and offered 52 million – one of D'Argenson's chief sources of income suddenly dried up.

Law now launched his biggest gamble of all. He offered to pay the national debt (the money the government borrows from various sources). The idea was that he would pay the government the sum of 1,500 million livres to enable it to repay all its creditors. The government in turn would pay Law a 3 per cent interest on his money instead of the usual 4 per cent. And what would the creditors do with the money that had been returned to them? They could re-invest it in Law's company. And Law guaranteed that he would repurchase at their original value in six months if the investors wanted to 'unload'.

Law's office in the Rue Qincampoix suddenly became the centre of a permanent scramble. In less than a year – between June 1719 and February 1720 – his shares increased eighteen times in value. Crowds packed the street and tried to push their way back to the desk where Law sat with a huge pile of shares in front of him. Anyone who could buy a few shares could walk outside and immediately sell them for several times what he had paid. Every house or shop in the dingy street rented rooms at thousands of francs a week to people who wanted to be outside the door the moment Law opened up in the morning. A poor cobbler made a fortune overnight; Law's own coachman became a rich man, and came to his master with two more coachmen, saying, 'Choose which one you want and I'll take the other.'

No one quite understood how money could be created so quickly, but it was obvious that Law had some secret. The result was a kind of frenzy. All over the country, the crime rate soared as people scrambled to lay their hands on the gold that could be doubled or trebled overnight. A young nobleman, the Comte de Horn, related to the Regent, lured a speculator to a house, and beat him to death to lay his hands on 150,000 francs the man had just made. He was broken on the wheel as an example but this example made no difference to the crime wave.

Shrewd speculators realized that the bubble was bound to burst and began smuggling their profits out of the country. One Dutch financier converted a million francs into gold and silver and smuggled it out in farm carts covered with hay; he himself dressed as a farm labourer. The word 'millionaire' was coined to describe a phenomenon that was becoming increasingly common.

It was the people without wealth enough to buy one share who suffered. Prices rose because most people had more money to spend while the poor could not afford the new prices. Law was causing mass starvation as well as crime.

His greatest problem was that speculators were bound to decide to take their profit while the going was good and every time this happened, it drained the bank's capital. Law persuaded the Regent to make it illegal for anyone to possess more than 500 livres in gold and silver. Goldsmiths were ordered not to make any gold articles that weighed more than one ounce. But this only increased the general anxiety to turn their paper money into gold. The Prince de Conti brought carts to carry away his gold. Law was forced to issue a statement saying that he would not change more than a 100-livre note per person. He issued an edict threatening shopkeepers who refused to accept his notes; they ignored it. There were still crowds outside Law's bank but they no longer had the same purpose; they wanted their money back. On 17 July 1720, a huge crowd waited all night – 15,000 of them. By morning, it was discovered that sixteen people had died of suffocation. A mob marched to the Palais Royal, carrying four of the dead on stretchers, to show the Regent what his policies had led to; they were finally persuaded to disperse. But revolution had been very close.

Law hid in the Palais Royal for ten days then escaped to one of his country houses. His family was taken under the protection of the Duc de Bourbon at his house at St Maur. Law was in a state of shock; he found it incomprehensible that the tremendous edifice had collapsed and seemed unable to understand what had gone wrong. He was still hoping that the Regent could save his bank with a huge loan but the French parliament flatly refused a loan. On 21 December 1720, Law finally left for Brussels in a post chaise. He had a shock at Valenciennes when he was arrested by the son of his old enemy D'Argenson, for if, as he suspected, the Regent had been deposed, then he would probably never escape from France alive. But within a few days, an order arrived from the Regent allowing him to proceed on his way.

In Brussels, he was approached by an agent of the Tsar of Russia, Peter the Great, who wanted him to take over the financial reorganization of the Russian empire. Law politely declined on the grounds that he needed a rest from his labours – in fact, his nerve was shattered.

In the following year, 1771, he journeyed to London and was received by King George I (who finally granted him a pardon). The news that he had been virtually the Prime Minister of France made the British decide that he deserved treating with respect. No one held it against him that it was his example that had led to England's greatest social disaster of the century, the South Sea Bubble (*see* page 382), which had left thousands bankrupt.

Law continued to be on good terms with the Regent – in fact, he received a pension from him. When he asked in a letter: 'What did you do about the bankruptcy?' the Regent replied: 'I disposed of it by simply making a bonfire of all the documents.' Law hoped to be recalled to France to take charge of its finances but the death of the Regent in 1723 dashed his hopes. He was separated from his wife but her relatives gave him a small allowance. And he made a small fortune by offering to bet anyone £1,000 to a shilling that they could not throw six double sixes in succession with dice; the number who tried was incredible. Law moved to Venice where he died on 21 March 1729, aged fifty-eight.

Napoleon later sold Louisiana to the Americans for $15 million.

McPHERSON, Aimée Semple
The Mystery Kidnapping

Aimée Semple McPherson – once described as 'the world's most pulchritudinous evangelist' – lost her immense following with dramatic suddenness after a farcical trial in which she was charged with 'a conspiracy to obstruct justice'.

She was born Aimée Elizabeth Kennedy, on a small farm in Canada, near Ingersoll, Ontario, on 9 October 1890. Her mother, a highly dominant woman, had been a Salvation Army lass until she married a devout farmer many years her senior. Aimée, like her mother, had a determined character, and there was a great deal of conflict between them in her childhood. Minnie Kennedy – later known as 'Ma' – found marriage to her elderly husband boring and frustrating and took it out on her family.

At the age of seventeen Aimée fell in love with a young English evangelist named Robert Semple and married him in spite of her mother's objections. Semple intended to become a missionary and apparently felt that she would make an ideal wife. She joined her husband in his evangelistic activities in Chicago, then they went to England to see his parents. But when they arrived in Hong Kong, where he intended to begin his missionary work, Semple was stricken with fever and died in the English hospital. Aimée gave birth to a girl soon afterwards. The China mission provided funds to send her back to America.

She joined her parents, who had moved to New York, tried life on the farm in Canada, then returned to New York and married a grocery clerk named Harold McPherson, by whom she had a son. Marriage bored her and within eighteen months she was on the move again, following the only profession she knew – that of evangelist. In Canada, she attracted a crowd by standing on a chair at a street corner, her eyes closed and her arms raised in prayer. As the crowd waited in silent expectation, Aimée suddenly opened her eyes and yelled, 'Follow me!' and rushed to the revival hall. Once the crowd was in she shouted, 'Shut the doors. Don't let anyone out.'

For the next few years, it was a rather discouraging routine of travelling around the country in a battered old car with a tent in the back. Her mother joined her and took the collections. Aimée preached the literal truth of every word in the Bible and the personal return of Jesus Christ. Slowly, she acquired a following. She began to hire lecture halls. Then, in 1917, at the age of twenty-seven, she made the momentous decision to head for California. In her old car, with her mother and two children, she made her way slowly across the country.

Aimée was not, in fact, 'pulchritudinous'; her features were too heavy, and her legs were like those of a Welsh dresser (so she always wore long skirts). But, by the usual standards of female evangelists, she was a welcome change. Within a week of arriving in Los Angeles, she was able to rent the Philharmonic Auditorium, which held over 3,000 people. Suddenly she was a celebrity. The rich contralto voice could hold the multitudes. On a new wave of confidence, she travelled to Canada, New Zealand and Australia. It seems to have dawned on her that American sales techniques could be used to sell religion. Back in California, this time in San Diego, she scattered evangelical tracts from an aircraft and held meetings in a boxing arena.

It was in San Diego that Aimée suddenly became far more than a successful preacher. San Diego was full of old and retired citizens and the suicide rate and the statistics for mental and physical illness were far higher than in the rest of California. At an outdoor meeting in Organ Pavilion, in Balboa Park, a middle-aged paralytic rose from her wheel chair in front of 30,000 people and took a few halting steps. Suddenly, hundreds of people were hobbling towards the platform, tears streaming down their faces, praising the Lord and Aimée Semple McPherson. The next day, everyone in San Diego was talking about the miracle.

Aimée embarked on another triumphant tour of the Pacific

coast. Then she realized it was time to stop moving around like a travelling showman. She would build a temple in Los Angeles. In 1923, Los Angeles was not the world's most sprawling city; it was still an enormous village, full of country folk. They welcomed the idea of an evangelical temple, and contributed generously. On 1 January 1923, trumpets blared, and Aimée unveiled the floodlit, electrically rotating cross that formed the heart of the Angelus Temple; by night it could be seen fifty miles away. The Temple, and Sister Aimée's house next door, had cost about $1½ million. The Temple had a seating capacity of 5,000, a broadcasting station, a theological seminary, an enormous organ, and a 'Miracle Room' full of discarded crutches. Groups of disciples engaged in non-stop prayer, participating in relays. Aimée, with a genius that owed something to Hollywood (and to which Billy Graham undoubtedly owes some of his own methods), held pageants with music, picture-shows of the Holy Land, and dramatized sermons, all accompanied by a vast choir. Her neighbour Carey McWilliams remarked felicitously that, 'Aimée kept the Ferris wheels and merry-go-rounds of religion turning night and day.' At the end of her sermons, she asked sinners to come forward to be saved; as the lights were lowered, and soft music soothed the audience, hundreds rose to their feet and moved down the aisles. Then Aimée would shout, 'Turn on the lights and clear the one-way street for Jesus,' and suddenly the music would turn into a brazen blare. Aimée was one of the earth's great showmen. For sheer entertainment her meetings surpassed anything that could be seen in the cinemas.

It was in 1925 that a new radio operator took over the Temple's radio station. His name was Kenneth G. Ormiston and he had a soothing, cultivated voice. At first, Aimée spoke to him only over the headpones; then they met by the Temple steps and she drove him home to his wife. But soon Ormiston was no longer hurrying home to his wife once the programmes were over. Instead, he went to a room in the Ambassador Hotel, where Sister Aimée was waiting. In 1926 Aimée went on a visit to the Holy Land, financed by 'love offerings' from her followers. Ormiston was absent from California during this period, although it is not known for certain whether he travelled with Aimée. She was back in Los Angeles in May 1926, and continued her clandestine meetings with Ormiston in various hotels. On 14 May Ormiston rented a cottage in Carmel, told the landlord that he would be returning with his 'invalid wife', and went back to Los Angeles.

Four days later, Aimée disappeared. She had gone to the beach at Venice for a swim. She sat in a beach tent, working on sermon notes, and after a while, she sent her secretary off on some errand. When the secretary returned, Aimée had vanished. Her mother proclaimed from the steps of the Temple, 'She is with Jesus – pray for her'. For the next thirty-two days, her followers mounted a frantic search. Aircraft flew close to the waves; men in diving suits looked for her body on the ocean floor. Two followers committed suicide – a young man yelled 'I'm going after her' and leapt into the sea. Aimée's mother had flowers scattered from an aircraft on the spot. A collection of $36,000 was taken for a memorial.

On 27 May, a newspaper mentioned that Ormiston had also vanished; his wife had reported him missing. Further probing by reporters revealed that he had also been absent when Aimée was in the Holy Land. As all Los Angeles began to buzz with indecent rumour and speculation, Ormiston strolled into the search headquarters, denied all knowledge of Aimée's disappearance and vanished again.

The police of California began to suspect that there might be a connection between Aimée and Ormiston, and that if they could find one they would find the other. Suddenly the search was intensified. On the morning of 29 May Ormiston called at a Salinas garage, near Carmel, to collect his car; he was accompanied by a woman, and later that day they registered as 'Mr and Mrs Frank Gibson' at a hotel in St Luis Obispo. That night, their car was stopped by a suspicious newspaper reporter. Ormiston turned and headed back towards San Francisco. Five days later, on 23 June 1926, a resident of a cottage in Agua Prieta, just across the Mexican border from Douglas, Arizona, was awakened by a knocking at the door, to be confronted by a woman who claimed she had been the victim of a kidnapping. It was Aimée.

Her story was that she had been kidnapped by two men and a woman – Rose, Steve and Jake. She had been taken to a shack in Mexico and had eventually escaped. When she returned to Los Angeles, 30,000 people were waiting at the station and she was carried to her car through lanes of flowers. Her followers showed a tendency to forgive and forget, and the rest of the world might have done the same, if Aimée had not tried quite so hard to prove her innocence.

She kept asking what the police were doing to find the kidnappers and issued challenges over the radio. A grand jury declared that there was no evidence to indict anyone. Soon after that, someone tracked down her 'love nest' in Carmel. Ormiston, who was still in hiding, sent an affidavit stating that although he had stayed in the cottage with a woman who was not his wife, that woman was not Aimée. This seemed to be confirmed when a woman announced that the lady in question was her sister; Aimée publicly declared herself vindicated. But when the lady proved to be wanted by the police for passing bad cheques, the Press once again showed a disposition to regard Aimée as an adulterous woman who had decided to brazen it out. Another grand jury was convened; this time, a follower of Aimée's vanished to the lavatory with a major piece of evidence – a scrap of paper found in the 'love nest' with Aimée's writing on it – and flushed it down the toilet. The grand jury was dismissed. Finally, Aimée was charged with conspiring with others to obstruct justice. She raised a 'fight the Devil fund' of $¼ million, explaining to her followers that she was being crucified by the forces of evil. The evidence against her looked overwhelming; chambermaids testified about her sessions in hotel rooms with Ormiston and the hotel registers left no doubt about it. She was identified as the 'Mrs McIntyre' of the Carmel 'love nest' and the cheque-bouncing lady who had supported Ormiston's story now admitted she had been paid by Aimée, who had carefully coached her in her story. And yet, in spite of all this, District Attorney Asa Keyes, suddenly moved to dismiss the case against her – there was talk of a $30,000 bribe. (Keyes was later sentenced to prison for corruption in office.) Aimée announced that the

Lord had rescued her and settled down to writing her autobiography, *In the Service of the King*, in which she repeated the kidnapping story.

Soon after this, Aimée set out on another lecture tour; this time the subject was her own life, and she expected her audiences to pay for admission. To her surprise, few people seemed inclined to do this. It was the same when she went on a European tour in 1928. The faithful continued to regard Sister Aimée as a saint and a wronged woman but the general public seemed to regard her with a cynical amusement. Her publicity stunts, her public quarrels (with her mother, among others) and her law suits began to bore even the American Press. She chartered a liner for a crusade to the Holy Land but only a hundred followers turned up. For this occasion, Aimée had her chestnut hair bleached to blonde; her mother was indiscreet enough to mention that she had also had her face lifted and this alienated more of the faithful than the kidnapping escapade. In 1931, she decided to ignore her own teaching on divorce – she had always insisted that no divorced person should remarry during the lifetime of the other partner – and married an overweight radio announcer named Dave Hutton. Two days after the wedding, another woman sued Hutton for $200,000 for breach of promise. When the case was tried, Hutton was ordered to pay $5,000. But when she heard the news, Aimée fainted and fractured her skull on the flagstone of the courtyard. She went to Europe to recuperate. Hutton sent her a telegram: 'Take your time, honey . . . Daddy wants a well woman.' But she and Hutton never lived together again.

During the remainder of her life she was sued fifty-five times in the courts of Los Angeles for unpaid bills, broken contracts, slander and other charges. There were a number of successful suits by relatives of Temple followers who had left their money to Aimée. She was as flamboyant as ever and as she grew older, her style in clothes became increasingly girlish, but the world had ceased to be interested in her.

On the morning of 27 September 1944, Aimée Semple McPherson was found unconscious in her hotel room in Oakland, California, with sleeping capsules scattered around her on the floor; she died later in the day. It was never established whether she had taken an overdose deliberately or accidentally.

MacPHERSON, James
The Ossian Scandal

There appeared in Edinburgh in 1760 a small volume entitled *Fragments of Ancient Poetry, collected in the Highlands of Scotland and translated from the Gaelic or Erse Language*. The translator was one James MacPherson. To say the work created a sensation would be an exaggeration, but it aroused warm interest. The classical spirit of the age of Dr Johnson was gradually giving way to an exciting new attitude that would be called 'Romanticism'. Poets like James Thomson and William Cowper were observing that nature was beautiful and the novel – virtually invented by a printer called Samuel Richardson less than twenty years earlier – was teaching a new generation to daydream. The world of mountains and mists and heroic simplicity of these 'fragments of ancient poetry' struck an immediate chord in the heart of all true Scots. It was almost an implicit criticism of the kind of stilted, artificial stuff that had passed for literature in England for the past half century.

James MacPherson, the son of a poor farmer, was only twenty-four at the time; he had studied divinity at Aberdeen and Edinburgh and was now working as a schoolmaster, being too young to become a minister. He had become a friend of a poet called John Home, whose play *Douglas* was popular and who had published a poem called 'The Highlander' two years earlier.

Now Home and other friends – like Hugh Blair and Dr Alexander Carlyle of Inveresk – urged him to go on a tour of the Scottish Highlands to gather more poetry. Blair had written the introduction to the *Fragments*, in which he had stated that these disjointed pieces were part of a longer epic. MacPherson was oddly reluctant; he pleaded lack of money. Whereupon some of his new friends invited him to a special dinner and proposed to raise enough money to send him to the Highlands. Since they included a distinguished peer – Lord Elibank – the poor farmer's son found it hard to refuse. A subscription was raised and more than £100 subscribed – the philosopher Hume was a donor. Armed with letters signed by distinguished people, James MacPherson set off for the Highlands. He was accompanied on his first journey by a relative, Lachlan MacPherson, who helped him to take down recitations in Gaelic. He later made a trip to Mull and the coast of Argyll and returned with still more transcriptions and manuscripts. Since he was not a Gaelic scholar, friends helped him to translate these. Finally, there appeared in 1762 a lengthy work called: *Fingal, an Ancient Epic Poem in Six Books, together with Several Other Poems composed by Ossian, the son of Fingal.*

It was this that made MacPherson famous, not simply in Britain, but all over Europe. It sold out and immediately reprinted. It was translated into German, French, Spanish, Italian, Dutch, Danish, Russian, Polish and Swedish. The Prince of Sweden was even named after Ossian's son Oscar and eventually succeeded to the throne as King Oscar I. MacPherson went to London and became a literary lion.

The Ossian poems were written in a kind of rhythmic prose which had a certain bareness and wildness that produced an effect like music. With its tales of heroic warriors, queenly maidens and 'battles long ago', it often brings to mind Tolkien's *Lord of the Rings* – particularly those appendices written in the style of the old sagas. MacPherson set out to create a mood of nostalgia:

A tale of the times of old! The deeds of days of other years!

The murmur of thy streams, O Lora! brings back the memory of the past. The sound of thy woods, Garmallar, is lovely in mine ear . . .

Who comes from the land of strangers, with his thousands around him? The sunbeam pours its bright stream before him; his hair meets the wind of his hills. His face is settled from war. He is calm as the evening beam that looks from the cloud of the west, on Cona's silent vale . . .

The English were less enthusiastic about Ossian than the rest of Europe. After the rising of 1745, the Scots were not popular. Critics like Samuel Johnson had a certain vested interest in the highly civilized 'classical' style of the 'age of reason'. Johnson was contemptuous; when Boswell asked him if any modern man could have written Ossian he replied, 'Yes, sir, many men, many women and many children.'

Fingal presented some baffling historical anomalies. Fingal was supposed to be king of a state called Morven, on the west coast of Scotland; he lived in the third century A.D., at the time of the Roman emperors Severus and Caracalla. But the poem is about a Viking invasion of Ireland. When the Irish hero Cuchulin is routed, Fingal rushes to help him and expels the Vikings. The Vikings, however, did not invade until the middle of the eighth century A.D. Moreover, as a learned clergyman called Warner pointed out in a pamphlet soon after *Fingal*'s appearance, the original of the Scottish hero Fingal is the Irish hero, Finn MacCool. It is unlikely that Finn ever saw a Roman in his life yet Ossian has him fighting the Romans in Scotland. As to Cuchulain, he was some three centuries earlier, at the time of Christ. While it is true that a few distortions might have crept into poems which, according to MacPherson, had been recited down the centuries by Gaelic bards, it seems unlikely that the bards would have committed such a howler as making an eighth-century Viking meet a first-century Irishman.

Two years after *Fingal*, MacPherson produced another Ossian epic called *Temora*. Purely as literature, this was much inferior to *Fingal*, being altogether more bombastic. Hume wrote to Blair that most people took it for 'a palpable and impudent forgery'. MacPherson had written a lengthy introduction to *Temora* and made the mistake of including a specimen of the original Gaelic poem; experts soon pointed out that it contained several modernisms.

There were other anomalies. MacPherson's earliest find was a poem called 'The Death of Oscar', and it gave a completely different version of the Oscar legend than the one based on Irish tradition. In MacPherson's version, Oscar kills his friend Dermid in a quarrel over a girl. There were many variants of the original legend but all of them have Dermid dying at a boar hunt from a poisoned bristle. It seemed highly unlikely that Ossian had produced a different version. MacPherson recognized the force of the argument and suggested that there were two Oscars, but this was also denied by Irish scholars.

In 1773, Dr Johnson travelled to Scotland with Boswell; his *Journey to the Western Isles* appeared in 1775, and contained some scathing words about Ossian which led MacPherson to write to the publisher and demand that they should be removed. He even sent Johnson an announcement to insert in the book; Johnson ignored him. When MacPherson sent him a challenge, he bought himself a large, stout stick. MacPherson's publisher had an announcement printed in the newspapers, declaring that MacPherson had deposited the originals of the Ossian poems in his own shop in 1762 for anyone to examine and that he had even tried to raise a subscription to publish them in the original Gaelic but without success. This story was disingenuous; the 'manuscripts' MacPherson had deposited were his own transcriptions of Gaelic poetry and would have proved very little.

Johnson, like most critics, was willing to accept that Ossian was not pure invention. There were many genuine fragments of ancient poetry there, as MacPherson's fellow collectors, who had accompanied him on his journeys to the Highlands, could testify. But there was no original 'epic.' MacPherson had stuck fragments of Gaelic poetry into his own composition as he felt inclined.

The clash between Johnson and MacPherson was the talk of literary London and Johnson's criticisms eventually led most people to conclude that Ossian was largely MacPherson's own composition. One of MacPherson's original patrons, David Hume, practically admitted as much when he described how MacPherson had visited him before his journey to the Highlands and had outlined the plot of *Fingal*.

MacPherson still had his supporters. One of these, William Shaw, set out for the Highlands in 1778 to gather materials for a Gaelic dictionary and to attempt to prove that the Gaelic legends of Ossian were genuine. It was his intention to submit any material he found to a minister or justice of the peace, so no one could question it later. He spent six months travelling around the Highlands, plying old gentlemen with snuff and whisky and persuading them to recite any fragments of Gaelic poetry they could recall. But although he heard many legends and fairy tales, there was no trace of the story of Fingal or Temora as told by Ossian. He continued his search in Ireland and met with little success. Then, finally, it dawned on him that MacPherson had been lying all along and that the poems were his own compositions. He published an *Enquiry into the Authenticity of the Poems ascribed to Ossian* and it added fuel to the flames of the controversy. MacPherson himself chose to remain silent which most people construed to mean that he had nothing much to add.

MacPherson had no reason to regret Ossian, even if he had been led into concocting it by the admiration of noble patrons. It laid the foundations of a prosperous career. He spent two years in Florida as secretary to the governor, wrote a history of Great Britain and Ireland that was mainly a glorification of the Celts and an attack on the English, translated the *Iliad* into Ossianic prose, and caused a scandal with a continuation of Hume's *History of England* in which he accused some of the most illustrious families of treachery and treason. He secured a place supervising the newspapers on behalf of the Court, moved into a house in Westminster, and bought another in Putney. Towards the end of his life – he died in 1796 – he became a Scottish landowner and built himself a mansion overlooking the River Spey. He left a considerable sum of money, some of which went to support five illegitimate children whom he had fathered on five different mothers. He was buried, at his own request, in Westminster Abbey.

After his death, at the age of fifty-nine, a commission of enquiry was set up by the Highland Society to try to settle the question of the authenticity of the poems once and for all. Their report in 1805 repeated what was already known: that there were many fragments of 'Ossianic' poetry around in the Highlands but no continuous epics such as *Fingal* or *Temora*. But in 1886–7, a series of articles in the *Celtic Magazine* by Alexander Macbain established beyond all doubt that the author of the Ossian poems was ignorant of Celtic history, that the life portrayed in the poems was totally unlike that known historically about the period, and that the Gaelic fragments quoted by MacPherson to prove their authenticity were a translation from MacPherson's English version, not vice versa. Finally, he pointed out that MacPherson's early poem, 'The Highlander', published four years before *Fingal*, bore a close resemblance to the Ossian poems. MacPherson had tried hard to suppress this later, without success.

Whether a fraud or not, the Ossian poems exercised a tremendous influence on a whole generation and led to the creation of the Romantic movement in literature.

MARCONI Affair

A Financial Scandal that Almost Wrecked a Government

This scandal, like most political scandals, was blown up out of all proportion by Opposition politicians. In retrospect, it seems a storm in a teacup.

The scandal concerned allegations that various Liberal politicians – the Liberals then formed the British government – had used their 'inside knowledge' to make money from a contract awarded by the government to the Marconi Company.

The charges had some slight basis in fact. In 1910, it was generally agreed that the British Empire needed to avail itself of recent scientific advances and set up a sophisticated communications system of telegraphs around the world. Disasters like the sinking of the *Titanic* and triumphs like the arrest of the murderer Crippen on the other side of the Atlantic showed the need to bring the Empire up to date. The Marconi Company – Guglielmo Marconi virtually invented radio – offered to set up six stations in England, Egypt, East Africa, South Africa, India and Singapore for £60,000 each. The Liberal government accepted this tender. The contract was signed on 19 July 1912. Almost immediately, there were rumours that members of the government – in particular, the Postmaster-General, Herbert Samuel, and the Attorney-General, Sir Rufus Isaacs – had received 'kickbacks' for their part in securing the contract. In August 1912 these charges were made publicly in a journal called *The Eye Witness*, edited by Cecil Chesterton (G.K.'s brother) and founded by Hilaire Belloc. Belloc was not only a cranky anti-Semite but seemed to regard the word 'financier' as synonymous with rogue. (Samuel and Isaacs were, of course, Jews.) In October 1912 the government was finally forced to set up a Select Committee to investigate these charges.

What soon became clear was that the rumours of kickbacks were totally unfounded. But it also emerged that Sir Rufus Isaacs had been foolish enough to buy shares in the American Marconi Company, of which his brother Godfrey was a director.

Godfrey Isaacs had come back from America in April 1912 with the intention of floating a new issue of Marconi shares on the London Stock Exchange, since the American company was in financial difficulties. On 9 April he had a lunch at the Savoy with his two brothers, Rufus and Harry – the latter another successful businessman – and offered to 'let them in on the ground floor'. Harry agreed to buy 50,000 Marconi shares but Rufus refused, in case he was accused of profiting from a government deal. Eight days later, he foolishly changed his mind and bought 10,000 of the shares at £2 each, from his brother Harry – apparently feeling that provided there was no direct connection with the Marconi Company, all was well. When the shares were offered publicly two days later their price was £4 per share, since it was now known that the government had signed a contract with the English Marconi Company, of which Godfrey Isaacs was Managing Director. Two more Liberal ministers, Lloyd George and Lord Murray, also bought shares. In fact, the price of the shares quickly sank below £4 after the original boom so no one made any money – Rufus Isaacs lost £1,300 when he sold some of his shares.

Unfortunately, the Select Committee was not deeply interested in getting at the truth. Its Liberal members wanted to prove the charges were nonsense and its Unionist (Conservative) members wanted to prove they were well-founded. The committee split on party lines. They grilled various journalists, one of whom, Leo Maxse of *The National Review* accused Ministers of being involved in the purchase of Marconi shares. Winston Churchill did the Liberals a good turn by persuading two leading Unionist politicians, Sir Edward Carson and F. E. Smith (later Lord Birkenhead) to represent Samuel and Isaacs in a suit for damages against a French newspaper, *Le Matin*, which had accused them of collusion and fraud over the Marconi contract. Samuel and Isaacs won damages but Carson admitted in court that they had bought American Marconi shares and this added fuel to the fire again.

Finally, the committee had to issue two reports. The Majority Report (Liberal) declared that Samuel and Isaacs had merely been guilty of a little misjudgment; the Minority Report (Conservative) accused Lloyd George and Isaacs of 'grave impropriety'. There was a passionate and noisy two-day debate in the Commons that ended with a government majority. Four months later Isaacs was raised by the Prime Minister, Asquith, to the office of Lord Chief Justice, which caused considerable scandal, and no doubt confirmed Belloc in his simplistic view that all politicians were crooks. In fact, his paper *The Eye Witness* was also sued for libel, and the editor, Cecil Chesterton, was found guilty but fined only £100; to many people this seemed an admission that he was right after all, which was not the case.

The only practical result of this storm in a teacup wa that the establishment of the chain of wireless telegraph stations was delayed until 1927.

MAYERLING AFFAIR

Double Suicide in a Hunting Lodge

The suicide of Archduke Rudolf of Habsburg after killing his eighteen-year-old mistress has been described as the greatest royal scandal of modern times.

If Rudolf had lived, he would have presided over a collapsing empire. The dynasty of the Habsburgs had dominated Europe for seven hundred years. But by the end of the nineteenth century, it had spread itself too far; it had too many ill-assorted subjects and great social changes were ripping apart the old fabric. Subject nations wanted their independence. The 1848 revolution had made the Emperor Franz Joseph determined to resist all change but it was like trying to hold on the lid of a pressure cooker by manual force.

Franz Joseph was a rigid disciplinarian, who rose at 4 A.M. to work on state papers; his life was one of exact routine. His empress, Elizabeth, was beautiful and sensitive and she found the atmosphere of her husband's court – dominated by her mother-in-law – impossible to stomach; she spent most of her time travelling over Europe, permanently dissatisfied.

Her eldest son Rudolf had his father's obstinacy and his mother's sensitiveness. Born in August 1858, he became an army officer and took pride in the number of his sexual conquests, entering their names in a ledger – red for aristocrats, black for commoners. He grew bored with seduction and flirted with left-wing ideas. Later, he wrote newspaper articles that revealed he had considerable literary talent. He was indeed highly intelligent.

It seems conceivable that at some point he contracted venereal disease. What is certain is that he contracted the rich dilettante's disease of boredom and a sense of meaninglessness. 'He seemed to doubt the validity of everything he did', says one commentator. His father declined to allow him any taste of responsibility. At twenty-three he was married to the seventeen-year-old Princess Stephanie of Belgium, a silly, selfish, empty-headed girl, who bore him a daughter. Rudolf became increasingly depressed and listless, and began to take morphine. When the German emperor inspected Franz Joseph's army in 1888, he protested that the infantry ought not to be in the charge of an incompetent like Rudolf; he was removed – one more blow to his self-esteem. To some brother officers he made the surprising proposal of a suicide pact, which they failed to take seriously, although it was reported to the police.

His relationship with his father became increasingly bitter. He began to plot, in a rather half-hearted manner, his father's downfall. His friend Count Stephen Károlyi was a Hungarian patriot and he planned to speak in the Hungarian parliament against granting funds to Franz Joseph's army. Rudolf seems to have agreed to a hare-brained scheme of Károlyi's to oust Franz Joseph and put him on the throne. (It might, in fact, have saved the Austrian empire if it had ever happened, since Rudolf's liberal tendencies may have defused the tensions.) A butler reported that the emperor bitterly upbraided his son for disloyalty.

Maria Vetsera was an attractive teenager of Greek extraction, whose mother had married into the minor Austrian nobility. She caught a few glimpses of Rudolf in society and decided she was passionately in love with him. Through her friend, Countess Marie Larisch, who was Rudolf's cousin, she succeeded in being presented to him in the Prater in Vienna. Rudolf was not one to turn down the opportunity to accept a girl's virginity when it was offered; the two became lovers in 1888. By this time he was already brooding on suicide.

On 28 January 1889, Rudolf received a telegram from Budapest. As he threw it aside he was heard to mutter, 'It has to be. There is no other way.' He spent the day writing farewell letters, then set out for his hunting lodge at Mayerling. He had arranged to meet Maria on the way; that morning, she slipped away from her mother and made off in a carriage sent by Rudolf. It seems likely that she had already agreed to the suicide pact. They met at an inn.

Rudolf had arranged a hunting party at his lodge and various friends were also there. But on 29 January, 1889, he protested that he had a cold and stayed indoors. That evening, he dined with Count Hoyos, while Maria stayed upstairs. When Hoyos left, Rudolf's valet, Loschek, entertained them by singing for them. They both wrote farewell letters – Maria told her sister: 'We are both going blissfully into the uncertain beyond . . .' They then discussed whether they preferred to die by poison or a bullet and decided on the revolver. Maria noted this decision on an ashtray. They went up to the bedroom where Rudolf shot Maria immediately. He himself waited until six in the morning, when he went downstairs and told Loschek to prepare breakfast. He returned to his room, drank a glass of brandy, and shot himself in the head. The bodies were discovered a few hours later.

Franz Joseph was deeply shocked by the news, and the empress broke down when she read Rudolf's farewell letter. At first the court insisted that Rudolf had died of heart failure but the truth could not be held back for ever. There was a wrangle with the Cardinal Secretary of State, Rampolla, as to whether Rudolf could be buried in consecrated ground as he had committed suicide. Eventually he was laid to rest in the Capucin Crypt in Vienna. Maria's naked body was thrown into a woodshed immediately after she was discovered and was not recovered for two days.

It is still not clear why Rudolf killed himself and why he, a Catholic, chose to die with the murder of Maria Vetsera on his conscience. The answer to the latter question may be that he was a physical coward and wanted someone else to die with him. He was probably not in love with Maria for he had spent the night before leaving Vienna with a prostitute named Mizzi Kaspter. It seems conceivable that she was as anxious to die with the man she adored as he was to have someone to die with him. He may even have felt he was conferring a favour on her by involving her in the suicide pact – after all, he was heir to the throne and she was a nobody.

In 1983, ex-Empress Zita, the last survivor of the Habsburg monarchy, caused a sensation when she announced that the double suicide was really a political murder. She claimed that she had received this information from her husband, Emperor Karl, and from Prince Rudolf's sisters, Archduchess Gisela and Archduchess Marie-Valerie and her aunts Archduchess Maria Theresia and the Duchess Marie-José. 'I have recorded precisely everything that was told to me under the seal of deepest sympathy. I intend to publish these documents which are among my personal papers when the time is right.' According to the ex-Empress, the assassination of Prince Rudolf was organized by no less a person than the French politician Clemenceau who had tried unsuccessfully to lure Rudolf into a republican plot against his father, and was afraid Rudolf would betray him. In a cloister built out of part of the hunting lodge, Carmelite nuns in a silent order still pray day and night for the 'three dead' of Mayerling. Why three, rather than two, remains another mystery; according to some, Maria Vetsera was expecting Rudolf's child.

The Empress points that that an enormous amount of documentation has disappeared from the state archives, including a 2,000-word telegram which the Emperor sent to Pope Leo XIII arguing that in spite of the official suicide explanation, his son had a right to a Christian burial. This telegram has also disappeared from the Vatican archives.

In September 1898, the Empress Elizabeth was stepping into a boat at Geneva when she was stabbed to death by a young anarchist named Luigi Lucheni. There were those who felt her death was a release. Since Rudolf's suicide she had been wandering all over Europe like an unhappy shade.

Rudolf was succeeded as heir to the throne by his cousin, Archduke Franz Ferdinand. It was the assassination of the archduke and his wife at Sarajevo on 28 June 1914 that precipitated World War I, and brought about the final destruction of the Austrian Empire.

MORELL, Marie de

The Rape Scandal

The Morell rape scandal was one of the great French *causes célèbres* of the 1830s. It is also a baffling unsolved mystery, to which various solutions have been offered.

At six o'clock on the morning of 24 September 1834, an English governess named Helen Allen knocked frantically on the door of a bedroom occupied by General Baron Charles Paul de Morell and his wife Solange, and told them that their sixteen-year-old daughter Marie had been raped in the night. They rushed to the girl's room and found her in her nightdress on which there was blood; there was also blood on the floor. The window pane had been broken and there were fragments of glass on the floor. Marie groaned with pain when she tried to move. She said that a soldier with a black handkerchief had broken into her bedroom in the middle of the night, tied her with a rope round her waist, then assaulted her. On the table there was a letter written on straw-coloured paper. It said: 'I am willing to marry your daughter and that will save her from disgrace. The solution . . . is to hand her over to me with a fine dowry . . .' It was signed 'Emile'. Emile de la Roncière was a young lieutenant in the lancers. Two days before, General de Morell had banned him from the house without explaining why.

The reason, in fact, was that for some weeks now, a series of disturbing anonymous letters had been arriving at the Morell house. Some came through the post, others were found hidden in such places as a sealed cigar box, suggesting that the author, or some accomplice, had regular access to the house.

The letters were written on the same straw-coloured paper as the one found in Marie's bedroom and were signed with an 'E'. One said: 'She is pure and innocent, of that I cannot rob her; but in the eyes of the world she will appear to be at the centre of a great scandal, and she will appear guilty. As I cannot win her for myself, this will be my revenge.' Other letters accused the general's wife of being unfaithful to him and said odious things about the governess, Helen. They were scattered with obscenities. Yet the young officer Emile de la Roncière was a regular visitor at the house of the general in Saumur, he was in charge of the cavalry school there and often sat next to the beautiful Marie at dinner. Why the handsome young man should try to win her by writing obscene letters was baffling. However, the general was finally convinced that it must be Emile who was writing the letters and when the young man showed up for an evening party on 23 September, two days before the alleged rape, he summoned him to his study and ordered him out of the house. It was a hard decision to take; Emile was the son of another famous French general, the Comte de la Roncière and might well have been an ideal match for Marie. It was true he was by no means a saint, being a gambler who kept at least two mistresses but these things could be overlooked in a good-looking young aristocrat.

Octave d'Estouilly, a lieutenant who had been seconded to the general's regiment to paint horses, had been asked by the general to compare the handwriting on the anonymous letters with that of Roncière's. He examined Emile's signature in the mess book and thought he detected a strong similarity. Apparently, Roncière learned about these efforts to incriminate him, for shortly afterwards d'Estouilly received a letter calling him a coward and threatening to mark his infamy on his face. Brother officers goaded d'Estouilly into sending a stinging reply, challenging Roncière to a duel. The encounter took place and d'Estouilly, who was an artist rather than a swordsman, was wounded twice. Yet Roncière, when told why he had been challenged, flatly denied writing the letters or even the letter calling d'Estouilly a coward.

As far as General de Morell was concerned, the duel was the last straw. He ordered Roncière to go to Toulon. The anonymous letters continued. One hinted that Marie de Morell would soon be showing signs of pregnancy.

A month after the events, the general and his family moved

to Paris for the winter. In her husband's absence, the baroness opened the box in which he kept the anonymous letters – he had refused to allow her to see many of them. No doubt she was driven by curiosity to know whether she was accused of any more infidelities. What she found astonished her. The box also contained two letters from Emile de la Roncière, one confessing to writing the insulting letter that had provoked the duel, the other to writing all the other anonymous letters. Solange de Morell decided to go to the police. The prefect recommended her to ask the advice of the celebrated lawyer, Maître Berryer. The box containing the letters was delivered to the advocate's house. The baroness merely wanted to stop the anonymous letters. Berryer's advice was that the Morell family should take the case to court. And, to make sure they had no alternative, he handed over the box of letters to the public prosecutor.

On 29 June 1835, the case against Emile de la Roncière opened in Paris. He had been arrested eight months previously. The allegations against him looked so strong that no advocate would agree to defend him in spite of the efforts of his father, the Comte. Finally, a young advocate, Maître Chaix d'Este-Ange, agreed to take the case. No one entertained much hope that he would secure an acquittal. And if the rape was proved, then Emile would be sentenced to execution.

The case against him certainly looked very serious. If he was innocent, then why had he written a confession to being the author of the letters? His own explanation, in court, was that since the experts had said he was the author of the letters, he felt he was 'done for'. The general has assured him that if he confessed in writing, there would be no further action taken against him. So he had confessed and accepted exile in Toulon.

Also charged with Roncière were two servants, Samuel Gilieron, the general's footman, and Julie Genier. They were both accused of helping Roncière 'plant' the letters in the general's house. One of the anonymous letters in the box had accused Samuel of being an accomplice. Another said that Julie was pregnant by Roncière, an accusation that had been proved untrue by her eight months in prison.

The high point of the trial was the appearance of Marie

herself in the witness box. She described how she heard glass break and how someone had jumped down into her room from the window-sill. She identified the man as Roncière. According to Marie, he had tied a rope round her waist and wrestled with her on the floor, trying to get on top of her. He managed to pull off her nightgown and made a number of cuts with a sharp instrument. She admitted that she had attended a ball only four days later, so it seemed clear that the attack had not caused the mental and physical breakdown that the prosecution alleged. Moreover, when she repeated that her assailant had worn a red forage cap, the defence pointed out that Roncière's regiment wore a blue one. She was by no means a convincing witness.

To the surprise and relief of Roncière, the trial was not going as badly as he expected. The glazier who repaired the window said that the glass had been found outside the room, indicating that it had been broken from the inside. He also said that the hole in the window was in such a position that no one would have been able to reach through and release the catch. The defence also pointed out that it would have taken an immensely long ladder to reach the window and that on a bright moonlit night, Roncière would certainly have been seen if he had carried it from the cavalry school.

At the beginning of the trial, feeling against Roncière had been strong and the distinguished spectators, including the artist, Honoré Daumier, and the writer, Victor Hugo, had evidently felt that the Morell family deserved the strongest sympathy. After Marie's evidence, that sympathy had clearly evaporated.

Despite this, the verdict was unexpected. Roncière was found guilty and sentenced to ten years' deportation. The two servants were unconditionally discharged. If they were innocent, then this suggested that the letters had been planted in the Morell household by someone else, someone who was not in the dock.

The case ruined the career of General Baron de Morell. There was a strong feeling that there had been a 'cover up' and that Roncière was innocent. But Morell's powerful patrons, including the king himself and his right-hand man, General

Soult, made sure the case was not re-opened. They suspected it might be used by the left-wing Press to cause trouble for the government and no doubt they were right – as the Dreyfus case was to show sixty years later (*see* page 164). Morell's wife left him, although she remained a source of intense gossip. The general continued to entertain in his Paris house, with his daughter as hostess, but his invitations were never returned. Marie herself married a Belgian diplomat and her father was not even invited to her wedding. Roncière spent eight years in prison in France, his sentence being reduced by the king to defuse the increasing demand for a retrial. He was later made a commandant in the National Guard and was awarded the Legion of Honour. He died in 1874.

What is the solution to this curious mystery? One thing seems very clear: Roncière was innocent. His diaries, published many years after the trial, show that he was in love with a mistress who had moved to Saumur to be with him, and the only reference to Marie comments that 'she is unattainable', being the daughter of his commanding officer. This does not indicate that Roncière wanted to attain her, only that, like any young officer, he considered her as a possible conquest. Nothing is more obvious than that Roncière had no reason to write the anonymous letters and that even if he was the author, he would not have continued to write them after being sent to Toulon. No one has suggested that he was mentally unstable or insane.

In his account of the case, in *French Crime in the Romantic Age*, Rayner Heppenstall suggests that the solution is that Helen Allen, the governess, was Roncière's mistress. On evidence published at the turn of the century, Heppenstall states that Helen Allen was sent to Roncière's lodgings to enquire why he had been rude to Marie at dinner the previous evening. The result was that Roncière began to spend nights in Helen's room, which was next to Marie's and connected to it by a door. Marie was intensely jealous. On the evening he was ordered out of the general's house Roncière got drunk and bet a fellow officer that he could seduce Marie the following night. Having got himself admitted to Helen's room, he slipped next door and drew the bolts, while Helen could only call 'Emile' in a low voice, afraid of waking the household. Emile then raised Marie's nightgown and proceeded to snip off some of her pubic hairs with a pair of scissors, intending to present these as evidence that he had won his bet. Marie presumably did not sleep throughout this 'assault' and may have been cut by the scissors as she struggled. Then, suggests Heppenstall, basing his speculations on a book by Gaston Delayen, the indignant girls decided to make him pay for his impudence and broke the window and invented the rape story.

The obvious objection to this theory is that there is no reason why a few pubic hairs should convince anyone that Roncière had slept with Marie. He might have persuaded his mistress to let him snip them off. Neither is there any reason why the girls should decide to break a window and invent the rape story; it would have been better to keep quiet. Heppenstall's version also fails to explain the anonymous letters unless Marie wrote them as a result of her jealousy of Roncière's sleeping with Helen Allen.

An altogether more plausible theory is advanced by Ian Messiter in his book *The Judgement*. He believes that Marie was the author of the letters and this is almost certainly true. Roncière had no reason to write them and certainly no reason to implicate himself by signing them 'E', and adding other indications of his authorship. If Marie had some reason to hate Roncière, then she is the likeliest suspect. She was in the general's household so could 'plant' various letters.

Why should she hate Roncière? Messiter believes that the answer is provided by the night of the 'rape'. What happened that night, he thinks, is that Marie had a miscarriage. This explains the four-hour delay between the 'rape' and the awakening of her parents. Helen was helping her to clean up her bedroom and ease her physical misery. Messiter has no suggestions to offer about the identity of the man who made Marie pregnant, although he doubts that it was Roncière. Saumur was full of young officers; the Morells entertained them several nights a week. Marie's mother cared for nothing but society and scarcely paid any attention to her daughter. When Marie discovered she was pregnant, she decided that the solution was immediate marriage and that Roncière was the perfect choice for a husband. Roncière, Messiter suggests, showed no interest in her advances, or simply regarded her as 'unattainable'. The anonymous letters, written in such a way as to suggest that Roncière was the culprit, were the revenge of a 'woman scorned'. The rape accusation, to cover up the miscarriage, was also directed, naturally, at Roncière.

But why did Roncière sign a confession? Messiter believes that the general bullied him into confessing, threatening him with disgrace if he refused, and promising silence if he agreed. This also fits in with Roncière's evidence in court.

If Messiter is correct, then Marie de Morell was one of the most neurotic and malicious women of the nineteenth century. And it must be admitted that all the evidence points in that direction.

NOVELLO, Ivor

The Red Rolls-Royce Scandal

In April 1944, a year before the end of World War II, newspapers all over England carried headlines: Famous Actor Jailed For Petrol Offence. Ivor Novello, Britain's most famous matinée idol, had been sentenced to two months' imprisonment for an offence that amounted to fraud.

Ivor Novello was born David Ivor Davies in Cardiff, Wales, the son of an accountant and a music teacher. He was taught singing by his mother and proved to be brilliantly gifted. At the age of ten he took first prize for singing at a National Eisteddfod and his soprano voice won him a singing scholarship to Magdalen College, Oxford. He wanted to become a composer and conductor. His first song was published when he was sixteen, and was performed – without much success – at the Royal Albert Hall in London with Novello as accompanist. His first successful song, 'The Little Damozel', appeared when he was seventeen, and was soon being sung by every soprano in the country. At this time, he also moved to London, supported by a modest income from his songs. He became famous at twenty-one, in 1914, with the song 'Keep the Home Fires Burning', which became almost a second national anthem during World War I. The singer, John McCormick, earned £20,000 from his recording of this song alone.

During the war Novello served in the Royal Naval Air Service but after two crashes he was transferred to the Air Ministry. There, in 1916, he wrote half the music for a show called *Theodore and Co.* produced by the actor George Grossmith. His fellow composer was Jerome Kern. The show ran for eighteen months at the Gaiety.

After the war, Novello was asked if he would act in a film *The Call of the Blood* which was filmed in Rome. It was an immense success. Novello had exactly the right kind of romantic good looks for a silent screen star and acting ability was hardly required – although he had his share of that too. In the 1920s he was a film star, an actor-manager, a composer and a playwright. People argued whether he or John Barrymore had 'the world's most handsome profile'. He starred in Hitchcock's 'first true film' *The Lodger* in 1926 – it has become a classic of the silent cinema. But it was in 1935 that he achieved a new dimension of fame with *Glamorous Night*, a combination of drama and musical with lavish spectacle. His formula was escapist romance and it was exactly what the audiences of the 1930s craved. *Careless Rapture* (1936) and *The Dancing Years* (1939) repeated the success. When World War II broke out in 1939, he had a luxurious flat in the Aldwych and a country home near Maidenhead. He was driven around in a red Rolls-Royce inscribed with his initials in black.

As the petrol shortage increased, it became increasingly difficult for Novello to travel from London to his country home for the weekend. His secretary wrote to the Regional Transport Commissioner's office to request extra petrol for him to drive to Maidenhead on the grounds that he needed to spend the weekends there writing his plays. The application was twice turned down. Just before Christmas 1942, Novello went into his dressing room where there was a crowd of admirers and asked despondently, 'Anyone want a Rolls? Mine's no good to me.'

Among the admirers in the room was a dumpy, middle-aged woman who had adored Novello from afar for years and gradually managed to get herself accepted among his retinue. He knew her as Grace Walton but her real name was Dora Constable. She now told Novello that she might be able to solve his problem. She was, she said, the secretary of the managing director of a firm with an office at Reading. She suggested that she might be able to apply for a special licence if the car was transferred to her firm for 'war work'. All this was arranged by Novello's secretary. The car was formally transferred into the firm's name; the firm even took over the insurance policy. Then Dora Constable wrote to the Regional Transport Commissioner to ask for a licence to 'facilitate speedier transport by the managing director and his staff between our many works and factories'. A few weeks later she collected the permit and handed it to Novello. He was effusively grateful and gave her a pair of earrings that had belonged to his mother, who had recently died.

Whether the firm actually made use of the initialled Rolls-Royce is not clear. Novello's biographer Peter Noble implies that it did, and that Novello then simply used the car 'from time to time' to take him from London to Maidenhead. But if this is so, then it is difficult to see why the firm was shocked to discover that it was supposed to be the owner of Ivor Novello's Rolls-Royce. For this is what happened in October 1943, almost two years after Novello had received his permit. The managing director of the firm rang Novello and asked him to come to his office. On arrival, he learned that his admirer was not called Grace Walton but Dora Constable, and that she was not the managing director's secretary but a filing clerk. The firm knew nothing whatever about the deal with the Rolls-Royce.

Novello realized that he could be in serious trouble. Not long before, the bandleader Jack Hylton had been fined £155 and sentenced to two weeks in jail for a similar petrol-rationing offence. (In the event the jail sentence was quashed.)

Novello decided against a cover-up – he felt it was not his fault. He informed the authorities what had happened and so did the firm. An inspector from the Fuel Ministry came to see him and Novello rather ungallantly put all the blame on Dora Constable, saying it was her idea and that he had no suspicion that he was doing anything illegal. This, of course, was nonsense; he knew he was using a false permit for his petrol. His waspishness backfired. When his remarks were repeated to Dora Constable, she replied indignantly that Novello was being unfair. He had known exactly what he was doing and even made various suggestions about the transfer. 'He was willing to do anything crooked as long as he had the use of the car.'

With a statement like that, the authorities had to act. On 24 March 1944, Novello was summoned to appear at Bow Street Court. He went to pieces and protested, 'The suggestion of my conspiring with a person of this woman's type is repugnant.'

But it was too late. On 24 April 1944, he stood in the dock at Bow Street alongside Dora Constable. His self-pitying remarks were quoted to the magistrate. The managing director of the firm went into the witness box and admitted, 'Novello was deceived as completely as I was.'

Novello gave one of his worst performances in the witness box. He was muddled and panic-stricken, and he gave the unfortunate impression that he was trying to unload the blame on to Dora Constable. The judge was an old-fashioned gentleman and there can be no doubt that Novello's attempt to dodge the blame revolted him. Dora Constable was fined £50 with £25 costs. Novello was fined £100. But, added Mr Justice McKenna, 'that would obviously be no punishment for a man like you, so I sentence you to eight weeks' imprisonment.' Novello was granted bail, pending an appeal. Shattered and stricken, he staggered from the court.

Two months later, on 16 May 1944, the appeal was heard at the London Sessions courthouse. The Chairman of the appeals committee was Mr Eustace Fulton who had quashed Jack Hylton's prison sentence. This time he was not in such a lenient mood. When Novello's secretary Fred Allen said that he had no suspicion there was anything wrong about the car transaction, 'otherwise I wouldn't have touched the damn thing', Fulton rebuked him for the use of 'damn'. Allen stammered nervously and Fulton snapped, 'Oh, get on!' The defending solicitor said, 'I am sorry your Lordship shows signs of impatience.' The judge snorted, 'I have shown every patience.' It did not bode well for Novello. And in spite of some distinguished character witnesses – Sir Lewis Casson, Dame Sybil Thorndike, Sir Edward Marsh – the most Fulton would concede was that Novello's sentence was perhaps too long and halved it to four weeks. As Novello left the court he turned and flung open his arms 'in a gesture of infinite despair'.

Novello was not a good prisoner. Although the authorities at Wormwood Scrubs leaned over backwards to treat him kindly – he was placed in charge of the prison choir – he almost went insane with despair and he plunged into extravagant self-pity. When he was released on 13 June 1944 he looked thin and haggard. A week later, he returned to the stage in *The*

Dancing Years and was cheered by a sympathetic audience who delayed the start of the show by ten minutes. His biographer Peter Noble is nevertheless convinced that the jail sentence should be regarded as a tragedy. Novello died seven years later of a heart attack at the age of fifty-eight. He was to write three more successes after his prison sentence: *Perchance to Dream, King's Rhapsody* and *Gay's the Word*. Noble believes the sentence shortened his life. In *Scales of Justice*, Fenton Bresler speculates that the prison sentence also cost Novello the knighthood that crowned the careers of most of his successful theatrical contemporaries.

Yet for the objective observer, it is hard to feel too much pity for Novello. His own behaviour was almost certainly responsible for the prison sentence. The obvious self-pity, the attempt to lay the blame on his admirer, who showed altogether more dignity when she decided not to testify, undoubtedly produced a mood of impatience in both judges. They probably felt that he was a spoiled brat who deserved a rap on the knuckles. Novello's real problem was that his life had been an almost unbroken run of success and until he was middle-aged he always had his adored mother to give him approval and moral support. The result was that he never really grew up. And, like a certain type of homosexual, he was prone to self-pity and self-dramatization. He once told Peter Noble, 'I have a suspicion that Fate has a sense of humour, and a rather malicious one. Fate says, "Ah, that boy's had a success. He is getting a bit above himself. Now for a few slips!"' A little more of this attitude might have averted the prison sentence or at least made it more bearable.

NOYES, John Humphrey

The Oneida Community – Promiscuity Justified by the Scriptures

To his disciples, John Humphrey Noyes was an inspired pro-
phet and a great spiritual leader but to most of his contemporaries he was a libertine whose doctrines of free love and 'complex
marriage' were a danger to the community. There were many
strange religious communities in America in the nineteenth
century: the Shakers (so called because they went into con-
vulsions of religious ecstasy that made them shake all over),
the Ephrata, the Rappites, Zoarites and many others. Most of
these were 'Perfectionists' – that is, they rejected the notion
that man is a miserable sinner as unnecessarily pessimistic and
taught that, through Divine Grace, man can achieve perfection.
The Shakers believed that God is both male and female by
nature, so women were as important as men in their religious
rites, many of which looked like orgies. But the Shakers taught
the importance of strict chastity.

The 1830s and 1840s were a time of tremendous religious
revivals in America, to such an extent that one portion of New
York State was known as the Burnt Over Region because the
fires of revivalism had burned so fiercely there. Men like Hiram
Sheldon, Erasmus Stone and Jarvis Rider preached their gospel
in the cotton village of Manlius and their converts adopted the
name of the Saints. One of the subjects that fascinated them
was whether the old marriage vows would still be binding when
the New Heaven and New Earth arrived. (Most of the great
religious revivals were based on the conviction that the Day of
Judgment was just around the corner.) It was John Humphrey
Noyes who provided a startling and controversial answer to
that question.

John Humphrey Noyes was born at Brattleboro, Vermont,
the son of a Congressman; he studied law, then divinity. He

was a man of considerable magnetism and remarkable intellect and he seems to have spent the two years following his conversion (at the age of twenty) in religious broodings and wrestlings. He found that he simply could not accept that he was a miserable sinner. Then, when he was twenty-two, the answer suddenly revealed itself to him in a blinding flash of revelation. Reading the Gospel of St John, he could see clearly that Jesus had announced the Second Coming within one generation of his own lifetime – that is, in the year 70 A.D. But if Jesus had already come to earth, then the Kingdom of God was already here. In that case, why was there so much sin on earth? The answer must be because people were unaware of the Second Coming. This, Noyes could now see and explained why he himself could never feel that he was a sinner. He wasn't. He was already saved. All he had to do was to live according to the gospels and nothing could go wrong.

The Bible said that in heaven there would be no marriage or giving in marriage. The Shakers also accepted this and for them it meant an obligation to celibacy. Noyes did not agree. Sex is obviously necessary to continue the race. What the Bible meant was obviously that all men were married to all women and vice versa. In *The Battle Axe*, the newspaper of the Perfectionists, he published in 1837 a letter in which he explained that 'at the marriage supper of the Lamb . . . every dish is free to every guest.' Sexual intercourse is one of the best things of life – men and women were intended to 'reflect upon each other the love of God'. Sexual shame was a consequence of the Fall, so all the Saved should now abandon it. Men and women should have sex together just as they felt inclined, regarding it as a sacrament.

At the age of twenty-three, Noyes returned to his home in Putney, Vermont, and preached his views; he converted a number of his own family. He married the daughter of the State Governor and one of his disciples, J. L. Skinner, married his sister. In 1840, Noyes and a number of disciples founded the Putney Community, which consisted of seven houses and a store on five hundred acres of fertile land. They spent the afternoons in manual labour to support themselves and the rest of the time in debate, prayer, reading, and teaching various subjects, including Latin, Greek and Hebrew.

Meanwhile, Noyes continued to brood on the problems posed by his doctrines of 'free love'. In 1846, he saw the answer. The problem with sexual intercourse was that it often produced unwanted results in the form of children. Mrs Harriet Noyes had produced five babies in six years and four had been stillborn. The answer was simple. Men and women should have full sexual intercourse, with orgasm taking place in the vagina only when they wished to produce children. For the rest of the time, the man must teach himself continence – not abstention. He could place his penis in the vagina but he must exercise severe self-discipline not to have an emission. It was a method that would later become known as the *karezza*, a term invented by Dr Alice Bunker Stockham of Ohio. Noyes pointed out that this method '*vastly increases* pleasure' (his italics). This doctrine was complemented by the notion of 'complex marriage' – that every man should regard all women as his wives and vice versa.

Noyes was not a man to keep his ideas secret – religious prophets seldom are – and he preached 'male continence' (i.e. the *karezza*) and 'complex marriage' quite openly. His neighbours were naturally outraged at what they took to be a public rejection of all decency. (Even nowadays, a community with these ideas would probably have a hard time of it if they lived in the vicinity of a small town.) There was a public outrage and the following year, Noyes was indicted on a charge of adultery. He decided that his great vision was too important to be destroyed by a few bigots. Fortunately, some of his disciples had already set up a community near Oneida Lake, about sixty miles away, with twenty-three acres of land. In 1847, Noyes and his disciples moved there and set up the Oneida Community.

What followed was a typical American success story – success preceded by disappointment and hard work. There were only two log houses, a log hut and an old sawmill; the disciples were obliged to sleep in garrets and outhouses for another twelve years. There were many hardships until an inventor called Sewell Newhouse joined the community; he saved it from bankruptcy by inventing a steel trap which the community proceeded to manufacture. They made travelling bags, satchels, preserved fruit and silk, and their workmanship made them widely known. They acquired more land and more people joined them. Two years after the community was formed, another branch was started at Brooklyn, and then others at Wallingford, Newark, Putney, Cambridge and Manlius. By 1878 there were over three hundred members. They had built a large brick house in which they all lived. They had factories, offices, a school, a carpenter's shop, barns and stables. The Mansion House – the main building – was centrally heated, with baths and labour-saving kitchens. The community also employed over two hundred workers from outside and treated them well.

The aspect that has chiefly interested posterity was the sexual innovation. Any man could propose love-making to any woman (or, indeed, vice versa) and she was free to reject him. Oddly enough, direct courtship was not allowed – a man who wanted to sleep with a woman had to approach her through the intermediary of a third person. What 'male continence' (or *coitus reservatus*) meant in practice was that the man put his penis into the woman's vagina, then lay still for anything up to an hour and a quarter. The woman was allowed to climax but the man was not expected to do so – even after withdrawal – Noyes denounced Robert Dale Owen's idea of *coitus interruptus* as 'Male incontinence plus evasion'. The male was supposed to stay in the woman until he lost his erection and this was believed to obviate any frustration and nervous tension. Noyes claimed that his community had a far better record of less nervous illness than the outside community while failing to recognize that there may have been other explanations for the situation.

As a system of sexual and moral hygiene 'complex marriage' seems to have been highly successful. Boys lost their virginity soon after puberty, girls somewhat later. An older person of the opposite sex was generally chosen to initiate the young – one of the aspects of 'complex marriage' that horrified the 'outside world' which felt a mixture of envy and moral indignation at the idea of a middle-aged man or woman being allowed to deflower a fifteen-year-old. One visitor wrote: 'The majority of the old women are hideous and loathsome in appearance and it seems to me the most horrible fate in the world to be linked with them.' But Noyes himself, as the father of the community (he was even known as Father Noyes), naturally had a wider freedom of choice than most – after the age of fifty-eight he fathered eight children. It is not clear whether this was accidental or intentional. The community practised eugenics – which Noyes called stirpiculture – and at one stage, twenty-four men and twenty women were selected for an experiment in selective breeding. But 'accidents' also happened – on average one every eighteen months.

Accounts of the community make clear that it was not a sexual free-for-all. The women dressed modestly, looking rather like the Chinese in long white trousers covered by a skirt. Any tendency by a couple to fall in love was regarded as selfish and 'idolatrous', and was discouraged by the system of 'mutual criticism', which usually meant that the person to be criticized was summoned before a committee, who then detailed his or her faults. People often requested mutual criticism just as someone today might go to a psychiatrist. One historian of the movement, Mark Holloway in *Heavens on Earth* (1951) has recorded that it was also used successfully to cure physical ailments, demonstrating that Father Noyes also understood about psychosomatic illness. There was one case in which 'mutual criticism' went further: when William Mills, a man in his early sixties – with an unattractive wife – tried to initiate more than his share of teenage virgins with the aid of sweets and alcohol, and as a result was hurled unceremoniously into a snowdrift.

Close attachments among children were also discouraged as selfish, which caused a certain amount of heartache. Otherwise, the children had an enviably pleasant time. They were allowed to sleep as late as they liked in the morning and there were dances, plays, pantomimes and other forms of entertainment for them. Nor were they deprived of parental affection. A mother weaned her child, then placed it in the Children's House where, until the age of three, it spent the daylight hours. After that children also spent the night there but parents could visit them as often as they liked and take them for walks. They left the Children's House at fourteen, when they were ready for sexual initiation and to join the adult community.

The adults also had a pleasant time of it once the community was well-established. Most members were supervisors rather than workers and they could change their jobs to avoid monotony. Times of meetings, amusements and meals were also changed for the same reason. There was fishing, hunting, boating and swimming at Oneida Lake, twelve miles away, and they could visit other communities.

The only real problem was the attitude of the outside world. The American constitution allowed for religious freedom but flagrant sexual immorality was quite another thing. One of the community's chief enemies was Professor John W. Mears, of Hamilton College, who denounced it as 'a Utopia of obscenity'. The Presbyterian Synod of Central New York appointed a committee of seven to investigate the activities of the community but was unsuccessful in destroying it. Eventually, the community began to decay from within. Many younger members thought that Noyes's religious doctrines were absurd; some were even agnostics (Noyes allowed members to study Huxley and Darwin). Noyes wanted to retire and appointed his agnostic son, Dr Theodore Noyes, to take his place but this caused dissension. Some members of the community even sided with the puritanical Dr Mears. Noyes finally slipped quietly away from Oneida and moved to Niagara Falls in 1876 at the age of sixty-five. It became clear that if Oneida wanted to survive, it would have to stop outraging the outside world with its sexual freedom. 'Complex marriage' was abandoned; the alternatives offered were celibacy or marriage and most preferred marriage. But to try to suppress 'complex marriage' was tantamount to removing one of the main foundations of the community. 'The Community sank step by step into its own Dark Ages' says one historian. The old generosity of spirit vanished, so that 'it was almost impossible to borrow a hammer from one's next door neighbour'. In 1881, the Oneida Community was reorganized as a joint stock company, and 'communism' was abandoned. Children were still educated free until they were sixteen, then they were given $200 to give them a 'start in life'. 'An arid commercialism' replaced the old communal spirit and the community began to split up. Yet the original Oneida branch remained commercially successful.

Noyes died in 1886 still believing firmly that the community had been ordained by God; praise and violent criticism continued long after his death. One English visitor had described him as 'a tall, pale man, with sandy hair and beard, grey, dreamy eyes, good mouth, white temples and a noble forehead.' But the secularist Charles Bradlaugh was to describe him as 'singularly unloveable, with his protruding, stuckout lower lip, his tired satyr-like leer . . . an eccentric goatish half-inch stripe of beard running from ear to ear.' Yet fifty-three young women had once signed a resolution declaring that they belonged to him as 'God's true representative', and that they were perfectly happy for him to decide which of the male members of the community were to father their children. It cannot be denied that Noyes was one of the most remarkable visionaries to come out of America in the nineteenth century.

PARKINSON, Cecil

The Sex Scandal that Destroyed Mrs Thatcher's Minister

The old adage that Hell knows no fury like that of a woman scorned brought the political career of handsome Cecil Parkinson, MP, crashing into ruin, as delegates to the 1983 Tory party conference met at Blackpool to celebrate their landslide victory at the hustings. He was a newly promoted senior cabinet minister and rising Parliamentary star in the second-term Thatcher government but also a married man with a family.

The text of a statement issued to *The Times* by colonel's daughter Miss Sara Keays, Cecil Parkinson's constituency secretary and pregnant mistress, was immediately relayed to the Premier at Blackpool after copies of Fleet Street's first editions reached number 10 Downing Street. In it, Miss Keays said she felt she had a public duty 'to put the record straight' about their affair, now that Mr Parkinson had seen fit to discuss it openly during a 'much-publicized' BBC television *Panorama* programme. Many observers, including Miss Keays, viewed his television appearance then as a calculated attempt by the government to influence public opinion and thus ward off any threat to Cecil Parkinson's political career. Now Miss Keays told how he had twice proposed – and twice jilted her – during their long affair, the second time after he had learned that she was carrying his child. 'The full facts have not been made public,' she asserted. 'Press judgment and public opinion have been influenced by inadequate information, speculation . . . and government's desire to restore Mr Parkinson's position, as someone put it to "rehabilitate" him.'

After a brief, poignant interview with Mrs Thatcher at two o'clock in the morning of Friday, 14 October 1983, Mr Parkinson returned to his own hotel room, and his wife Ann, to mull over his future. Six hours later he called on the Prime Minister again to tender his resignation which she accepted 'with regret'. Unusually following a ministerial resignation, the customary exchange of letters was not made public. Political observers were quick to point out, however, that it was still a resignation in disgrace and that, had he not resigned, Cecil Parkinson would have been dismissed from office.

The scandal of the tall, debonair, 52-year-old Minister's affair with his secretary had become public knowledge only days earlier. It was sparked off by a paragraph in the satirical magazine *Private Eye*, which referred to 'marital difficulties' and the fact that Miss Keays was shortly expecting a baby. That night a statement was put out by Mr Parkinson's solicitors in which he admitted that he had conducted a long affair with Miss Keays and that she was expecting his child. Next morning it was headline news in every paper and Britain was left to debate the fourth sex scandal involving a Tory Minister in twenty years (War Minister, John Profumo's affair with call-girl Christine Keeler in 1963, the scandal of Lord Lambton, Under Secretary for Defence, RAF, ten years later, and close on its heels, another call-girl scandal involving Lord Jellicoe, the Lord Privy Seal and Leader of the House of Lords).

Although gossip about Cecil Parkinson's affair with Sara Keays was already the topic of endless conversation at the Tory conference, following the *Private Eye* disclosure and subsequent statement from Mr Parkinson's solicitors, the announcement of his resignation stunned not only the Party faithful but the nation as a whole. He was personally popular. After only thirteen years in politics, nothing seemed beyond him. Some had expected him to be named Foreign Secretary in the new Thatcher administration, although Trade and Industry in itself meant promotion to Cabinet rank; he was even seen as a possible future Prime Minister, so meteoric had been his rise.

Cecil Parkinson came from a working-class background and was born in Carnforth, Lancashire, in 1931, the son of a railwayman. After winning a scholarship to Cambridge, he entered business as a trainee manager with the Metal Box Company and later joined a firm of City accountants. His marriage two years after leaving Cambridge led to his success both in business and politics. His wife Ann's family company, Jarvis Harpenden (Holdings) – a prosperous housebuilding firm with a turnover of millions of pounds – was founded by her grandfather at the turn of the century. After his marriage, Mr Parkinson succeeded first with a property company which he set up with a friend and then in the construction industry. By 1979 he was a chartered accountant and a wealthy man in his own right after selling one of his business interests to a Swiss engineering firm. Mrs Ann Parkinson was also an active Young Conservative. After unsuccessfully contesting Northampton in the 1970 General Election Cecil Parkinson entered Parliament a few months later when he won the Enfield West seat left vacant by the death of Mr Iain Macleod. By 1974 he had risen to junior whip in the Heath administration. Mrs Thatcher recognized his considerable ability by promoting him Paymaster-General and party chairman when she first came to office and he enhanced his growing reputation with the success of his 'Impact 80s' Central Office campaign. The transformation from Party esteem to national regard came during the difficult days of the Falklands fighting, when he served as a member of Mrs Thatcher's 'War Cabinet' and radiated calm, quiet confidence in the outcome at each televised appearance. Later he was a leading advocate of an early election and when that advice resulted in a landslide Tory victory, the Prime Minister rewarded his political loyalty and acumen with promotion to senior rank.

In direct contrast to his public image, however, Cecil Parkinson led a double life in private. Outwardly happily married, he conducted an affair with Miss Keays over several years. Moreover, the man who had exhibited such rock-steady confidence during the 'war' with Argentina apparently displayed only vacillation when confronted with his self-inflicted domestic problems. According to Miss Keays, he first offered to leave his wife and marry her in 1979. Instead he stayed with his wife and family while Miss Keays, then aged thirty-two, left Westminster in 1980 to work for Mr Roy Jenkins, then President of the European Commission, in Brussels. She and Cecil Parkinson resumed their affair on her return but when she told him she was pregnant, in May 1983, he declined either to marry her or inform Mrs Thatcher of the situation. According to Miss Keays, he then changed his mind again on Polling Day (9 June 1983), proposed to her a second time and informed the Prime Minister.

The public, unaware of the drama, saw him on Election Night alongside Mrs Thatcher at Central Office, waving to the crowds who cheered her victory. Political commentator, Graham Paterson of *The Daily Telegraph* said:

In retrospect, it was the highlight of his political life. He appeared to face a glittering political future . . . and was even being mentioned as possible future Prime Minister. Until September, when Mr Parkinson said he had changed his mind yet again and was staying with his wife, the issue seemed relatively clear-cut. For the government it would be a divorce by a senior and trusted Cabinet minister. The pressures of political life would doubtless be blamed.

There was no question, until September, of the affair becoming a scandal. But, by wavering between his family and his mistress, Mr Parkinson embittered relations between himself and Miss Keays so that public disgrace became almost inevitable . . .

In August, Mr Parkinson left for a holiday abroad with his wife and family. By now tongues were wagging, and by 23 August reporters from the *Daily Mirror* called on Miss Keays at her London home to ask if it was true that she was pregnant by the Trade and Industry Secretary. Then on 1 September, said Miss Keays, Cecil Parkinson asked her to meet him secretly in a London office when he told her that he had decided while abroad that he would not after all marry her. Then came the *Private Eye* disclosure and the inevitable newspaper headlines following his statement, via his solicitors, that '. . . I have had a relationship with Miss Keays for a number of years. During our relationship, I told Miss Keays of my wish to marry her. Despite my having given Miss Keays that assurance, my wife, who has been a great source of strength, and I decided to stay together to keep our family together.' As the public wondered what would happen next, a brief statement issued from No 10 Downing Street contained the assurance that 'Resignation does not . . . and will not arise.'

Downing Street – and Mr Parkinson – had reckoned without Sara Keays, however. According to newspaper reports, she was 'determined' to defend not only her own reputation but also that of her family. In doing so, the statement she issued to *The Times* landed with all the deadly effect of a dagger thrust between the minister's political shoulder-blades. It said:

> I agreed for the sake of my family that we would not discuss with the Press the statement made by Mr Parkinson last week. I hoped that it would not become necessary for me to say anything. However, I now feel that I have a duty to do so.
>
> On Friday, October 7 *The Times* said that Mr Parkinson had made a sad and silly blunder. Like the government, the editor believes this should have remained a 'private matter'. For the *Daily Telegraph* (Monday, October 10) 'the moral logic is that a quiet abortion is greatly to be preferred to a scandal . . .' I was not aware that political expediency was sufficient grounds for an abortion under the 1967 Act, quite apart from the fact that I would not have contemplated it.
>
> On Monday night, in spite of the understanding expressed in his statement (on Friday, October 14, that it would be in no one's interest that his differences with Miss Keays should be discussed publicly) Mr Parkinson saw fit to answer questions about the matter in a much-publicized *Panorama* programme. It appeared from the programme that the Prime Minister had been kept fully informed and that the statement issued by Mr Parkinson contained the full facts.

Miss Keays then went on to say that the full facts had not been made public and public opinion influenced accordingly. Her statement continued:

> 1. It has been implied that I tried to trap Mr Parkinson into marriage
> 2. That I sought to destroy his reputation
> 3. That the matter should have remained private
>
> This last presumes that I should hide from public view and declare on the baby's birth certificate 'father unknown', so casting further doubt on my reputation and denying the child his fundamental right to know the identity of his father.
>
> According to the view expressed in the *Telegraph*, I should have sacrificed my baby's life for Mr Parkinson's career and the Government's reputation. [This was denied by the editor, who claimed that a leader in the newspaper had been misquoted.]
>
> I wish to make known the following chronology of events.
> 1. My baby was conceived in a long-standing, loving relationship

which I had allowed to continue because I believed in our eventual marriage. It has been suggested that Mr Parkinson only asked me to marry him after I became pregnant, when in fact he first did so in 1979.

2. In May, when I knew of my pregnancy, Mr Parkinson decided he no longer wished to marry me. I told him that, while I had to accept the fact that he was not going to marry me, I could not deny my baby his right to know the identity of his father.

3. I did, however, implore Mr Parkinson, during May and early June to inform the Prime Minister, because his name and mine were sufficiently linked in political circles for speculation to be inevitable and it was essential that the Prime Minister was made aware of the situation before forming her new Government. He would not agree to this.

4. On Polling Day Mr Parkinson sought a reconciliation and asked me to marry him. I gladly accepted. He said he was about to see the Prime Minister to inform her of our relationship, and to tell her that he would be obtaining a divorce in order to marry me. That evening he told me he had so informed her. He also told other members of my family of his intention. He asked me to give him time to arrange matters and to leave my job at the House of Commons, which I did at the end of June. I and my family assured him of our full cooperation and that we would give him such time as he needed.

5. On August 5, Mr Parkinson went on holiday abroad with his wife and family, having reassured me of his intention to marry me.

6. On August 23 I was visited at my London home by reporters from the *Daily Mirror* who demanded to know if it was true that I was pregnant by Mr Parkinson. At that very moment others from the same newspaper called on my father and young sister. Later that night, as I was driving a girlfriend to her home, I was pursued by two cars which I believed to be driven by reporters from the *Daily Mirror* who tried to force me to stop and one of their cars collided with mine. I had to take refuge in Rochester Row Police Station.

7. On August 24 I informed Mr Parkinson, who was still abroad, of the incident with the *Daily Mirror*. I assured him that neither I nor my family had told them anything, but I was concerned that the Press would shortly confront him. He advised me to leave London, which I did, and he said he would speak to me again on his return to England the following week. He gave me no indication that matters between us had in any way changed.

8. On September 1, Mr Parkinson asked me to meet him secretly at an office in London, where he informed me that he had decided while abroad that he was not going to marry me after all. Later that day I telephoned him to say that I thought it was essential that he should inform the Prime Minister.

9. I subsequently instructed solicitors with a view to Mr Parkinson and myself issuing a joint statement. In the ensuing weeks it became clear that other newspapers were pursuing the story, and that it was being talked about in political circles.

10. On Wednesday, October 5, when I was informed of what had been published in *Private Eye*, I telephoned Mr Parkinson and told him that if he did not issue the statement which solicitors had been discussing for some weeks, then I would be obliged to defend myself.

Press comment, government pronouncements, and the continued speculation about this matter have placed me in an impossible position.

I feel that I have both a public duty and a duty to my family to put the record straight.

On the last day of the Tory conference, Cecil Parkinson resigned as Trade and Industry Secretary. A year later Mrs Thatcher publicly hinted that a time might come when he could be recalled to office, but there was no job for him in her ministerial reshuffle of September 1985. Then whatever hopes may have remained for his 'political rehabilitation' were dealt a second blow with the publication by the *Daily Mirror* of extracts from Sara Keays's book about the affair, *A Question of Judgment*, on the eve of the 1985 Tory party conference (which Mr Parkinson did not attend). The *Mirror* commented: 'The Tories bitterly complain that the serialisation has been timed to coincide with their conference . . . Why not? This week we are going to see the glossy, professionally polished, so-called caring face of the Conservative Party. But there is another side to the image-makers . . .'

Later, the Director of Public Prosecutions ordered a police investigation into the allegation in the book that Mr Parkinson discussed War Cabinet 'secrets' with Miss Keays during the Falklands crisis. This moved the *Mirror* to protest: 'The scandal is not that Mr Parkinson talked to Miss Keays. No one doubts the loyalty of either. The scandal is that this absurd Act . . . should still be a part of the law of the land. It protects every secret, even the colour of the Minister's braces, provided he shows them on duty . . .' Whatever the outcome of that inquiry, the serialization itself fuelled Press speculation that, far from regaining Cabinet rank, Mr Parkinson might resign as an MP at the next General Election and return to industry.

PARNELL, Charles Stewart

Ireland's Greatest Politician Destroyed by Adultery Scandal

Charles Stewart Parnell, perhaps the most remarkable political leader to come out of Ireland, was virtually destroyed by the divorce scandal that erupted in 1890. He was hardly the type of leader that one associates with Irish nationalism: a reserved, silent, withdrawn man, whose speeches were cool and unemotional. In the House of Commons he was regarded as an English gentleman and English politicians found it strange that such a man should take up the cause of the oppressed Irish tenantry.

Parnell was born on 27 June 1846, at the family estate of Avondale, in County Wicklow. His mother was an American who hated the English. Parnell's ancestors were English. He became squire of the estate at the age of thirteen after the sudden death of his father. He attended prep school in England, then went on to Cambridge University. An oversensitive young man, he became convinced that the English despised him for being Irish. At the age of nineteen, he seduced the pretty daughter of a local fruit farmer, then abandoned her. She committed suicide by drowning and, according to Parnell's sister Fanny, he happened to be boating when her body was fished out of the river. After that, she said, he was subject to fits of nervous depression. At the age of twenty-three, he knocked down two drunks who tried to push him off the footpath and was sent down from the university.

The decision to enter politics seems to have been taken suddenly and unexpectedly. One evening in 1874, Parnell joined his brother John for dinner in Dublin; he was in an uncharacteristically gay mood (being normally introverted and withdrawn). The discussion turned to politics and the coming elections for Parliament and Charles suddenly remarked, 'By jove, it will be a grand opening for me to enter politics.' His

family were astonished, not only because he had so far shown
no interest in politics, but because he proposed to stand for
Parliament, not as a Conservative or Liberal but as a 'Home
Ruler'. The expression 'home rule' had been invented only
four years earlier; the leader of the party was a barrister named
Isaac Butt. When asked his opinion of the Home Rulers by his
brother, Parnell had replied haughtily that he wouldn't have
anything to do with 'that set'. The mystery of why he decided
to enter politics has never been solved; the likeliest answer is
that he needed some purpose into which he could divert his
considerable energy and intellect. A Dublin journalist
described him as 'a nice gentlemanly fellow, but so hopelessly
ignorant . . .' and added that he seemed to have no political
capacities whatsoever. Nevertheless, he was elected in 1875
and took his seat in Parliament. At first he merely sat and
watched. He soon became convinced that there was no chance
of persuading an English parliament to vote for Home Rule by
sweet reason; it would have to be done by creating such a
nuisance that the English would be glad to send the Irish back
to their own parliament in Dublin. He took a hint from the
tactics of a fellow Irish member, Joseph Biggar, who delayed
an Irish Coercion Bill in 1875 by talking at inordinate length.
(In America, the same technique was known as filibustering,
although there it was possible for a politician to talk about
anything he liked, or even read a newspaper aloud; in England,
he had to stick to the point.) Now Parnell becan to use these
'obstructing' tactics to the fury of the English. The Home Rule
party talked non-stop on every possible subject of debate – in
1877 seven Irish members held up the bill to annexe the
Transvaal for twenty-six hours with continuous speeches. All-
night sittings became commonplace. Isaac Butt continued to
oppose these aggressive tactics and within two years, Parnell
was the acknowledged leader of the Home Rule party. His
coldness and contempt impressed the English; on 30 June 1876,
he created a sensation by interrupting the Secretary of State
for Ireland, who referred to the 'Manchester murderers' by
commenting icily that neither he nor Ireland would ever regard
these men other than as martyrs. (The 'murderers' were three
Fenians who had been executed after a policeman had been
accidentally killed in an attempt to rescue arrested Fenians

from a police van.) It made Parnell the hero of the Fenians – Irish revolutionaries – who had so far regarded the Home Rule movement as a contemptible compromise with the British.

One of the leading Fenians, Michael Davitt, had been in prison since 1870 on a charge of distributing arms; in 1878 he was released and sent back to Ireland. There was a crop failure that year. Davitt preached that the only genuine solution was to abolish landlordism; he advised tenants not to pay rents. The 'Land War' began. The Land League was formed in 1879 and Parnell was persuaded to become its president. Davitt was soon arrested for urging tenants to seize food. Parnell immediately organized protests. The trial in Sligo was a farce. Davitt and his two fellow prisoners were on bail; they were given a torchlight procession every evening and taken to court every morning by a brass band. When a judge mispronounced a word, the defence attorney leapt to his feet to ask whether it was lawful for judges to murder the Queen's English. After a week of these absurd proceedings, the case was dropped. When the first tenant was due for eviction in November 1879, 8,000 armed peasants turned up and only a speech by Parnell avoided a bloody riot. He was swiftly becoming the 'uncrowned king of Ireland'. A month later, Parnell sailed for America, and collected $200,000 for the Land League.

In 1881, the British government passed a Coercion Bill, which amounted virtually to declaring martial law in Ireland. Inevitably, it played into the hands of the Irish rebels. The Land League was declared illegal. Parnell was thrown into jail for 'incitement' in a speech he made; so was Davitt. The Land League retaliated with a manifesto advising tenants to stop paying rent. Parnell won again; after seven months, the government had to agree to release him on condition of withdrawing the No Rent manifesto and trying to keep the Land Leaguers in order.

Then, on 6 May 1882, Parnell received his most serious setback yet. As Lord Frederick Cavendish was walking in Phoenix Park, Dublin, with the British Under Secretary Thomas Burke, they were attacked by a gang of seven men and stabbed to death. The scandal was tremendous. Parnell promptly denounced the murders in the House but the Home Rule party had been seriously undermined and it was generally believed that Parnell had organized the murders. In fact, the assassins were members of a secret society that called itself the Invincibles. In the following year, one of their members, a Dublin town councillor named James Carey, was induced to confess by means of a trick (he thought someone had already betrayed them) and he turned Queen's Evidence. Nine men were brought to trial for the murders and five of them were hanged. Carey himself was later shot to death on a ship at sea by a member of the Invincibles, who in turn was executed.

Parnell's immense popularity was demonstrated again in 1883 when a public subscription to pay off his mortgage – he was deeply in debt – raised £37,000, in spite of an attempted intervention by the Pope.

In 1885, Gladstone and the Liberals fell from power partly as a result of the defeat of General Gordon at Khartoum, for which Gladstone was blamed. Parnell united with the Conservatives and received some important concessions in return. In the following year, the Conservatives were defeated, in spite of the support of the Home Rulers. Gladstone decided it was now time to propitiate Parnell and the Liberals introduced the first Home Rule Bill in 1886. It was defeated but it was a start.

Parnell's greatest triumph was at hand: the affair of the Piggott forgeries. Richard Piggott was a violently nationalist Irishman who gradually turned scoundrel and blackmailer. In 1867, as editor of three nationalist newspapers, he was imprisoned for attacking the execution of the Manchester murderers. It was only a short step to extorting money from Isaac Butt, the founder of Home Rule, by threatening to publish Fenian attacks on him. He was a bouncy, florid man who looked like an alcoholic Santa Claus, a seducer of women and collector of pornography. By 1881 his reputation was so foul that the circulation of his newspapers plunged and he was forced to sell them to Parnell. Piggott now claimed to be a reformed Fenian and wrote articles for the *St James Gazette*. He made the acquaintance of Edward Houston, secretary of an Irish 'patriotic' organization financed by the English to fight Irish nationalism. Houston was convinced that Parnell was behind the Phoenix Park murders. He paid Piggott to become a private detective to try and prove it. Piggott declined until

Houston promised him unlimited hotel and travelling expenses; then he proceeded to spend the money on trips to Paris and America. Finally, Houston got suspicious and threatened to cut off the funds. Then Piggott produced the 'evidence' he wanted: a letter signed by Parnell, admitting that he had denounced the Phoenix Park murders for purely political reasons and saying that Thomas Burke deserved what he got. This was published in *The Times* in April 1887 in an article – one of a series – entitled 'Parnellism and Crime'. Parnell saw it, declared contemptuously that it was a forgery, and took no further action. It seriously damaged his reputation.

In the following year, another 'Parnell letter' was read aloud in a court case when a former friend of Parnell's named Frank O'Donnell was suing *The Times* for libel. This new letter was apparently written from Kilmainham jail, when Parnell was imprisoned in January 1882, and seemed to be urging his followers to violence: 'What are these fellows waiting for?' Two words were misspelled: 'inexcuseable' and 'hesitency'. Parnell demanded that the House set up a committee of investigation. The Attorney-General agreed readily; Parnell's enemies felt that this would be an ideal opportunity to throw a great deal of mud. In effect, Irish nationalism was going on trial. The man behind this was probably the wily Joseph Chamberlain, a Liberal who had broken with Gladstone because of his dislike of Home Rule.

The Special Commission began on 17 September 1888 and dragged on for month after month. It was not until 15 February 1889, that Richard Piggott finally stepped into the witness box and Parnell muttered audibly, 'The rat caught in the trap at last.' Piggott was asked by the celebrated advocate Sir Charles Russell to spell a number of words, including 'hesitancy'; he spelt it 'hesitency'. Then various letters were read aloud in court, proving that Piggott was a man who changed his political opinions every time he could make any money by doing so. The court roared with laughter at the revelations of his scoundrelism. As he left the stand that day Piggott muttered, 'I don't pretend to be very virtuous.' Two days later, he went to the home of the celebrated radical editor Henry Labouchere ('Labby') and confessed to forging the letters. When the trial reopened on the following Tuesday, Piggott was not in court;

he had fled. When Parnell went to Bow Street to swear out a warrant for Piggott's arrest, he was followed by a cheering crowd. It was a new experience for him to be cheered by Englishmen. Three days later, Piggott shot himself with a revolver as Spanish police went to arrest him in his Madrid hotel room. The next time Parnell entered the House of Commons, most members stood up in respect. He was elected a life member of the Liberal Club.

This was to be the last of his triumphs. That Christmas in 1889 he was served with papers naming him as co-respondent in the divorce of Captain William O'Shea and his wife Katherine. Parnell had met 'Kitty O'Shea' in July 1880 and had fallen immediately and violently in love with her. In spite of her Irish name, she was a member of the English aristocracy, a daughter of Sir John Page Wood of Gloucestershire. In 1867, at the age of twenty-one, she had married Captain William Henry O'Shea of the Hussars, a glib, jaunty character who was an intellectual lightweight. He sold his commission and tried his hand at various businesses, all of which failed. In 1880 'Willy' succeeded in getting himself elected to Parliament as a Whig, by promising a more influential candidate £2,000 for his support. Katherine had to beg the money from a rich relative to pay the debt. By the time O'Shea became an MP, he and his wife were virtually estranged.

As a Member of Parliament, O'Shea needed his wife as a hostess; he was hoping to recoup his fortune by making important connections. Parnell promised to attend one of Kitty O'Shea's dinner parties but failed to turn up. Then, according to her later autobiography, Mrs O'Shea went to the House of Commons and demanded to see him. He came out to the Palace Yard and both were impressed. What she saw was a tall, gaunt man with a pale face and burning eyes while he saw a rather short, plump, round-faced woman with beautiful hair. As she leaned out of the cab, a rose fell from her bosom; Parnell picked it up, kissed it, and put it in his buttonhole. He promised to be present at her next dinner and he was. He kept the rose and it was placed in his coffin after this death.

This is Kitty O'Shea's story but it is probably romanticized. Parnell's friend Justin McCarthy claims that he was present at their first meeting, which was at a lunch party – this is probably closer to the truth.

What seems clear is that Kitty O'Shea was the woman Parnell had been waiting for. He seems to have been celibate since the affair that had resulted in the suicide of the farmer's daughter. Now he experienced immediate infatuation. It is conceivable that Kitty O'Shea reminded him of his mother. Kitty seems to have been a non-stop talker with the manner of a bouncy schoolgirl; Parnell's mother has been described as a 'bright and incisive' talker with a determined character and strong opinions. Within months of meeting Kitty, Parnell was writing from Dublin: 'I cannot keep away from you any longer, so shall leave tonight for London.' In the following month they became lovers, probably at her house in Eltham.

The attitude of Captain O'Shea is something of a mystery. Kitty O'Shea later claimed that her husband knew perfectly well that she and Parnell were lovers and that he encouraged it for his own political advancement. A Parnell disciple named Henry Harrison later made the same claim in a book called *Parnell Vindicated*. Jules Abels, a recent biographer of Parnell, examines the evidence and totally rejects this view.

When Parnell went down to Eltham, he was a sick man, worn out by his political responsibilities and endless fund-raising for his party. He spent much time in bed and Kitty usually joined him, in spite of the presence of her three children in the house. It seems clear that he felt he was married to her for she had told him that sexual relations with her husband had ceased long ago.

In July 1881, Captain O'Shea went down to Eltham unexpectedly, found Parnell's luggage in a bedroom and challenged him to a duel. Kitty's sister made peace and Parnell assured O'Shea that he was mistaken in his assumption that they were lovers. O'Shea, so it seems, believed this, or at least pretended to.

It was in 1885 that Parnell had to pay a heavy price for his mistress's favours. Her husband was highly unpopular with other Irish members; disappointments had turned him into a whiner and a sneerer. His chances of being returned to Parliament as a Liberal candidate in 1885 were minimal. Kitty O'Shea pulled all the strings she could. Since she was known as Parnell's mistress and his party now held the balance of power in the House, she succeeded in getting her husband nominated as Liberal candidate for a division of Liverpool. Unfortunately, he was defeated. O'Shea now asked Parnell to find him a Home Rule seat – a difficult task, since the Home Rulers all loathed O'Shea. Parnell swallowed hard but decided he had to do it for the sake of his mistress. He used all his influence to persuade a popular Galway candidate to withdraw and two of his own followers, Joseph Biggar and Tim Healy, to stop opposing O'Shea. It cost him every ounce of his authority but he succeeded. O'Shea was not in the least grateful and was later to be the only Irish nationalist who did not vote for Home Rule. (The bill was defeated.)

In 1886, O'Shea was on the Continent when he saw an item in the *Pall Mall Gazette* stating that Parnell's carriage had collided with the truck of a market gardener while he was on his way down to Captain O'Shea's house in the early hours of the morning. Once again, O'Shea demanded to know whether Parnell was his wife's lover and again she denied it although her last two children were Parnell's. O'Shea resigned his seat in Parliament – a clear indication that he was now certain she was Parnell's mistress.

O'Shea and Joseph Chamberlain had been friendly for the past year or so. Chamberlain had been a former friend of Parnell's but had hated him since he decided to support the Conservatives in 1885. It seems to have been Chamberlain who first saw the possibility of destroying Parnell by persuading O'Shea to cite him as co-respondent. In August 1889, O'Shea wrote to Chamberlain: 'He who smashes Parnell smashes Parnellism.' It is conceivable that Chamberlain hinted at some reward – such as a safe seat in parliament – if O'Shea 'smashed' Parnell.

When Parnell was served with the papers that cited him as co-respondent, on Christmas Eve 1889, he does not seem to have been particularly worried; neither, oddly enough, were his followers. Parnell's popularity was now at its height; the Piggott forgery case had confirmed his position as 'the uncrowned king of Ireland'. Parnell told Michael Davitt that he would emerge from the case 'without a stain on his character', which Davitt took to mean that he was innocent.

A scheme to 'buy off' O'Shea for £25,000 came to nothing when Kitty was unable to raise the money from the estate of a deceased aunt. The case came to court on 15 November 1890. Parnell made the mistake of not being represented – over the years he had maintained this habit of indifference to threats but now was the wrong time. From the beginning, Parnell and Kitty had spent an enormous amount of time together; the incident of the market-gardener's truck would have been enough to convince most judges that they were lovers. A maidservant told how Parnell came to visit Kitty under the name of Stewart, and how, when she wanted to deliver a message, she had to knock at the door of the room where Parnell and Mrs O'Shea were closeted and wait ten minutes before it was opened a crack wide. She said that when O'Shea came unexpectedly, Parnell would escape down the fire escape, then come and knock at the front door ten minutes later.

This and similar testimony remained unchallenged. The result was that after two days, the judge decided that Parnell was 'a man who takes advantage of the hospitality offered him by the husband to debauch the wife'. He granted the decree nisi and gave O'Shea the custody of all the children, including the two Parnell had fathered.

In the eyes of the general public, Parnell was a trickster, a deceiver, a libertine. The fire-escape testimony made him a laughing stock – there were music hall songs and sketches about it. Parnell had so far been regarded as something of a mystery man, a remote, silent figure who kept his own secrets. When he stood up to speak, the bars and restaurants of the House emptied as members rushed to hear him. Now he was seen as a lecherous clown.

Yet at first, it looked as if Parnell was correct in believing that it would all make no different to his political standing. A few days after the divorce, he was unanimously elected chairman of the Home Rule party. But Gladstone let it be known that if Parnell would not consent to retire for the moment, the second attempt to push through the Home Rule Bill would end in failure. Parnell refused to resign as chairman and his own party split with the anti-Parnellites in the majority. When he heard of the split, Gladstone said, 'Thank God, Home Rule is saved.'

In Ireland, there was uproar. The Church had always been ambivalent about Parnell and now denounced him as a depraved adulterer. At the new elections, there were riots and disorders, and Parnellites and anti-Parnellites hurled abuse and bricks at one another. Davitt had become an anti-Parnellite and during the Kilkenny election campaign, Parnell lost his temper and poured out a stream of invective that was totally unlike the aristocratic reserve for which he had become famous. The anti-Parnellites won an overwhelming victory.

Parnell married Mrs O'Shea and continued to be active in Parliament. He further undermined his health by rushing between London and Ireland. There the clergy continued to denounce him; one clergyman is reported to have threatened to turn a man into a goat if he voted for Parnell's candidate. Ally after ally turned against him, until he presented an image like a St Sebastian shot full of arrows. The Conservatives, who were in power, made various concessions to the Irish but refused to consider Home Rule. In September 1891, he made a speech in pouring rain without an umbrella, his left arm in a sling because he had a pain in it. From then on there was a steady decline, and he died in Brighton on 6 October. The official cause of death was given as 'rheumatism of the heart'. His followers, of whom there were still hundreds of thousands, believed he had died of a broken heart.

PAYNE, Cynthia

The 'Sex-for-Luncheon-Vouchers' Scandal

In April, 1980, dark-haired Mrs Cynthia Payne, was jailed for eighteen months for keeping a disorderly house in Ambleside Avenue, Streatham, in South London. She was a middle-aged lady christened 'Madam Sin' in a play on names by the popular Press. Her sentence was reduced on appeal to six months, of which she served only four – to the chuckles of the public at large, most of whom found more to laugh at than lecture in the scandalous goings-on at her suburban establishment.

Male clients there paid £25 a time for luncheon vouchers which were traded in for sex plus 'generous helpings' of food and drink. Customers and scarlet women broke the ice at Madam Sin's over a glass or two of wine and sandwiches in rooms furnished with fitted carpets. At the subsequent court hearing, even the prosecution was moved to admit that it was 'a well-run brothel'. Down in the kitchen, Mrs Payne nailed her colours to the mast with a sign which proclaimed: 'My House Is CLEAN Enough To Be Healthy . . . And DIRTY Enough To Be Happy.' It all sounded so genteel, more of a mini-scandal than any outrage on morality.

Mrs Payne, who was forty-six at the time of her arrest, revealed that she numbered several vicars, barristers, an MP and a peer of the realm among her regular customers. Clutching their luncheon vouchers, they whiled away their nervous first moments in Ambleside Avenue at a bar in the conservatory, decorated with red fairy lamps and a stuffed parrot perched in a gilded cage. Later the girls – described by Mrs Payne as 'dedicated amateurs' mostly, housewives out to make a little pin-money – received £6 for each voucher they handed in. There were more than fifty men present when police raided the house. Later, while Mrs Payne was detained elsewhere, a man of seventy-four who gave his name as Squadron Leader

Robert Smith, Retd., acted as caretaker and took journalists on conducted tours.

In March 1983 the name Madam Sin featured in more newspaper headlines when renewed activity was reported at the house in Ambleside Avenue. This time, however, no luncheon vouchers were issued, while Mrs Payne was quoted as saying, 'I'm doing it for love.' She told a *News of the World* reporter, 'These days neighbours sometimes see a lot of cars parked outside my house, and say "Oh, so you're at it again, are you, Cynthia?" Alas, I'm no longer in business . . . but I feel I'm still doing a service, even though I'm not making a living out of it. It's like real, genuine welfare work.' She harked back briefly to the good old luncheon-voucher days, 'I'd like to think that I'll be remembered for running a nice brothel . . . not one of those sordid places like they have in Soho. I should have been given the OBE for what I did for the country.'

Profumo Affair

The Minister and the Russian Spy

Few if any politico-sex scandals in British history have titillated the public's imagination as much as the Profumo-Christine Keeler affair of the so-called 'swinging sixties'. It centred on a real-life situation which, on the face of it, seemed so absurd as to sound more like a plot for some particularly bawdy West End farce; one in which John Profumo, MP, Her Majesty's Secretary of State for War, took turn and turn about in call-girl Christine Keeler's bed with (among others) Captain Eugene Ivanov, the assistant Soviet naval attaché in London and, allegedly, a Russian spy bent on gathering nuclear secrets from any resultant pillow talk.

So seriously was the possibility taken that a judicial inquiry was appointed and charged, among other things, with considering '. . . any evidence there may be for believing that national security has been, or may be, endangered . . .' And, if that were not enough, the affair also had racial undertones, arising from the trial and imprisonment of two of Miss Keeler's former lovers, both West Indian. The resultant scandal was sparked off by her disappearance on the eve of the first trial, in which she was due to appear at the Old Bailey as chief witness for the prosecution; instead she was discovered, by the Press, in Spain. As all Britain laughed behind its hand, questions were asked in Parliament. After first strenuously denying allegations of any impropriety in his dealings with Miss Keeler, War Minister Profumo later resigned – when he had confessed that he had lied to the House, the Cabinet and the Prime Minister about their relationship. Soon there was talk in the foreign Press of 'widespread decadence' in British public life, while the most scurrilous and salacious rumours (never substantiated) began to circulate at home of sexual orgies in upper-crust circles, attended by 'The Man in the Mask' – always naked, carrying a whip, and popularly supposed to be another Tory Cabinet Minister. This particular rumour gained such credence that it became common gossip in pubs, clubs and homes throughout the country.

Then came tragedy, when Dr Stephen Ward – osteopath, talented portrait-artist, procurer of women for his rich and famous friends (who all deserted him after his arrest) and a central character in the whole Profumo Affair – committed suicide during his own Old Bailey trial, in July 1963. Ward took an overdose of barbiturates when the court adjourned for the night after part-hearing the judge's summing up, and died in hospital without knowing the verdict. Miss Keeler herself was later jailed for committing perjury at the trial of the second of her two West Indian former lovers. Finally, a year after the resignation in October 1963 of Prime Minister Harold Macmillan, on health grounds, the Tory party was beaten at the polls after more than twelve years in power; a defeat, said the pundits, which was hastened by the odium of the Profumo Affair.

At the time the scandal began, 'Dr' Stephen Ward – he was an osteopath, not a medical practitioner – had for several years rented a cottage *orné*, on peppercorn terms, at Cliveden, the country estate owned by his friend Lord Astor. Ward's guests were allowed use of the swimming pool and it was there that he introduced Christine Keeler to both Mr Profumo and Captain Ivanov in the summer of 1961. Unconfirmed reports that Profumo, the husband of actress Valerie Hobson and a wealthy man in his own right, was competing with Ivanov for Miss Keeler's favours were already circulating in Fleet Street by mid-1962. Only *Queen* magazine dared, however, to hint at the incredible situation that was said to be developing. It printed a brief but barbed reference to a chauffeur-driven Russian Zis limousine arriving at an unnamed lady's front door, just as a government chauffeur-driven Humber pulled away from the back. That flat was in Wimpole Mews in central London, provided by Stephen Ward at nominal rent for Christine Keeler's use. But since no identification was made, the article caused no great stir beyond a privileged readership.

Then on 14 December 1962 a West Indian called Johnny

Edgecombe was arrested after firing a revolver at the door and window of the flat. Inside were Christine Keeler and a friend, Mandy Rice-Davies, likewise destined soon to become a household name. They rang Dr Ward at his consulting rooms nearby and he called the police. On 14 March 1963 Edgecombe stood trial at the Old Bailey. The charges included one of attempted murder and another of wounding 'Lucky' Gordon, a fellow West Indian who had supplanted him in Christine Keeler's affections. Chief prosecution witness Keeler failed to appear; unknown to the court she was in Spain. However, no request was made for a postponement and of the two women present in the flat at the time of the shooting, only Miss Rice-Davies gave evidence. Edgecombe, who had previous convictions, was found not guilty of attempted murder, or of wounding Gordon, but guilty on a lesser charge, of possessing a firearm with intent to endanger life. For this he was sentenced to seven years' imprisonment and the scandal now moved into the open.

Two national newspaper reporters who had refused to name their informants to the Vassall (spy) Tribunal were already in jail, so Fleet Street, although fully aware of Mr Profumo's association with Christine Keeler, was obliged to proceed cautiously. It, therefore, printed stories about the Edgecombe trial and its missing prosecution witness, alongside apparently unconnected stories concerning John Profumo. *The Sunday Pictorial* printed an exclusive interview with Dr Stephen Ward, in which he said: 'Now it looks as though somebody – no doubt a loyal friend – has spirited her away . . .'

Who that 'loyal friend' may have been and what if any were his motives, has never been established. In his official report, Lord Denning, who had examined the bank accounts of both Mr Profumo and Dr Ward, found no evidence to suggest that either man had assisted her in leaving the country. However, on 22 March *Private Eye* published a mock 'report' under the byline 'Lunchtime O'Booze' which read:

Mr Silas Jones, a West Indian immigrant of no fixed abode, was today sentenced at the Old Bailey to twenty-four years Preventive Detention for being in possession of an offensive water-pistol. The chief 'witness' in the case, gay fun-loving Miss Gaye Funloving, a 21-year-old 'model', was not actually present in Court. She has, in fact, disappeared. It is believed that normally, in cases of this type, a Warrant is issued for the arrest of the missing witness.

Parties. One of Miss Funloving's close 'friends', Dr Spook of Harley Street, revealed last night that he could add nothing to what had already been insinuated. Dr Spook is believed to have 'more than half the Cabinet on his list of patients'. He also has a 'weekend' cottage on the Berkshire estate of Lord —, and is believed to have attended many 'parties' in the neighbourhood. Among those it is believed who have also attended 'parties' of this type are Mr Vladimir Bolokhov, the well-known Soviet spy attached to the Russian embassy and a well-known Cabinet Minister.

Resignation? Mr James Montesi, a well-known Cabinet Minister, was last night reported to have proffered his 'resignation' to the Prime Minister, on 'personal grounds'. It is alleged that the Prime Minister refused to accept his alleged 'resignation'. Mr Montesi today denied the allegations that he had even allegedly offered his alleged 'resignation' to the alleged 'Prime Minister'.

That night, outspoken Socialist MP Colonel George Wigg – no friend of Mr Profumo's and with whom he had already clashed in the House on another unrelated matter – addressed the Commons as they debated the affair of the two reporters jailed by the Vassall Tribunal. Colonel Wigg said,

There is not an Honourable Member in the House, nor a journalist in the Press Gallery, nor do I believe there is a person in the Public Gallery, who in the last few days has not heard rumour upon rumour involving a member of the Government Front Bench. The Press has got as near as it can – it has shown itself willing to wound, but afraid to strike. This all comes about because of the Vassall Tribunal. These great Press Lords, these men who control great instruments of public opinion and power, do not have the guts to discharge the duty that they are now claiming for themselves. That being the case, I rightly use the privilege of the House of Commons – that is what it is given to me for – to ask the Home Secretary, who is the senior member of the government on the Treasury Bench now, to go to the Dispatch Box – he knows that the rumour to which I refer relates to Miss Christine Keeler and Miss Davies and a shooting by a West Indian – and, on behalf of the government, categorically deny the truth of these rumours. On the other hand, if there is anything in them, I urge him to ask the Prime Minister to do what was not done in the Vassall Case – set up a Select Committee, so that these things can be dissipated and the honour of the Minister concerned freed from the imputations and innuendoes that are being spread at the present time.

Home Secretary Henry Brooke refused to pick up the gauntlet, while Mr Profumo himself was not in the House. He was, however, informed of what had happened and promptly made a personal statement to the Commons. The 'personal statement' is a device used by MPs, including Ministers, for a variety of reasons (including the denial of rumours, repeated under the cloak of Parliamentary privilege). By tradition, the speaker is never questioned about the personal statement so that he in turn becomes honour-bound to tell the truth, the whole truth, and nothing but the truth. To betray this mutual trust is to commit political *hara-kiri*. Mr Profumo made his personal statement with his wife watching from the Stranger's Gallery, and himself on the Front Bench flanked by Prime Minister Harold Macmillan and Iain Macleod, the Leader of the House.

He said,

I understand that my name has been connected with the rumours about the disappearance of Miss Keeler. I would like to take this opportunity of making a personal statement about these matters. I last saw Miss Keeler in December 1961 and I have not seen her since. I have no idea where she is now. Any suggestion that I was in any way connected with or responsible for her absence from the trial at the Old Bailey is wholly and completely untrue. My wife and I first met Miss Keeler at a house party in July 1961 at Cliveden. Among a number of people there was Dr Stephen Ward, whom we already knew slightly, and a Mr Ivanov, who was an attaché at the Russian Embassy. The only other occasion that my wife or I met Mr Ivanov was for a moment at the official reception for Major Gagarin [the first man in Space] at the Soviet Embassy. My wife and I had a standing invitation to visit Dr Ward. Between July and December 1961, I met Miss Keeler on about half-a-dozen occasions at Dr Ward's flat, when I called to see him and his friends. Miss Keeler and I were on friendly terms. There was no impropriety whatsoever in my acquaintanceship with Miss Keeler. Mr Speaker, I have made this personal statement because of what was said in the House last evening by the three Honourable Members, and which of course was protected by privilege. I shall not hesitate to issue writs for libel and slander if scandalous allegations are made or repeated outside the House.

Later that day the Minister and his wife were photographed at the races in the company of the Queen Mother. Press reaction was restrained, although *The Guardian* declared: '. . . only the most compelling evidence to the contrary could warrant any suspicion now, after such explicit statements from

Mr Profumo . . . They ought to end the talk.' Christine Keeler, found at last by the Press in Spain, said somewhat obliquely, 'I have nothing to be ashamed of; I know that now.' When she returned to Britain, the only penalty she incurred was to forefeit the £40 recognizance put by the court on her duty to appear as witness at the Edgecombe trial. Mr Profumo himself made good the threat he had uttered earlier in the Commons, by commencing actions for libel against *Paris Match* and *Tempo Illustrato* magazines. (He gave the £50 out-of-court settlement paid by *Illustrato* to charity.) 'Dr' Stephen Ward said on television that Mr Profumo had told the truth about Miss Keeler; to all intents and purposes it seemed as if the 'scandal' was no more than Press invention. And yet it stubbornly refused to die down.

On the night of 18 April 1963, Christine Keeler complained to the police that she had been attacked by 'Lucky' Gordon as she left a woman friend's house in London. He was arrested and bail was opposed. One week later Mandy Rice-Davies was arrested at London airport *en route* to Majorca and charged with possessing a forged driving licence. The licence enabled her to drive the Jaguar car given to her on her seventeenth birthday by slum landlord and racketeer, Peter Rachman. (In her memoirs, *The Mandy Report*, published in 1964, Miss Rice-Davies claimed that the real reason for her arrest was to persuade her to make a statement concerning Stephen Ward. She then gave evidence at his trial, which began on 22 July 1963.) Also in 1964, author and broadcaster Ludovic Kennedy wrote in his book *The Trial of Stephen Ward* that: '. . . [Ward] felt, naïvely perhaps but not altogether unreasonably, that as he had done his best to protect the Government's War Minister, the Government might do their best to call their dogs off him. He wrote to the Home Secretary, his local MP Sir Wavell Wakefield, and the Leader of the Opposition, Mr Harold Wilson. To Mr Wilson he wrote: "Obviously my efforts to conceal the fact that Mr Profumo had not told the truth in Parliament have made it look as if I myself have something to hide. It is quite clear now that they must wish the facts to be known, and I shall see that they are . . ."'

Copies of some of the letters Ward wrote were also sent to the Press and further questions were tabled in the House. The

Prime Minister thereupon instructed Lord Dilhorne, the Lord Chancellor, to investigate. Meanwhile Johnny Edgecombe's appeal had been dismissed; now it was 'Lucky' Gordon's turn to stand trial at the Old Bailey. This time Christine Keeler was present to give evidence. Gordon claimed that she had been pregnant by him when she went to Spain. As he attempted to talk matters over with her on her return, she fell over her suitcase and so caused the injuries she had sustained. Miss Keeler denied the pregnancy allegation and protested so vehemently when Gordon said she had given him a venereal disease that the judge ordered her from the court. Gordon, who dismissed his counsel and then conducted his own defence, asked for a number of witnesses to be called, including John Profumo and Stephen Ward. Neither was called. Only two men (said by Gordon to have been in the flat as Miss Keeler left) were sought but could not be found. Gordon was found guilty and sentenced to three years' imprisonment. A few weeks later, that sentence was quashed and he was freed. In his book *The Profumo Affair, Aspects of Conservatism*, author Wayland Young wrote: 'Six weeks later the Lord Chief Justice, having heard some new evidence which was not made public, upset the verdict and released [Gordon]. But already on the second day of the trial the whole grumbling, menacing mess of happenings and rumours of happenings had been lifted to the level of a duly constituted scandal by the resignation of the Secretary of State for War . . .'

After telling his wife the full story of his association with Christine Keeler, Mr Profumo had cut short their holiday in Venice, returned to England and resigned both as Minister and MP. The interchange of letters between himself and the Prime Minister revealed that he had committed the unpardonable sin of lying to Parliament when he made his personal statement.

John Profumo wrote:

Dear Prime Minister,
    You will recall that on 22 March, following certain allegations made in Parliament, I made a personal statement. At the time rumour had charged me with assisting in the disappearance of a witness, and with being involved in some possible breach of security. So serious were

these charges that I allowed myself to think that my personal association with that witness, which had also been the subject of rumour, was by comparison of minor importance only. In my statement I said that there had been no impropriety in this association. To my very deep regret I have to admit that this was not true, and that I misled you, and my colleagues, and the House.

I ask you to understand that I did this to protect, as I thought, my wife and family, who were equally misled, as were my professional advisers. I have come to realize that, by this deception, I have been guilty of a grave misdemeanour and despite the fact that there is no truth whatever in the other charges, I cannot remain a member of your Administration, nor of the House of Commons. I cannot tell you of my deep remorse for the embarrassment I have cause to you, to my colleagues in the Government, to my constituents, and to the Party which I have served for the past twenty-five years.

Your sincerely,
Jack Profumo.

To which Mr Macmillan, then on holiday in Scotland, replied:

Dear Profumo,

The contents of your letter of 4 June have been communicated to me and I have heard them with deep regret. This is a great tragedy for you, your family, and your friends. Nevertheless, I am sure you will understand that in the circumstances, I have no alternative but to advise the Queen to accept your resignation.

Yours very sincerely,
Harold Macmillan.

The Times commented acidly: 'There can be few more lamentable documents in British political history than Mr Profumo's letter of resignation. In his reply the Prime Minister says: "This is a great tragedy for you, your family, and your friends." It is also a great tragedy for the probity of public life in Britain . . .'

If that was undeniable, the moral question was now overtaken by a more sinister aspect of the affair; had the national security been put at risk by Mr Profumo's conduct? It was clear that he had laid himself open to possible blackmail, but even before the Commons could debate the matter Mr Michael Eddowes, a former solicitor and member of the Thursday Club, published the contents of a letter he had written earlier to the Prime Minister. In it Mr Eddowes claimed he had warned MI5 in March 1963 that Miss Keeler had told him Ivanov had asked her to find out from Mr Profumo the date on which nuclear warheads were to be delivered to West Germany. (Christine Keeler herself maintained later the suggestion had come from Stephen Ward, not Ivanov, and had not been intended seriously; nor had she put any such question to the War Minister.) However, the disclosure came at a time when everything Miss Keeler said, or did, or was said to have done, was news. Her 'Confessions' were appearing weekly in the mass-circulation *News of the World*. She was said to have turned down an offer of £5,000 per week (for twelve weeks) to compère a cabaret show called 'Turkish Delight'. Against all the backcloth of rumour and known scandal there was also talk in political circles of more threatened Cabinet resignations, even a move to oust Premier Macmillan.

The highly responsible *New York Times* declared that: 'A political crisis even more profound than the storm over Suez which blew Anthony Eden out of office and brought Prime Minister Macmillan to power is now shaking Great Britain to its foundations. The Suez crisis forced a change in Conservative Prime Ministers but left the Conservative Government intact. The present crisis threatens to end the twelve-year rule of the Conservative party . . .'

During the Commons debate – which was held while Stephen Ward was awaiting trial – Mr Macmillan revealed that Ward had called on his Private Secretary on 7 May of that year, in the presence of an MI5 officer. During the course of his complaints, 'Mr Ward let drop the remark that Mr Profumo had not told the truth' (in his personal statement). Later, when the Lord Chancellor began his inquiries, he learned that '. . . Christine Keeler had told the police on 26 January (1963), while they were questioning her about the Edgecombe affray, that Stephen Ward had asked her to discover from Profumo the date on which certain atomic secrets were to be handed to West Germany by the Americans – this was at the time of the Cuba crisis – and that she did not put this question to Mr Profumo . . .' The Prime Minister added, 'I think it very unfortunate that this information was not given to me, but the head of the security service, in considering these reports, did not take that as of great importance.'

Ironically, the then head of MI5 was Sir Roger Hollis, who was himself later accused by some of his senior officers of being a Soviet agent (*see* page 47). (There was another 'spy' connection, unknown at the time. On 22 July 1963, the day on which Ward's trial began at the Old Bailey, an exhibition of his drawings opened in London. Among his portraits of the famous were some of members of the Royal Family. As the trial proceeded a mysterious caller who declined to give his name bought the lot for £5,000 – paid in cash, with £5 notes. He was later identified as Professor Anthony Blunt, then Keeper of the Queen's Pictures. Another year was to pass before he confessed to being a long-term Soviet agent – *see also* page 47.)

At the lower court hearing, the magistrates found that no *prima facie* case of brothel keeping had been made against Dr Ward; by the time his Old Bailey trial began, the Crown had further decided to leave two abortion charges on the file. Ward pleaded not guilty to five counts of poncing and procuring. On the seventh day of his trial, held in the Bailey's famous No 1 Court and packed to capacity throughout, proceedings were adjourned before the judge had completed his summing-up. Ward was allowed home on bail. After sending for a *Daily Express* reporter, to whom he confessed that he was afraid of the outcome, he later took an overdose of barbiturates. For the ensuing three days he hovered between life and death at St Stephen's Hospital. Meantime the trial continued. He was found guilty on two counts (of living off the immoral earnings of three prostitutes, including Christine Keeler and Mandy Rice-Davies), not guilty of the other three. Dr Ward died before he knew the verdict or could appear before the judge for sentence.

However, he left several suicide notes, including one each to his trial judge and both leading counsel, as well as Lord Denning, who had been appointed by the Prime Minister to inquire into the whole Profumo Affair. He also wrote thanking a prostitute named Ronna Ricardo for having told the truth at the trial and directed that she should be paid £500 from his estate. (She had retracted much of the evidence she gave earlier at the magistrates' court, claiming she was under police pressure.) To prostitute Vickie Barrett, another Crown witness, he wrote, 'I don't know what it was or who it was that made you do what you did. But if you have any decency left, you should tell the truth like Ronna Ricardo. You owe this not to me, but to everyone who may be treated like you or like me in future.'

Mr Wayland Young said apropos the Denning Report, which was published in September 1963,

> But many questions remain to worry the public. Was Ronna Ricardo telling the truth when she said she had been threatened by the police into giving false evidence? Why did Vickie Barrett break down when Ward died, confess to a journalist that she too had been lying, and then retract her confession? On whose instructions and with what right had Mandy Rice-Davies been forcibly kept in the country to give evidence against Stephen Ward? And, a question which seems to sum up the others, why did the police find it necessary to interview 140 people before they moved against Stephen Ward? How many people do they usually think it worth interviewing in order to prepare charges of poncing?

In general, Lord Denning found there had been no damage done to the national security, while he was 'satisfied' MI5 had not known in 1961 of Mr Profumo's affair with Christine Keeler (as Ward claimed). He confirmed, however, that MI5 knew in February 1963 about Miss Keeler's statement to the police, claiming that Ward had asked her to discover from the War Minister the date on which atomic secrets were to be handed to West Germany. 'They (the Special Branch Commander and a senior MI5 officer) decided that there was no security interest involved such as to warrant any further steps being taken.' He was, however, critical of the government's failure to face facts and take the appropriate action. 'The conduct of Mr Profumo was such as to create, amongst an influential section of the people, a reasonable belief that he had committed adultery with such a woman in such circumstances as the case discloses. It was the responsibility of the Prime Minister and his colleagues, and of them only, to deal with this situation: and they did not succeed in doing so . . .'

Stephen Ward said, at his trial, of Christine Keeler, 'I don't think she ever had intercourse with Ivanov.' In his official Report, Lord Denning came to the same conclusion – although

Miss Keeler, who should know, stated categorically in her book *Nothing but* . . . (with Sandy Fawkes, 1983) that, 'He gave me the kiss we had both been waiting for and we made marvellous, passionate love. He was gorgeous, so utterly masculine, we were for a while totally swept away . . .'

Whoever was telling the truth, Ivanov was the only one of the central characters in the Affair who got away scot-free. He simply stepped on a plane back to Russia. In December 1963 Christine Keeler was jailed for nine months for committing perjury at 'Lucky' Gordon's trial. Some thought it a stiffer sentence than she might have received for absconding and flying to Spain a second time. Stephen Ward was dead, while Mr Profumo disappeared from public view and has dedicated the rest of his life to running Toynbee Hall, the East End of London settlement and community workshop.

RAMPA, Lobsang
The 'Third Eye' Hoax

Some time in 1955, a man arrived at the office of the publisher Secker and Warburg in Great Russell Street, London, and managed to persuade its chairman, Fred Warburg, to see him. The man, who wore a tonsure, introduced himself as Dr T. Lobsang Rampa, and explained that he had written his autobiography and wanted Mr Warburg to publish it. He declared he was a medical doctor and produced a document, in English, which he said was issued by the University of Chung-king. Mr Warburg agreed to look at the manuscript, which thereafter arrived in sections. It was a fascinating document describing how the young Rampa, child of wealthy parents, had been singled out by astrologers at the age of seven to become a monk and how he had trained in a monastery. At the age of eight, he had submitted to a brain operation to open the 'third eye' – the source of man's psychic powers. A hole was drilled in his forehead, then a sliver of very hard wood poked into his brain, so he saw 'spirals of colour and globules of incandescent smoke'. 'For the rest of your life you will see people as they are and not as they pretend to be.' And Rampa saw, to his astonishment, that all the men in the room were surrounded by a luminous golden flame, the vital aura.

Warburg had his doubts; the details seemed authentic, but the style was curiously English and colloquial. 'I really did not think so much of kite-flying. Stupid idea, I thought. Dangerous. What a way to end a promising career. This is where I go back to prayers and herbs . . .' It didn't sound Tibetan. Various experts expressed contradictory opinions. But Rampa stood by his story of being a Tibetan. Warburg submitted him to a test: a few words of Tibetan. Rampa agreed that he could not understand it but explained that there was a perfectly good reason. During World War II he had been a prisoner of the

Japanese, who had tortured him for information about his country; he had used his psychic powers to blot out all his knowledge of Tibetan.

Warburg swallowed his doubts and published, and the results vindicated his commercial sense. The book became a bestseller. It went into many languages and made Rampa a rich man.

A body of 'Tibetan scholars' was doubtful about its authenticity and hired a private detective, Clifford Burgess, to find out about Lobsang Rampa. What he discovered was that Rampa was in reality Cyril Henry Hoskins, a Devon man who now lived in Thames Ditton. Hoskins had been born in Plympton, near Plymouth, in 1911, and entered his father's plumbing business. He was apparently deeply interested in psychic matters and claimed to have been taken to China as a child. It seemed that Hoskins was given to fantasizing about China and things Chinese; a journalist on *Psychic News*, John Pitt, tracked down a couple who had known him when he was a clerk in Weybridge and was told that Hoskins had claimed to be a flying instructor in the Chinese air force and had had an accident when his parachute failed to open. Later still, Hoskins changed his name to Carl Kuon Suo, called himself Dr Kuon, and claimed to have been born in Tibet.

Fred Warburg was understandably dismayed by these revelations but pointed out that he had published a note in the book saying that the author took full responsibility for all statements made in it. And he hinted at an alternative theory. 'But is the truth, the whole truth, out? . . . Did he believe his own fantasies? Was he, perhaps, the mouthpiece of a true Lama, as some have alleged?' Rampa/Hoskins was tracked down to a house outside Dublin, where he was living with a lady whom he had, apparently, seduced away from her Old Etonian husband. Rampa declined to be interviewed; so did the Old Etonian husband.

Quite undeterred by the furore, Rampa went on to write a second book, *Doctor From Lhasa* (1959), which was accepted by Souvenir Press. The publisher's note in this book acknowledged that *The Third Eye* had caused great contention but went on to state that the author's explanation was that he had been 'possessed' by the Tibetan lama Rampa since a blow on the head had caused mild concussion, and that Rampa now wrote his books through the author. Whatever the truth of the matter, the publisher added diplomatically, it is right that the book should be available to the public . . . *Doctor From Lhasa* continued the story where *The Third Eye* left off but is even more incredible. There is, for example, a chapter describing how Rampa jumped into an aircraft and, without any flying lessons, flew around for an hour or so, then brought the plane in to land.

Doctor From Lhasa revealed that Rampa had an audience who would believe anything he said. In a third book, *The Rampa Story*, he continued Rampa's autobiography from the point where he had left off at the end of the previous book – where Rampa was a prisoner of the Japanese and narrowly escaped execution – and described how he crossed into Russian territory, was imprisoned in the Lubianka prison in Moscow, then escaped, via Europe, to America. But the high point of the book is its seventh chapter, where Rampa described leaving his body and soaring to the astral plane, where his old teacher, the Lama Mingyar Dondup, was awaiting him. Dondup tells him: 'Your present body has suffered too much and will shortly fail. We have established a contact in the Land of England. This person wants to leave his body. We took him to the astral plane and discussed matters with him. He is *most* anxious to leave, and will do all we require . . .' Later, in London, Rampa is able to study the history of this Englishman in the Akashic record – the record on the 'psychic ether' of everything that has ever happened (Madame Blavatsky invented the phrase). Then Rampa goes to the Englishman's bedroom – in his astral body – and converses with the Englishman's astral body, agreeing to the swap. The Englishman tells him how he fell on his head and stood up to find himself standing by his physical body, connected to it by a silver cord. Then he saw a Tibetan walking towards him. 'I have come to you because I want your body . . .' And, after thinking it over, the unselfish Mr Hoskins decided that he had had enough of life anyway, and that he might as well hand over his body to someone who could make better use of it. The lama instructs him to climb the tree again and fall on his head in order to loosen the cord. Then a lama takes Hoskins by the arm and floats away with him to heaven, while Lobsang Rampa squeezes himself into the vacated body with a sensation of suffocating. Rampa finds himself confronted with such problems as riding a bicycle and claiming unemployment benefit. Life was difficult and painful until he met a literary agent and outlined the story of *The Third Eye* . . .

The book should end there, but there is more to tell. After finishing *The Third Eye* he has a heart attack, and he and his wife move to Ireland. (It is not clear why the climate of Ireland should be better for heart ailments than England.) There he wrote *Doctor From Lhasa*. But the task was still not completed; he had to go on and tell *The Rampa Story*. Driven out of Ireland by income tax problems, he moves to Canada. There he receives a telepathic message: he must go on writing and tell the *Truth*. 'Write it down, Lobsang, and also write of what *could* be in Tibet.' And he continues to tell a story of how Truth found it difficult to obtain an audience until he borrowed the coloured garments of Parable. After that, Truth was welcome everywhere . . . (This, presumably, is intended as a reply to people who claim that Rampa's Tibet is unlike the real place; he can always claim he is talking in parables.) The book ends with a nasty vision of an atomic rocket, launched from Tibet by the Chinese. 'Is it fantasy?', he asks. '*It could be fact.*' The placing of the quotation suggests that it could refer to the whole Rampa story.

Rampa's explanations about his body swap must have convinced a fair number of readers, for he has gone on to produce several more books: *Cave of the Ancients*, *Living with a Lama*, *You-Forever*, *Wisdom of the Ancients*, and a book called *My Visit to Venus* in which he describes how he was taken to Venus in a flying saucer and spent some time studying the history of Atlantis and Lemuria in its skyscraper cities. (Space probes have since shown that Venus is too hot to support any form of life.)

It seems that Hoskins has constructed a story that cannot be disproved by the sceptics, since he has an answer to every objection. Yet there still remain a few matters that need explaining. Why did Hoskins tell his neighbours, a Mr and Mrs Boxall, in 1943 or 1944 that he had been a pilot in the Chinese air force? This was some years before his first 'meeting' with Lobsang Rampa. And why, in 1948, did he change his name to Dr Carl Kuon Suo, rather than to Lobsang Rampa? Of one thing we can be sure: Rampa would have no difficulty providing answers that would satisfy the faithful.

RUSSELL, Bertrand

Sex Life of a Logical Philosopher

Bertrand Russell was a lifelong philanderer of whom one biographer wrote his 'private life was a chaos of serious affairs, secret trysts and emotional tightrope acts that constantly threatened, if never quite exploded into, ruinous scandal.'

Russell's father, Lord Amberley, was not quite so fortunate. At the age of twenty-two, his tutor recommended him to read a book on the overpopulation problem and four years later, Amberley took the chair at a meeting of the London Dialectical Society, in which he criticized the clergy for being opposed to the prevention of overpopulation and said that if women had more say in the latter they would be opposed to large families. Ten days later, the *British Medical Journal* repudiated birth control, and Lord Amberley, with 'indignation and disgust'. The *Journal*, and other organs that took up the attack, seemed to believe that Amberley was advocating abortion or infanticide. (Victorian delicacy made it hard for anyone to say openly what Amberley had advocated.) He was called a 'filthy, foulmouthed rake', and when he stood as a Liberal for Parliament, a placard of 'a scandalous and indecent character' was flourished at him. Understandably, he failed to gain the seat.

Russell was born in 1872. He tells in his autobiography how his father hired a tutor named Spalding to teach his elder brother science. The tutor was in an advanced stage of consumption but Lord and Lady Amberley decided that, although he ought to remain childless, it was unfair for him to remain celibate. So Lady Amberley gallantly offered Spalding the use of her own body to allay his frustration, 'though', adds Russell, 'I know of no evidence that she derived any pleasure from doing so.' This seems a naïve remark; no woman, particularly the daughter of a peer, is likely to consent to allowing a young man to use her like a prostitute unless she has some sneaking admiration for him. The affair started soon after Russell was born. However, two years later, Lady Amberley died of diphtheria, and her husband, soon after, of bronchitis.

Russell was raised by a Presbyterian grandmother and brooded a great deal on his sinfulness. At fifteen he was 'constantly distracted by erections' and learned to masturbate. Then, at twenty, he fell in love with Alys Pearsall Smith, an American Quaker. At the same time he became involved with Alys's sister, Mary, who had just left her husband. He later told intimate friends that he had had an *affaire* with Mary. This seems to contradict the statement in his autobiography that until 1911 he had never had 'complete relations' with any woman. The solution may lie in the word 'complete'. As a child, Russell had fallen out of a carriage and hurt his penis and there is a suggestion that this induced periodic impotence. He mentioned later that he 'failed totally' to give his first wife a child. So he and Mary may have tried hard but failed to achieve any result.

Russell married Alys, who was five years his senior, and they seem to have been reasonably happy, in spite of her conviction that 'sex was beastly' and that 'all women hated it'. After some initial sexual problems, which he found 'merely comic', they seem to have overcome problems of mutual adjustment. Even so, Russell describes 'a day after three weeks of marriage, when, under the influence of sexual fatigue, I hated her and could not imagine why I had wished to marry her.' This is a highly revealing comment, which throws some light on the curious paradox of Russell's mental life. Intellectually he was brilliant, with a natural capacity for abstract reasoning. But he always seemed to handle emotional problems with a clumsiness that shows a total lack of imagination. This is why his writings, particularly on moral and social questions, often seem naïve.

Russell was himself capable of recognizing this emotional inadequancy. When he began to work on his monumental *Principia Mathematica* with Alfred North Whitehead, he fell in love with Whitehead's wife Evelyn. She often suffered intense pain from heart trouble. One day Russell walked into the room to find her undergoing a severe bout of pain: 'She seemed cut off from everyone and everything by walls of agony, and the sense of the solitude of each human soul suddenly overwhelmed me. Ever since my marriage, my emotional life had been calm and superficial. I had forgotten all the deeper issues, and had been content with flippant cleverness. Suddenly the ground seemed to give way beneath me . . .' The result was a sort of religious conversion, which turned him into a pacifist and, socially speaking, an idealist.

One day out bicycling, he suddenly realized he was no longer in love with Alys and that she irritated him profoundly. With typical unconscious cruelty, he decided he had better tell her so immediately. The poor woman was naturally shattered and went on clinging pathetically to him for several years, periodically begging him to come to her bed. (He did, but found it unenjoyable.)

Then one day he fell in love. He had been canvassing for his friend Philip Morrell, a Liberal candidate. In March 1911 he went to stay the night at the London home of the Morrells and found that his host had had to go elsewhere. He was entertained by Lady Ottoline Morrell, Philip's wife, who had red hair and a face like a horse. But both she and her house were intensely feminine and Russell was tired of Quaker plainness and flannel nighties. 'Making timid approaches, I found them to my surprise not repulsed. I found to my amazement that I loved her deeply and that she returned my feeling . . . For external and accidental reasons [he means presumably that she was menstruating] I did not have full relations with Ottoline that evening but we agreed to become lovers as soon as possible.' The opportunity came when Russell went to visit her at her country house, Studland. Russell's dentist had told him he thought Russell had cancer and he describes how this knowledge heightened his happiness by giving it greater intensity. A specialist reassured him about the cancer and he and Ottoline remained lovers for five years to the fury of Alys and the disgust of Philip Morrell.

Russell, having embarked on a career of adultery, never looked back. In 1913, on holiday in Italy, he saw a young German woman sitting alone and induced one of the ladies in the party to invite her to join them. 'I made friends with the lady and we made an expedition into the country. I wished to make love to her, but thought that I ought first to explain about

Ottoline. Until I spoke about Ottoline, she was acquiescent but afterwards she ceased to be so. She decided, however, that for one day her objections could be ignored.' In the following year Russell visited America, and met a surgeon's daughter named Helen Bradley in Chicago. He confessed to Ottoline that they had spent the day in the woods 'and I found that I care for her a great deal. It ended by our spending the night together and she will come to England as soon as she can.' Helen Bradley came to England with 'hopes and preparations for a honeymoon'; but Russell had already tired of her. Helen had to pour out her miseries to Ottoline, with whom she was staying. When Russell and Helen went together to Garsington – the Morrells' new country home – Helen could be heard knocking on Russell's bedroom door in the middle of the night; but he refused to open up. And back in London, Russell was making love to Ottoline in his new flat when Helen came and knocked on the door – and again received no answer. Meanwhile, Ottoline had introduced him to the beautiful Irene Copper Willis, a research assistant who worked with him on a political pamphlet. Russell made love to her, then wished that he hadn't for she was afraid of scandal and refused to go away with him. 'I do like people to be willing to shoot Niagara,' said Russell, conveniently overlooking his tendency to fall out of love with women when they were struggling in the water.

During World War I, Russell was dismissed from his lectureship at Trinity College, Cambridge, for his pacifist views. In 1916 his pacifism brought him into contact with a pretty twenty-year-old actress, Lady Constance Malleson, who was married to the actor Miles Malleson. When Russell had delivered a pacifist speech and received an immense ovation, they dined together and afterwards he went back to her flat – her husband was away – where they became lovers.

In 1915, Russell had bumped into T. S. Eliot in London – he had met him earlier in America (and Eliot had written a poem about him called 'Mr Apollinax'). Eliot was now about to marry a beautiful but rather unstable young lady named Vivien Haigh-Wood and they had nowhere to live. Russell offered to let them share his Bury Street flat. Apparently Eliot had no objection to Russell staying in the flat with Vivien when he himself happened to be away. Vivien seems to have preferred

Russell to Eliot in many ways – Eliot was undervitalized (a doctor remarked that he had the thinnest blood he had ever come across). Even when the Eliots found their own flat, Russell would sometimes take Vivien out to dinner or lunch. He had decided that his relations with the Eliots should be purely 'paternalistic', but in 1918, he finally gave way and made love to Vivien. He told Constance Malleson that the experience was 'hellish and loathsome' and that he had to disguise his antipathy. He took the first opportunity of breaking with Vivien, who later went insane.

In 1919, Russell moved to Lulworth, in Dorset, for the summer. Among many visitors there was a personable young lady named Dora Black, a Fellow of Girton. She was also a campaigner for women's rights who was 'outspoken in her advocacy of greater sexual freedom.' She found Russell 'enchantingly ugly' and thought he looked like the Mad Hatter. The next time they met they talked about her aversion to marriage and he asked her what she wanted to do about children. She replied that they should be entirely the concern of the mother. Two weeks later there was a ring at her doorbell and Russell asked her if she could catch the 12.30 train to Lulworth on Monday. 'Am I to understand . . . ?' asked Dora breathlessly and Russell nodded. 'But I understand you are already in love with a lady?' Russell assured her it was all over. (In fact, it was to be another two years before he threw over Lady Constance.) Typically, halfway through their weekend, Lady Constance sent a telegram announcing her arrival so Russell informed Dora she would have to leave immediately . . .

In spite of this bad start, when he was offered a post at Peking University, it was Dora Black Russell decided to take with him. When they returned in 1921 she was pregnant. They agreed to marry but both insisted that they should retain their individual freedom. And when, in 1926, the Russells decided to start their own experimental school, one of the things they advocated was that free love should be allowed to the staff. Russell regarded the female staff as his private harem and thoroughly enjoyed himself. He explained to his staff that it was impossible for a man to know a woman until he had slept with her (a view also held by his contemporary Professor

Joad). 'He had no hesitation putting his beliefs to the test,' says Russell's biographer Ronald Clark, who also quotes him on the subject of his 'inability to restrain his abnormally strong sexual urges.' He had one fairly regular affair – a girl with whom he disappeared most weekends to his London flat, explaining blandly to his staff, 'As we both have to go to London it saves a chauffeur if we both go at the same time.' This can have fooled few of them, since Russell was in the habit of propositioning the more attractive females. One new teacher turned him down on her second evening at the school (he seems to have borne her no ill will). When Dora Russell was finally granted a divorce in 1935 the judge commented that Russell had 'been guilty of numerous acts of adultery . . . with persons in the household.' He added, 'in circumstances which are usually held to aggravate the offence,' implying that Russell did not confine his activities to 'dirty weekends' in London, but carried on under his wife's nose. Dora Russell describes how she had been spending a weekend with a young man in London when she received a note from the cook saying she must return home at once – she was refusing to let the governess come near the children because she had caught her sleeping with 'the Masther'. 'Bertie had an aristocratic attitude to the servants', says Dora, recording that the cook had to go but that the governess, 'who was a charming girl', should stay on. Russell had by this time broken with Lady Constance Malleson after several unsuccessful attempts that had ended in brief reconciliation. Russell remarked that philosophers in love 'are exactly like everybody else, except, perhaps, that the holiday from reason makes them passionate to excess.'

Russell had discovered that his ugliness – the prim but weak mouth, the receding chin, the large nose – made no difference where women were concerned; his fame was an aphrodisiac. Clark records that even as he approached sixty he was still endangered by 'an insatiable appetite for personable and intelligent young women'. There was, for example, the case of a Miss Joan Folwell, whom he met after addressing a political meeting in Salisbury. She was twenty-one. Russell was a guest in the house of her parents and he asked her to read aloud an essay she had written. 'I then realized,' wrote Miss Folwell, 'that he was more interested in me than my writing.' Letters soon progressed from 'My Dear Joan (may I call you so?)' to 'My darling Joan', and after a short time he was inviting her to spend the night with him. 'My only fear is lest you may find me sexually inadequate, as I am no longer young . . . but I think there are ways in which I can make up for it. And I do want you dreadfully . . .' Problems intervened; he had to send her a telegram and cancel. Then he went to America but when he returned he renewed the pursuit. They met – the second time for dinner, the third to stay the night together. It had taken Russell three years to get her into bed. 'He was very tenacious . . . But the sleeping wasn't a success, so I gave him up.' More than forty years later, Miss Folwell recorded her conviction that Russell was largely responsible for the permissive society and that he would have hated it.

The marriage to Dora ended after she had had two children by an American journalist. Dora hired a pretty governess named Patricia Spence, known as Peter; inevitably, Russell became attracted to her and when Dora Russell's American journalist visited, they formed a *ménage à quatre*. Eventually, he and Patricia married but there continued to be other women. It made no difference whether they were already married or married to men with whom he was friendly – like Gamel Brenan, wife of his friend Gerald Brenan, whom Russell pursued with customary tenacity for years. Then there was the young wife of a Cambridge lecturer, who moved into Russell's house with her husband to look after him when Patricia was in hospital after an accident. Although now in his mid-seventies, Russell bombarded her with letters suggesting clandestine meetings in London or elsewhere. The philosopher Sidney Hook, who knew Russell well, records that the marriage with Patricia broke up when Russell declined to make a pledge of mutual fidelity. 'That was the last straw for Patricia who had suffered humiliation enough because of Russell's roving eye and affections.' Hook also recorded (in *Encounter*, March 1984):

He volunteered confessions about his sexual powers, and related matters about which I would no more have enquired of him than I would of my own father. He seemed always on the prowl when attractive and vivacious young women were around and he assumed that my interest in extracurricular matrimonial activity was as keen as his own. On occasions I was rendered speechless by his unsolicited advice on how to 'make' a girl and what to do after one made her. 'Hook', he once advised, 'if you ever take a girl to an hotel and the reception clerk seems suspicious, when he gives you the price of the room, have her complain loudly, "It's *much* too expensive!" He's sure to assume she is your wife . . .' At another time when I commented on his remarkable memory, he mildly demurred and observed that it was not what it used to be. Seconds later, as if to illustrate the point, he turned to me and asked, 'Hook, what's been the most embarrassing moment of your life?' Without waiting for a reply from me, he went on, 'Mine was the failure to remember at breakfast the name of an attractive woman to whom I had made ardent love the night before. I really knew it, of course, but it came to mind too late!' Like George Bernard Shaw, Russell was apparently an eloquent vocaliser in his love-making ecstasies.

Hook offers some interesting insights into the paradox that was Bertrand Russell: the brilliant mind, the penetrating intellect, allied to a curious emotional immaturity. He lists the three things that prevent him from classifying Russell as one of the 'great minds who were also great human beings'. 'The first was Russell's vanity. He once told me that whenever he met a man of outstanding intellectual reputation, his first unuttered reaction was: "Can I take him or can he take me? . . ." There was more than a touch of exhibitionism in the riskless sit-downs of his last years, when he made well-publicized gestures to Ban The Bomb that were as futile as they were ill-advised.' The second trait Hook found unpleasant was Russell's greed. 'I was shocked to find what Russell was prepared to do for a little money . . . He always seemed strapped for money and tended to blame it on Patricia's extravagance which seemed hardly plausible to me.' He cites an article Russell wrote for a magazine called *Glamour* entitled 'What To Do If You Fall In Love With a Married Woman'. When Hook asked him why he did it, Russell replied, 'For fifty dollars.' The third trait Hook disliked was a certain cold-bloodedness. 'I reluctantly came to the conclusion that Russell's religion of truth overlaid a strong streak of cruelty.' He cites many examples, including Russell's treatment of Helen Bradley. 'Sensitive readers of Russell's autobiography will have been revolted by the cruelty of some of its pages, not only his account of his treatment of the infatuated young woman who followed him to England, but particularly by the reproduction of a letter from a harmless German savant who after making some contributions to the philosophy of mathematics had become insane. Publication of that letter was like jeering at a cripple.'

Dora Russell made the interesting comment, 'In love, too, Bertie was a perfectionist; the "spiritual" bond must exist, if it were broken then love might come to an end. In this, as in other matters, Bertie was not fully aware of his underlying motives; that spiritual bond might well mean that a wife must agree with him in every detail, so that she might be fully possessed.' It is the nearest she comes to admitting that Russell was an adept in self-deception.

SCHLIEMANN, Heinrich
The Great Troy Hoax

During his lifetime and for more than eighty years after his death, in 1890, the name of Heinrich Schliemann – 'the man who found Troy' – remained untainted by the slightest breath of scandal. The discovery in the late 1970s that he was, in fact, a pathological liar and a crook caused tremendous reverberations in the world of archaeology.

Heinrich Schliemann, the man who was to be described as 'the creator of prehistoric Greek archaeology', was born on 6 January 1822 at Neu-Buckow, Germany, the son of a country parson. It was from his father that young Heinrich first heard about ancient history. In his autobiography, he tells of the crucial event of his childhood: how, at the age of seven, he received for Christmas a copy of Jerrer's *Universal History*, with an illustration showing Troy in flames. Surely, reasoned the young Heinrich, walls so mighty could not have been destroyed? They must still be there . . .

His childhood was not happy. One of seven children, he was shattered by the death of his mother and by the scandal when his father took a maidservant as a mistress, and later when his father was accused of misappropriating church funds and dismissed (he was later exonerated). Heinrich and his father had many bitter arguments. At the age of fourteen, Heinrich became a grocer's assistant and had to work fourteen hours a day. Suffering from tuberculosis, he gave up his job and became a cabin boy on a boat sailing for South America; it was shipwrecked and he found himself eventually in Amsterdam. There he became a clerk, taught himself English and went on to learn nine foreign languages in six years. At the age of twenty-four, he was sent to Russia as the chief agent of an Amsterdam merchant. In 1850, he sailed for America to claim the estate of his brother Louis, who had died in California. He records in his diary that he called on the President of the United States, Zachary Taylor, and had an hour-and-a-half's conversation with him, meeting his family and being treated with great kindness. Then he went on to Sacramento, where he set up an office to buy gold dust from the miners for the gold rush was at its height at that time. He amassed a fortune of $350,000 as a result. He noted in his diary that he was in San Francisco during the great fire of 1851. Back in Europe, he married a Russian beauty but she did not care for archaeology or travel and they eventually divorced. Schliemann visited Greece for the first time at the age of thirty-seven. Four years later, he was rich enough to realize the ambition of a lifetime and to become an archaeologist. He studied archaeology in Paris and travelled extensively in the Mediterranean area. In 1868 he visited Mycenae, in Greece – the home of Agamemnon – and propounded a startling theory that the royal tombs would be found within the ruined walls of the citadel, and not, as the Greek geographer Pausanius stated, outside the walls. Soon after this he was awarded his doctorate by the University of Rostock, writing his thesis, according to his autobiography, in classical Greek.

An old friend, Archbishop Theoclitus Vimbos of Athens, helped him find a Greek wife. A sixteen-year-old schoolgirl, Sophia Engastromenos, was selected for him; her parents agreed, and the couple was married. Her parents were much impressed by his tales, particularly the story about the fire of San Francisco.

Schliemann was convinced that Troy really existed and that it was no legend, as many scholars believed. Those scholars who accepted the existence of Troy – ancient Ilion – thought that it was situated three hours from the sea near Bunarbashi, on the Balidagh, in a mountain fastness. On the evidence of Homer, Schliemann disagreed – Homer's heroes had ridden between Troy and the coast several times a day. He decided that the site of Troy was probably a mound at a place called Hissarlik, an hour from the sea. He obtained permission from the Turkish authorities to dig there and started in 1871, with a gang of eighty men.

It must be admitted that, as an archaeologist, Schliemann does not rate very highly. His method was as subtle as a bulldozer. He simply ordered his men to cut a deep trench through the mound. He soon discovered that the mound contained several cities, one on top of the other. Convinced that ancient Troy must be the lowest, he ordered his workmen to dig straight down to it, destroying all the ruins above, including those of the city archaeologists now known to be the Troy of Homer. The city Schliemann thought was the Troy of King Priam was in reality many centuries earlier.

In the following year, Schliemann's workmen sliced the top off the mound. Many discoveries came to light, but so far, there was no sign of the gold that Homer talked about. At least he found structures he identified as the royal palace, the walls of the gods, and the ramp leading to the Scaean Gate.

By the spring of 1883 he was becoming worried; he had still found no gold and he had agreed to end the excavations in June. Then, one day in May, he thought he glimpsed a copper vessel through a hole in a wall. What followed has been told in breathless detail by more than twenty biographers of Schliemann. Afraid that his workmen would make off with part of his find, he waited until they were eating, then asked Sophia to help him remove the 'treasure'. Indifferent to his danger for the wall above was made of loose masonry, he tore out the stones, aided by a large knife and, piece by piece, handed the marvellous gold objects – drinking vessels and jewellery – to his wife, who wrapped them in her shawl. Later, behind closed doors, Sophie was dressed in the jewels of Helen of Troy – Schliemann was later to take a photograph of her draped in the gold ornaments. In June he returned to Athens and finally announced his discovery of the treasure. It made him world famous. He was later to excavate Mycenae, where his guess about the situation of the tombs proved correct. He died in 1890, at the age of sixty-eight. Sophia survived him by forty years.

That is the story of Heinrich Schliemann, and it has been retold many times. Guides at Hissarlik still show fascinated tourists the spot where Schliemann discovered the treasure of Priam, only a few weeks before he was due to leave Troy for ever.

In 1972, William Calder, Profesor of Classics at the University of Colorado, was asked to go to Schliemann's birthplace,

Neu-Buckow, to give a lecture on the hundred-and-fiftieth anniversary of his birth. Studying the various biographies of the great man, he realized that about 90 per cent of their material came from Schliemann himself. As soon as he began to check source material, he discovered that Schliemann was rather less trustworthy than his admirers had assumed. Checking at the University of Rostock, Calder discovered that the doctoral thesis was not, as Schliemann had declared, written in classical Greek; it only had a short section in classical Greek and this was atrocious. Calder checked on the story about calling on the President of the United States and being kindly received; the reception at which Schliemann claimed he was presented to six hundred guests would certainly be mentioned in Washington newspapers. There was nothing whatever – Schliemann had invented it.

Calder's lecture about these saddening discoveries was read by David Trail, a classics professor at the University of California. In San Francisco, he was able to check the records of the bankers who had stored the gold dust that Schliemann had bought from the miners in Sacramento and found suggestions that Schliemann had systematically cheated them by sending them short-weight consignments. Checking Schliemann's account of the great fire of San Francisco, Trail discovered that Schliemann had quoted the wrong date – he gave it as 4 June 1851 when it had taken place on 4 May. Schliemann's papers are stored in Athens, and Trail checked the diary. The page with the account of the fire proved to have been glued in later. The page preceding it has an entry in Spanish, which continues on the following page. The account proved to have been culled from newspapers of the time.

Calder's opinion was that Schliemann was a pathological liar – a liar so convinced of his own romances that a lie-detector test would probably have indicated he was telling the truth. Even the story about seeing the pictures of Troy in a book he was given for Christmas proved to be an invention, fabricated later for Schliemann's book *Ilion*.

The diaries also revealed that there were doubts about the finding of the treasure. There was no entry for the discovery of the treasure; he speaks about it for the first time in an entry dated 17 June. In the published account, this entry is datelined from Troy. In the diary, 'Athens' has been crossed out and 'Troy' substituted. An entry that was a draft-account of the discovery for his German publishers fails to describe the treasure, with the exception of one gold cup, noted as having large handles and being shaped like a champagne glass, with a rounded bottom (the shape we would now describe as a hock glass). There is no such vessel among the treasure. The nearest to it is a kind of gold sauce boat with handles and the descriptions do not correspond. But Schliemann had unearthed many terracotta vessels that looked exactly like the 'champagne glass' he described. It seems that he simply invented the item in order to give his publisher a foretaste of the treasure.

Further investigation revealed that Sophia was not present at the time Schliemann claims he found the treasure. She was in mourning for her father in Athens and did not return to Troy. And although excavations continued for two weeks after Schliemann claimed to have found the treasure – giving him plenty of time to describe it – there is nevertheless not a single description in his diary. The inference is that he did not find any treasure – at least, not in the manner he described.

But where did the treasure come from? Trail's conclusion was that the 'treasure' was already back in Athens at the time Schliemann claims he discovered it. He was obliged by contract to share anything he found with the owners of the site, a Pasha and an American named Frank Calvert. What almost certainly happened is that Schliemann systematically cheated them, claiming he had found nothing, and smuggling his finds back to Athens – his letters often refer to objects that he failed to show to Calvert. In March, before the 'finding' of the treasure, a letter mentions sixty gold rings – precisely the number of rings in the treasure.

That Schliemann found something is proved by the testimony of his trusted overseer, Nicolaos Yannakis, who later told an English antiquarian, William Borlase, that he had been with Schliemann at the time of the find and not Sophia. And the find contained no gold or jewellery – only a quantity of bronze objects, found in a stone enclosure outside the city wall.

So why did Schliemann do it? Psychoanalysts who have considered the problem have talked about his relationship with his father – the admiration combined with fear and dislike that compelled him to seek fame so that he could finally feel he had outstripped his father. This may or may not be true. All that is certain is that Schliemann craved fame and applause – his lie about the meeting with the President reveals the desire to impress. 'We all bid for admiration with no intention of earning it,' says Shaw. In his own devious way, Schliemann set out to earn it. He wanted to believe that he had found Homer's Troy; to complete the triumph, he needed to find King Priam's treasure. And if the treasure did not exist, then it had to be made to exist. Only in this way could Schliemann achieve the kind of celebrity he craved.

But although these revelations reveal Schliemann as a crook and a liar, they leave one part of his reputation untouched: that strange, intuitive genius that led him to dig in exactly the right place, first at Hissarlik and later at Mycenae. He may have been a confidence man, but he was still, in spite of everything, 'the creator of prehistoric Greek archaeology'.

SCOTLAND YARD
The Great Bribery Scandal

Harry Benson, one of the most ingenious swindlers of all time, is remembered chiefly for his leading role in the great Scotland Yard scandal of 1877.

Benson was the son of a well-to-do Jewish merchant with offices in the Faubourg St Honoré in Paris. He had charming manners, spoke several languages, and liked to represent himself as a member of the nobility. Soon after the Franco-Prussian war of 1870–71, he approached the Lord Mayor of London, calling himself the Comte de Montague, Mayor of Châteaudun, seeking a subscription for the relief of citizens made destitute by the war. He collected £1,000 but his forged receipt gave him away and he was sentenced to a year in prison. He found prison life so intolerable that he attempted suicide by trying to burn himself to death on his prison mattress. He was crippled by it and had to walk with crutches thereafter.

When he came out of prison, Benson advertised for a secretarial position, mentioning that he spoke several languages. The man who answered his advertisement was a certain William Kurr who specialized in swindles connected with racing. His crude method was to decamp hastily with his customers' winnings. The ingenious Benson soon convinced him that there were better and less risky ways of making a fortune. Members of the French aristocracy were the chosen victims. Kurr and Benson issued a newspaper called *Le Sport* which contained articles about racing translated from British newspapers. It also contained many references to a wealthy Mr G. H. Yonge, who was so incredibly successful in backing horses that British bookmakers always shortened their odds when they dealt with him. *Le Sport* was sent out, free, to dozens of French aristocrats interesting in racing; they had no earthly reason for suspecting a prospective swindle.

One of the aristocrats who became a victim was a certain Comtesse de Goncourt. She received a letter from Mr Yonge of Shanklin, Isle of Wight, asking her if she would agree to act as his agent in laying bets. All she had to do was to send the cheque he would send her to a certain bookmaker; if the horse won, she would receive his winnings, which she would forward to Mr Yonge, and would receive a 5 per cent commission. Madame de Goncourt agreed to this arrangement and received a cheque for a few hundred pounds, which she posted off to the bookmaker in her own name. In due course, she received a cheque for more than a thousand pounds in 'winnings' and after she had sent this off to Mr Yonge, she received her £50 or so commission. It seemed a marvellously easy way of earning £50. What she did not realize was that the 'bookmaker' to whom she forwarded the cheque was simply another of Mr Yonge's aliases. When she had sent Mr Yonge several more lots of winnings and received more lots of commission, she decided that he was obviously a financial genius and entrusted him with £10,000 of her own money to invest on her behalf. That was the last she saw of it.

Although Scotland Yard was a relatively new institution in the 1870s (it was established in 1829), its methods of crime-fighting depended a great deal on underworld 'narks' who betrayed fellow criminals. Police officers, then as now, were forced to cultivate the acquaintance of many criminals. It also meant that an underpaid police officer – in those days the salary of a detective was a mere £5 6s 2d a week – might be subjected to the temptation of accepting presents, favours and open bribes for protecting his own 'narks'. This may well be how a certain detective officer named John Meiklejohn became friendly with William Kurr and then began to accept money from him in exchange for not pressing his investigations into Kurr's earlier swindles. When Chief Inspector Nathaniel Druscovich, a naturalized Pole, confided to Chief Inspector Meiklejohn that he was in financial difficulties, Meiklejohn told him he knew a 'businessman' who could help him. The businessman was Benson and all he wanted in return for the £60 he 'lent' Druscovich was a little information – prior warning if the Yard intended to arrest him. Soon a third detective had been drawn into the net – Chief Inspector William Palmer. Not long after this, Meiklejohn warned Kurr and Benson that the Yard was getting close. Meiklejohn's superior, Chief Inspector Clarke, had been tracking down sham betting offices and was hot on the trail of Gardner and Co., the name under which Kurr and his confederates had been operating.

Among these confederates was a man called Walters who belonged to a gang that Clarke had recently broken up. Now Benson wrote to Clarke from his pleasant home in the Isle of Wight – he kept a carriage, and had an excellent cook and many servants – saying that he had some interesting information about Walters. Unfortunately, he explained, he was crippled and could not come to Scotland Yard but if Clarke would be kind enough to come down to Shanklin . . . In those days, policemen stood in awe of the aristocracy and were likely to treat a wealthy suspect with obsequious respect. So Clarke hurried down to Shanklin and was duly overawed by Mr Yonge's magnificent home. He was worried when Mr Yonge told him that Walters was going about saying that he had bribed Clarke and that he had in his possession a letter to prove it. Indeed Clarke had written Walters a letter; he was not a very literate man and he might easily have expressed himself in a way that could be open to false interpretation. Mr Yonge promised to try to get hold of the letter and he and Clarke parted on friendly terms. But Clarke then reported to his own superior that Yonge was a scoundrel. They had some correspondence and Yonge addressed Clarke as 'My Dear Sir and Brother' for they were both freemasons. They met several times and 'Yonge' later claimed he had given Clarke £50.

With this network of 'police spies', the Benson-Kurr gang should have been untouchable. But Benson now overstepped himself. He wrote to the Comtesse de Goncourt saying that he had a marvellous and unique opportunity to invest a further large sum for her. The Comtesse had no more ready cash and she called on her lawyer, a Mr Abrahams, to ask him to turn certain securities into cash. Mr Abrahams took the precaution of contacting Scotland Yard and asking whether they knew anything about a certain Mr Yonge of 'Rose Bank', Shanklin. Druscovich, who was in charge of frauds connected with the

Continent received the message and hastened to warn Benson that trouble was brewing. Scotland Yard had been asked by the Paris police to intercept letters containing money from various dupes – but the telegram containing this request was pocketed by Druscovich. Druscovich could see that he was playing a dangerous game; he would be expected to make an arrest soon. He begged the swindlers to remove themselves beyond his reach as soon as possible.

The gang, which included Kurr's brother Frederick, and two men named Murray and Bale, had put most of its ill-gotten gains into the safest place, the Bank of England. They could, of course, withdraw it without difficulty. The only problem about that was that English bank notes are numbered and for such a large sum of money, they would be numbered consecutively and would, therefore, be easy to trace. If the gang escaped to the Continent, they would be leaving a trail of bank notes behind them like a paperchase. Benson withdrew about £16,000 from the bank and hastened up to Scotland where he opened an account in the Bank of Clydesdale in Greenock; he also withdrew £13,000 in Bank of Clydesdale £100 notes. These had the advantage of bearing no number but they were still easily traceable. Benson was eating dinner with the manager of the Clydesdale Bank when he received a telegram from Druscovich warning him that he was on his way to arrest him. Benson fled, forfeiting the £3,000 still in his account at Greenock.

The detectives were rewarded with about £500 each (although Clarke does not seem to have been included). Meiklejohn immediately made the mistake of cashing one of his £100 notes and giving an office of the gang as his address. A week later he cashed another note with a Leeds wine merchant. The Leeds Police discovered this and since they were on the lookout for the gang sent a telegram to Scotland Yard. Druscovich intercepted the telegram and burnt it.

Scotland Yard found it baffling that, in spite of all their efforts, the Benson gang had slipped through their fingers. The bribed detectives were still not suspected. Clarke's superior Williamson set it all down to sheer bad luck. In fact, most of the gang was now in hiding at Bridge of Allan in Scotland.

When the Comtesse's lawyer, Abrahams, traced them to Scotland, Detective Officer William Palmer sent them a letter warning them to scatter.

It was Druscovich who was made responsible for rushing around the country to trap the swindlers. He met Kurr at the Caledonian Station in Edinburgh and was offered £1,000 by him if he did not go to Bridge of Allan. Druscovich had to decline for he had been ordered to go to Bridge of Allan to collect certain letters that had been addressed to one 'Mr Giffard' at the Queen's Hotel. Mr Giffard was William Kurr.

Inevitably, the birds had flown by the time Druscovich reached Bridge of Allan. Williamson was understandably disappointed. He was astounded to learn that his subordinate Meiklejohn had been seen in the company of the swindlers at Bridge of Allan. This was surely the point when Scotland Yard had to smell a rat . . . But Meiklejohn explained that he had no idea he had been wining and dining with crooks. He had met Yonge by chance and believed him to be a perfectly respectable gentleman. Williamson accepted his story.

Now the gang found themselves with thousands of pounds in uncashable £100 notes and with no ready cash. Murray was sent off to cash a cheque at one of the banks in Scotland where they had opened an account; the police were waiting for him. Benson went to Rotterdam and tried to cash a note at his hotel but Scotland Yard had alerted the Dutch police and he was arrested. Druscovich passed on the news to Kurr who persuaded a crooked attorney named Froggatt to send the Dutch police a telegram signed 'Scotland Yard', ordering them to release Benson on the grounds that his arrest had been a mistake. It almost succeeded but the Dutch police decided to wait for a letter confirming the telegram, and this never came.

It was Druscovich, the expert on Continental crime, who was sent to Rotterdam to bring back Benson – and Bale, who had also been arrested there. There was nothing he could do about it except to look at them sternly and mutter under his breath that he would do his best. There was no opportunity to allow them to escape. Besides, his own position was now in danger. Williamson had now heard about the letter from the Leeds Police, telling them that Meiklejohn had cashed a £100 note there. He wanted to know if Druscovich had seen it.

Druscovich denied all knowledge of it and he realized that any attempt to allow Benson to escape was now out of the question.

The swindlers finally stood in the dock and were found guilty. Benson received fifteen years and Kurr received ten. As soon as they reached Millbank Prison, they asked to see the governor and told the story of the corrupt detectives. A short time afterwards, Druscovich, Meiklejohn, Palmer and Clarke all stood in the dock – and, for good measure, the police had also arrested the crooked attorney, Froggatt. Many letters from the detectives were produced, warning the crooks of the activities of Scotland Yard. Druscovich had also been seen talking to Benson and Kurr at St Pancras Station, London.

All except Clarke were convicted – the evidence against Clarke was inconclusive. Druscovich, Meiklejohn and Palmer all received two years' hard labour, the maximum sentence for conspiring to defeat the ends of justice.

Clarke was retired on a pension. Meiklejohn became a private detective. Palmer used his savings to become a publican. What happened to Druscovich is not known but he disappeared from sight; while Froggatt died in a workhouse.

The two principal swindlers still had many successful years before them. Benson and Kurr both received a third remission of sentence for good conduct. They teamed up again and slipped across the Atlantic where they became mining company promoters. Benson returned to Belgium and continued in business selling stock in non-existent mines. The Belgian Police found out more about him from Scotland Yard and arrested him. Huge quantities of postal orders and cheques, apparently sent to him by gullible investors were found in his lodgings. He spent another two years in jail then moved to Switzerland. There he again set out to give the impression he was a wealthy stockbroker. He met a girl in his hotel, whose father was a retired general and surgeon of the Indian army. He persuaded the girl to marry him and induced the father to sell his shares and hand over the proceeds of £7,000 for 'investment'. Then he tried to disappear to America. His father-in-law managed to have him arrested at Bremen but decided not to prosecute when Benson gave back £5,000. Jewellery that Benson had given his fiancée proved to be made of paste.

His last great coup was in America. The singer Adelina Patti was arriving in New York for a tour. Benson, calling himself Abbey, bribed Customs officials to let him on the boat ahead of the Patti Reception Committee. He introduced himself to her as the head of the committee. When the committee arrived, he was deep in conversation with her and they assumed he was her manager. She left the boat on his arm. He then went to Mexico and sold thousands of bogus tickets of Patti concerts. He was arrested when he went back into the States and committed to the Tombs. Apparently, unable to face the prospect of another long period in prison, he leapt from a high gallery and fell 50 feet snapping his spine. At the time of his death he was little more than forty years of age.

SHOLOKHOV, Mikhail

The Quiet Flows the Don *Plagiarism Scandal*

The most eminent Russian author to emerge since the Revolution in 1917 is undoubtedly Mikhail Alexandrovitch Sholokhov, born in the hamlet of Kruzhlino, on the banks of the Don, in 1905. Like Gorky, Sholokhov led a varied life – soldier, handyman, statistician, food inspector, goods handler, mason, book-keeper and finally journalist – before he hurtled to literary fame at the age of twenty-three with the first volume of *Tikhi Don, The Quiet Don* (translated into English as *Quiet Flows the Don*). When compared with the great Russian novels of the nineteenth century, it seems full of 'shock tactics' of the kind associated with cheap popular novels in England and the United States. The book begins with a scene in which the Turkish wife of a Cossack is trampled by a mob who believe her to be a witch. As a result she dies in premature childbirth. Shortly thereafter there is a description of how a seventeen-year-old girl is raped by her father and how her brother and mother then beat and kick him to death. Seductions, rapes and various forms of violence follow at regular intervals. But the nature writing is as fine as anything in the work of the novelist Turgenev.

Sholokhov's first book *Tales of the Don* appeared when he was only twenty. It is interesting to note in these tales of the civil war and shortly after that the village leaders are portrayed as isolated from the people; later, as he learned communist conformity, Sholokhov showed them integrated with the people.

Sholokhov began work on *Tikhi Don* when he was twenty-one. When it appeared two years later – and became an instant bestseller – critics were amazed that anyone so young could write so powerfully; it eventually sold four and a half million copies before its fourth and final volume appeared fourteen years later. The later volumes are generally admitted to be inferior to the first. *Virgin Soil Upturned* (1932), about a collective farm, was a success in Russia but it is considered inferior to the earlier parts of *Tikhi Don*.

Soon after the first volume of *Tikhi Don* appeared in 1925, rumours began to spread around Moscow literary circles to the effect that Sholokhov was not the true author and that he had found the manuscript or a diary on which he based the book. In 1929, *Pravda* published a letter from a number of proletarian writers denouncing the 'malicious slander'. It even threatened prosecution. Nevertheless, Sholokhov was generally regarded as Russia's most important writer. In 1965 he was given the Nobel Prize for literature. By then, Sholokhov had become spokesman for the Soviet literary establishment, denouncing writers like Pasternak and Solzhenitsyn and taking an aggressively anti-intellectual stand that has caused young writers to regard him with distaste. This may be fuelled by envy for his life style on a large estate at Rostov-on-Don, where he has a private aeroplane and theatre, and hunts regularly.

Alexander Solzhenitsyn, who was forced into exile in Zurich in 1974, brought out of Russia a number of documents about Sholokhov's work by a friend whom he identifies simply as 'D'. 'D', according to Solzhenitsyn, engaged in painstaking literary analysis of *Tikhi Don* but died before he could complete it. Solzhenitsyn explained that he could not reveal 'D's' real name for fear of reprisals against his family but he published the manuscript and appealed to Western scholars to help complete the research.

'D's' textual analysis revealed two different authors of *Tikhi Don*: some 95 per cent of its first two volumes belong to the 'original author', while less than 70 per cent of the second two are his work. 'D's' scepticism was apparently aroused by the fact that the first two volumes, which showed intimate acquaintance with pre-Revolutionary society in the Don region and described World War I and the Civil War, were allegedly written by a young man between the ages of twenty-one and twenty-three. Sholokhov was too young to have witnessed either war. Even the speed of composition seems incredible – a novel of well over a quarter of a million words had been written in two years. Yet it took another fourteen years to complete the remaining two volumes and the first part of *Virgin Soil Upturned*. Sholokhov seemed to have 'dried up'. His collected works, issued in honour of his seventy-fifth birthday in 1980, amounted to a mere eight volumes.

According to Solzhenitsyn (introducing 'D's' book *The Mainstream of the Quiet Don*), the true author of *Tikhi Don* was a historian of the Don region, one Fyodor Dmitrievitch Kryukov, born in 1870, the son of a local 'ataman' (village leader). By the end of the nineteenth century he had achieved great popularity as a recorder of Cossack life and was elected to the state parliament (Duma). Solzhenitsyn believes he began writing his major work, *Tikhi Don*, in Petrograd during World War I. As a Cossack, he was opposed to the Bolsheviks who seized power in 1917 and fought with the army of the Don. When this collapsed, he retired to the Kuban and died there of typhoid at the age of fifty. 'D's' analysis of Kryukov's earlier works, which were never printed by the Soviet regime, convinced him that he was the true author of *Tikhi Don* and that as a journalist Sholokhov somehow came across Kryukov's manuscript and used it as a basis for his own book, deleting whole chapters where they did not suit his purpose and inserting material of his own. This, according to 'D', explains the unevenness of the style and various internal contradictions.

Understandably, the Soviet view is that Solzhenitsyn is merely concerned with slandering and undermining the greatest Soviet novelist. But if this is so, at least he has presented his evidence in full so it can be studied by literary scholars and experts who can decide on its merits.

SIMPSON, Mrs Wallis
The Royal Abdication Crisis

No single incident in all that fateful year of 1936, which saw Hitler's troops march into the Rhineland, Mussolini's forces conquer Abyssinia, and the outbreak of civil war in Spain, caused a bigger sensation in the Old World or the New than a love affair between a middle-aged couple, and its aftermath; the love of King Edward VIII for American divorcee Mrs Wallis Simpson. It developed into the greatest of all British royal scandals, since it was seen as a possible threat to the monarchy and thus to the Constitution itself, and it ended in the King's abdication and exile.

The King's love for twice-married Mrs Simpson, which began when he was still Prince of Wales, was an open secret for years within the Royal Family, the Establishment and café society circles in London, New York, and the capitals of Europe. Yet incredibly, even when it had progressed to the stage where American newspapers were openly predicting 'King to marry "Wally"' – and naming the date – all mention of the royal romance was deliberately withheld from the ordinary people of Great Britain until the constitutional crisis it had engendered reached flashpoint; a cover-up without precedent in the nation's history. Then, unable to have the woman of his choice proclaimed Queen at his forthcoming Coronation, denied the alternative of a morganatic marriage, and presented by his Ministers with the stark choice of renouncing either the woman he loved or the Crown, the King chose to abdicate in favour of his brother Albert, Duke of York (later George VI). The former King sailed into exile on the night of 11 December 1936, aboard a British destroyer, after addressing the nation by radio. He married Mrs Simpson in France at the Château de Candé, near Tours, in June 1937. No member of the British royal family attended the wedding and most of his former friends stayed away. The service was conducted by an unknown, volunteer Anglican priest from Darlington.

On his wedding eve, the ex-King was officially informed that while he would henceforth be styled His Royal Highness the Duke of Windsor, the magic initials HRH were to be denied his wife, the Duchess – 'a damnable wedding present', he called it. For the rest of their lives together (the Duke died of cancer in May 1972) the Windsors remained objects of curiosity – and gossip – wherever they went.

Prince Edward was born to be King on 23 June 1894, the eldest son of George V and Queen Mary, at White Lodge, Richmond Park. He was christened Edward Albert Christian George Andrew Patrick David (but known to his family simply as 'David'). Mrs Simpson was born on 19 June 1896 at Blue Ridge Summit, Pennsylvania, USA, and christened Bessie Wallis (Warfield) – she was known throughout her childhood as 'Bessiewallis'. Both her parents came from good stock, contrary to scurrilous rumour once her name became linked with the King's. Her mother was a Montague from Baltimore, of Virginian ancestry, and her father Teackle Wallis Warfield from Maryland. Both were of British descent.

'David' became the most popular Prince of Wales in history, idolized not only in Britain but throughout the Dominions and Empire. He travelled extensively as heir to the throne, winning instant acclaim with his good looks and boyish charm from the crowds who welcomed him everywhere. Bessie Wallis Warfield's father died at twenty-seven, leaving very little money. Mother and daughter moved to Baltimore, where relatives paid Bessie's boarding-school fees. The widowed Mrs Warfield remarried in 1908, and following the death of her second husband, for a third time in 1926.

In 1916 Bessie Wallis Warfield met and married her first husband, US Navy pilot Lieutenant Earl Winfield Spencer, Jr. They separated five years later and she was granted a divorce in 1927. That petition was already pending when she met the man who was to become her second husband and accompany her into the pages of history – Ernest Aldrich Simpson. His mother was American, his father an Englishman who headed a prosperous firm of shipbrokers with offices in New York and

London. During World War I young Ernest Simpson sailed for London to enlist in the British forces; in June 1918 he was commissioned in the Coldstream Guards (but did not serve in France). His own first marriage, to divorcee Mrs Dorothy Parsons Dechert, also ended in divorce; that suit, too, was pending when he met Mrs Wallis Warfield Spencer in 1926. Both went separately to Europe in 1928, when they met in London and were married at the Chelsea registrar's office on 21 July.

The Simpsons' flat in Bryanston Court became a rendezvous for businessmen, diplomats and influential journalists, and for the first years their marriage was a happy one. Husband and wife were introduced to the Prince of Wales in the winter of 1930, at a cocktail party given by Thelma, Lady Furness, at her home in Grosvenor Square.

The Prince of Wales fell in love three times before he was forty, on each occasion with someone else's wife. The first was Mrs Freda Dudley Ward, wife of Liberal Whip, William Dudley Ward, MP. She was caught in an air raid in 1918 as she was being escorted through Belgrave Square, in London, and sought refuge in a house there. Among those in the cellar which served as makeshift air raid shelter was the young Prince of Wales, on leave from France (where he served as staff officer). It was the beginning of a romance which lasted sixteen years and – by astonishing coincidence – the hostess who introduced them was the then unknown Ernest Simpson's married sister. Mrs Dudley Ward took an entirely practical view of her own affair with the Prince and wrote later: 'I never met either the King or the Queen. They regarded me as a scarlet woman. They were always after David to leave me and marry within his rank – some Princess or other . . . Heavens, it wasn't as if I were *trying* to marry David! Or even wanted to. He asked me often enough, ardently too. But just as often I said no . . . the whole idea was ridiculous. I was already married, of course, so there'd have to be a divorce, and his parents and friends and the Church would never have allowed it . . .'

The Prince's second love was Thelma, Lady Furness. She was an American who had eloped at sixteen, divorced her first husband, and married again at twenty-one to the widowed

Marmaduke, Viscount Furness, the shipping magnate. (They, too, were divorced in 1933.) She had known the Prince of Wales for more than two years when he gave the Simpsons a lift home, from a party at the Furness house, early in 1931. Soon the Prince was a regular visitor to Bryanston Court and in January 1932 he invited the Simpsons to join him as his guests at Fort Belvedere, his residence on the outskirts of Windsor Great Park.

In the autumn of 1933, when Thelma, Lady Furness, sailed for New York, she asked her friend Wallis Simpson to 'look after' the Prince while she was away. By the time she returned to London the following spring, the Prince had become infatuated with Mrs Simpson. Angered by reports of Thelma, Lady Furness's friendship with Prince Aly Khan, he soon broke with her. His final break with Mrs Freda Dudley Ward came at about the same time, as he fell more and more under Wallis Simpson's influence.

Royal biographer Frances Lady Donaldson wrote of this period: 'Within a matter of weeks more gossip and scandal had been created than in the whole of his previous forty years. Until now . . . there is no doubt that the Prince had added more to the brilliance of the Crown, to the magic of the monarchy, than he had taken away. From now on he was to behave with a senseless recklessness in minor matters, an imperviousness to other people's opinions and feelings, which, carelessly and publicly proclaimed, could not for long have been covered by his Household and must in the end have undermined even his extraordinary popularity . . .'

In August 1934 the Prince invited both Simpsons to join him on holiday at Biarritz. Ernest Simpson declined because of business commitments. Mrs Simpson, who was therefore obliged to decline also, later changed her mind and travelled to Biarritz with her aunt, Mrs Bessie Merryman, as chaperone. From Biarritz the Prince's party set sail on *Rosaura*, a yacht owned by Lord Moyne (of the Guinness family), for a fortnight's Mediterranean cruise. In the Duchess of Windsor's own words years later, it was on this cruise that her association with the Prince '. . . crossed the line that marks the indefinable boundary between friendship and love'. On their arrival at Cannes he gave her a diamond and emerald bracelet charm, the first in a cascade of precious stones he was to lavish on his new love.

The Prince holidayed twice in Europe in 1935, the first time at winter sports in Kitzbuhel, followed by a visit to Vienna and Budapest, then a leisurely summer vacation spent in the South of France, Switzerland, Austria and Hungary. On each occasion, both Simpsons were invited to join him. Each time Ernest Simpson declined while his wife accepted – and the inevitable scandal grew. The second time Ernest Simpson sailed for America to discuss his crumbling marriage with his wife's aunt, Mrs Merryman. At Balmoral, George V met with the Archbishop of Canterbury, the lugubrious Cosmo Lang, to mull over the situation. In a later talk with his Prime Minister, Stanley Baldwin, the King predicted with uncanny accuracy, 'After I'm dead the boy will ruin himself in twelve months.' He died on 20 January 1936; David became King Edward VIII – and was on his way into exile, as ex-King, within the year.

Some observers, like his aide and cousin Lord Louis Mountbatten, always maintained that the Prince would have liked to discuss the possibility of marriage to Mrs Simpson during the King's lifetime, but was too much in awe of his disciplinarian father to do so. Once he was King himself, he was free to marry whom he wished within the bounds of the Royal Marriages Act. Given all that, there was still one major obstacle to overcome before he could entertain any hope of marrying Mrs Simpson: the fact that she was already married. At what stage the first steps were taken to obtain that essential divorce – and at whose instigation – has always been a subject of debate. Under the divorce laws then obtaining in England, a successful appellant would first be granted a decree nisi. (Literally 'nisi' means unless.) Then, if no evidence was brought within six months to warrant the attention of the King's Proctor – evidence of collusion, perhaps, or some miscarriage of justice – the decree became absolute and both parties would be free to remarry. That unavoidable six months' interval would inevitably have been an important consideration if, as some were beginning to suspect and fear, the King intended to have Mrs Simpson crowned Queen on 12 May 1937, the date set for his Coronation.

American authors J. Bryan III and Charles J. V. Murphy

state categorically in their book *The Windsor Story* that: '. . . the King stage-managed the divorce from beginning to end. Wallis's attitude was depicted in her bland assurance . . . a few months later . . . that the divorce was "at Ernest's instigation", and at no wish of hers. Precisely when the King decided to start preparations for her suit is not clear. The vague, but best available, date is "one evening in February 1936".' A close friend revealed that he was present, at Ernest Simpson's request, at a meeting between the two men at the time. He said Simpson asked the King, 'Are you sincere? Do you intend to marry her?' and the King replied, 'Do you really think I would be crowned without Wallis by my side?' At that, say the authors: 'The bargain was struck. And kept.'

Certainly the King's subsequent conduct would appear to indicate that henceforth he took marriage to Mrs Simpson almost for granted, although there has never been any suggestion that either his own or Mrs Simpson's legal advisers were in any way involved. On 27 May 1936 he gave a dinner party at St James's Palace. The guests included the Mountbattens, Prime Minister Stanley Baldwin and his wife, the Duff Coopers and the Simpsons, husband and wife. Years later, as the Duchess of Windsor, she wrote that the King said he was inviting the Baldwins that night because 'Sooner or later my Prime Minister must meet my future wife . . .' What is beyond dispute, in the light of the divorce action that was then being prepared, is that the King's Mediterranean cruise that summer, with Mrs Simpson in the royal party but not her husband, was positively reckless, so much international publicity and speculation did it arouse.

Before the King left Britain, the Palace asked Fleet Street to respect his privacy on holiday, as usual. No such obligation rested upon the American and European press however, Unfortunately no one could accuse the King of discretion. First he hired a 250-foot luxury yacht, the *Nahlin*, complete with crew of fifty. When the royal party sailed in her from the Jugoslav port of Sibenik, with two Royal Navy destroyers in attendance, a crowd of many thousands turned up to see them off, shouting *Zivila Ljubav!* ('Long live love!'). Wherever they went the King and Mrs Simpson were photographed together; in Greek waters, at Istanbul, where they were fêted by Turkish dictator Kemal Ataturk, at every stop on their long return journey across Europe by train. True to its word, the British Press, almost alone, made no open reference to Mrs Simpson's presence, although *The Times* was stung into commenting that a sovereign '. . . should be invested with a certain detachment and dignity . . .' Authors Bryan and Murphy summed up by saying: 'The King returned to London no longer the invincible figure he had appeared when he left to join the *Nahlin*. The world publicity had done for him. Within the Establishment, his reputation was in ruins . . .'

Back in Britain, Mrs Simpson's name then appeared in the Court Circular as one of the King's house guests at Balmoral. On this occasion, however, it was not only members of his family and the Establishment who were offended; now it was the turn of the public. The King had been asked earlier, by the trustees of the Royal Infirmary at Aberdeen, to open a new hospital extension on his arrival at Deeside. He had refused on the grounds that the Court would still be in mourning for his dead father. Since then he had been seen at Ascot and holidayed on the *Nahlin*; now, on the day that his brother, the Duke of York, deputized for him at Aberdeen, the King drove to Ballater railway station to meet Mrs Simpson on arrival there. This royal snub caused deep resentment, not only in Deeside but wherever the incident was related, in Scotland and south of the Border.

Soon after the King's return from Balmoral to London, a date was set for the hearing of the Simpson divorce action – 27 October. Already the American newspapers were showing an almost obsessive interest in the royal romance. Those papers were finding their way into Britain and the Dominions, and angry letters of protest were reaching the leaders of the Establishment in London, at Downing Street, Lambeth Palace and the Foreign Office. Behind the scenes, pressure grew to try to have the divorce proceedings stopped but the King would have none of it. He told Prime Minister Baldwin that the divorce was the lady's private business, adding, 'It would be wrong were I to attempt to influence Mrs Simpson just because . . . she happens to be a friend.'

On 12 October 1936 Lord Beaverbrook, Canadian proprietor of the all-powerful *Express* group of newspapers, learned that the divorce was to be heard at Ipswich. He thereupon rang Mrs Simpson's solicitor, Theodore Goddard, and told him he intended to publish a report on the forthcoming petition in the *Evening Standard*. Goddard then called personally on Beaverbrook, to deny that the King intended to marry Mrs Simpson. Later the King invited Lord Beaverbrook to call on him and asked him not only to suppress all comment before the case was heard but for his help in 'limiting publicity' afterwards, on the grounds that Mrs Simpson was 'ill, unhappy and distressed by the thought of notoriety . . . Notoriety would attach to her only because she had been his guest on the *Nahlin* and at Balmoral.'

Lord Beaverbrook agreed and together with Esmond Harmsworth (son of Lord Rothermere, owner of the *Daily Mail* group), persuaded the rest of the British Press to agree to this unprecedented voluntary pact of silence. Beaverbrook wrote later that: 'While I was engaged in these activities directed to regulating publicity, I had no knowledge that marriage was in the mind of the King. He himself had given me no hint of the matter, and, at the same time, I had been told by Mrs Simpson's solicitor, Mr Theodore Goddard, that His Majesty had no such intention. I repeated that assurance to other newspaper proprietors. And I believed it . . .'

The divorce was heard at Ipswich where Mrs Simpson had taken up residence, presumably as a further deterrent to possible publicity. She was awarded a decree nisi against her husband, with costs, on the grounds of his adultery (with a professional co-respondent called Buttercup Kennedy but not named in court). As the former Mrs Simpson left with her solicitor, Theodore Goddard, so the courtroom doors were locked to keep the Press inside. Outside, two photographers had their cameras smashed by the police as they attempted to photograph her. In the confusion, the King's chauffeur drove off with Mrs Simpson: yet next morning, as agreed, the divorce proceedings were reported without comment.

On 13 November, after a visit to the Fleet at Southampton – where he was given a rousing ovation – the King returned to Fort Belvedere to find a terse, coldly polite letter awaiting him from his Private Secretary, Major Alexander Hardinge. In it the King was warned that the Press was about to break its pact

of silence and told that Prime Minister Baldwin had called a
Cabinet to decide what action should be taken 'to deal with
the serious situation which is developing'. Hardinge spoke of
the possible resignation of the government and the damage
which could result from an Election fought on the issue of the
King's private life. His letter ended: 'If Your Majesty will
permit me to say so, there is only one step which holds out any
prospect of avoiding this dangerous situation, and that is for
Mrs Simpson to go abroad *without further delay* and I would
beg your Majesty to give this proposal your earnest consideration before the situation has become irretrievable . . .'

The King met with Prime Minister Baldwin and was told
that his marriage to Mrs Simpson would not meet with the
approval of the Cabinet. The King's response was that his
mind was made up and that he was ready to abdicate if need
be to marry her. Baldwin called it 'grievous news'. Later
Queen Mary, Edward's mother, wrote to her son saying: 'I do
not think you have ever realized the shock which the attitude
you took up caused your family and the whole nation . . . It
seemed inconceivable to those who had made such sacrifices
during the war that you, as their King, refused a lesser
sacrifice . . .'

By now gossip was rife in the Commons. MPs, already
restive under the self-imposed Press censorship, were becoming
increasingly concerned with the government's own deliberate
attempts to hide the truth from the people. On 17 November
1936 Socialist MP Ellen Wilkinson put a leading question to
Sir Walter Runciman, President of the Board of Trade, 'Can
the Right Honourable Gentleman say why, in the case of two
American magazines of the highest repute imported into this
country in the last few weeks, two and sometimes three pages
have been torn out; and what is this thing the British public
are not allowed to know?' To which Runciman replied equivo-
cally, 'My department has nothing to do with that . . .'

Next day the King put private cares aside, and carried out
the tour by which he is still best remembered in Britain –
through the distressed areas of the Rhondda and Monmouth
valleys of South Wales. The unemployed, who knew nothing
of the pending crisis, turned out in their thousands to cheer
him and sing hymns of praise in Welsh. The King, who was

deeply and visibly moved, declared passionately as he looked at all the poverty around him that, 'Something must be done.' If it was an empty promise, it was still the charismatic King at his best, establishing instant rapport with his subjects, so that he and his closest advisers were greatly impressed by the obvious public support he commanded.

Equally, no one who was aware of the fast-approaching constitutional crisis wanted the King to go, but most were determined that Mrs Simpson should not become Queen of England. Their objections had nothing to do with the fact that she was an American, or a commoner; they were that she was a twice-divorced woman, with her two ex-husbands still alive. Similarly, even those who supported the King's desire to marry the woman of his choice, believed his best course was not to challenge the Establishment head-on, but to proceed with his Coronation and then, at some unspecified future date, when Mrs Simpson had won public approval by example, to raise the issue again. This was unacceptable to the King, who felt it meant 'being crowned with a lie on my lips'. Instead, he approved the suggestion of a morganatic marriage, which meant that Mrs Simpson would become Consort of lesser rank (possibly Duchess), and with a proviso that their children if any could not enter the line of succession.

Again Prime Minister Baldwin, who knew what the answer must be, tried to dissuade the King from forcing the issue. He pointed out that the morganatic marriage proposal would have to be put, not only to the Cabinet at home but also to the governments of the Dominions. (Under the terms of the Statute of Westminster of 1931, '. . . any alteration in the law touching the Succession to the Throne or the Royal Style and Titles, shall hereafter require assent as well of the Parliaments of all the Dominions as of the Parliament of the United Kingdom.') Baldwin then asked the King if that was his wish: the answer was 'yes' and at once abdication loomed that much closer.

Lord Beaverbrook, who had been recalled from a trans-Atlantic holiday by the King, immediately advised to withdraw his request. Beaverbrook realized that if Baldwin's cabinet colleagues advised against a morganatic marriage – and the King refused to accept that advice – then his Ministers would have to resign. A General Election would then be fought on the very issue Hardinge had warned against, the King's marriage to twice-divorced Mrs Simpson and the title she should assume. However, after Lord Beaverbrook was telephoned by the King late that night and told, 'Mrs Simpson . . . prefers the morganatic marriage to any other solution . . .' he realized the battle was lost.

Baldwin, who was later accused of slanting the vital telegrams to the Dominion Prime Ministers, received the answer he expected. None was in favour of the morganatic marriage proposal, although some were less emphatic than others. From talks with Opposition leader Clement Attlee, Baldwin also knew that, with the exception of a few back-benchers, Parliament at home was against it. Since the voluntary 'Pact of Silence' still held in the Press, however, there had been no opportunity to sound out public opinion as late as the end of November. Then dramatically – and in all innocence, he later claimed – the silence was broken by the Bishop of Bradford, Dr Alfred Blunt, in an address to his diocesan conference. After a reference to the essential religious nature of the Coronation ceremony, the aptly named Bishop went on to say, 'The benefit of the King's Coronation depends under God upon two elements – firstly, on the faith, prayer and self-dedication of the King himself. On that it would be improper for me to say anything except to commend him, and ask others to commend him, to God's grace, which he will so abundantly need – for the King is a man like any other – if he is to do his duty properly. We hope he is aware of this need. Some of us wish that he gave more positive signs of such awareness . . .'

Although Dr Blunt later protested that at the time he had not heard of Mrs Simpson, the Press clearly thought otherwise. The provincial newspapers examined the speech first. 'Dr Blunt must have good reason for so pointed a remark,' insisted the influential *Yorkshire Post*. 'Most people by this time are aware that a good deal of rumour regarding the King has been published of late in the more sensational American newspapers . . . But certain comments which have appeared in reputable United States journals, and even we believe in some Dominions newspapers, cannot be treated with quite so much indifference. They are too circumstantial, and plainly have a foundation in fact . . .'

On the same morning the *Yorkshire Post* was published, the Cabinet in London formally rejected the proposal of a morganatic marriage between the King and Mrs Simpson. Prime Minister Baldwin called on the King that night to discuss the situation. In their varying accounts later of what took place at that meeting, both parties agreed on one thing: that Baldwin urged the King not to abdicate. However, he was obliged to point out that the King had three courses only left open to him. They were: to give up the idea of marriage to Mrs Simpson altogether, to marry against his government's advice – and plunge the country into constitutional crisis – or to abdicate, and marry. As the King considered his position, so Fleet Street joined in the great debate, at long last. Press reaction in the critical week that followed was mixed, with more newspapers against the marriage than for it. In the end the King, disheartened by Press comment generally, and increasingly worried by anonymous threats made against Mrs Simpson, arranged for her to leave for the South of France accompanied by his Lord in Waiting, Lord Brownlow, and his personal bodyguard.

Before she left, Mrs Simpson suggested the King might borrow an idea from the American presidency and discuss his dilemma with his subjects direct – through a 'fireside chat' broadcast. The King was enthusiastic but when he showed the proposed draft to Baldwin, the Premier warned him that, although he was willing to discuss the idea with his ministerial colleagues, he was in no doubt what their decision would be. He further pointed out that any such appeal to the public, over the heads of the elected government, would be unconstitutional. (Baldwin's opponents later claimed that he had already discussed the draft with his Cabinet who rejected it before he called on the King).

According to Baldwin, the King replied, 'You want me to go, don't you? And before I go, I think it is right for her sake and mine that I should speak.' To which the Premier responded, 'What I want, Sir, is what you told me you wanted: to go with dignity, not dividing the country, and making things as smooth as possible for your successor . . . You will be telling millions throughout the world – among them a vast number of women – that you are determined to marry one who has a husband living . . . You may, by speaking, divide opinion; but you will certainly harden it.'

Shortly afterwards the King left Buckingham Palace for the last time as sovereign and drove to Fort Belvedere. As always in critical moments in the nation's history, crowds began to gather outside the Palace and Number 10, Downing Street. Denied information for so long by Press silence, their understandable confusion was reflected in the placards they carried: some for, some against the marriage. 'After South Wales, You Can't Let Him Down . . . Come To The Palace Now!' Opponents of the marriage in their turn spread the crudest anti-Simpson jokes. 'Heard about the King's new job? He wants to sign on as Third Mate on an American tramp!'

On 4 December, Baldwin told the House bluntly that there was no such thing as morganatic marriage in English law. 'The lady whom [the King] marries . . . necessarily becomes Queen. The only way in which this result could be avoided would be by legislation dealing with a particular case. His Majesty's Government are not prepared to introduce such legislation.' According to the *Daily Telegraph* (which was pro-Baldwin) the Prime Minister was cheered so loudly at this, 'that for a little while, [he] could not continue . . .' Mrs Simpson telephoned from France and urged the King to 'fight for his rights', but all to no avail. On the morning of 5 December he sent Walter Monckton, his barrister friend and adviser, to Downing Street to inform Baldwin officially that he intended to abdicate. When Beaverbrook heard the news he told Winston Churchill, the King's political champion, 'Our cock won't fight.' On 7 December Churchill himself was howled down in the Commons when he sought an assurance from Baldwin that no 'irrevocable' steps should be taken by the government. Behind the scenes there were real fears that the King's Proctor might yet be asked to intervene and quash the decree nisi awarded to Mrs Simpson (and so thwart the intended marriage), but an attempt to have the divorce made absolute forthwith by Act of Parliament was resisted by the government, who believed that any such Bill could only provoke an even greater scandal.

Desperate eleventh-hour attempts were made to try to prevent the abdication. In Cannes, Mrs Simpson (under pressure, it was said, from Lord Brownlow) put out a Press statement which read: 'Mrs Simpson, throughout the last few weeks, has invariably wished to avoid any action or proposal which would hurt or damage His Majesty or the Throne. Today her attitude is unchanged and she is willing, if such action would solve the problem, to withdraw from a situation that has been rendered both unhappy and untenable.' When told of its contents, the King, who was anxious that she should not be blamed for the crisis, said simply, 'Go ahead if you wish. But it won't make any difference.' Shortly afterwards Mrs Simpson's solicitor, Theodore Goddard, flew to Cannes to call on his client. Different reasons have since been given for his visit. One was that he had learned that an affidavit was about to be served on the King's Proctor, allegedly accompanied by 'evidence' of collusion, by a private individual. Another, widely circulated within the Establishment, was that he had been requested to recover jewellery left by Queen Alexandra (wife of Edward VII), and since given to Mrs Simpson by the King. In the event, Mr Goddard telephoned the following message to the Prime Minister, after meeting with Mrs Simpson in Cannes: 'I have today discussed the whole position with Mrs Simpson – her own, the position of the King, the country, the Empire. Mrs Simpson tells me she was, and still is, perfectly willing to instruct me to withdraw her petition for divorce and willing to do anything to prevent the King from abdicating. I am satisfied that this is Mrs Simpson's genuine and honest desire. I read this note over to Mrs Simpson who in every way confirmed it.' It was signed by Mr Goddard, and counter-signed by Lord Brownlow.

In their turn the Cabinet sent a formal message to the King, asking him to reconsider his intention to abdicate. This he refused to do. 'His Majesty has given the matter his further consideration but regrets he is unable to alter his decision.' All that remained now was for the parties concerned to settle the King's future finances (never officially disclosed but said to be very considerable) and his rank. On Thursday, 10 December he signed the Instrument of Abdication. It read: 'I, Edward the Eighth, of Great Britain, Ireland, and the British Dominions beyond the Seas, King, Emperor of India, do hereby declare My irrevocable determination to renounce the Throne for Myself and My descendants . . .' It was witnessed by his three brothers, Albert (York), Henry (Gloucester) and George (Kent).

On 11 December he sailed into exile. Only now that he was ex-King could be broadcast to his former subjects without first seeking government sanction. However, as a matter of courtesy, he sent an advance copy of his farewell speech to No 10 Downing Street. Walter Monckton drove with him from Fort Belvedere to Windsor Castle, whence the broadcast was to be made. Sir John Reith, Director General of the BBC, introduced him, on the personal instructions of the new King, his brother George VI, as 'His Royal Highness Prince Edward'. It was a moving, memorable speech and occasion, and his voice was heard wherever English was spoken.

You all know the reasons which have impelled me to renounce the Throne. But I want you to understand that in making up my mind I did not forget the country or the Empire which as Prince of Wales, and lately as King, I have for twenty-five years tried to serve. But you must believe me when I tell you that I have found it impossible to carry the heavy burden of responsibility and to discharge my duties as King as I would wish to do, without the help and support of the woman I love.

Authors Bryan and Murphy described the scene 3,000 miles from Windsor Castle: 'In New York, taxi drivers pulled over to the kerb and stopped, to hear him through. The whole English-speaking world all but stood still for seventy seconds. People wept. There never has been its match for pathos: a king – a King of England! – renouncing his imperial splendour for love alone . . .'

SOUTH SEA BUBBLE, The

England's Greatest Financial Scandal

'One of the most terrible social disasters that had ever fallen upon England', as one historian calls it, the South Sea Bubble was a 'get-rich-quick' scheme that brought ruin and misery to the whole country.

Unlike John Law's Mississippi Company (*see* page 262), which was equally disastrous, the South Sea Company had thoroughly respectable beginnings. It was the idea of that born intriguer, Robert Harley, the Earl of Oxford (1661–1724). Harley was a Tory and as Chancellor of the Exchequer, he brooded on the problem of how to cause trouble for the newly formed Bank of England, which was run by Whig shareholders. In 1969 he tried to form a rival Land Bank but it failed to gain support. In 1711, Harley's friend and co-conspirator, Daniel Defoe – later the author of *Robinson Crusoe* – suggested another money-making scheme. Defoe had always been romantically fascinated by South America. Why not form a company to trade with South America, import slaves from Africa and develop that vast and rich continent? It was basically a sound idea. There was only one problem: Spain was already in South America and Spain's ally France had been granted the concession to trade with the colony.

However, this was by no means an insuperable problem. It should be possible to persuade France to surrender its concession to England. For Louis XIV had been at war with England, and most of the rest of Europe, for the past twenty years and he badly wanted peace. The British Tories also wanted peace, for they bore the burden of war taxes while their rivals the Whigs were merchants who made money from the war. If Harley could secure peace, he could also probably make the South American concession a part of the bargain with Louis.

He secured his peace, by a shameful trick. Britain and her allies – the Dutch, the Austrians and various German states – were winning the war, so had no desire for a peace treaty. They knew they would soon be able to state their own terms. Harley communicated the Allied plan of campaign to the French and also sent secret instructions to the English general, Ormonde, telling him to avoid engaging the enemy until he had direct orders from Queen Anne. Then Harley's friend, Lord Bolingbroke, announced a truce between England and France. All Europe was stunned by the treachery – it was as if Britain had announced a truce with Hitler immediately after VE Day. But Harley got what he wanted from France as part of the deal: the South American concession. The South Sea Company was formed in 1711 and hailed as 'the Earl of Oxford's masterpiece'.

The company did Harley no good, for during its first few years it was not particularly successful. Queen Anne had died and was succeeded by George of Hanover, one of the allies Harley had betrayed. Bolingbroke took warning and hurried off to France while Harley stayed behind in England and was arrested and sent to the Tower. He was kept waiting so long for his trial that the feeling against him evaporated and he was released. He was allowed to live out the rest of his life quietly on his estate.

The Spanish king, Philip V, was distinctly mean about the concessions he was willing to grant. African slaves died by the hundred on their way to South America. Pirates spoiled the traffic by smuggling thousands of Negroes into the plantations. By 1715, four years after its foundation, the South Sea Company was barely profitable although it had immense prestige. The Prince of Wales – later George II – was persuaded to become a shareholder and a ship was named after him. But when, in 1717, a bitter quarrel blew up between the Prince of Wales and his father about the christening of the Prince's child, the king accepted the role of Governor of the Company merely for the pleasure of striking off his son's name as Deputy Governor. But George I also had another motive. He was badly in debt and hoped the South Sea Company would make him a fortune.

Through various machinations, the king's chief minister,

Lord Townshend, was dismissed, and his protégé and brother-in-law, Robert Walpole, felt obliged to resign as Chancellor of the Exchequer, but he was also to play an important part in the South Sea affair. These two were replaced by Lord Sunderland and the Earl of Stanhope.

In Paris, meanwhile, that extraordinary Scottish adventurer John Law was creating tremendous excitement with his Mississippi scheme. People were making vast fortunes overnight. In England, an unscrupulous little man named John Blunt, self-made and a director of the South Sea Company, was fascinated by Law's success and decided he could do even better. Why should not the South Sea Company take over the British national debt – the £50 million the government had borrowed from the British public? Twenty million of this had been borrowed from the Bank of England and the East India Company, and the South Sea Company could only benefit by a close alliance with these.

What would the investors do with the money the South Sea Company returned to them? The answer, of course, was to invest it in South Sea stock. Here there was a marvellous opportunity to make a vast profit. Suppose an investor had £1,000 worth of government bonds: South Sea shares were worth £100 each so the Company would print ten new shares to hand over to the investor. But suppose the price of the shares went up, say, for example, that it doubled in the meantime. The shareholder would only need five shares, worth £200 each, to replace his securities. And the South Sea Company would have £1,000 worth of shares to sell to someone else.

Of course, everything would depend on the price of the shares rising. Blunt was impressed by John Law's publicity methods. He was a master showman. He made sure that everyone in France talked about his Mississippi Company. Blunt decided to make sure that the South Sea Company benefited by the same methods – what is known in America as 'ballyhoo'. When Blunt suggested the idea to his fellow directors they were impressed. The national debt was a subject of deep concern. Before the war with Louis XIV, Britain had always managed to balance its books; now this vast debt was always being compared to a millstone around a swimmer's neck. Anything that might remove it would be sure to win the widest possible support. There was only one problem, as the board pointed out to Mr Blunt: the Bank of England and the East India Company were owned by Whigs and they would fight tooth and nail to prevent a takeover by the Tory South Sea Company.

The proposals were put to the House of Commons on 22 January 1720 by John Aislabie, Chancellor of the Exchequer. The terms were much the same as those proposed by John Law to the French parliament: the government would only pay the Company 4 per cent interest, instead of the present 5 per cent, so it would save an immense amount of money and the debt could be wiped out in twenty-five years.

Parliament liked the idea. But, predictably, the Bank of England was indignant. Why should this upstart company enter into such a profitable deal with the government? The Bank offered the government nearly £6 million for the privilege of taking over the national debt; the South Sea Company outbid them by £2 million. There was a debate in Parliament, the opposition to the South Sea Company being led by Robert Walpole. But after much argument, the government won by four votes. The South Sea Scheme was under way.

Hundred-pound shares in the Company immediately soared to £400, then settled down at £330. There was a frantic rush to buy. Dukes and lords laid their hands on every penny of spare cash they possessed and turned it into shares; country gentlemen mortgaged their homes; the working people of England took their hard-earned savings from socks under mattresses. In April 1720, Blunt announced that another 20,000 shares would be available to the public. This was, in fact, illegal; the only shares he was entitled to sell were the 'leftovers' when government pensioners and other creditors had been 'paid' in shares. But no one seemed to worry. This new issue of shares sold for £300 each. At the end of April, another 10,000 shares were issued and sold at £400 each. A great deal was handed out in bribes to various Ministers and other influential people, including the king's mistress, the Duchess of Kendal. The king bought £20,000 worth of shares at the first subscription and soon parted with them for a handsome profit of £86,000. He was so pleased that he made John Blunt a knight. Blunt became a celebrity; he was treated like a king, and he behaved like one, treating lords and ladies with magnificent condescension. Most of the court made large sums of money, for they all returned to Hanover when the king went on his annual visit and sold their shares before they left.

What seems incredible, in retrospect, is that no one realized that if money is to earn money, it must be 'put to work'. The South Sea Company seemed to have no intention of making its money 'work'. In Paris, John Law had done his best to put his new capital to work overseas and had made large profits. But the directors of the South Sea Company seemed to feel that all they had to do to make more money was to offer more shares for sale; it never seems to have struck anyone that there would have to be a reckoning. The idea of 'credit' was so new that no one quite understood it.

With the whole country anxious to buy shares, dozens of smaller companies sprang up. Most of these were illegal, for a company needed a royal charter, but no one gave this a second thought. There were companies for building pirate-proof ships, for importing jackasses from Spain, for building a 'wheel of perpetual motion', for insuring marriages against divorce, for breeding silk worms in Chelsea Park, even a company whose aim was to invent an 'expeditious and cleanly manner' of emptying lavatory buckets (for these were the days before water closets). One man announced that he was selling shares in 'a company for carrying on an undertaking of Great Advantage but no one to know what it is'. He sold £2,000 worth of shares in a single day – not surprisingly, since he was promising to give £100 a year income for each £2 deposit on a share – and vanished the same evening.

It seems strange that no one was warned by the crash of John Law's Mississippi Company in Paris. But news travelled slowly in those days and, in any case, no one understood why Law's company had collapsed, including Law himself.

The South Sea Company had soon sold over £12 million worth of shares. But since most of these had been bought on a hire-purchase plan, less than £3 million had gone into the coffers of the Company. It still owed the government £7½ million for the privilege of starting the Company, but Blunt dismissed the idea of using the three million to keep the

government quiet. Instead, he set out to sell more shares. If
people didn't have the money to buy them, he would lend it to
them. Everybody who possessed a £100 share could borrow
£250; within a short time he had lent over £1 million, and all
this had come back in the form of payments for shares. The
price of his stock soared to £400 a share. A new issue of shares
sold at £1,000 each, and still there were plenty of takers. By
August 1720, the price had slumped slightly, due to profit-
taking, but shares were still worth £900.

By now, the Company's resources were severely over-
strained. It had taken £8½ million, but it was owed another
£60 million by shareholders. Then as some of the 'bubble'
companies went to the wall, confidence began to ebb and the
money stopped flowing in so fast.

Then Sir John Blunt made a mistake that revealed his total
lack of understanding of the market forces. He decided to
prosecute four of his large river companies on the grounds that
their charters were not in order. In fact, their charters were
legal but dated back so many years that it may have been
possible to allege they had lapsed. The Prince of Wales was a
governor of one of these, the Welsh Copper Company, but
was persuaded to resign.

Writs were served and the Lords Justices ruled that three or
four companies were operating illegally. The stocks of these
companies became worthless. But what Blunt had forgotten is
that many shareholders in these companies were also shareholders in the South Sea Company and that if they found
themselves in financial difficulties, they would sell their South
Sea stock for ready cash. And this is exactly what happened.
Since the market had already been badly shaken by the
bankruptcy of these 'illegal companies, public confidence suddenly evaporated, and everybody wanted to sell. Blunt had not
realized that the very essence of a 'credit economy' is confidence. Successful rivals of the South Sea Company – like the
Royal Exchange and the London Assurance Company – were
badly hit. But the South Sea Company fared even worse: its
shares slumped from £900 to £190 within days. The Bank of
England at first agreed to help then changed its mind. Now
nothing could stop the South Sea bubble from bursting.

Thousands were ruined. The Duke of Chandos lost £300,000.

The Duke of Portland had to flee from England; the king appointed him governor of Jamaica. Practically every country family – those who had mortgaged their homes to buy shares – was left penniless. The most successful portrait painter of the day, Sir Godfrey Kneller, lost his fortune and had to start looking for commissions again. Poets like Alexander Pope and Matthew Prior also lost heavily. John Gay, author of *The Beggars' Opera*, had declined the advice of friends to sell £2,000 worth of shares given to him by a patron; he was ruined and took to his bed in despair. There were suicides by the score. Second-hand coaches and gold watches became a drag on the market. The daughters of country squires had to look for jobs as governesses.

All the rage was directed at the directors of the South Sea Company. It was assumed that the whole thing was a deliberate swindle. The King returned from Hanover in November, and Parliament met in December. Robert Walpole was now Prime Minister (the first man to hold that title) and he did his best to keep the fury under control. Most MPs had lost heavily and it never seemed to strike them that they were responsible for giving the scheme their vote in the first place. Robert Knight, the Company's cashier, escaped abroad to everyone's rage, and although he was arrested in Belgium, the Emperor of Austria, who owned Brabant, refused to extradite him. (It was only later realized that the king was behind this refusal: his mistress had taken a huge bribe to help launch the Company and he was anxious not to have its affairs made public.)

Finally, a parliamentary committee interviewed all those closely involved and they were heavily mulcted. John Blunt's fortune of over £185,000 was taken away from him and he was left with only £1,000. Sir John Fellows, sub-governor of the Company, was left £10,000 out of a £¼ million. More than thirty other directors had their fortunes confiscated and were left with a pittance. The MP John Aislabie, who had first raised the question of the South Sea Company, was expelled from the House and sent to the Tower. One unfortunate director was only allowed to keep £31 out of more than £40,000.

The government pensioners who had sold their annuities for worthless stock, on the advice of Parliament, hoped that they would somehow be 'rescued'. They were unlucky. Walpole made it clear that all obligations would have to be met. There was a riot in the lobby of the House and the police had to read the Riot Act twice to disperse the mob. The King even considered bringing over his German troops from Hanover in case of a revolution. But in spite of the chaos and misery, England remained prosperous. Overseas trade was booming and although thousands were now poorer, thousands had also become rich. It was a radical redistribution of wealth rather than a national bankruptcy. Most of the directors whose fortunes were confiscated built new fortunes: the grandfather of the historian Edward Gibbon was among them. Walpole was the hero of the hour for he had always opposed the South Sea scheme (although he profited from it). As a result of the scandal, the Whigs were in power for the next four decades. England had learned about credit the hard way and it now proceeded to become one of the wealthiest nations in Europe.

TANAKA, Kakuei
The Japanese Bribery Scandal

On 12 October 1983 Kakuei Tanaka, aged sixty-five, a former Prime Minister of Japan and still the country's dominant political figure, was found guilty by a Tokyo court of accepting a colossal 500-million-yen bribe (then worth £1.4 million, or $2.1 million) in the early 1970s from America's giant Lockheed Corporation. The trial, which involved a total of fifteen defendants, had lasted nearly seven years. The sheer size of the alleged bribes, and coverage by a hostile Press, meant that long before a verdict was reached the 'Tanaka Case' had become Japan's biggest scandal since the end of World War II. The main plank of the prosecution's case, which turned on depositions taken in America from Lockheed officials, was that Tanaka had abused his political clout to push through sales of Lockheed Tristar airliners to a Japanese domestic airline, in return for the massive bribe.

A panel of three judges found him guilty, although the ex-Premier protested his innocence throughout. He was sentenced to four years' imprisonment and in addition ordered to pay a 500-million yen fine to match the alleged bribe. If the verdict was not unexpected after so many headlines, the harshness of the sentence shocked and surprised politicians in every part of Japan. There was a sense of national shame too: Tanaka was the first Japanese Premier to be convicted by a Japanese court for a crime committed while in office. He appealed immediately, and was released on bail in the sum of 300 million yen (then about £780,000).

Four other defendants who stood trial with him, including his former personal secretary and three officials from the trading company through which the bribes were said to have been channelled, were likewise released on bail. Altogether the separate trials involving all the defendants (the others had already been found guilty) spanned six years and eight months, in nearly two hundred sessions.

Mr Tanaka was first accused of involvement in the Lockheed bribes scandal in July 1976. He had previously served as Prime Minister of Japan from July 1972 to December 1974, when he resigned the premiership following a separate controversy alleging irregularities in financial deals. However, even after his resignation as Prime Minister and throughout the Lockheed bribes case, he remained the power behind the political scene in Japan, by controlling the biggest faction (119 strong) within the ruling Liberal Democratic Party; and it was Tanaka who master-minded the election of Prime Minister Yasuhiro Nakasone, in 1983.

Although the four-year sentence he was awarded fell one year short of the penalty demanded by the prosecution, it was still the heaviest sentence for any alleged bribery offence in Japanese legal history. It also held immense potential political significance. As soon as sentence was announced, Opposition MPs demanded Tanaka's resignation as a member of the Diet (Parliament). The motion was really aimed at Prime Minister Nakasone, who – although personally untarnished by the scandal – was maintained in power only by a coalition vote led by the Tanaka faction. Tanaka promptly responded by issuing a statement as soon as bail was posted making it clear that he intended to hold on to his Parliamentary seat as long as he retained 'the support of the public.'

After a period of uneasy political calm Mr Tanaka – whose health was said to have been undermined by the strain of the marathon trial – was admitted to hospital in February 1985. A medical bulletin was issued saying he had suffered a mild stroke, causing some temporary impairment of speech and the ability to move. By now he was 68, and facing an unprecedented challenge from within his own faction. This became apparent in January 1985, with the formation of a 'study group' known as *Soseika* (creative political society) under the leadership of Finance Minister Noburu Takeshita. Not until 84 out of the 119 MPs who made up his king-maker faction applied to join *Soseika* did the ailing Tanaka realize that here was a threat not only to the premiership of his nominee Nakasone, but also to his own hitherto undisputed control of the faction itself. He managed to clip *Soseika*'s wings temporarily, by reducing the number of applicants from his faction to between 30 and 40 – but then came the disclosure that his illness was more serious than had at first been thought. Doctors now said he had suffered a cerebral infarction rather than a mild stroke, adding that it would be months rather than weeks before he could resume normal activities. But amid doubts of Mr Tanaka's ability to make a complete recovery in time for the hearing of his appeal (said to be due in late 1985), so the political pressure on Prime Minister Nakasone mounted once more.

TEAPOT DOME SCANDAL
The Ohio Gang Hijacks America

Warren Gamaliel Harding was probably the worst President the United States has ever had. The best that can be said of him is that the Teapot Dome scandal that erupted after his death was none of his doing; it was simply the result of his failure to do anything except play poker and make love to his mistress in a room behind the Oval office.

Warren Harding's only asset was his ruggedly handsome face and a square jaw that made him look like a President. He was born in the small town of Corsica, Ohio, in 1865. He made half-hearted attempts to become a schoolteacher and a lawyer, and finally acquired a newspaper on the verge of bankruptcy. At about this time he met Florence Kling de Wolfe, the daughter of a leading citizen, who married him in spite of her father's bitter opposition. She was the driving force in their marriage for Harding was lazy, good natured and easy going. It was largely due to her hard work that the Marion *Star* became a successful newspaper.

As editor, Harding met many politicians, including Harry Daugherty, who lacked the personality to achieve the political ambitions he dreamed about. But Harding looked like a politician and with Daugherty as his campaign manager, he soon became a Republican State sentator, then Lieutenant-Governor of Ohio. That was as far as Harding wanted to go, but his wife and Daugherty continued to push him until, to his bewilderment, he found himself elected to the United States Senate with a large majority.

Harding had no real interest in politics. He spent more time on the golf course or attending baseball games than in the Senate. He also took a mistress. A schoolgirl named Nan Britton had fallen hopelessly in love with him back in Marion and when she moved to New York they began meeting secretly. Soon she was pregnant and bore him a daughter.

In 1920, a presidential election was due; Woodrow Wilson had suffered a breakdown in 1919 and had no intention of running again. The Republicans had no clear favourite among their candidates. At the Convention in Chicago in June, none of the three main contenders was able to command a clear majority. Harding, a 'dark horse', seemed an acceptable alternative. He was asked if there was any scandal in his life that might cause the party embarrassment; he emphatically denied this and was nominated on the tenth ballot. In November, he beat the Democratic candidate James J. Cox and became twenty-ninth President of the United States. At the Convention, his wife had been heard to mutter, 'I can see only one word written above his head if they make him President, and that word is "Tragedy".'

It was not quite as bad as that; rather something closer to farce. Presidents do not need to be intellectual giants but Harding was barely an intellectual gnat. He was bewildered by all the tasks he ought to be tackling; post-war disarmament, world monetary problems, tariffs, tax proposals; he was like a schoolboy faced with a page of quantum equations. He invited all his cronies to the White House where they drank and played poker in his study. When Nan Britton arrived, they retired to a private room. Harding liked to sit with his waistocat unbuttoned, his feet on the desk and a spitoon by his side, in a room thick with tobacco smoke.

Meanwhile, all his old political cronies – 'the Ohio gang' – had moved to Washington and set up a kind of alternative White House on K Street. Harry Daugherty, now Attorney-General, sold government jobs and other favours, using a jobber named Jesse W. Smith as a go-between with the men who wanted to buy favours. Smith, a coarse, genial man used to love to sing: 'My God, how the money rolls in.'

Another member of the Ohio gang was the Secretary of the Interior, Albert Fall. Fall itched to get his hands on an enormous oil reserve known as Teapot Dome, an area of land in Wyoming, north of the town of Caspar. Woodrow Wilson had decided that Teapot Dome should be held in reserve in case of future national emergencies and it was under the control of the Naval Department. Fall persuaded the Secretary of the Navy, then the President, to transfer the lease to his Department of the Interior. Then it was secretly leased to Harry F. Sinclair, president of the Mammoth Oil Company, for more than $¼ million. Another oil reserve at Elk Hills, California, was leased to another friend, Edward Doheny, for $100,000. Fall was soon able to pay nine years of back-taxes that he owed on a New Mexico ranch, and to stock it with prize cattle. Another Harding crony, Charles R. Forbes, was head of the Veterans' Bureau, and was in charge of purchasing supplies for hospitals for ex-servicemen and awarding contracts for new hospitals. Hospital supplies bought with public money were promptly sold as government surplus – a million towels that had cost 34 cents each were sold at 36 cents a dozen; sheets costing $1.35 a pair were sold at 27 cents a pair. Vast sums were paid to him in exchange for hospital contracts. He also received 'kickbacks' from real estate dealers from whom he bought land for the hospitals at far more than its value.

Sooner or later, this empire of corruption had to collapse under its own weight. Washington journalists began to hint more and more openly at what was going on. The Attorney-General's office under Daugherty became known as the Department of Easy Virtue. Finally, the rumours reached Harding's ear. His health was breaking down – no doubt due to his intake of Bourbon – and now his nerve began to crack. A visitor to the White House took the wrong turning and was startled to come upon Harding grasping a man by the throat and shouting, 'You yellow rat! You double crossing bastard!' The man was Charles Forbes, head of the Veterans' Bureau. Soon after, Forbes took a trip to Paris and sent in his resignation 'for health reasons'.

Jesse Smith, the go-between who liked to sing, 'My God, how the money rolls in', had been sent back to Ohio by Daugherty because he talked too openly. Harding summoned him to the White House and listened, aghast, as Smith told him the extent of the skulduggery. When he had finished, he asked the President what would happen now. 'Go home. Tomorrow you will be arrested.' Smith went back to his hotel and shot himself.

Harding was due to make a trip to Alaska and he decided

that this might be an opportune moment to escape from Washington. There was talk of a Congressional Enquiry; Charles Cramer, Forbes's right-hand man, also shot himself; there was an increasing number of resignations. As Harding returned from the Alaska trip, down the Pacific coast, he fell ill, his doctor diagnosed food poisoning from crab meat. On 2 August 1923, he died of pneumonia. His wife died in the following year. The Teapot Dome scandal now erupted and Nan Britton added to it by writing a bestselling book about her affair with Harding called *The President's Daughter*.

When a Harding Memorial Association raised $700,000 for a monument in Marion, Ohio (where the President was buried), it was decided that it should take the form of a huge marble cylinder with colonnades. Others greatly preferred a design that was closer to a sphere. This idea was dropped when someone pointed out that it only needed a spout and a handle to look like a teapot.

THORPE, Jeremy
The Liberal Leader and the Male Model

The trial of Jeremy Thorpe, leader of the British Liberal Party, on a charge of conspiracy to murder was the greatest political scandal in England since the Profumo case (*see* page 326). The charge was that Thopre had incited three men – who stood beside him in the dock – to murder the former male model Norman Scott, with whom Thorpe was alleged to have had a homosexual affair.

Until the Scott case, the career of John Jeremy Thorpe, born on 29 April 1929, had been an unbroken success story. The son of a Conservative Member of Parliament, he was educated at a private school in Connecticut (during World War II), then at Eton College and Oxford University. He was obviously a man of driving ambition and became President of the University Liberal Club, then the Law Society, and finally – the most coveted post of all – of the Oxford Union, the debating society whose presidents have often become distinguished politicians. He was called to the bar in 1954 and contested the North Devon constituency as a Liberal in the following year. His flair for politics was obviously great, and he conducted his campaign 'with all the panache of an American congressional campaign', in the words of his biographers (Lewis Chester, Magnus Linklater and David May, in their book *Jeremy Thorpe, A Secret Life*). The same biographers quote various Oxford contemporaries of Thorpe to the effect that he could be too ruthless in achieving his aims and was capable of 'cutting corners'. This first political campaign ended in failure, but he cut the Tory majority in half. When he contested the seat again in 1959, he won by 362 votes. He made an immediate impact on the House of Commons with his wit and oratory. There was only one small cloud on the horizon: in March 1960, a routine security check into his background concluded that he was believed to have homosexual tendencies – at that time, homosexual activity was a criminal offence. It was also in 1960, on a visit to a riding stable in Oxfordshire, that Thorpe made the acquaintance of the man who was to be his political downfall, Norman Josiffe, later to be known as Norman Scott.

Josiffe, eleven years Thorpe's junior, was the child of a broken marriage and was emotionally unstable. The most important thing in his life was his pony. At the age of sixteen he was found guilty of larceny and placed on probation. In the following year he became a riding instructor. By this time he was having severe emotional problems: he was subject to crying fits and was in the habit of inventing tragic stories about his background to arouse pity. A doctor prescribed tranquillizers and he was admitted to a clinic. In 1961 he took an overdose of Largactil and had to be rushed to hospital. It was when he came out that he recalled Jeremy Thorpe's remark that if ever he was in difficulties, he should feel free to look him up at the House of Commons. Josiffe went there on 8 November 1961, and had an interview with Thorpe. Afterwards, they went down to Oxted, in Surrey, where Thorpe's mother had a house. According to Josiffe, their homosexual affair began that night.

Josiffe alleged that on the way to Oxted, Thorpe asked if he would mind being introduced as a member of a television camera crew, with whom he would be travelling abroad the next day. At Mrs Thorpe's house, Josiffe signed the visitor's book with a false name. That night, when Josiffe was in bed, Thorpe visited him with a book by James Baldwin, the homosexual novel *Giovanni's Room*. Later, he returned to Josiffe's room in a dressing gown and pyjamas, and sat on the bed. 'He said I looked like a frightened rabbit . . . he just hugged me and called me "poor bunny" . . . he got into bed with me.' Thorpe went out to get some Vaseline which he put on his penis. Then he put a towel on the bed and made love to Josiffe, with Josiffe as the passive partner. According to Josiffe, when Thorpe left, 'I just lay there with my dog . . . crying.' But although Josiffe declared that he did not enjoy being sodomized ('I just bit the pillow and tried not to scream'), the affair continued apace. Josiffe was given a job on the staff of Len Smith, a Liberal Party official, and moved into a small service flat near the House of Commons where, according to him, Thorpe went to make love to him. They went down to Mrs Thorpe's house four or five times. They would meet in the Reform Club and go to a Chelsea restaurant for dinner. Josiffe went down to Devon with Thorpe at Christmas and while their hosts were walking in the garden, Thorpe made love to Josiffe in the bathroom.

Problems began to arise. A Mrs Ann Gray accused Josiffe of stealing her suede coat and when the police wanted to question him, Thorpe insisted on the interview taking place in his office in the House of Commons, explaining that he was 'more or less' Josiffe's guardian since Josiffe had lost both parents. Soon after, Josiffe moved to a position with a farming family in Somerset, and Thorpe wrote him a letter in which he told him that he could 'take the Ann Gray incident as over and done with'. The letter concluded: 'Bunnies *can* (and *will*) go to France.' There was a postscript: 'I miss you.'

But when Thorpe began to look into the matter of Josiffe's 'lost' parents and discovered that they were both alive and well, the relationship began to cool – at least, on his side. There was the additional problem that the farming family found Josiffe too nervous and highly strung. Josiffe moved to the home of a Dr Keith Lister and when the doctor wrote Thorpe a letter enquiring about the young man's background, he was told rather brusquely that he should consult Josiffe's parents, whose addresses were enclosed. But Thorpe continued to help Josiffe and sorted out a problem about his national insurance card.

Unfortunately, as Thorpe seems to have found himself losing patience with the 'bunny', Josiffe decided he was in love with Thorpe. When Josiffe's dog Tish killed Dr Lister's ducks, Josiffe was asked to leave. He tried confessing his 'sins' to a Catholic priest but was refused absolution unless he broke off his association with Thorpe. Josiffe felt himself torn in several directions at once and began to feel increasingly bitter. One day, in a fit of wild self-pity, he began talking to a young lady about his plan to kill Thorpe and commit suicide. The result was that Josiffe was interviewed at the Chelsea police station in December 1962, and began a statement: 'I have come to the police to tell you about my homosexual relations with Jeremy

Thorpe . . .' The police took the 'Bunnies will go to France' letter and another, and these ended up in the file of the Assistant Commissioner of Police. The police made no attempt to follow up the allegations about the homosexual affair. Josiffe soon went to Ireland to take another job involving horses. When a West End outfitter, Gieves Ltd., wrote to Thorpe asking payment for a pair of silk pyjamas that Josiffe had ordered on his account, Thorpe refused to pay, and said he had no idea of Josiffe's present whereabouts. It was obviously his fervent wish never to hear from Josiffe again.

It was not to be. In 1964, Josiffe contacted Thorpe to ask for his help in getting a job on the Continent. Thorpe advanced him the money to go to Switzerland. Josiffe went there, disliked the job, and returned promptly without his luggage. With exemplary patience, Thorpe offered to help him retrieve the luggage. By now, Josiffe had upgraded himself; he called himself the Honourable Lianche-Josiffe and declared that his father, who had died tragically, was a peer of the realm. He also claimed that his wife had died in a car crash. He went back to Ireland, ran into more employment problems and finally wrote Jeremy Thorpe's mother a letter telling her in some detail about his homosexual affair with her son, and alleging that he felt himself shamefully mistreated. Mrs Thorpe passed the letter on to her son.

Thorpe was worried and his reaction was to confide in a fellow Liberal MP, Peter Bessell, the Member for Bodmin. Bessell's political career had been, in some ways, as meteoric as Thorpe's own, and Thorpe had helped him in the crucial campaign. Bessell listened sympathetically and then flew off to Dublin, carrying a legal letter threatening Josiffe with a libel suit. He met Josiffe and found him, on the whole, likeable. Bessell told him firmly that he could not believe that there had been a homosexual relationship with Jeremy Thorpe and asked if he had any proof. Josiffe replied that he did – that there were letters from Thorpe in the luggage that was still in Switzerland. Bessell promised to help him retrieve this. Bessell's secretary finally located the luggage and sent it on to Dublin. When it arrive, Josiffe telephoned Bessell to report that the letters from Jeremy Thorpe were missing . . . Bessell was less concerned than he might have been; he was on the verge of bankruptcy and all his efforts were directed at borrowing $15,000 or so. Eventually, with some help from Jeremy Thorpe, he succeeded.

In 1966, the Labour Party won the Election, dashing the hopes of the Liberal leader, Jo Grimond, for a pact with the Labour Party. Grimond decided to resign. To many Liberals, Jeremy Thorpe was the obvious choice as a replacement. He had proved himself a brilliant fund-raiser and had become party treasurer. There were many who felt he was too lightweight, that for all his charm and eloquence, he lacked the qualities of a future Prime Minister. And, regrettably, there were also rumours about his homosexuality – largely the result of Bessell's inclination to gossip. A 'Stop Jeremy' movement was formed among Liberals. But it made no difference and Thorpe was elected leader of the party in January 1967 by a unanimous vote of the executive. He was thirty-seven.

Meanwhile, Josiffe had changed his name to Norman Scott and had found work as a male model. Three months after Thorpe became leader, Josiffe-Scott wrote to Peter Bessell explaining that he wanted to go to America but had burned his passport during the 'upset' over Jeremy – could Bessell help? Josiffe also lacked insurance cards, which meant he could not apply for unemployment benefit. In August 1967, Josiffe came to London and Bessell arranged to pay him a 'retainer' of between £5 and £10 a week until he could either find a job or obtain another passport. There was, of course, no reason why Josiffe should not apply for a new passport and insurance card. But he had come to the conclusion that Jeremy Thorpe should have put insurance stamps on his old card and this was the basis of yet another grudge.

Bessell was not sure that it would be a good idea for Josiffe to go to America. Although homosexuality had ceased to be a criminal offence in England in July 1967, there was still a stigma attached to it. If Josiffe accused Thorpe of being homosexual in England, Thorpe could sue him for libel, and since Josiffe now had no proof that he had known Thorpe, Thorpe would undoubtedly win. In America, Josiffe could say anything he liked, and the results could be embarrassing for everyone, including Bessell, who had business interests there. And as far as Thorpe was concerned, this was certainly no time for a scandal. Many Liberals were dissatisfied with him; his style of oratory had become dull and pompous, and some fellow party workers felt he was too dictatorial.

In May 1968, Jeremy Thorpe married 29-year-old Caroline Allpass, whom he had met through a friend named David Holmes, a businessman who became his honorary deputy. While he was on honeymoon, there was an attempt to unseat him as Liberal leader and he had to rush back to London. All this aroused sympathy for him and the threat temporarily receded. But Scott remained a menace in the background. And some time in the autumn of 1968, according to the prosecution case, Thorpe began to seriously consider the idea of killing Scott. In December, he and Bessell had a discussion in the House of Commons just before the division bell rang. When Bessell said it seemed to be impossible to find Scott a job in America, Thorpe replied, 'In that case we have got to get rid of him.' Bessell asked, 'Are you suggesting killing him off?' and Thorpe answered, 'Yes.'

In May 1969, Thorpe had a temporary respite from his worries about Scott when the latter married. But his relief was short-lived. Scott and his wife had moved to a Dorset cottage and she was pregnant. Soon cash was short and although an emergency insurance card was issued, so that the expectant mother could claim maternity benefit, Scott became increasingly angry and hysterical. He rang Jeremy Thorpe's house in Devon, and found himself speaking to Caroline Thorpe. He poured out his story to Caroline who was understandably shocked. Scott also rang Bessell, threatening to give his story to a Sunday newspaper; Bessell did his best to soothe him. Eventually, Scott's marriage came to an end when he confessed to his wife that, during her absence, he had been sleeping with a former boyfriend. Once again, Thorpe was in the firing line.

Matters began to come to a head when Scott's wife sued him for divorce in the autumn of 1970. Both Bessell and Thorpe knew what that could mean. Anything a man says in a court of law is 'privileged' – he cannot be sued for libel. Both knew Scott well enough to believe that he would seize his opportunity to denounce Thorpe. But denounce him for what? For having 'seduced' him in 1961? But a seduction involves two people and besides, Scott had since become a practising homosexual.

Scott was, in fact, trumping up a number of absurd and hysterical charges against Thorpe. Thorpe's increasing irritation and desperation were justified. These were undoubtedly increased by the personal tragedy that took place soon after the summer election of 1970 (which Labour lost to the Conservatives). On 29 June, Caroline Thorpe set out to drive to London from Devon. Near Basingstoke her car struck an oncoming lorry and she was dead by the time she reached hospital. Later gossip asserted that Scott had gone to Thorpe's house the previous day and told her the full story of the homosexual affair, and that this was preying on her mind. Scott flatly denied this story. But it does seem likely that Thorpe's problems with Scott were preoccupying her mind on that last journey.

The next time Scott put on the pressure, he received an irritable rejection. With Bessell's help, Scott had moved to Talybont, in Wales. He decided to start a horse-training school and asked Bessell to help him with money. But Bessell had serious troubles of his own; his own money worries were enormous and he was struggling to avoid bankruptcy. He finally announced that he was unable to help him. Scott persuaded a new friend in the village to write to Thorpe, explaining that Scott's financial situation was now critical. Thorpe's personal assistant replied that he did not know a Mr Scott but that if he was the same person as Mr Josiffe, then Mr Thorpe was under no obligation to him.

Scott now persuaded another gullible acquaintance, a Mrs Gwen Parry-Jones, to write to a local Liberal MP, Emlyn Hooson, to say that a certain well-known Liberal had shamefully wronged a young man of her acquaintance. Hooson thought that the MP referred to was Peter Bessell. A meeting was arranged between Scott and Liberal MP David Steel who was shaken to learn that the accused man was Jeremy Thorpe. Hooson's reaction, when he was told, was 'Thorpe must go'. But when Thorpe learned about this, he protested angrily. Scott, he said, was an unbalanced young man whom he had helped in earlier days and who had concocted this whole absurd fantasy. Four Liberal MPs now interviewed Scott; one of them openly accused him of blackmail. Scott walked out indignantly. He began telling his story to the Press: 'I was deeply in love with Jeremy. I thought our idyllic friendship would last forever. But he discarded me. That's why I loathe him now.' (Hooson was to say, 'I formed the strong impression that Norman Scott had a definite fixation about Jeremy Thorpe, somewhat in the manner of a jilted girl . . .') But the newspapers declined to touch it.

In March 1973, Thorpe married the former concert pianist Marion Harewood. At about this time, Scott attempted suicide by slashing his wrists. In the autumn of that year, he met Thorpe's Tory opponent Tim Keigwin and told him the long, sad story. Clearly, he had no intention of fading into the background. And when, in the following year, Edward Heath called his emergency Election in an attempt to break the miners' strike, Thorpe began to feel that Scott was a ticking time-bomb that would blow up the Liberal Party. Scott no longer had Thorpe's own letters but he had all the letters from Peter Bessell, which constituted strong evidence for his claims – after all, why should Bessell have paid him several hundreds of pounds unless there was a guilty secret somewhere? It was certainly not Bessell's guilty secret – Bessell's own extra-marital affairs were strictly heterosexual. The result was that Thorpe's friend David Holmes paid Scott £2,500 for the 'Bessell file'. Thorpe was re-elected with an increased majority. But the Election was otherwise a tie, in which the Tories lost their majority. For a while it looked as though Heath would propose a Liberal-Tory pact and Thorpe would at last attain some real political power. It was not to be, but the long discussions at 10 Downing Street were an indication of Thorpe's crucial political importance.

Meanwhile Scott had spent most of the £2,500. He was living in squalor in a cottage on the edge of Exmoor, taking various drugs and drinking heavily. He was now convinced that his life was in danger and that he had been a fool to part with the Bessell file. He even started to institute proceedings to recover it from the well-meaning doctor who had acted as intermediary with David Holmes. (In fact, Holmes had burned Bessell's letters.) Odd incidents terrified Scott. He alleged that a helicopter landed near his remote cottage and two men came and knocked on his door and that he stayed quiet until they went away. A man who claimed to be a foreign journalist, interested in his story, arranged an appointment in a hotel lounge in Barnstaple. Scott went along with his briefcase and was called to the telephone by the journalist, who said that he had to cancel the appointment because Mrs Margaret Thatcher had been appointed head of the Conservative Party and he had to rush to London. When Scott had finished the telephone conversation, he found his briefcase was missing. A week later he was beaten up by two assailants as he came out of a pub in Barnstaple. Then a man who called himself Peter Keene came to see him and told him he was in great danger because a hired killer was on his way from Canada to assassinate him. Scott was too nervous to go with Keene to meet the unknown benefactor who, according to Keene, was trying to protect him. However, he agreed to meet him in the centre of Combe Martin on 24 October 1975. Scott decided to take his Great Dane along.

'Keene' was a junior pilot officer with British Airways called Andrew Newton. They met at a hotel, as arranged, and Newton persuaded Scott to drive with him to Porlock, where he had business. They could discuss the 'assassin' on the way. Newton left him in Porlock for an hour, then collected him with apologies for being late. Scott was now beginning to feel at ease with 'Keene'. Newton seemed to be driving very badly and explained that he was tired. Scott offered to drive. On the edge of the moor, Newton stopped the car. Scott got out and ran through heavy rain to the driver's side of the car. As he arrived there, he found the door open and Newton standing outside the car. The Great Dane, Rinka, was barking excitedly. 'This is it,' said Newton, producing a Mauser pistol. He shot the dog through the head, then placed the gun against Scott's head, saying, 'It's your turn now.' Scott froze, terrified. But the gun seemed to have jammed; Newton was swearing loudly. Scott began to run over the moor, then decided it was useless to run away and went back to his dog. Newton pointed the gun at him again and said, 'Fuck it.' He jumped into his car and drove away. Soon after, another car drove up and Scott flagged it down. Its occupants included an AA scout who contacted the police for Scott.

Newton was easily traced: a suspicious landlady had noted the number of his car the first time he came to see Scott and it proved to have been hired from a firm in Blackpool. Newton was arrested and told the police that Scott had been trying to blackmail him, and that he had shot the dog to 'scare him off'. In due course, Newton was sentenced to two years in prison – he served slightly more than a year.

In January 1976, Norman Scott was charged with defrauding the Department of Health and Social Security of £58.40. On 29 January, he finally did what he had been threatening to do for so many years. In court in Barnstaple, he blurted out that he was being hounded because he had once had a homosexual relationship with Jeremy Thorpe.

Now the story was out. Inevitably, Thorpe promptly denied it. He told the Liberal chief whip, Cyril Smith, in confidence, that Scott was a common blackmailer and that he had been blackmailing Bessell about an affair he was having with his private secretary. Bessell had been persuaded to write a letter to this effect – it would explain the sums of money he had paid to Scott over the years. But Bessell had been told that his 'confession' would only be used in a case of extreme emergency. When away in America a friend told him on the telephone that the letter had been leaked to the press; Bessell's first reaction was to deny it. Thorpe telephoned him and persuaded him to withhold his denial for a few days. 'Peter, I'm begging for time.'

But by now the Press felt they had an important story. The Prime Minister, Sir Harold Wilson, added a new dimension of scandal to it when he produced his belief that sinister forces from South Africa were behind the attack on the Liberal leader – Thorpe being an outspoken opponent of apartheid. From Thorpe's point of view, this intervention was less than helpful, for it led investigative journalists to probe deeper than ever into his own background. A 'Get Rid of Jeremy' movement began to snowball – one of its supporters was the now disillusioned Peter Bessell, who was living in Oceanside, California, where he had fled from his creditors. Finally, Thorpe had to give way. On 10 May 1976, he sent in his letter of resignation as party leader.

For another year, the scandal again became dormant; it began to look as if, in spite of losing his position as party leader (he was succeeded by David Steel), Thorpe was going to survive politically. But in April 1977, Andrew Newton was released from prison. He felt that someone owed him something for his year of discomfort and began trying to sell his own story to the Press. On 19 October 1977, the scandal exploded again when the London *Evening News* came out with a headline: 'I Was Hired To Kill Scott, *Exclusive*. Gunman tells of incredible plot – a murder contract for £5,000.' The newspaper had paid Newton £3,000.

A week later, Thorpe gave a press conference in which he read aloud a statement giving his own version of his relationship with Norman Scott. He admitted asking Bessell to act as his intermediary with Scott but insisted that he had no knowledge of the purchase of the 'Bessell file' for £2,500. He added: 'As far as Mr Bessell is concerned, it is my considered opinion that if he had credible evidence to offer, he should have gone to the police rather than the Press.' This was virtually a declaration of war on the man who had helped him so much.

Matters now came quickly to a head. The Director of Public Prosecutions now had to decide whether to prosecute. By now, the newspapers had sniffed out what they called 'The South Wales Connection' – the allegation that Newton had been hired to kill Scott by two businessmen from Port Talbot, Wales – John Le Mesurier, who ran a discount carpet firm, and George Deakin, who had made a fortune from one-armed bandits. On 2 August 1978, warrants were issued for the arrest of Jeremy Thorpe, David Holmes, John Le Mesurier and George Deakin. On 20 November, the four men appeared in court in Minehead, the nearest court to the place where Norman Scott's dog had been shot. The magistrate had to decide whether there was a case to answer. The chief witness was Andrew Newton, with his assertion that he had been hired to kill Scott. The story that emerged was that in October 1974, David Holmes had gone to visit an old friend, John Le Mesurier, in Port Talbot, and was introduced to George Deakin, the 'one-armed-bandit king'. At the third or fourth meeting, Holmes mentioned that a friend was having trouble with a blackmailer. Could Deakin find someone to frighten this man? Deakin in turn went to a friend called David Miller, who ran a printing shop in Cardiff; it was Miller who recommended his friend Andrew Newton. Newton had at first been promised £15,000 to frighten Scott; this later dropped to £10,000, then to £5,000. When Newton came out of prison in April 1977, he was summoned to a lonely moorland road by Miller and Le Mesurier and given his £5,000. A private detective hired by Miller roared past in a car and photographed the transaction – Miller was hoping he might some time sell his story to the Press.

This, then, was the background to how Newton came to shoot the dog. (Newton insisted he had no intention of killing Scott and that he had deliberately pointed the gun away from him before pulling the trigger a second time.) The magistrate decided that all this amounted to a conspiracy to murder. The trial of the four men opened at the Old Bailey on 8 May 1979.

All four – Thorpe, Holmes, Le Mesurier and Deakin – pleaded not guilty. The counsel for the prosecution, Peter Taylor, QC, told Norman Scott's story of how he had been seduced by Thorpe and the gradual breakdown of their relationship. According to Scott, the affair with Thorpe had continued for five years and he had frequently come back from Ireland to have sex with Thorpe. The turning point in the relationship came when Scott wrote to Thorpe's mother, telling her that he and Jeremy had been lovers for the past five years.

The most startling evidence came from Peter Bessell on day four of the trial. He described acting as intermediary between Thorpe and Norman Scott, then went on to tell of the day in the House of Commons in 1968 when Thorpe had first suggested 'getting rid' of Scott. They had then discussed various methods of disposing of Scott's body – it could be buried, dropped in a river, concealed in the rubble of a new motorway. When Bessell mentioned the tin mines in his Cornish constituency, Thorpe took him by the shoulders and exclaimed, 'That's it!' The body could be dropped down an empty mineshaft. Bessell said he thought killing was immoral and Thorpe replied, 'It's no worse than shooting a sick dog.'

A few months later, according to the prosecution, Bessell and Holmes attended another meeting in the House, and this time, Thorpe proposed that Holmes should pose as a reporter and invite Scott to Plymouth. On the way he could get him drunk in a pub, kill him in a lonely spot and dispose of him. Bessell remarked that shooting Scott would be noisy and messy. 'In that case', said Thorpe, 'it will have to be poison. You can slip it into his drink, David, in a pub.' Holmes said it might be awkward if Scott dropped dead off his bar stool. Bessell said, 'You can apologize to the landlord and ask for directions to the nearest mineshaft.' Thorpe snapped, 'This is a serious matter.'

According to Bessell, they regarded Thorpe's murder plans as something of a joke. In any case, they were dropped when Scott got married. But Thorpe anticipated more trouble from Scott, and began to discuss luring him to America to kill him in some remote place.

In 1971, Holmes and Bessell met in New York to discuss a 'charade' that would convince Thorpe they meant to kill Scott. Holmes bought a toy pistol that would fire plastic pellets a few feet so he could report he had acquired a murder weapon. Holmes telephoned Thorpe from New York to explain that the plan had failed because Scott had not turned up.

The prosecution told the story of how Andrew Newton had been hired and how he had asked Deakin privately, 'I understand you want somebody bumped off?' Newton was apparently not particularly competent and went to Dunstable instead of Barnstaple. He contacted Holmes, who explained he would be happier if Scott vanished from the face of the earth. Newton described how he tried to lure Scott to the Royal Garden Hotel in Kensington and had gone there with a chisel hidden in a bunch of flowers – he intended to kill Scott with the chisel in a hotel room. But Scott failed to show up. Finally, Newton described how he had contacted Scott under the name of Peter Keene and had taken him for a drive that ended in the death of the dog. He again insisted that he had only pretended that the gun had jammed. It was for this abortive attempt that he was paid £5,000.

Where had this money come from? It was part of the prosecution's case that it had been syphoned off from Liberal Party funds, supplied by a millionaire named Jack Hayward, who had been a generous benefactor of the Liberals. After the 1974 Election, Thorpe had written to Hayward, explaining that he needed £50,000 for election funds, but that it would be best if he could have two cheques, one for £40,000 and one for £10,000. The £40,000 went into the Liberal funds; the £10,000 into an account on Jersey belonging to Thorpe's friend, and the godfather of his son, Nadir Dinshaw. Dinshaw sent the money on to David Holmes; in March 1975 the procedure was repeated, and a further £10,000 went to Holmes via Dinshaw. (The latter was dubious about the proceeding but was reassured by Thorpe that it was all perfectly above board.)

When the prosecution had finished presenting its case, things looked very black for the accused. The evidence that Thorpe had wanted Scott 'disposed of' had been precise and circumstantial. But when the defence presented its case, things began to look better. In the witness box, Peter Bessell agreed that he was hoping to make a great deal of money from a contract with a newspaper; if Thorpe was convicted, the total payment would be £50,000; if not, only £25,000. The defence's inference was that Bessell had good reason to want to see a conviction. Bessell was made to admit in court that he had 'disappeared' in 1974 to escape his creditors. It also emerged that the prelude to this disappearance had been an unsuccessful ploy to swindle Jack Hayward of $½ million. Thorpe had been heavily involved in this scheme according to Bessell. In a brilliant cross-examination, George Carman QC succeeded in conveying a strong impression that Bessell was a swindler and a habitual liar.

He was equally impressive with Norman Scott. He scored a vital point when he made Scott admit that he had been boasting about a sexual relationship with Jeremy Thorpe before he went to see Thorpe in the House of Commons for the first time. Scott admitted that he had been mentally ill at the time and was suffering from a delusion. The implication was obvious: that Scott might have invented the whole story of his sexual relations with Jeremy Thorpe. And even if he hadn't, he had gone to the House of Commons with the idea of an affair in his mind – so the story of being dragged unwillingly into homosexuality by Thorpe must be untrue. This admission may well have been the turning point of the trial.

Scott made a thoroughly bad impression in court – one of a hysterical neurotic who had persecuted a public man out of malice. The impression made by Andrew Newton was equally bad. He began by admitting that he had lied on oath at his original trial for shooting the dog. Carman pressed him to admit that he had been hired simply to 'put the fear of God' into Scott and not to kill him. Newton disagreed but by the time he had finished giving his evidence, his general credibility was also badly dented.

Of the four accused, George Deakin was the only one who chose to go into the witness box. He insisted that he had merely helped to find someone to frighten a blackmailer and that he had been totally incurious about who was being blackmailed. He denied any subsequent involvement in intimidating Scott – he had been named as the man who had gone to Barnstaple to steal Scott's briefcase.

The prosecution and defence took five days to summarize their cases. Thorpe's counsel emphasized that the fact he had chosen not to go into the witness box did not prove him guilty. He had a perfect right to remain silent. The summing up by Mr Justice Cantley was, on the whole, in favour of the accused. He was scathing about the credibility of the prosecution witnesses and he also explained that the refusal of Thorpe, Holmes and Le Mesurier to go into the witness box should not be regarded as evidence of guilt. When he spoke of Bessell the judge further emphasized that his evidence about Thorpe's 'ultimate solution' to the problem of Scott was uncorroborated. When he spoke of Scott, he obviously found it impossible to hide his distaste. He spoke of his 'hysterical, warped personality', and described him as an accomplished liar and a crook. He pointed out that the 'Bunnies can go to France' letter might be seen as evidence of a homosexual relationship or it might not. It was possible that when Scott first went to see Thorpe at the House of Commons, he had blackmail in mind. 'He is a fraud. He is a sponger. He is a whiner. He is a parasite. But of course, he could still be telling the truth. It is all a question of belief.'

When the jury retired, they were divided six to six for and against acquittal. An hour later, they were two to ten in favour of acquittal. By the following day, only one man held out for a guilty verdict. Finally, after two days, that one man was convinced. On Friday, 22 June 1979, the four accused filed back into the dock. The foreman read out the verdicts of acquittal for all the four. Thorpe looked rigid and stunned. Then he tossed the three cushions he had been sitting on over the side of the dock and leaned forward to embrace his wife.

The authors of *Jeremy Thorpe, A Secret Life*, add one curious footnote to the case. The turning point had probably been Scott's admission that he had boasted about a sexual relation with Thorpe even before he went to the House of Commons. The authors traced Scott's psychiatrist and asked about this. The psychiatrist, Dr Anthony Willems, assured them that this was not true; Scott had discussed his sexual fantasies very fully during his treatment, in the days before he went to meet Thorpe in the House. But Thorpe's name had never been mentioned. So Scott had, in effect, unnecessarily undermined his own case – another example, as the authors point out, of his being his own worst enemy.

TRESTRAIL, Commander Michael
The Palace Homosexual Scandal

The summer of 1982 was a torrid time in Britain for Palace scandal and none of it to do with the Royal Family, except by association. On 19 July of that year, at a time when Scotland Yard was already in sackcloth and ashes over the intruder-in-the-Palace fiasco (*see* page 174) Her Majesty's personal police bodyguard, Commander Michael Trestrail, MVO, resigned because he was found to be a promiscuous homosexual.

Commander Trestrail was fifty-one years old and would normally have expected to serve for a further six years. He had successfully passed a positive vetting check only four months earlier, following a change in security procedure. His resignation was announced to a shocked House of Commons by Home Secretary William Whitelaw, after Trestrail's association with a male prostitute named Michael Rauch had been reported to Buckingham Palace by a Fleet Street newspaper.

Yorkshire-born Rauch, aged thirty-eight, had known the Queen's bodyguard since he was a detective-sergeant. According to newspaper reports, they continued their homosexual affair after Trestrail's promotion and appointment to the Royalty Protection Group. Rauch was said to have visited him at Buckingham Palace, as well as at his flat in Teddington, Middlesex. The two men were also alleged to have holidayed abroad together. The Commander broke off the association when Rauch tried to blackmail him and after reading Press reports of the intruder-in-the-Queen's-bedroom scandal, Rauch attempted to sell the story of his relationship with Trestrail to a Fleet Street newspaper for a reported £20,000. Instead, the newspaper reported the matter to Buckingham Palace and Rauch was interviewed by Scotland Yard detectives on 17 July 1982.

Shortly after the Commander's resignation, his solicitor, Sir

David Napley, said his client wished to express his 'deep sorrow' for the embarrassment he had caused both the Royal Family and the Force, 'towards whose service his only objective has been to devote himself, including ensuring the safety of Her Majesty'. Questions arising from the failure of the positive vetting system were tabled in the Commons but a Security Commission chaired by Lord Bridge of Harwich found that: 'If a man in a public position leads a secret double-life and succeeds, as Trestrail did for so long, in maintaining a total and effective separation between the two sides of his activities, this must present the positive vetting investigator with an almost impossible task . . .' Lord Bridge added that there was no connection, 'direct or indirect', between Commander Trestrail's resignation and Fagan's break-in at Buckingham Palace. His report did reveal, however, that the Palace had twice previously been warned that Trestrail might be homosexual and, therefore, a security risk. These warnings came from a fellow police officer (referred to only as 'X') soon after Trestrail joined the Royalty Protection Group, but were ignored. Although the positive vetting check in April 1982, also failed to uncover his double-life, the Commander resigned immediately he was confronted with Rauch's evidence.

The Commission decided that neither his association with Rauch, nor a series of other secret liaisons over the years had breached security, even though Rauch made one attempt to blackmail him. Security at the Palace 'was not put at risk. Commander Trestrail carried out his duties as Queen's Police Officer loyally and efficiently, but led a secret double-life in that he indulged in promiscuous homosexual activities, mostly with prostitutes.' He also met casually with other homosexuals, especially when he had been drinking. Lord Bridge said that Trestrail, who had been aware of his homosexuality from teenage, had been reluctant to acknowledge it to himself and sought to repress it. 'In the result, the occasions of his homosexual activity have been spasmodic and infrequent, separated by intervals of "months", according to his own account . . .' Even when he had been drinking and felt unable to control his urge, '. . . there was no breach of security, and in my judgment, security was not put at risk . . .'

Only two of the homosexuals with whom he consorted knew he was the Queen's personal bodyguard, Rauch, whom he knew as 'Michael Pratt', was one; the other was a Spaniard from the Canary Islands he met in Hyde Park. The report said Rauch had tried to blackmail him (for £2,000) two or three years earlier, but 'nothing came of it and the two did not see each other again.' Of 'X's' warnings the report commented: 'On hearing of Trestrail's resignation, X very properly communicated with Scotland Yard, volunteered a statement and in due course gave evidence before me. The substance . . . was . . . that twice after Trestrail's joining the Royalty Protection Group (X) reported to Commander Perkins, who was then the Queen's Police Officer, his suspicion that Trestrail was a homosexual. According to X, Commander Perkins simply brushed the matter aside, telling X in effect that it was nothing to do with him.' Commander Perkins was now dead and Lord Bridge took the view that while X was a completely honest witness, he was unable to provide Commander Perkins with hard evidence to back up his suspicions.

The Report criticized the media for its 'singularly unpleasant publicity' about the scandal, but found that the authorities were right to accept Commander Trestrail's resignation. He had clearly laid himself open to blackmail, while, 'Doubts as to the soundness of his judgment, and public opinion with regard to indiscriminate promiscuity would, in any case, have made it impossible for him to continue.' Lord Bridge also said that the Metropolitan Police were unable to provide him with an authoritative account of how its officers were selected for service with the Royalty Protection Group. Apart from routine steps to ensure that they were not known criminals or security risks, no special checks on character or background were made.

Michael Trestrail, the son of a Cornish greengrocer, and a slim, balding man who accompanied the Queen on overseas tours as well as domestic engagements, was seconded to the Royalty Protection Group in 1966. He was made a member of the Royal Victorian Order eleven years later. On his resignation in 1982 he was paid a lump sum of £25,000 plus a (reduced) pension of £600 a month. Male prostitute Michael Rauch was later found dead in his hotel room in Notting Hill Gate, after taking an overdose of drugs. He was said to have died penniless. An unnamed friend was quoted as saying, 'No one wanted to know him because he had betrayed Michael Trestrail and embarrassed the Queen. The gay community loathed him . . .'

VICTORIA and BROWN, John

The Widow of Windsor and the Scottish Ghillie

Scandal involving the widowed Queen Victoria and her Court favourite, ghillie John Brown, reached such proportions in the 1860s that there were genuine fears for the future of the monarchy in Britain. Republicanism had already swept Europe in 1848, the year of the Communist manifesto of Marx and Engels. Now it was on the rise in Britain, feeding off poverty and the struggle for electoral reform. Disenchantment with the monarchy stemmed from the Queen's virtual disappearance from public life following the death of the Prince Consort in 1861. Now rumours of her 'affair' with John Brown, the one-time stable lad who had been appointed Victoria's Personal Highland Servant – with explicit instructions to take orders from no one but herself – fell on doubly fertile ground, both within the Establishment and with the mob.

That Queen Victoria and John Brown loved each other is a matter of record. After Brown's death in 1883, she wrote to his brother Hugh: 'So often I told him that no one loved him more than I did or had a better friend than me . . . and he answered, "Nor you than me. No one loves you more." ' What has always remained the subject for speculation, and scandal, is if that love was strictly platonic. When rumour was at its height the Press sailed as close to the wind as it dared, pillorying Brown personally and the Queen by inference, in savagely slanted reports and cartoons. One Swiss newspaper, the *Gazette de Lausanne*, 'reported' their secret marriage, adding for good measure that Victoria was pregnant by Brown. An American diarist visiting Britain in 1868 wrote in *Tinsley's Magazine*: 'Soon after my arrival in London at a table where all the company were gentlemen by rank or position, there were constant references to and jokes about "Mrs Brown" . . . I lost the point of all the witty sayings and should have remained in blissful ignorance throughout the dinner, had not my host kindly informed me that "Mrs Brown" was an English synonym for the Queen . . .' And if, after all that and much more, there were those left who still harboured any doubts about the relationship between the Queen and John Brown, their doubts must surely have been dispelled after her death in 1901, when her eldest son now King Edward VII, ordered all his mother's treasured photographs of John Brown to be burned, his busts destroyed, and – pettiest of all – the ghillie's apartment at Windsor Castle, undisturbed since his death, to be turned into a billiards room.

John Brown, second of a family of eleven children, was born at Crathienaird, opposite Balmoral on the north bank of the Dee, on 8 December 1826. His father was the local schoolmaster, his mother a blacksmith's daughter. He started working life as ostler's boy at a coaching inn, joined the staff on Balmoral estate (then rented by a Scottish knight) as a thirteen-shillings-a-week stable hand and was retained as an under-groom when it passed into royal ownership in 1848. His rise in royal favour was swift. By 1858 'Johnny Brown' had been specially appointed to attend on the Queen, doubling as 'keeper' to Prince Albert. When the Queen and her husband began their 'Great Expeditions' in the Highlands in 1860, travelling incognito from Balmoral to stay at country inns and shooting lodges, Brown accompanied them as Victoria's valet. She wrote gushingly of him to her uncle, King Leopold I of the Belgians: 'He takes wonderful care of me, combining the offices of groom, footman, page and maid, I might almost say, as he is so handy about cloaks and shawls.'

Victoria's mother, the Duchess of Kent, died in March 1861 and her husband, Albert, of typhoid fever in December the same year. At forty-two she found herself in that unique, gilded-cage isolation known only to Monarchy, as mother of nine children as well as Queen of the world's greatest power. Perhaps not surprisingly she became so overwhelmed by grief and responsibility that many considered her behaviour unbalanced, even a little mad. Henceforth a photograph of her dead spouse was to hang a foot above every bed she slept in, with a plaster cast of his hand on the dressing table nearby. The royal servants laid out a clean nightshirt each night for his ghost and as solemnly brought in hot shaving water every morning. Albert's rooms at Buckingham Palace, Windsor, Osborne and Balmoral were sealed and their contents photographed, so that after cleaning each article could be restored to the exact spot it occupied at the moment of his death. So overwrought did she become that she blamed her son Bertie, the Prince of Wales (and a notorious rake) for hastening his father's death by his affairs. Tearful and brooding, she went into a *purdah* of mourning for several years, wilfully neglecting her royal duties to the point of forfeiting public sympathy and even loyalty.

It was into this unreal world of permanent mourning and near madness that John Brown was summoned in December 1864. He arrived at Osborne, the Queen's home on the Isle of Wight, in kilt and bonnet and leading her favourite pony through the snow, harnessed to her own carriage brought from Balmoral. As medicine, it worked from the start. According to author E. E. P. Tisdall: 'It was said that the smile which lit the Queen's face was the first which had been seen since that dreadful night.' Unfortunately while Brown's presence signalled the start of the Queen's return to normality, it also gave rise to gossip. She was still only forty-five and a passionate woman. Brown was thirty-eight, a handsome, red-headed giant of a man, already devoted to her. If it was only natural that she should rely more and more on this one man who was never far from her side, it was perhaps also inevitable that tongues should soon start to wag; especially as Brown had a positive genius for upsetting all but Her Majesty with his gruff, no-nonsense manner.

Within two months of his arrival at Osborne he had been appointed the Queen's 'Personal Highland Servant', at a salary of £120 a year, with instructions to attend her both indoors and out and to take his orders 'from none but herself'. This he interpreted literally and while his respect for his royal mistress was sincere, no one could ever accuse him of kow-towing to her. He addressed her as an equal, calling her 'wumman', openly scolding her for taking insufficient care with her appearance. ('What are ye daein' wi' that auld dress on ye agen?') No one else in Britain would have dared to speak to her in such a way and when extended to senior members of the Household it caused the deepest resentment. General Sir Charles Grey, her Personal Secretary, bristled at Brown's offhand manner when bearing royal messages. A clash with equerry General Sir John M'Neil brought a fiery retort from Brown, 'Dinna be abrupt wi' me, I'm nae one of ye're private sodgers' and, within hours, an implied rebuke from the Queen, offering the General a remote command in India should he choose to accept it. Ministers-in-waiting knew better than to offend this former ghillie who wielded such immense influence with the Queen but few loved him for that.

The Queen's first, reluctant efforts to regain goodwill by appearing in public served only to worsen the situation. In February 1866, she opened Parliament for the first time since Albert's death in 1861 but disappointed the crowds by eschewing all pomp and pageantry, even entering the Palace of Westminster by a side door. The following month she reviewed a parade of troops at Aldershot, likewise for the first time in years; but instead of sitting on her own horse to take the salute, as of yore, she remained in her carriage – leaving John Brown in full view, on the box above.

Rumours of the 'association' were already rife; now they multiplied, with Brown the target for attack. In June, rumour said, 'Brown was to blame' for the Queen's failure to return immediately to London from Balmoral, following the defeat of Lord John Russell's government. In July, their mutual fondness for whisky ('Begg's Best', distilled on the Balmoral estate, was a favourite tipple) was used as a weapon by the reporters keeping watch on the royal holiday there. According to rumour, John Brown had been mortally offended by a mock Court Circular in *Punch* which debunked him, so much so that he tendered his resignation in drunken fury when the Queen dared to laugh at the article. Soon the *John O'Groats Journal* published a letter from its London correspondent:

I suppose all my readers have heard of the great Court favourite John Brown. His dismissal some weeks ago was generally talked about at the time, and I observe that the fact has now found its way into print, coupled with the suggestion of John Brown's probable restoration to power before long. The reason assigned for his dismissal is an inordinate indulgence in the national taste for whisky, and the restraining of that appetite is mentioned as a likely condition of his readmission to favour. Far be it from me to question Mr Brown's powers of suction. They may rival those of Dickens' character, the elder Weller, I think, who would have made an uncommon good oyster if he'd been born in that sphere of life . . . But Brown's fall has been more commonly ascribed to *Mr Punch* than to any shortcomings of his own . . .

In September 1866 an anonymous 'Special Correspondent' of the *Gazette de Lausanne* said in print what the rumour-mongers in London society were saying at their dinner tables – that the Queen had secretly married Brown in a morganatic ceremony, and was avoiding public appearances to try to hide the fact that she was pregnant again. 'They say that with Brown and by him she consoles herself for Prince Albert, and they go even further. They add that she is in an interesting condition, and that if she was not present for the Volunteers Review, and at the inauguration of the monument to Prince Albert, it was only in order to hide her pregnancy. I hasten to add that the Queen has been morganatically married to her attendant for a long time, which diminishes the gravity of the thing . . .'

In his book *Queen Victoria's Private Life* author E. E. P. Tisdall (who discounted the notion that the affair was platonic) says that a pamphlet entitled *Mrs John Brown* was privately printed in Britain '. . . to circulate very widely in stately homes and servants halls . . . The pamphlet declared that the Queen had married John Brown at a secret ceremony. It was never discovered who had paid for the printing and organized the distribution of the pamphlet, but a suggestion was made that the money came from the funds of the Republican party, which was active and growing, as might be expected with such a queer state of affairs existing around the Throne . . .'

To boost circulation, the satirical magazine *Tomahawk* lost no time in joining the anti-royalist pack. In its first issue of May 1867, the caption to a caricature of Landseer's painting of Victoria on horseback at Osborne, attended by John Brown, read slyly: 'All is black that is not Brown.' In his painting, the artist had over-emphasized the Queen in mourning; not only did he show her in full widow's weeds, mounted on a black charger, he even put Brown into a black kilt. The public, who flocked to the Royal Academy's Spring Exhibition – and had heard all the rumours – first giggled and finally laughed out loud on seeing the painting. Press comment was brutal. Said the *Saturday Review*: 'We respect the privacy of Her Majesty but when Sir Edwin Landseer puts the Queen and her black favourites into what are, during the season, the most public rooms in England, he does more harm to her popularity than he imagines.'

Tomahawk's June edition carried a more spiteful cartoon. This time it portrayed an empty Throne, with the royal robes flung across it and alongside, an equally neglected Crown – under a glass dust-cover. The caption asked bluntly: 'Where is Britannia?' The magazine's August cartoon was downright vicious. Captioned: 'A Brown Study', it showed kilted John Brown leaning indolently on the vacant Throne, with a clay pipe in his hand, wearing a bonnet and hobnailed ghillie's boots, staring down unconcernedly at an angry British Lion. Tisdall called it '. . . the most daring and ferocious cartoon ever seen in Britain, or possibly anywhere, in a public journal . . . If such an insult to the Sovereign appeared today in the Press, questions in Parliament and assurances from the Prime Minister would doubtless be followed by a sensational prosecution. But nothing followed the publication of "A Brown Study" . . . except an uproar of bitter laughter . . . Nobody called attention to it in the House; Ministers of the Crown kept their silence. They suspected that *Tomahawk* with its "Brown Study" was more or less telling the truth.'

By July 1867, government fears of a hostile demonstration against the Queen were such that an excuse was invented to cancel a military review in Hyde Park rather than risk her attendance there in the company of John Brown. Although she had agreed, reluctantly, to the Prime Minister's suggestion to leave Brown at home to avoid possible incidents 'of an unpleasant nature', the Cabinet feared she might defy ministerial advice and take Brown anyway. So the assassination in far-off Mexico of the Emperor Maximilian (a distant relative, by marriage, of the Queen) was used as a pretext to put the Court back into mourning and cancel the review altogether.

The year 1871 saw the Republican movement reach its zenith in Britain and not only because of her supposed dalliance with Brown. In an age when 15s a week was a factory hand's wage, a request that Parliament should approve a dowry of £30,000, plus an annuity, on the Queen's daughter, Princess Louise's marriage to the Marquis of Lorne, dismayed even the most ardent royalist supporters. The Queen herself was even accused in a pamphlet of misappropriating public funds. Signed by a critic styling himself 'Solomon Temple', and headed 'What Does She Do With It?', the pamphlet complained that cash saved from Civil List funds was diverted to her own account.

Neglect of royal duties was still the main weapon in the Republican armoury, however. *The Times* labelled Queen Victoria 'The Great Absentee', while to the *Pall Mall Gazette* she had become 'The Invisible Monarch'. When she fell ill in the autumn of that year no medical bulletins were issued, so that the country remained unaware of her condition even though, at one stage, she was apparently not expected to live another twenty-four hours. In contrast, when the Prince of Wales (himself no stranger to scandal) went down that winter with typhoid fever – the same illness which had killed his father ten years earlier – the whole nation prayed for his recovery. This time bulletins were issued and as the Prince's condition reached crisis point, so the public attitude to the Royal Family changed to one of compassion and sympathy. ('An epidemic . . . of typhoid loyalty', sneered the anti-royalist *Reynold's News*.) So complete was the turn-around, however, that by mid-December 1871, when the royal recovery was assured, republicanism in Britain was a spent force.

Now it was Brown's turn to benefit from the wind of change. On 27 February 1872 a Thanksgiving Service for the Prince's recovery was held at St Paul's Cathedral. Two days later the Queen drove through Regent's Park in an open carriage, accompanied by her sons Alfred and Leopold, to thank her subjects for their demonstrations of loyalty. Brown was on the box, as always. As the carriage re-entered Buckingham Palace a young man scaled the railings, ran up and pointed a pistol at the Queen's face. In the split-second of confusion which followed the two Princes hesitated, as did the mounted equerries nearby. Brown alone proved equal to the occasion. As the Queen screamed, 'Save me!' and flung herself against her Lady-in-Waiting, Lady Jane Churchill, he leapt down and shouldered the gunman aside, then pursued him as he made for the other side of the carriage. He described what happened next to Bow Street magistrates, 'I took hold o' him wi' one o' my hauns, and I grippit him wi' the other by the scruff o' the neck . . . till half a dizzen had a grip o' him, grooms, equerries, I kenna' how many there was . . .'

The pistol was later found to be defective, the intruder mentally unstable, but none of that detracted from John Brown's courage or presence of mind. In the eyes of the public, at least, he was transformed at a stroke from villain to hero. The Queen presented him with a new award, the Devoted Service Medal, which carried with it an annuity of £25 (but lapsed with his death; John Brown was the sole recipient). She later made him 'John Brown, Esquire' and he was listed in *Whitaker's Almanack* as a member of the Household, at a salary of £400 a year.

After his death (from erysipelas) in 1883, aged only fifty-six, he lay in state for six days, in the Clarence Tower at Windsor. His Court Circular obituary occupied twenty-five lines, compared with Disraeli's five lines, two years earlier. The Queen attended his funeral service at Windsor, although most of her family found excuses to be elsewhere. Her card on his coffin read: 'A tribute of loving, grateful, and ever-lasting friendship and affection from his truest, best and most faithful friend, Victoria. R & I.' Five hundred mourners attended his burial at Crathie, on 5 April 1883. His opponents within the Establishment were to have the last word, however. Encouraged by the success of her previous book, *More Leaves from the Journal of a Life in the Highlands*, which she had dedicated to Brown, the Queen now declared her intention of writing *The Life of Brown*. Her household was appalled, knowing it could only revive the scandal, but lacked the courage to say so. It was left to the Dean of Windsor (The Reverend Randall Davidson, later Archbishop of Canterbury) to urge her, after reading the rough draft, not to publish. When she persisted, he offered to resign – and the Queen gave in.

After his mother's death in 1901, Edward VII inflicted the final indignities on Brown's memory, as mentioned above, by ordering her photographs of him to be burned, and his quarters at Windsor turned into a games room. Author Tom Cullen wrote a fitting epitaph for the best-loved and most hated of all

British royal servants in his book *The Empress Brown*: 'Although John Brown has been dead for eighty-six years, his bones still rattle in the Royal closet at Windsor, where, as a subject for scandal he is regarded as second to the Abdication . . .'

VOIGT, Wilhelm

'The Captain of Kopenick'

The story of the bogus 'Captain of Kopenick' made all Kaiser Wilhelm's Germany rock with laughter. On the morning of 17 October 1906, a troop of ten soldiers, headed by a sergeant, was marching through Tegel (now in West Berlin). Suddenly, a man in a captain's uniform stepped in front of them and roared, 'Halt!' The captain was a plump man with a drooping moustache, in his late fifties. He inspected the squad, then ordered the sergeant to accompany him to Kopenick, a dozen or so miles away, where he had official business at the town hall. Being Prussians, they obeyed without question. When they arrived at Kopenick, the captain gave them a mark each and told them to fall out for the midday meal. After their meal, he lined them up outside the town hall and set guards at the doors, ordering them to keep callers from entering. Then he marched the remaining seven men into the building, set some of them as guards on stairs and in corridors, and marched into the mayor's office. The captain informed the mayor that he was under arrest. Then he demanded to be shown the cash box with the municipal funds. It contained 4,000 marks which he confiscated, after carefully counting them.

The captain ordered his men to lead the prisoner away, while a soldier was told to requisition three vehicles. Into the first two of these, the soldiers and the mayor were ordered; their destination was a police station some fifteen miles away. The captain and the cash box entered the other cab. It was this cab that failed to arrive at the police station. It took more than two hours of confusion and mutual recriminations before it dawned on the police and the mayor that they were victims of a hoax.

The 'captain' was an old lag named Wilhelm Voigt, who had spent twenty-seven of his fifty-seven years in jail. He had walked into a pawn shop, shortly after his release from his latest spell in prison, and purchased the second-hand captain's uniform. It is not clear whether the robbery was planned, or whether it was a spur of the moment decision as he saw the soldiers marching through Tegel.

The news of the comic-opera robbery spread round the world. Even the kaiser is said to have roared with laughter when he heard about it and said, 'Such a thing could only happen in Germany.' From the description, it didn't take the police long to identity the captain as Voigt. While all the Berlin police searched for him, the city was flooded with picture postcards of the exploit showing the trembling mayor standing before the ferocious captain, while another showed Voigt winking and smoking a fat cigar. The newspaper *Berlinger Tageblat* said that he ought to be rewarded, not punished, for teaching the Germans a lesson.

Voigt was arrested ten days later in his room in a Berlin slum. Most of the 4,000 marks was still unspent. He was sentenced to four years in jail but this was later reduced to twenty months – on the direct intervention of the kaiser, it was whispered.

Voigt came out of prison in 1908 and discovered that a dramatist called Kalnberg had written a successful play called *The Captain of Kopenick*. Voigt requested, and received, a free seat for a performance of the play.

The case had political echoes. In 1910, Herr von Oldenburg-Januschau, a fire-eating right winger, defended Prussian militarism against the dangerous liberalism that seemed to be undermining the country. He declared, 'It must always be possible for the German Emperor and King of Prussia to tell the nearest lieutenant: take ten men and close down the Reichstag (parliament).' This sentiment backfired as comedians all over Germany parodied the statement. After the exploit of Wilhelm Voigt, Prussian authoritarianism was no longer treated with quite the same respect.

WATERGATE
The US Presidential Scandal

The Watergate scandal, which racked America in the early 1970s, grew out of a unique political conspiracy directed from within the White House and aimed at subverting the legal presidential electoral processes in order to secure a second term in office for the incumbent Richard Nixon. The courts of law, the CIA, and the FBI were all caught up in its octopus-like tentacles of corruption. The conspiracy and subsequent cover-up involved not just senior members of the White House executive staff, but even the President himself; though to what degree, no one is sure to this day. But, after admitting his part in the affair – by directing FBI agents away from the White House, when their inquiries into the Watergate burglary pointed towards his own aides – Nixon resigned as President, the only man to do so in US history. By his disgrace, the whole nation was shamed.

'Watergate' took its name from a plush, office-apartment-hotel complex on the banks of the Potomac River in Washington, DC, scene of a sixth-floor break-in of the Democratic National Committee headquarters at 2.30 A.M. on 17 June 1972. What transported it from the realms of common burglary to incipient national scandal was the revelation that the five burglars, who were caught red-handed by the police, were led by a former CIA agent and carried electronic 'bugs', 35-mm camera, a walkie-talkie, as well as lock pick and James-Bond style tear-gas pen-guns; and there were new $100 notes in abundance in their wallets – all evidence suggesting political spies rather than ordinary thieves.

Both Nixon's campaign manager and the White House were quick to deny any involvement. But thanks to a stubborn and courageous Press investigation led by the *Washington Post*, the trail led inexorably back to the White House and, eventually, to the President himself. The scandal finally culminated in August 1974 with President Nixon's resignation, followed by the imprisonment of a number of his former senior executive officers. They included his chief of staff, Bob ('I'm the President's son-of-a-bitch') Haldeman, his chief adviser on domestic affairs, John D. Ehrlichman, and his former Attorney-General and campaign manager, John Mitchell Jr, along with the 'Watergate Seven' who organized and carried out the original break-in.

Many questions arising from the scandal still remain unanswered. To this day no one really knows what the burglary was meant to achieve, who tampered with the President's secret tape-recording of a conversation between Haldeman and himself three days later, or how much Nixon may have known in advance about Watergate and its attendant 'dirty tricks' campaign.

The five men arrested at the 1972 Watergate break-in were led by James McCord, aged forty-eight, Oklahoma-born but raised in Texas, a former USAAF Lieutenant Colonel who had also served as an FBI special agent, as well as Chief of the CIA's Physical Security Division. His four associates all came from Miami. They were: Bernard Barker, fifty-five, born in Cuba of American parents, and a World War II US Air Force prisoner-of-war who had been recruited by the CIA after Fidel Castro seized power in Havana in 1959; locksmith Virgilio Gonzalez, aged forty-six, and Eugenio Martinez, forty-nine, both exiled Cubans; and former US Marine Frank Sturgis, a soldier of fortune who had fought in Cuba both for and against Castro.

When they first appeared in court, one of the accused gave their joint profession as 'anti-communists'. None of the others disagreed. Police who searched them after their arrest found two address books containing the name and telephone number of E. Howard Hunt Jr, a novelist and World War II OSS officer who later joined the CIA. Hunt had worked for the CIA in Europe and South America, and assisted in planning the abortive 'Bay of Pigs' invasion of Cuba by anti-Castro forces. It was Hunt who recruited the four from Miami for the Watergate break-in, and directed the ground operation – under the overall command of an organization called The Committee for the Re-Election of the President or CRP for short (but known as CREEP to the Press). At the time, CRP was regarded as a bona fide Republican campaign organization, legitimately working to secure Nixon a second term. In fact, it covered a multitude of sins, including the direction of under-cover operations by a 'dirty tricks' squad known as 'The Plumbers', paid from a secret fund siphoned off from legitimate campaign contributions, and whose carefully hidden chain of command stretched far back into the White House.

James McCord, CRP's security co-ordinator, physically led the Watergate burglary team. Hunt supervised the operation by walkie-talkie contact with McCord and a look-out named Alfred C. Baldwin (another former FBI agent, who later turned witness for the prosecution). However, a legitimate security guard found doors leading to the Democratic Commit-tee rooms taped open and raised the alarm. The five intruders caught inside offered no resistance.

Next day, former US Attorney-General John Mitchell – campaign manager in President Nixon's bid for re-election – put out a tongue-in-cheek statement disowning the five bur-glars. 'The person involved [McCord] is the proprietor of a private security agency which was employed by our Committee months ago to assist with the installation of our security system. He has, as we understand it, a number of business clients and interests, and we have no knowledge of these relationships. We want to emphasize that this man and the other people involved were not operating on our behalf or with our consent. There is no place in our campaign or in the electoral process for this type of activity and we will not permit or condone it.'

Democratic national chairman Lawrence O'Brien, who was convinced he knew better, retorted that the break-in 'raised the ugliest questions about the integrity of the political process that I have encountered in a quarter of a century of political activity', and filed a million-dollar suit for damages against CRP. On 22 June 1972 President Nixon stated firmly that, 'The White House has had no involvement whatever in this particular incident.' Nine days later John Mitchell announced his resignation as campaign manager, on the grounds that his wife Martha, an outspoken woman, had insisted that he step down. As far as the ordinary American voter was concerned, the Watergate burglary appeared to be just one more, isolated, 'dirty trick' among the many which so frequently seem to disgrace US party politics.

However, Press inquiries as the five burglars awaited trial revealed that a total of $114,000 had been paid into Bernard Barker's bank account in Miami, some two months before the break-in. While most of it was 'laundered' (untraceable) money, paid in via Mexico City, the signator of one cheque (for $25,000) told the *Washington Post* that it represented campaign contributions collected in his capacity as mid-West finance chairman for CRP. The cheque, he said, had been handed to the Committee in Washington at an earlier meeting. For the first time, a link had been established between the Watergate burglary and CRP.

In August 1972, a new name emerged in the growing scandal: that of G. Gordon Liddy. Liddy, who was later to spend fifty-two months in jail – longer than any other Watergate conspirator – was a brash, heavily moustachioed former FBI agent and Assistant District Attorney. He had later joined the US Treasury's Bureau of Narcotics and Firearms Control, where his work had brought him to the notice of the Nixon White House staff. In July 1971 he joined Edward Hunt in the White House 'Special Investigations Unit', alias 'The Plumbers', the organization which carried out the Watergate burglary.

The Special Investigations Unit acted on authority which extended from the President, via John Ehrlichman, his chief domestic adviser. The aide appointed head of the unit was named Egil Krogh Jr, a Christian Scientist of such reputed probity that he was mockingly nicknamed 'Evil' Krogh by his associates. The Special Investigations Unit was set up on White House orders after the *New York Times* began publishing the damaging 'Pentagon Papers' files, to reveal hitherto unknown facts about America's involvement in the Vietnam war. Its intended task originally was to trace and suppress all such Press 'leaks', hence its nickname of the 'Plumbers'. Later its activities expanded to include bugging, wiretapping, personal surveillance of suspects and their families, theft, the planting of provocateurs at political rallies, muck-raking into the private lives of political opponents, and more. Its ultimate objective was to discredit anyone who opposed the re-election of President Nixon, no holds barred. (Krogh himself was later disbarred and served four months in jail for his role in an earlier, associated scandal: the break-in to steal psychiatrist Dr Lewis Fielding's confidential files on his patient Daniel Ellsberg, named as a source in the vexatious 'Pentagon Papers' leak.) Krogh's assistant in Room 216 at the Executive Office building, next door to the White House, was another young aide named David Young, on loan to Special Investigations from Dr Kissinger's staff. 'Chief Plumber' Gordon Liddy and Edward Hunt supervised the burglary (or 'black-bag job', as it was known in Watergate jargon) of Dr Fielding's office in Los Angeles, after he refused to hand over his files to the FBI on ethical grounds.

Following its disclosure that Watergate burglar Bernard Barker had had $114,000 paid into his account, the *Washington Post* concentrated its inquiries into the 'secret fund' which it believed was being used to pay for CRP's 'dirty tricks'. In September 1972, the newspaper named John Mitchell as the original controller of that fund. It said 'John N. Mitchell, while serving as US Attorney-General, personally controlled a secret Republican fund that was used to gather information about the Democrats, according to sources involved in the Watergate investigation. Beginning in the spring of 1971, almost a year before he left the Justice Department to become President Nixon's campaign manager . . . Mitchell personally approved withdrawals from the fund. Four persons other than Mitchell were later authorized to approve payments from the fund, the sources said. Two of them were identified as former Secretary of Commerce Maurice H. Stans, now finance chairman of the President's campaign, and Jeb Stuart Magruder, manager of the Nixon campaign before Mitchell took over, and now a deputy director of the campaign . . .'

On 29 August 1972, President Nixon told America that White House counsel John Dean III had conducted his own Watergate inquiry, and reported: 'I can say categorically that his investigation indicates that no one on the White House staff, no one in this administration, presently employed, was involved in this very bizarre incident. What really hurts in matters of this sort is not the fact that they occur, because

over-zealous people in campaigns do things that are wrong . . .
what really hurts is if you try to cover it up.'

On 15 September, Liddy, Hunt, and the five men arrested
on the night of 17 June in the Watergate complex, were
charged with numerous counts relating to conspiracy, burglary,
and bugging the Democratic National Committee headquarters.
The date of the trial was set for January 1973 – by which time
the Presidential election would already have been decided.
Significantly, no one in the CRP command structure had been
charged in connection with the break-in; it looked as if the
'buck would stop' with Liddy and Hunt. And, behind the
scenes, there was talk that the Watergate Seven had all been
promised swift 'executive clemency', should they be jailed by
Judge Sirica at their forthcoming trial.

On 10 October the *Washington Post* reported that the
Watergate burglary was linked to a far wider campaign of
political 'espionage and sabotage', orchestrated by certain
White House officials and members of CRP, and named lawyer
Donald Segretti as one of the leading 'dirty tricks' activists.
Segretti, who had studied law at Cambridge University,
England, eventually served four and a half months in prison
for his role in Watergate. He was a former captain in the US
Army's Judge Advocate General Corps, and had served in
Vietnam. A staunch Republican, he started working for 'The
Plumbers' in June 1971 – three months before he left the army
– under the auspices of White House aide Dwight Chapin,
President Nixon's appointments secretary. Chapin himself, who
was also a close friend of White House chief of staff Bob
Haldeman, subsequently spent eight months in prison for
offences arising from his Watergate activities.

Segretti's salary was to be $16,000 a year, plus expenses,
paid by the President's personal lawyer Herbert Kalmbach
from the special fund. Segretti's role was to disrupt campaign
rallies in a number of ways, and serve as 'double agents' by
posing as Democrats, while feeding back any 'dirt' concerning
the various presidential candidates to CRP. (Leading Democratic contenders Senators George McGovern, the party's
eventual nominee, and Ed Muskie both became targets for
dirty tricks tactics during the 1972 campaign.)

The *Washington Post*'s principal informant on Watergate

affairs was an anonymous source within the Executive, known even now only by the pseudonym 'Deep Throat'. This source told the newspaper that more than fifty people were employed by CRP as political spies, campaign saboteurs and muck-rakers, saying, 'Some of [their activity] is beyond belief, kicking at the opposition in every imaginable way.' But when the *Post* reported, accurately, that hundreds of thousands of dollars in Nixon campaign contributions had been set aside to pay for 'an extensive undercover campaign, aimed at discrediting individual Democratic presidential candidates and disrupting their campaigns', a CRP spokesman dismissed the report as, 'Not only fictions, but a collection of absurdities.'

The American electorate, like the law-abiding silent majority in any democracy, not unnaturally felt more inclined to accept the word of officialdom than that of an anonymous newspaper source. As a result, the Press disclosures were not enough to influence the result of the 1972 US Presidential election. Nixon and his running mate, Vice-President Spiro Agnew (who himself resigned from office in 1973, paying a $10,000 fine for income tax evasion), were re-elected in a landslide victory, gaining 61 per cent of the vote and capturing every state except Massachusetts and the District of Columbia.

A few days before the Election Charles W. Colson, a senior White House aide, boasted to a *Washington Star* reporter that as soon as the Election was won, they were '. . . really going to shove it in to the *Post* . . . all the details haven't been worked out yet, but the basic decisions have been made – at a meeting with the President.' Shortly afterwards, challenges aginst the newspaper's ownership of two television stations in Florida were lodged with the Federal Communications Commission by various 'citizens', including some with long associations with Nixon. At the same time, the value of *Washington Post* stock dropped by almost 50 per cent on the American exchange. Then on 8 January 1973, the trial of the 'Watergate Seven' opened, before US District Court Chief Judge John J. Sirica. Judge Sirica, aged sixty-eight and known as 'Maximum John' – from his reputation for handing down the stiffest of sentences to convicted offenders – had warned at the pre-trial hearing, 'This jury is going to want to know: what did these men go into that headquarters for? Was their sole purpose political espionage? Were they paid? Was there financial gain? Who hired them? Who started this?'

Not one of these questions was solved at the trial, however. Chief prosecutor Earl Silbert told the court he would be able to account only for $50,000, from a total of $235,000 in presidential campaign funds which had been handed to Liddy in $100 notes. Liddy, he said, had been given the money to conduct 'legitimate intelligence-gathering inquiries and had acted on his own initiative in planning and executing the Watergate operation. After hearing the opening statement, Howard Hunt changed his own plea to guilty – and told reporters outside the courtroom that to his personal knowledge, no 'higher-ups' were involved in the conspiracy. Persistent rumours immediately began to circulate that the Miami four, Barker, Gonzalez, Martinez and Sturgis, were likewise about to change their pleas to guilty.

The *Washington Post* discovered that Hunt had called on all four before the trial to promise that their families would be 'taken care of financially' if they all pleaded guilty. The *New York Times* declared that all four were 'still being paid' by persons as yet unnamed. *Time* magazine issued a press release saying that the four men had been promised $1,000 for each month they spent in jail. Next day all four witnesses discharged their attorney and engaged a new one, who promptly entered pleas of guilty on behalf of his clients. Amid the smell of corruption, Judge Sirica called the four Miami defendants before him and asked about 'these $100 bills that were floating around like coupons'. As his companions nodded agreement, Barker said he didn't know; 'I got the money in the mail in a blank envelope.' The judge retorted, 'Well I'm sorry, I don't believe you.'

All four maintained they had been under no pressure to change their pleas and denied that there had been any promise of executive clemency. The judge also asked if any of them had worked for the CIA. Gordon Liddy and others in court laughed out loud when that, too, was denied, by Martinez. (According to the *Washington Post* Watergate investigators, reporters Carl Bernstein and Bob Woodward, in their best-selling book *All the President's Men*, Martinez '. . . had been on a CIA retainer of $100 a month until the day after his Watergate arrest.')

Gordon Liddy was depicted by the prosecution as the 'Mister Big' behind Watergate and on 30 January 1973 he was found guilty on six charges arising from the break-in, McCord on eight. Judge Sirica deferred sentencing the seven men until March. As public unease about the proceedings mounted, Senator Sam J. Ervin Jr, a no-nonsense 76-year-old Democrat from North Carolina, was appointed head of a Senate Investigation Committee. His brief was a wide one. The Committee's duties were defined on 7 February 1973 under Senate resolution No 60 '. . . to conduct an investigation and study of the extent, if any, to which illegal, improper, or unethical activities were engaged in by any persons, acting individually or in combination with others, in the presidential election of 1972, or . . . any campaign, canvass, or other activity related to it.' Specifically, Senator Ervin and his committee were charged to investigate Watergate in all its circumstances and to determine if there was evidence of a subsequent cover-up. At last the cooking of the White House goose had begun.

At about the time Senator Ervin was appointed to head the Watergate investigation committee, the Press in America began to question the wider activities of the FBI under the successive Nixon administrations. Until the Supreme Court had ruled such conduct illegal on 19 June 1972, two days after the Watergate break-in, a number of persons suspected by the administration of so-called 'subversive activity' had been put under electronic surveillance without court authority. On 11 February 1973 *Time* magazine disclosed that several newspapermen, as well as certain government and White House aides, had had their telephones tapped by the FBI over a period of four years. The tapping began, said *Time*, in 1969, with the reluctant consent of veteran FBI chief J. Edgar Hoover and was continued under his successor Patrick Gray until the Supreme Court issued its ruling in 1972.

In March 1973, Gray (Nixon's appointee as acting-Director of the FBI, following Hoover's death in May 1972) urgently requested White House support over testimony he had given at his Senate confirmation hearing. There he disclosed that John Dean, counsel to the President, had sat in on all FBI interviews with White House personnel concerning the Watergate burglary, and that he himself had later handed over all the relevant files to Dean. The Judiciary Committee then wanted to know what other FBI favours, if any, had been shown to the White House. The Nixon camp's fury over Gray's disclosures was revealed by the transcript of a telephone conversation between John Ehrlichman, the President's chief domestic affairs adviser, (later to serve eighteen months in jail for perjury and conspiracy), and Dean (who served four months for conspiracy to obstruct justice) released later. It read:

Ehrlichman Hi. Just had a call from your favourite witness.
Dean Which is?
Ehrlichman Patrick J. Gray.
Dean Oh, really?
Ehrlichman And he says to make sure that old John Dean stays very, very firm on his story that he delivered every document to the FBI, and that he doesn't start making nice distinctions between agents and directors.
Dean Yes, he's really hanging tough. You ought to read the transcript. He makes me gag.
Ehrlichman Let him hang there. Let him twist slowly, slowly in the wind.

Ten days later the Watergate Seven appeared for sentencing and the text of a letter wiritten by James McCord to Judge Sirica was read out in court. McCord wrote: 'Several members of my family have expressed fears for my life if I disclose knowledge of the facts in this matter', but said he was prepared to tell all 'in the interests of restoring faith in the criminal justice system'. He claimed that there had been political pressure on the Watergate defendants to plead guilty, and further alleged that perjury had been committed, while 'higher-ups' in the conspiracy had not been named. 'Maximum John' thereupon handed down some harsh sentences.

Gordon Liddy was sentenced to 'not less than six years eight months, and not more than twenty years' imprisonment. Barker and his three associates from Miami, Gonzalez, Martinez and Sturgis, were 'provisionally sentenced to forty years apiece, Hunt to a 'provisional' thirty-five years. To non-legal observers, the underlying message appeared to be plain – tell the truth, or rot in jail. McCord was released on surety of $100,000, with sentence postponed. He eventually served four months in prison for conspiracy, burglary and wire-tapping. (All the Watergate Seven sentences were subsequently commuted. Liddy served fifty-two months in jail, the longest of all; Hunt thirty-three months, and the Miami four between thirteen and fifteen months apiece.)

McCord's letter to Judge Sirica destroyed the last remaining hope of a successful cover-up. He later told the Senate Watergate Committee that both Dean and Jeb Magruder (the deputy director of CRP) had had advance knowledge of the burglary and were involved in the planning. On 15 April the *Washington Post* reported that Magruder had revealed, 'Mitchell and Dean . . . later arranged to buy the silence of the seven convicted Watergate conspirators', while on the same day, the *New York Times* said the grand jury was turning its attention from the burglary to the 'obstruction of justice' by administration officials thought to be involved in the cover-up. The newspaper added that Dean was said to be ready to implicate others, if he himself was indicted.

Also on 15 April, President Nixon summoned Dean. Later Dean himself told the Senate Investigating Committee what transpired at their meeting. 'Almost from the beginning,' he said, 'the President began to ask me a number of leading questions which made me think that the conversation was being taped, and that a record was being made to protect himself.' At the time, Dean issued a statement warning: 'To date I have refrained from making any public comment whatsoever about the Watergate case. I shall continue that policy in the future. It is my hope . . . that those truly interested in seeing that justice is done will be careful of drawing any conclusions as to the guilt or involvement of any person . . . Finally, some may hope or think that I will become a scapegoat in the Watergate case. Anyone who believes this does not know me, know the true facts, nor understand our system of justice.'

Then on 26 April 1973, the New York *Daily News* reported that acting FBI director Patrick Gray had earlier destroyed a number of files belonging to Howard Hunt of the Watergate Seven. Gray, who later told the Senate investigating committee he kept the Hunt papers at his Connecticut home for six months before burning them with the 'Christmas trash' in December 1972, resigned next day. According to the *Sunday Times* Insight Team's definitive book *Watergate: The Full Inside Story*, in his call to Ehrlichman, Gray had '. . . begged him to tell John Dean to keep absolutely mum about the fact he had personally taken delivery of the "sensitive" material found in Howard Hunt's White House safe . . .' Now, on the night before he tendered his resignation, Gray said to Henry Petersen, a senior member of the Justice Department, 'I'm scared . . . because it seems that you and I are expendable, and Haldeman and Ehrlichman are not . . .'

The FBI role in Watergate aside, it also emerged that the CIA had been involved in CRP's 'dirty tricks' campaign almost from the start – at the behest of the White House. In 1971 John Ehrlichman telephoned General Robert E. Cushman Jr, then deputy-director of the CIA and President Nixon's former chief adviser on national security. According to the *Sunday Times* Insight Team, 'Ehrlichman informed the general that the White House wanted Howard Hunt ("a bona fide employee, a consultant on security matters") to be given some assistance by the agency.' The general, a Marine veteran, took a precautionary tape recording of his subsequent conversation with Hunt, and later submitted a transcript in evidence to the Senate Watergate Committee. Part of their conversation read:

Hunt Could we make this just the two of us?
Cushman All right, sure. We certainly can.
Hunt Thank you very much. I've been charged with quite a highly sensitive mission by the White House to visit and elicit information from an individual whose ideology we aren't entirely sure of, and for that purpose they asked me to come over here and see if you could get me two things: . . . documentation . . . and some degree of physical disguise, for a one-time op – in and out . . .

Later, at a CIA 'safe house', Hunt was provided with a false driving licence, a Social Security card and other cards in the name of Edward Joseph Warren, a device shaped like a false-tooth plate which distorted his normal speech, and a reddish wig. On a second occasion he drew a set of false papers for Liddy, together with a mini-camera hidden in a tobacco pouch.

These items formed their basic 'alias equipment' for the Ellsberg psychiatrist break-in.

When the Democrats later raised Watergate as a legitimate campaign issue, CBI director Richard Helms assured Nixon's chief of staff, Haldeman, that his agency had not been involved in the failed operation. The *Sunday Times* Insight Team said in their Watergate book that, according to a memorandum prepared after that meeting on Helm's instructions: 'Haldeman's instructions were quite specific . . . [He] said "the whole affair was getting embarrassing, and it was the President's wish that Walters" – General Cushman's successor as deputy director of the CIA – "call on acting director L. Patrick Gray and suggest to him that since the five suspects had been arrested, this should be sufficient and that it was not advantageous to have the inquiry pushed, especially in Mexico . . ."' Later General Walters went beyond Helm's instructions and told Gray that '"if the investigations were pushed south of the border it could trespass on some of our covert projects . . ."'

Patrick Gray's forecast that Haldeman and Ehrlichman were 'not expendable' was soon proved wrong. On 27 April 1973 President Nixon left for Camp David with his speech writer and private secretary but without his two senior White House aides, sometimes referred to as his 'German shepherds' (Alsatians). At 9 P.M. on 30 April he was back in the White House to appear on television, flanked by a Nixon family photograph on one side of his desk and a bust of Abraham Lincoln – the President who coined the phrase 'Government of the people, by the people, for the people' – on the other. He admitted that there had been a cover-up and announced the resignation of both Haldeman and Ehrlichman, 'two of the finest public servants it has been my privilege to know . . .'

'I want to talk to you straight from my heart,' he began, saying there had been '. . . an effort to conceal the facts from the public, from you and from me.' After saying that he had accepted the two resignations in one of the most difficult decisions of his Presidency, he continued, 'The easiest course would be for me to blame those to whom I delegated the responsibility to run the campaign. But that would be a cowardly thing to do. In any organization, the man at the top must bear the responsibility. I accept it . . . It was the system that brought the facts to light . . . a system that in this case has included a determined grand jury, honest prosecutors, a courageous judge, John Sirica, and a vigorous free press . . . There can be no whitewash at the White House . . . two wrongs do not make a right.'

In addition to the departure of his chief of staff, Bob Haldeman, and senior domestic affairs adviser, John Ehrlichman, the President fired his White House counsel, John Dean III and accepted the resignation of his Attorney-General, Richard G. Kleindienst, successor to John Mitchell. Next day, White House Press Secretary, Ronald Ziegler, publicly apologized to the *Washington Post* and its two investigative reporters, Bob Woodward and Carl Bernstein, for his previous criticism of their reporting of the Watergate affair.

Worse was to come. On the same day the President made his broadcast, Judge Matthew Byrne – presiding over the trial in Los Angeles of Daniel Ellsberg, defendant in the Pentagon Papers case – revealed that he had been offered the directorship of the FBI following Patrick Gray's resignation. When FBI witnesses told him that John Ehrlichman had known about the burglary of Ellsberg psychiatrist Dr Fielding's office since September 1971, the judge immediately ordered further inquiries to be made. Then, after being told that the FBI tapes of a telephone call said to have been made by Ellsberg from a friend's home 'could not be found', Judge Byrne ordered Ellsberg to be released, saying, 'The conduct of the Government . . . precludes the fair and dispassionate consideration of the issues by the jury . . .'

The sudden collapse of the Pentagon Papers trial, coming on top of the resignations of three senior White House executives and the firing of a fourth, pushed the beleaguered Presidency to the brink. One of the problems facing Justice Department lawyers probing the scandal, however, was a constitutional issue: whether an incumbent President could be indicted and brought before a grand jury. And that most delicate problem was brought to a head on Friday, 13 July 1973, when Alexander Butterfield, one of Haldeman's aides, told the Senate Investigation Committee that he was in charge of 'internal White House security', and reluctantly revealed that Nixon had a secret tape-recording system which had been in operation for more than two years. John Dean had already testified that he thought his own conversation with the President had been bugged. Now, here was proof.

The first shots in the struggle which ensued between Executive and Legislature were fired by Senate Committee chairman Sam Ervin. On 14 July he wrote to President Nixon (by then in Bethesda Military Hospital recovering from transient viral pneumonia), respectfully asking for the relevant tape-recordings and wishing him a speedy recovery from his illness. Special Watergate prosecutor Archibald Cox, a professor of law from Harvard, who had been appointed by the (new) Attorney-General, Elliot Richardson, to conduct a judicial inquiry, also sought access to the hitherto unknown tapes. Nixon claimed executive privilege. In reply, a subpoena was served on 22 July, calling on him to produce the tapes – the first time in American history that Congress had so challenged an incumbent President. While a decision was awaited, the Committee continued its investigation and heard the evidence of both Haldeman and Ehrlichman. In essence, both pleaded ignorance of the Watergate break-in.

In mid-October, while the Senate Investigation Committee stood adjourned for the summer recess, a federal appellate court ordered that the tapes be handed over to a judge to determine their relevance, if any, to the grand jury hearing. President Nixon countered with an offer to provide a summary of the contents, but, when Prosecutor Cox refused to halt the judicial process, Nixon ordered his discharge. Attorney-General Richardson, who had only recently succeeded Kleindienst, thereupon resigned rather than carry out the President's order. His deputy, William D. Ruckelshaus, was in turn also discharged for a similar refusal. Professor Cox was finally dismissed by Nixon's Solicitor-General.

The incredible sequence of events caused such uproar that the President finally surrendered seven tapes. On 21 November 1973, lawyers acting on Nixon's behalf told Judge Sirica that one of the tapes contained an eighteen-and-a-half-minute gap; according to a panel of experts who then carried out an examination, that gap could not have been made accidentally. (Ten years later, *Newsweek* magazine published an article headed 'The Legacy of Watergate'. Under a sub-heading, 'The

Unanswered Questions', *Newsweek* said: 'The discovery that someone had erased eighteen-and-one-half minutes of a taped conversation between Nixon and Haldeman three days after the Watergate burglars were caught was a turning point in the road towards Nixon's resignation. Most accounts say only three people had ready access to the machine: White House aide Stephen Bull, Rose Mary Woods, Nixon's long-term personal secretary, and Nixon himself. Woods has admitted she erased about five minutes of the tape accidentally. Experts found that the eighteen-and-a-half-minute gap, in fact, consisted of five separate erasures – and Dean (John Dean III) thinks that very clumsiness was the signature of Nixon. "The only man I know who couldn't get his desk drawer open or take the top off his pen – someone who had no conception of how the machine worked."')

By the spring of 1974, several of his former Executive, including Haldeman, Ehrlichman, Dean, Mitchell, Magruder and others, had either pleaded guilty to, or been charged with, offences arising from Watergate. The combined effects of these charges, together with the ugly questions left by the several erasures on the secret tapes, led to a formal Impeachment Inquiry by the House Judiciary Committee. On 30 April, Nixon released edited transcripts of conversations recorded in the White House between 15 September 1972 and 27 April 1973, protesting that for him to go further would irreparably damage the institution of the Presidency, with its need for confidentiality. Other tapes were subpoenaed, none the less, and on 24 July 1974 the Supreme Court ruled unanimously that Nixon must hand over all potential evidence, including tapes of recorded conversations, ready for the forthcoming criminal trial of his former senior staff.

After listening to those recordings the President consented to release, between 27 and 30 July the Judiciary Committee voted that he should be impeached on three charges. The first article of impeachment, approved by all twenty-one Democrats and six Republicans on the Committee, charged him with engaging in a course of conduct 'designed to obstruct justice', by trying to conceal the role played by the White House in the Watergate scandal. And, although he had consistently denied allegations of a cover-up, on 5 August – after handing over three of the transcripts ordered by the Supreme Court – he finally admitted that, as shown in the tapes, he had taken steps to direct the FBI agents away from the White House, when their inquiries in fact were leading them to his executive staff. Already his popularity with the electorate had dwindled from 61 per cent to 27 per cent in less than a year. Now his admitted role in the cover-up cost him all support in Congress. And on 8 August 1974, when his impeachment was in no doubt, he resigned the Presidency (effective next day when Gerald Ford, who had succeeded the disgraced Spiro Agnew as vice-President on 6 December 1973, was sworn in as America's thirty-seventh President).

After declaring that he would withhold a final decision until there had been an indictment or conviction, President Ford changed ground and granted Nixon 'a full, free and absolute pardon' one month after assuming office. By so doing he saved his predecessor from certain impeachment by the House of Representatives and almost certain conviction in the Senate. He denied there had been any 'deal' and in a voluntary appearance before the House Judiciary Sub-Committee he referred to Nixon's 'shame and disgrace'. However, his act of clemency cost him dear in terms of public and Congressional support. A Gallup Poll showed that his public rating had plummeted from 71 per cent to 50 per cent by September 1974. His request for payment of $850,000 to meet Nixon's expenses during transition from President to private citizen was slashed to $200,000 while stringent campaign reforms were brought in by Congress, effective the following year.

Following the pardon, a suggestion was floated that all Watergate defendants should be pardoned, but was dropped in the face of hostile Congressional and public reaction. Nixon's own resignation speech had contained no specific admission of guilt. He said merely, 'I regret deeply any injuries that may have been done.' However, there were those (including President Ford) who felt that both the granting and acceptance of pardon was in itself a presumption of guilt.

Harry Robbins (Bob) Haldeman, Nixon's former chief of staff, later served eighteen months in prison for perjury and obstruction of justice. In his book *The Ends of Power*, which he wrote in 1978 – and, ironically, which made him a rich man

– he said Nixon had been involved in Watergate from the start.
John Ehrlichman also spent eighteen months in jail for perjury
and obstruction. Charles W. Colson, who had boasted that the
White House would 'shove it into' the *Washington Post* for its
Watergate investigation, was sentenced to seven months for
obstruction of justice. John Dean served four months for
conspiracy. (His book *Blind Ambition*, later televised, made
him a millionaire.) Richard Kleindienst, former Attorney-
General, was given a thirty-day (suspended) sentence on
charges arising from the Justice Department's anti-trust case
against ITT (the International Telephone and Telegraph Corporation). Jeb Stuart Magruder spent seven months in prison,
during which he became a born-again Christian. He was
later made an associate pastor. John Mitchell served nineteen
months in jail for his part in the cover-up. Maurice Stans, the
CRP finance chairman, was fined $5,000 on charges of technical
campaign violations. All will be swiftly forgotten but the one
man history will remember is America's disgraced President
Richard Milhous Nixon – almost certainly by his lasting nickname 'Tricky Dicky'.

WELLS, H.G.

The Love Life of a Literary Don Juan

As a lifelong seducer of women, H. G. Wells was the subject of a great deal of scandalous gossip – Arnold Bennett recorded in his journal, perhaps with a touch of envy, that Wells openly displayed photographs of his various mistresses on the mantelpiece. However, the gossip never reached the general public; perhaps the nearest thing to an open disclosure was a malicious story of M. P. Shiel called 'The Primate of the Rose' in which Wells is represented as a popular but mediocre journalist-philosopher whose self-esteem depends upon sexual conquest. (Wells had once stretched the truth in the opposite direction when he described Sheil as 'a flaming genius'.)

Wells was the son of a gardener and a maidservant. He experienced a great deal of poverty during his childhood in Bromley, Kent, where his father ran an unsuccessful crockery shop; his mother deserted the family when he was thirteen and became a housekeeper in a country mansion. 'Bertie' (as he was known) was apprenticed to the drapery trade, which he hated as much as Dickens hated the blacking factory, and he ran away at the first opportunity. (His mother forced him to return just as promptly.) He became a schoolmaster, gained a scholarship to the South Kensington School of Science, had a few articles accepted, and became a writer. (His first book was a textbook of biology.) He came near to dying of tuberculosis, married his cousin, and slowly achieved success. But during the period when he was struggling to make a living, his marriage broke up, and he ran away with one of his students, Amy Catherine Robbins. Unfortunately for Wells, who was sexually insatiable, Catherine was only mildly interested in lovemaking, so he remained sexually obsessed with his first wife. (In his autobiography, he even admits to going over to see her a few years after their separation and imploring her to give herself to him again; she refused.)

Soon after marrying Catherine in October 1895, Wells was unfaithful for the first time. He was alone in the house with a Miss Ethel Kingsmill, to whom his wife was teaching the retouching of negatives. 'I forget by what excuse Ethel Kingsmill flitted from her retouching desk upstairs to my study. But she succeeded in dispelling all the gloomy apprehensions I was beginning to entertain, that lovemaking was nothing more than an outrage inflicted upon reluctant womankind . . . The sound of my returning aunt's latch-key separated us in a state of flushed and happy accomplishment.' Wells had been virtually sex-starved up to the age of thirty but he set out to make up for it in the remaining fifty years of his life.

In the posthumously published postscript to his autobiography (*H. G. Wells in Love*, 1984), Wells describes how it was the renewal of acquaintance with a childhood friend, Sidney Bowkett, who had become an actor, that converted him from a romantic attitude towards women into a determination to 'get' them. Bowkett boasted about his own conquests.

The first girl Wells tried to 'get' was apparently a teenager named May Nisbet, the illegitimate daughter of a journalistic colleague, E. F. Nisbet, who had died suddenly. Wells paid the girl's school expenses and invited her to his house at Sandgate for holidays. He describes her as a 'gawky and rather sullen girl' of fifteen or sixteen, to whom he was not particularly attracted until 'one day upon the beach at Sandgate she came down towards me wearing a close-fitting bathing dress; instantly she seemed the quintessence of sunlit youth to me, and I was overwhelmed with a rush of physical desire . . .' He goes on to say, 'I never gratified that physical desire', and then adds, rather puzzlingly, 'I made love to May Nisbet, but quite vaguely and inconclusively . . .' But this inconclusive love affair aroused a desire 'that had to be assuaged'.

He met a writer named Violet Hunt at some literary gathering, who experienced 'the same restless craving for the clasp of an appreciative body as myself'. They became lovers. 'There were one or two other *passades* about this time.' One was with Ella D'Arcy, who wrote short stories in *The Yellow Book*; another was Dorothy Richardson, a schoolfriend of Catherine

Wells, whose mother had committed suicide, and who had become a dentist's receptionist. 'For me, it was a sensuous affair, for Dorothy was then a glowing blonde . . . But a vein of ego-centred mysticism in her had always made her mentally irritating to me; she seemed to promise the jolliest intimate friendship; she had an adorable dimple in her smile; she was most interestingly hairy on her body, with fine golden hair, and then – she would begin intoning the dull clever things that filled that shapely, rather large, flaxen head of hers; she would lecture me on philology and the lingering vestiges of my Cockney accent, while there was not a stitch between us.' Dorothy Richardson later gave an account of her love affair with Wells – calling him Hypo Wilson – in a volume of her autobiographical novel *Pilgrimage (Dawn's Left Hand)*. He also recalls a woman from Australia who had read *Kipps* and asked him to come to her lodgings, and a black prostitute in America with whom he talked literature after their lovemaking.

In 1901, a book called *Anticipations*, containing Wells's vision of the future, was a considerable success, and Wells was invited to join the Fabian Society, a socialist group run by Sidney Webb, Bernard Shaw, Graham Wallas and Hubert Bland. Bland, who looked the typical English gentleman, with his monocle and bristling moustache, was himself an incorrigible Don Juan. He was married to Edith Nesbit, the writer of children's books, and his wife's best friend, Miss Hoatson, also lived with them. When Miss Hoatson announced that she was pregnant, Edith was warmly sympathetic until she found out that her husband was the father of the baby. She ordered Miss Hoatson out of the house but Bland threatened to go too so they continued as a *ménage à trois*. In due course, Bland turned to seducing his daughters' schoolfriends. Then, according to Wells, he began to contemplate incest with Rosamund, his illegitimate daughter, a 'dark-eyed sturdy girl'. Wells decided that the best way to save Rosamund was to seduce her himself. Bland found out his intention before this was accomplished and was furious, while Edith Nesbit wrote letters to Catherine Wells denouncing her tolerance of her husband's affairs. 'Rosamund was hastily snatched out of my reach.'

Wells was becoming a leading figure in the Fabian Society, challenging Shaw and the 'old guard' for leadership. His heady teachings about sexual freedom inspired a number of young ladies with ardent admiration. One of these was Amber Reeves, a teenage student at Cambridge, who was the daughter of two Fabians, Maud and Pember Reeves. Maud Reeves encouraged the development of a friendship between Wells and her daughter, a pretty, dark-haired girl. They used to go for long walks and discuss social questions. Wells called her Dusa (short for Medusa). One day, Amber told Wells she was in love and when Wells asked 'With whom?', she hurled herself into his arms. Wells was never one to decline an invitation to lovemaking. They stripped and climbed into bed although without lovemaking. In Soho shortly thereafter, Amber surrendered her virginity – probably in one of the hired rooms that Wells had learned about from Violet Hunt. They spent some days together in a lodging at Southend while Amber was supposed to be with friends in Epping and then Wells took a room in London where they could spend a day together every week or so. He describes how they would snatch opportunities for lovemaking on country walks and how they obtained the key of a church belfry from the sexton and made love in the room below the bells.

Wells told himself that this was the ideal situation for a writer: Amber, the mistress, Jane (as he called his wife), the understanding mate, and his work. Amber told her mother about the relationship and Maud Reeves did her best to be broad minded. (For some reason, this always seems to be easier for the mother of a seduced girl than for the father.)

Soon Amber Reeves became aware that she was pregnant. Her father had to be told and this was done by a young man called Rivers Blanco White, who was in love with Amber himself, and wanted to marry her. Pember Reeves 'became all that an eighteenth-century father should be', declared his intention of shooting Wells and made the whole affair a public scandal – at least, among the Fabians.

Wells was greatly torn. His ideal *ménage à trois* was turning into a nightmare and there was no doubt that for Amber, the ideal solution would have been for Wells to divorce Jane and marry her. But Wells was too fond of his home and children. The worst of it was that he was physically addicted to Amber. Wells installed her in a chalet in Le Touquet and rushed over to see her as often as possible. Finally, he told her that the best solution would be for her to accept the offer of marriage from Rivers White. She was shocked and indignant. Wells left her. On her way back to England on the Channel packet, she attempted to jump overboard but was saved by a steward. Finally, exhausted, she agreed to marry Rivers White.

Beatrice Webb, a leading Fabian, was particularly outraged by Wells's conduct and began writing poison-pen letters to other members of the Society who had teenage daughters, warning them to keep them out of Wells's reach. One of these letters was sent to Sidney Olivier, a member of the 'old guard' who had four pretty daughters. Olivier liked Wells and showed him the letter saying, 'Here's something that will make you laugh.' Wells was furious and wrote the Webbs a letter so full of abuse that it made Sidney Webb recognize that his wife was running the risk of a libel suit. Beatrice ceased to write the poison-pen letters, but continued her campaign verbally. She was even more outraged to learn that Wells was a frequent visitor at the cottage at Woldingham, in Surrey, in which the young married couple had settled. Rivers White must have been either an admirer of Wells or a singularly weak man, for he allowed Wells to live with them in a *ménage à trois* for several weeks. Wells and Amber still contrived to meet after she had had the baby, a daughter, and in later life, she and Wells and Rivers White once again resumed an open friendship. Wells remarks in his autobiography that, 'I do not see much of Blanco White because I find him sententious and argumentative in an unimaginative way. I prefer . . . to entertain her alone. I take her to a theatre or opera at times or we dine at a restaurant . . .'

His wife's attitude was equally accommodating. Wells implies that she was perfectly happy to see her husband having affairs with other women. 'Jane was wonderful. She betrayed no resentment, no protesting egotism. She had never seen or felt our relationship as being primarily sexual . . . She had always regarded my sexual imaginativeness as a sort of constitutional disease; she stood by me patiently, unobtrusively waiting for the fever to subside. Perhaps if she had not been immune to such fevers, I should not have gone astray . . .' This, at all events, was Wells's rationalization. Unfortunately, we have no direct insight into how Jane Wells felt about it. We only know that she died of an abdominal cancer in 1927.

Wells further scandalized the Fabians by publishing a novel called *Ann Veronica*, which had been written during his affair with Amber, about a girl who proposes to her college teacher that she should become his mistress. Every reviewer in London knew that Ann Veronica was Amber Reeves and it seemed that Wells was flaunting his immorality. The reading public was shocked at the idea that a 'nice' young, middle-class girl should offer her virginity to her teacher and that he should accept it. The chorus of outrage made *Ann Veronica* something of a bestseller. There was further trouble two years later with Wells's novel *The New Machiavelli*, about a politician who deserts his wife for his mistress – the mistress was again clearly based on Amber Reeves. (There was also an acid portrait of the Webbs.) When the book appeared, after being turned down by several publishers, it was banned by a number of booksellers and libraries but the controversy did the sales no harm.

It was as well that Jane lacked the proprietorial temperament. After the break with Amber, Wells set himself up in a flat in Candover Street and tried to get the 'fever of Amber' out of his blood by sleeping with as many young women as possible. One of these was Elizabeth von Arnim, a successful authoress who had left her German husband, the Count von Arnim, because he wanted to keep her in a perpetual state of pregnancy. She had called on the Wellses at Sandgate, was apparently fascinated by Wells's reputation as a lady-killer, and became his mistress at the first opportunity. They went abroad together several times and made love on the pine needles at her villa near Montana. While he was still having an affair with her, he met another young woman who showed an immediate inclination to become his mistress. Her name was Cicely Fairfield; she wrote under the name of Ibsen's heroine, Rebecca West. She had attacked one of Wells's books and he asked her to come and see him. She spent a weekend with Wells and his wife. The next time they met, 'face to face with my book-shelves, in the midst of a conversation about style or some such topic, and apropos of nothing, we paused and suddenly kissed one another.' She went to see Wells at his flat in St James's Court and they became lovers. 'It was our second enounter and she became pregnant.' Rebecca declined to have an abortion, so Wells rented a villa at the seaside town of Hunstanton and persuaded her to go there. In due course a son, Anthony West, was born. Rebecca made a series of moves from place to place but it was only after an unpleasant episode in a house at Leigh-on-Sea, when it dawned on her that an unmarried mother was regarded with contempt even by the servants, that she decided to replace Jane as Wells's wife. Jane's reaction was simply to pass the word round that Rebecca was behaving badly. When this got back to Rebecca, she gave way to violent emotions that thoroughly alienated her lover. He flatly refused to divorce Jane and marry her. So the stormy relationship dragged on until, after World War I, it gradually broke apart. In the biography of his father, Anthony West suggests that she was a mythomaniac – not so much a liar as a person who totally believed her own fantasies.

In 1923, Wells's private life almost became public property. A 'pretty young woman with a face like the *Mona Lisa*' came to see him from Vienna, to tell him about what was happening in Austria. She also asked if she could translate Wells's *Story of a Great Schoolmaster*, which provided a further excuse to see Wells. One day when Jane was absent 'she passed rather suddenly and skilfully from an intelligent appreciation of my educational views to passionate declarations . . . I hate to snub an exile in distress, and she was an extremely appetizing young woman . . .' He was soon forced to recognize yet again that there is probably no such thing as a love affair without 'strings' attached. She bombarded him with letters about her adoration and Wells gave way and 'assuaged her sufferings on various occasions'. One weekend she came down to Felsted, near Easton, where Wells was living, and asked him to call one afternoon to meet her hosts. When Wells called, he found her alone for the hosts had gone away, leaving her in charge of the house. She was wearing a tea gown and nothing much besides. '"This must end," said I, "this must end," – allowing myself to be dragged upstairs.'

She went back to Austria for a while and, when she returned, Wells had decided it was time to call a halt to the affair. He instructed his maid that if she called he was not at home. One evening he was about to leave his Whitehall Court flat to go to dinner when the woman called and a temporary housemaid let her in. Wells went into his study and found her lying on the hearthrug naked except for a waterproof – which she had opened – and her shoes and stockings. It is a proof of how far she had exhausted Wells's patience that he declined the invitation and went to summon the hall porter. While his back was turned, she produced a razor, and slashed her wrists and armpits. Two policemen were summoned and she was taken off to Charing Cross Hospital. The carpet was covered with blood. Wells realized that this was the kind of story that could ruin him if it got into the newspapers. He had recently published his bestselling *Outline of History* and was planning a further two immense volumes covering biology and sociology. How could readers take him seriously if the sight of his name conjured up visions of a woman wearing only shoes and stockings lying with her legs apart on a hearthrug? Fortunately, Wells knew two of the leading Press barons, Lord Beaverbrook and Lord Rothermere. He telephoned them and explained the problem. They gave orders to all their newspapers that Wells had ceased to be news for the next few weeks. And apart from a couple of brief mentions in other newspapers, the affair was suppressed. Later, Wells learned that the woman made a habit of trying to commit suicide in front of lovers who had decided to get rid of her – she had learned how to cut her veins without bleeding to death. On his seventieth birthday, Wells had a friendly note from her, she was now happily married, and met her without unpleasant repercussions.

Yet Wells never seemed to learn by experience. It was at about this time that he started yet another affair with a woman who was to cause him endless trouble – Odette Keun. The telephone rang and a woman's voice explained that she had come from Grasse to see him; she asked him to come to her hotel. She had been writing to him for several years and made it clear that she wanted him to become her lover so Wells knew what he was letting himself in for. 'I found myself in a dimly lit apartment with a dark slender young woman in a flimsy wrap and an aroma of jasmine.' She told him that he was all she had to live for. '"If you feel like *that*," said I . . .' And in writing of the episode, Wells makes the acute observation: 'This sort of free gift is one that no one should accept.' He was beginning to suspect at last that this kind of bait usually had a fish-hook attached.

But not soon enough. Odette Keun proved to be his biggest mistake so far. She was highly intelligent but aggressive, emotional and quarrelsome. Anthony West says that her 'profound seriousness was masked . . . by a rather childish desire to shock and by a degree of sexual exhibitionism.' She liked to repeat the story of her 'seduction' of H.G. in mixed company. Fortunately, she was unable to obtain a visa to come to England, having had differences with the British authorities in Constantinople, so Wells was able to keep his life with her apart from Jane and his family. He built a house for her in the South of France and had inscribed over the fireplace: Two Lovers Built This House. (Wells told Charlie Chaplin, who visited him there, that he had had it removed and restored several times, after each violent quarrel.) But he soon began to find her an intolerable nuisance. She began by regarding him as a kind of superman. 'My god-like quality diminished with every freedom I gave her . . . The danger of losing me, which had had the most salutary influence on her behaviour at the beginning of our liaison, seemed to have passed altogether.'

Wells tells a typical story of her craving to shock. A highly respectable Englishman, Sir Wilfred Grenfell, was dining with them and Odette was hoping he was going to invite her to Labrador, where he was in charge of various missions. The conversation turned to Casanova, and Sir Wilfred asked vaguely, 'Now let me see – what exactly did Casanova do?' Wells saw an ominous brightness in Odette's eyes and knew there was nothing he could do about it. 'She told him in a word.' An awful silence fell. Wells hastily intervened with more general information. Odette was not invited to Labrador.

Wells was sick of her by 1928. But it was not until 1933 that she gave him the excuse to break with her, by opening a letter from a woman friend who was not a mistress, but who began her letter 'Darling'. Odette threatened to tell the woman's husband. Wells told her that if she opened his letters, he was finished with her. But when he started to write the postscript to his autobiography in 1934 he had to admit: 'So Odette is receding out of my life down a *diminuendo* of parting shots.'

The 'parting shots' were violently abusive letters which, according to Wells, were Odette's normal way of letting off steam.

Ironically, the only woman Wells really loved deeply in the last years of his life refused to marry him. She was Baroness Moura Budberg, whom Wells had first met in St Petersburg in 1914. He met her again in 1920 when he went to Russia to visit Lenin; she was now the secretary of Maxim Gorki. Wells learned later that, because of her connection with a British secret agent, Bruce Lockhart, she had been blackmailed by the secret police into working for them and spying on Gorki. She decided to tell Gorki the truth; the result was that he became her protector. When Wells was in Moscow she became his official interpreter. 'I fell in love with her, made love to her, and one night at my entreaty, she flitted noiselessly through the crowded apartments in Gorki's flat to my embraces.'

In 1929, at a time when Odette was making his life a misery, Moura turned up at a lecture Wells gave in Berlin, and he decided instantly that he was in love with her. In 1932, Odette exploded when Wells told her he expected to see Moura at a writers' conference in Dubrovnik and told him that if he went, he need never come back. Wells seized on the excuse to leave their home in the South of France for ever. Even his discovery that Moura was still a Russian spy made no difference to his feelings. But he went through a crisis of misery and jealousy when he discovered that she had been staying with Gorki at a time when she wanted him to believe she was at her home in Estonia. By the time he wrote about her, in the postscript of his autobiography, in 1934, he had decided that 'she does not cheat deliberately. It is just her easy way with fact . . . Like a child she believes a thing as she says it . . .' Their relationship lasted, on and off, until Wells's death in 1946.

WILDE, Oscar

'One must seek out what is most tragic'

Oscar Wilde's father, Sir William Wilde, was a constant subject of Dublin gossip and scandal. Known as 'the Wilde knight', he was reputed to be the father of many illegitimate children – Bernard Shaw said he had a child in every farmhouse. In 1864 (when Oscar was ten), a libel case against his wife, Lady Jane Francesca Wilde, turned into a trial of Sir William, a leading physician, on a charge of raping a female patient.

Lady Jane had written a furious letter to a Dr Travers, Professor of Medical Jurisprudence at Trinity College, accusing his daughter of blackmailing Sir William and disseminating a pamphlet accusing him of 'an intrigue' with her. The daughter, Miss Mary Josephine Travers, decided to sue; she wanted £2,000 damages.

When the case came up on 12 December 1864, the prosecution lost no time in informing the jury that 'the particulars . . . are of so shocking a description that I wish to God it had devolved upon some other counsel to present them . . .' Having cured Miss Travers of ear trouble, Sir William had lent her books and money, bought her bonnets and dresses, taken her to lectures and exhibitions, and finally raped her in his consulting room. (One lady fainted and had to be carried out of the courtroom.) She had gone to him to be treated for a burn on her neck and in the course of the treatment had fainted. She had awakened to realize that, alas, she was no longer a maid. Sir William had urged her to keep this quiet. Miss Travers had gone to Lady Wilde to complain but had been treated with scorn. She had attempted suicide with a dose of laudanum (opium) but had recovered. To redress her wrongs, she had printed the pamphlet accusing Sir William of taking advantage of her. When Miss Travers was called to the witness box, the judge told the ladies in the gallery that any who wished to do so might leave; no one did. Then the prosecution asked the question, 'When you were unconscious was your person – er – violated?' and Miss Travers replied, 'It was.'

But the cross-examination was damaging. Why, Miss Travers was asked, did she accuse Sir William of violating her after administering chloroform? Miss Travers agreed that it had not happened like that but could give no excuse for printing a false version. Then Sergeant Sullivan, in Sir William's defence, went in for the kill. Had the alleged assault happened on other occasions? Blushing, Miss Travers admitted that it had. She explained that Sir William had led up to it with 'rudeness and roughness'. But the jury must have found it a little odd that a girl who had been raped while unconscious should give the rapist the opportunity to do it several times more – even with rudeness and roughness. The jury returned to say that they found Lady Wilde's letter libellous, which implied that her husband was guilty, but they awarded Miss Travers only one farthing in damages. The Wildes had to pay the considerable costs. Oscar should have learned from the example of Miss Travers that it can be dangerous to accuse someone of libel; it can lead to embarrassing counterclaims.

Oscar Wilde was born on 16 October 1854. At seventeen he won a scholarship to Trinity College, Dublin. There he came under the influence of the remarkable Professor of Ancient History, the Reverend John Pentland Mahaffy. It was from Mahaffy that Wilde picked up his passionate love of the classics, particularly those of ancient Greece. At this time, Wilde's sexual inclinations were basically heterosexual, with a mild touch of ambivalence, such as may also be noted in Lord Byron. And, as with Byron, his intellectual and emotional appreciation of Mediterranean pederasty laid the foundations for his later development.

At Trinity, and later at Oxford, Wilde was brilliant rather than hardworking. He had the typical charm of those born under Libra. At Oxford he came under the influence of John Ruskin, who taught him to appreciate painting and architecture, and Walter Pater, who taught that the basic aim of life is to live with 'a hard gem-like flame' and who revived Victor Cousin's phrase 'Art for art's sake'. Pater confirmed Wilde in that intellectual elitism he had picked up from

Mahaffy, the feeling that the true aristocrats of this world are the men of brilliance and imagination. And when, at the age of twenty-three, he accompanied Mahaffy on a tour of Greece, the experience confirmed his conviction that beauty is the only ultimate value.

In his last year at Oxford, Wilde wrote to a friend: 'I'll be famous, and if not famous, I'll be notorious.' And when he went to join his mother in London – his father had died – he decided to become both at once. His elder brother Willie, who had become a journalist, introduced him to editors, and Wilde published some poems. He fell in love with the famous beauty Lily Langtry, mistress of the Prince of Wales, and wrote her a number of poems. When a volume of verse failed to bring him fame, he announced that a revolution in dress was more important than a revolution in morals, and began to call attention to himself with a velvet coat edged with braid, knee breeches and black silk stockings. He was one of the first great modern experts in the art of self-publicity. By 1880, he was being regularly satirized in *Punch*. In the following years, W. S. Gilbert portrayed him in *Patience* as the mediocre poet Bunthorne. Gilbert no doubt thought he was being cruel but Wilde was delighted with the notoriety it brought him. This led to a request to go on a lecture tour of America. Wilde arrived in New York with the typical comment, 'I have nothing to declare but my genius.' He was not particularly fond of America. Later, when he heard that Rossetti had given someone the money to go to America he commented, 'Of course, if one had enough money to go to America, one wouldn't go.'

In 1883, after a lecture tour of Scotland, he announced his engagement to Constance Lloyd, daughter of an Irish barrister, a beautiful and sweet-natured girl. They were deeply in love and on the morning after his wedding night, Wilde strolled in Paris with his friend Robert Sherard and described his sexual pleasures with embarrassing detail. Two sons were born of the marriage.

It was about two years after his marriage that Wilde made a shattering discovery. At Oxford he had contracted syphilis from a prostitute and had been 'cured' with mercury treatment (which had discoloured his teeth). Now he learned that the spirochetes were still in his bloodstream. With modern treatment he would have been cured in a weekend. As it was, he felt that he had to give up sex with Constance. At about this time, he met a seventeen-year-old youth named Robert ('Robbie') Ross, who was amusing, cultivated and amiable. Ross later claimed that he was the first male Wilde had been to bed with.

Success was slow in arriving; early plays like *Vera, or the Nihilists* and *The Duchess of Padua* failed to make an impression. He was literary critic for the *Pall Mall Gazette*, and he became the editor of a magazine called *The Lady's World* (renamed *Woman's World*). He wrote short stories, children's stories, poems and essays. Finally, in 1891, when he was thirty-seven, *The Picture of Dorian Gray* appeared and caused a degree of public outrage that he must have found highly satisfying. In the following year, *Lady Windermere's Fan* went on at the St James's Theatre and finally made Wilde rich as well as famous.

In the year of *Dorian Gray*, Wilde met a handsome young aristocrat of twenty-two, Lord Alfred Douglas, son of the Marquess of Queensberry (responsible for the Queensberry Rules in boxing). Soon they were inseparable, dining in expensive restaurants, spending weekends at country houses, attending art exhibitions and first nights. Inevitably, they slept together, although Douglas later insisted that there was no sodomy – only mutual masturbation and a certain amount of oral sex. 'Bosie' (as Wilde called Lord Alfred) was himself a pederast and preferred boys to older men. The French novelist André Gide has described how Wilde and Douglas were responsible for his own downfall. For years he had been struggling against his homosexuality. In Algiers, he discovered that Wilde and Douglas were staying in the same hotel – he had met Wilde in Paris. Before they set out for the evening, Douglas remarked to Gide, 'I hope you are like me. I have a horror of women. I only like boys.' Wilde told the 'vile procurer who came to pilot us through the town' that he wanted to see some Arab boys and added 'as beautiful as bronze statues'. But a brawl broke out in the café the procurer took them to and they went home disappointed. Soon after, Douglas went off to Blidah, where he was hoping to buy an

Arab boy from his family (in fact, the boy ran away with a woman). Wilde took Gide out for another evening in the Casbah, and in a little café, a beautiful Arab youth came and played on a flute for them. Then Wilde led Gide outside and whispered in his ear, 'Dear, would you like the little musician?' and Gide, his voice choking, answered, 'Yes.' Later, the youth came to a hotel room and Gide wrote: 'My joy was unbounded, and I cannot imagine it greater even if love had been added.'

Back in London, Wilde met Alfred Taylor, an upper-class young man who had spent his way through a fortune. Taylor was a homosexual who liked to dress as a woman; he burned incense in his dimly lit apartment and spent his days picking up young men – many of them telegraph boys of the kind who figured in the Cleveland Street scandal (*see* page 131) – and taking them back to his room for sex. The first youth Taylor picked up for Wilde was a twenty-year-old named Sidney Mavor – known in his own circle as Jenny. The following evening, Wilde took Taylor, Douglas and 'Jenny' to dinner at Kettner's and afterwards Wilde and Mavor went to a hotel room together. It emerged later that Wilde's idea of sex was to have the boy seated on his knee, While he fondled his genitals and occasionally indulged in oral sex. Wilde would tell them to imagine they were women and that he was their lover, which suggests that his role was fundamentally masculine and dominant. He disliked obviously feminine youths – he commented once that having sex with coarse, masculine types gave him a feeling of 'dining with panthers'. His appetite seems to have been enormous – he told Beardsley once that he had had five messenger boys in one evening and had kissed them all over their bodies. 'They were all dirty and appealed to me for that reason.'

Some time in 1893, Douglas gave a suit of clothes to an unemployed clerk, who found in the pockets a number of letters from Wilde. The result was an attempt to blackmail Wilde. 'A very curious construction can be put on that letter,' said the blackmailer, to which Wilde replied, 'Art is rarely intelligible to the criminal classes.' When the blackmailer said he could get £60 for the letter from a certain man, Wilde advised him to go and sell it immediately. The astonished blackmailer relented and gave Wilde the letter back for nothing

– an example of Wilde's extraordinary charm, which was based upon a fundamental kindliness.

Unfortunately, a copy of the letter fell into the hands of the Marquess of Queensberry who was particularly outraged by the sentence: 'it is a marvel that those rose-red lips of yours should have been made no less for music of song than for the madness of kisses.' Queensberry was an eccentric Scottish aristocrat – in *The Trial of Oscar Wilde* Montgomery Hyde calls him 'arrogant, vain, conceited and ill tempered', and says that he was probably mentally unbalanced. One day when Queensberry saw Wilde and his son dining together at the Café Royal, he allowed himself to be persuaded to join them, and was dazzled by Wilde's charm, and told 'Bosie' afterwards that he could understand why he loved him. The 'rose-red lips' letter seems to have changed his mind and he wrote a furious letter ordering Douglas never to see Wilde again. Douglas replied with a telegram: 'What a funny little man you are.' Queensberry began to haunt the restaurants where Wilde and Douglas dined, threatening to thrash Wilde. One afternoon, the Marquess came to Wilde's house to order him to stop seeing his son. Wilde ordered him, and his bodyguard, out. Queensberry continued to persecute Wilde. He tried to get into the theatre on the first night of *The Importance of Being Earnest*, but was kept out by police. On 18 February 1895, he left his card at Wilde's club, the Albemarle, with a note written on it: 'To Oscar Wilde, posing as a somdomite' [*sic*]. When he received it two weeks later, Wilde decided to sue. He went to see a solicitor, Charles Humphries, and assured him that the accusation of being a sodomite was untrue. (He may well have felt he was being honest – he was not, as we know, inclined to sodomy.) Humphries agreed to prosecute.

The first trial proved a disaster for Wilde. His old schoolfellow Edward Carson was defending. Wilde was brilliant and amusing in the witness box but when Carson declared in court that he would prove that Wilde brought boys to the Savoy Hotel, it was obvious that Queensberry had done his homework – or paid private detectives to do it – and the prosecution realized it would have to withdraw or suffer defeat. The Marquess was acquitted.

Now Wilde's friends begged him to flee the country. Homosexuality was a criminal offence. Wilde refused and there was undoubtedly a touch of masochism in his refusal. In fact, he seemed to identify himself with Christ and to believe that he had to live out a tragic destiny. ('One must always seek what is most tragic', Wilde had told Gide.) On the day the Marquess was acquitted, a warrant was issued for Wilde's arrest, on a charge of committing acts of indecency with various male persons. Taylor, who had refused to betray Wilde, was also charged with him. This, Montgomery Hyde insists, was unfair to Wilde, since the case against Taylor was a great deal stronger than that against Wilde. The second trial lasted from 6 April to 19 April 1895. The judge's summing up was in Wilde's favour – at least, he urged the jury to take into account every possible doubt of Wilde's guilt. The jury failed to reach an agreement. For the next three weeks Wilde was out on bail.

The third trial began on 20 May 1895, and this time Taylor was tried separately. He was soon found guilty of indecent acts with males. Then Wilde stepped into the dock. Again, a succession of working-class young men described being taken back to Wilde's room. Sodomy sometimes took place; more often, mutual masturbation and fellatio. Wilde was again brilliant and amusing in the box but seldom convincing. Finally, as everyone by now expected, Wilde was found guilty on every count but one. He and Taylor were sentenced to two years' imprisonment with hard labour.

Wilde was taken to Reading jail. Standing around on the station platform he remarked to the guard, 'If this is the way Her Majesty treats her prisoners, she doesn't deserve to have any.' But the old sparkle had gone. The experience of prison almost drove Wilde insane. He wallowed in self-pity and wrote a long letter – in fact, a short book – to Alfred Douglas, accusing him of his ruin. It was later published, in an expurgated version, as *De Profundis*. His hard labour consisted in picking oakum (that is unpicking old ropes for caulking boats). He served every day of his sentence and was finally released on 19 May 1897.

The desire to write had vanished. 'Something is killed in me', he told Robbie Ross. Constance Wilde died in a nursing home in Genoa after an operation to correct a spinal injury, soon after reading Wilde's long poem *The Ballad of Reading Gaol*. Wilde went to Dieppe, where he bumped into the poet Ernest Dowson, who persuaded him to go to a brothel. Wilde did not enjoy it. 'The first in these ten years – and it will be the last,' he told Dowson. 'It was like cold mutton.' He lived in Paris under the name of Sebastian Melmoth – borrowing the name from the Gothic novel *Melmoth the Wanderer* by Maturin – and died in poverty in a cheap hotel on the Left Bank on 30 November 1900, telling a friend who came to see him, 'I am dying beyond my means.'

WISE, Thomas J.

The 'First Editions' Scandal

In 1932, two young London booksellers, John Carter and Graham Pollard, were intrigued to discover that both had been investigating the same curious bibliographical problem. They decided to pool their information. The problem concerned certain rare pamphlets by John Ruskin and other Victorian writers. In the notes to their complete edition of Ruskin, his editors, Cook and Wedderburn, had asserted that certain pamphlets were undoubtedly forgeries. The reason, they said, was that the text of the pamphlets, which were supposed to be 'first editions', was that of later revised editions of Ruskin, not of earlier ones.

But there were many other pamphlets that puzzled Carter and Pollard — more than fifty. For example, there was a pamphlet of *Sonnets by E.B.B.* (Elizabeth Barrett Browning) dated 'Reading 1847'. These were the famous *Sonnets from the Portuguese*, and there is a romantic story of how Mrs Browning came shyly down to breakfast one morning and slipped a sheaf of papers into her husband's pocket, then ran back to her room, terrified of his verdict on her poetry — on which, of course, he was able to reassure her. What was slightly puzzling about this 'first edition' of the sonnets was that they were printed at Reading. Why should the Brownings send them all the way to England when they could have had them printed more easily in Italy, where they were living?

The answer to this question had apparently been provided by the eminent literary critic Edmund Gosse, who, in turn, had had it from some 'unnamed friend'. Gosse said that the poems had been sent to Mrs Browning's friend Mary Russell Mitford and that she had arranged the printing. By the 1920s, a few copies that had been kept back by Miss Mitford were selling to collectors for as much as $1,250 each.

It was while they were trying to find out how the copies had come on to the market that the investigators came upon the name of the eminent bibliographer, Thomas J. Wise, who had published a bibliography of the works of Elizabeth Barrett Browning. He told how the copies had been given to a doctor friend, who had in turn sold them to Browning collectors.

Carter and Pollard decided to call chemistry to their aid. They had the paper of the 1847 pamphlet analyzed and discovered that it was made of wood pulp, which had not been used in paper-making until the early 1880s. The type itself also afforded a clue in the form of the f's and j's which were of a kind known as 'kernless font'. In this font no part of the type projects beyond the rest of the letter (as with the curled top of an f or the curled tail of a j). Research revealed that these had not been introduced into the type in which the 1874 pamphlet was printed until 1880.

But if the pamphlet was a forgery, who was responsible? The first task was to try and track down the printer. The pamphlet bore no printer's name but the detectives were lucky enough to stumble on another pamphlet in exactly the same type. It was of a poem by Matthew Arnold and this was not a forgery but an ordinary collector's facsimile reprint of the first edition. In the back, they found the address of the printer: Richard Clay and Son, a respectable London firm. But there the trail petered out. Clay and Sons told the investigators that their records before 1911 had been destroyed in a fire so they had no way of finding out who commissioned them to print the 'E.B.B.' pamphlet.

Carter and Pollard went on to study many more pamphlets by the famous such as George Eliot, Tennyson, Swinburne, Thackeray and Matthew Arnold; they found more forgeries. It seemed that the 'forger' usually took a poem or article from the works of the literary celebrity, had it reprinted as a pamphlet, and explained on the title page just how it had come to be printed before the genuine 'first edition'.

When two similar pamphlets had been questioned years earlier, Thomas J. Wise had pointed the finger of suspicion at two deceased bibliophiles, Richard Herne Shepherd and John Camden Hotten. Wise, who was now in his seventies, was so universally respected that it seemed unlikely that he could be the forger. Yet Wise was a friend of Gosse and could have been the source of Gosse's story about the Browning pamphlet. Wise had also been closely connected with both the Shelley and the Browning Societies and had often commissioned reprints of their first editions. If such a man asked the printers to run off a pamphlet by Ruskin or Elizabeth Barrett Browning, they would do it without the slightest suspicion.

Again and again the investigators came upon Wise's name in connection with pamphlets that proved to be forgeries. Eventually, they traced the source of supply of many of the pamphlets. The man who had launched them upon the rare book market was an antiquarian bookseller named Herbert Gorfin. At first the investigators suspected that Gorfin was the forger but when they interviewed him, his shock convinced them that he had no idea he had been selling fakes. He gave them full access to his records. Just as they had expected, it became clear that Gorfin had bought hundreds of copies of forged pamphlets from Thomas J. Wise.

Carter and Pollard now went to visit Wise, an ailing man of seventy-three. He stonewalled; he had no idea how it had happened – his memory was rather poor. They told him they intended to publish their evidence and asked for his side of the story. Wise said he would try to find records of the sales. But they heard no more from him and, in 1934, Richard Clay and Company issued *An Enquiry into the Nature of Certain Nineteenth-Century Pamphlets*, which pointed the finger at Wise. They stopped short of accusing Wise of the forgery and pretended to believe that he was the victim of some unknown master forger.

Wise, meanwhile, had offered to buy all the remaining pamphlets from Gorfin at a good price – £400 on condition he declared he had received the pamphlets from another noted bibliographer, now deceased, called Harry Buxton Forman. Gorfin accepted the offer of the £400 but declined to support the Forman story.

Publication of the book about the forgeries caused a sensation far beyond the world of rare books, and reporters rushed to interview Wise. He was evasive. In letters to *The Times Literary Supplement* he insisted that the pamphlets had come from Harry Buxton Forman but Gorfin denied this story.

Carter and Pollard now told Wise that unless he stopped trying to pin the blame on Forman, they would tell the story of his attempt to persuade Gorfin to lie about it. Wise subsided into silence; he died in 1937, three years after the exposure, still refusing to admit his guilt.

Why did he do it? In his chapter on Wise in *The Scholar Adventurers* (1950), Richard D. Altick suggests that it was because he was himself an obsessive book collector, who started life as a clerk in an essential-oils firm. When he began to have a hand in the printing of facsimile editions of Shelley and Browning, he realized how easy it would be to sell reprints as originals. Later in life, he made such a success of the essential-oils business that there was no need for him to carry out the forgeries. Altick also cites some evidence that suggests Wise was telling at least half the truth when he accused Forman. The men seem to have known one another in the 1890s and Wise commented in a note to Forman: 'We print *Last Tournament* in 1896, and want "some one to think" it was printed in 1871.' *Last Tournament* was proved by Carter and Pollard to be another of the forgeries.

Bibliography

Alexander, Marc *The Outrageous Queens* (Frederick Muller, 1977)

Altick, Richard D. *The Scholar Adventurers* (The Free Press, New York and Collier-Macmillan, 1966)

Anger, Kenneth *Hollywood Babylon* (Dell Publishing New York, 1975)

Barkeley, Richard *The Road to Mayerling* (Macmillan, 1959)

Barrow, Andrew *International Gossip* (Hamish Hamilton, 1983)

Bloch, Michael *The Duke of Windsor's War* (Weidenfeld & Nicolson, 1982)

Blythe, Ronald *The Age of Illusion* (Penguin Books, 1963)

Boyle, Andrew *The Climate of Treason* (Hutchinson and Coronet, 1979)

Bresler, Fenton *Scales of Justice* (Weidenfeld & Nicolson, 1973)

Bryan III, J. and Murphy, Charles J.V. *The Windsor Story* (Granada, 1979)

Chaplin, Lita Grey with Cooper, Morton *My Life with Chaplin* (Bernard Geis Associates, USA, 1966)

Chapman, Guy *The Dreyfus Case* (Rupert Hart-Davis, 1963)

Clark, Ronald W. *The Life of Bertrand Russell* (Jonathan Cape and Weidenfeld & Nicolson, 1975)

Connolly, Cyril *The Missing Diplomats* (The Queen Anne Press, 1952)

Cullen, Tom *The Empress Brown* (Bodley Head, 1969); *Maundy Gregory, Purveyor of Honours* (Bodley Head, 1974); *The Prostitutes' Padre* (Bodley Head, 1975)

De Mille, Richard *Castaneda's Journey* (Capra Press, USA, 1976); *The Don Juan Papers* (Ross-Erikson, USA, 1980)

Di Fonzo, Luigi *St Peter's Banker* (Mainstream Publishing, Edinburgh, 1983)

Donaldson, Frances *Edward VIII, The Road to Abdication* (Weidenfeld & Nicolson, 1974)

Evans, Christopher *Cults of Unreason* (Rampa, etc.) (Harrap, 1973)

Fryer, Peter *Mrs Grundy* (Corgi Books, 1963)

Gurwin, Larry, *The Calvi Affair* (Pan Books/Macmillan, 1983)

Harris, Frank *Oscar Wilde* (Constable, 1938)

Harrison, Michael *London by Gaslight 1861–1911* (Peter Davies, 1963)

Higham, Charles *Errol Flynn: The Untold Story* (Granada, 1980)

Holland, Vyvyan *Oscar Wilde: A Pictorial Biography* (Thames & Hudson, 1960)

Holloway, Mark *Heavens on Earth* (Dover Publications, New York, 1966)

Hyams, Joe *Bogart and Bacall, A Love Story* (Sphere Books, 1976)

Hyde, H. Montgomery *The Cleveland Street Scandal* (W. H. Allen, 1976)

James, Robert Rhodes (Ed.) *Chips, The Diaries of Sir Henry Channon* (Weidenfeld & Nicolson, 1967)

Kayser, Jacques, *The Dreyfus Affair* (William Heinemann, 1931)

Keeler, Christine with Fawkes, Sandy *Nothing But* (New English Library, 1983)

Kennedy, Ludovic *The Trial of Stephen Ward* (Gollancz, 1964)

Leighton, Isabel *The Aspirin Age 1919–1941* (Simon & Schuster, New York, 1949)

McCormick, Donald *Temple of Love* (Jarrolds, 1962); *Murder by Perfection* (John Long, 1970)

Mackenzie, Jeanne and Norman *The Time Traveller, The Life of H. G. Wells* (Weidenfeld & Nicolson, 1973)

Mayersberg, Paul *Hollywood, The Haunted House* (Allen Lane and The Penguin Press, 1967)

Messiter, Ian *The Judgement* (Michael Joseph, 1981)

Middlemas, Keith and Barnes, John *Baldwin* (Weidenfeld & Nicolson, 1969)

Moorhead, Alan *The Traitors* (Hamish Hamilton, 1952)

Noble, Peter *Ivor Novello, Man of the Theatre* (Falcon Press, 1951); *The Fabulous Orson Welles* (Hutchinson, 1956)

Noyes, John Humphrey *Strange Cults and Utopias of 19th-Century America* (Dover Publications, New York, 1966)

Olsen, Jack *'Son' A Psychopath and His Victims* (Atheneum, New York, 1984)

Philby, (Kim) H.A.R. *My Silent War* (MacGibbon & Kee, 1968)

Pincher, Chapman *Their Trade is Treachery* (Sidgwick & Jackson, 1981)

Ramsaye, Terry *A Million and One Nights* (Frank Cass, 1954)

Ray, Gordon N. *H. G. Wells and Rebecca West* (Macmillan, 1974)

Rees, Goronwy *A Chapter of Accidents* (Chatto & Windus, 1972)

Schulberg, Budd *Moving Pictures: Memories of a Hollywood Prince* (Souvenir Press, 1982)

Seaman, Donald and Mather, John *The Great Spy Scandal* *(Daily Express,* 1955)

Seth, Ronald *Encyclopedia of Espionage* (New English Library, 1972)

Skeat, M.A., Rev. Walter W. *The Poetical Works of Thomas Chatterton, Vols I and II* (George Bell, 1883)

Tisdall, E.E.P. *Queen Victoria's Private Life* (Jarrold, 1961)

Watkins, Glenn *Gesualdo* (Oxford University Press, 1973)

Welcome, John *Cheating At Cards* (Faber and Faber, 1963)

Wells, G.P. *H. G. Wells In Love* (Faber and Faber, 1984)

White, T.H. *The Age of Scandal* (Penguin Books, 1962)

Yallop, David A. *In God's Name* (Jonathan Cape, 1984)

Young, Wayland *The Profumo Affair, Aspects of Conservatism* (Penguin, 1963)

Index